ISBN 978-1-330-14383-4
PIBN 10036541

Forgotten Books is a registered trademark of FB &c Ltd.
Copyright © 2015 FB &c Ltd.
FB &c Ltd, Dalton House, 60 Windsor Avenue, London, SW19 2RR.
Company number 08720141. Registered in England and Wales.

For support please visit www.forgottenbooks.com

# 1 MONTH OF
# FREE
# READING

## at

## www.ForgottenBooks.com

By purchasing this book you are
eligible for one month membership to
ForgottenBooks.com, giving you
unlimited access to our entire
collection of over 700,000 titles via
our web site and mobile apps.

To claim your free month visit:

www.forgottenbooks.com/free36541

THE QUEEN OF THE SOUTH.

# ADVANCE AUSTRALIA!

AN ACCOUNT OF

EIGHT YEARS' WORK, WANDERING, AND AMUSEMENT

IN

QUEENSLAND, NEW SOUTH WALES, AND
VICTORIA.

BY

THE HON. HAROLD FINCH-HATTON.

LONDON:
W. H. ALLEN & CO., 13 WATERLOO PLACE,
PALL MALL. S.W.

1885.

PRINTED BY W. H. ALLEN AND CO., 13 WATERLOO PLACE.

# CONTENTS.

1179883

vi CONTENTS.

# LIST OF ILLUSTRATIONS.

# ADVANCE AUSTRALIA!

## CHAPTER I.

### THE VOYAGE.

In January, about nine years ago, I climbed on board the Messageries Maritimes steamer *Irouaddy*, for the purpose of getting to a cattle-station in Queensland. Like many others of the same line, the *Irouaddy* is a grand boat, clean, well ventilated, very fast, and steady in bad weather.

Three days after leaving Marseilles we got to Naples. I had been there before, but as I never can be twenty minutes in a steamer without wanting to get out, of course I went ashore. There was nothing fresh to be seen, and certainly nothing fresh to be smelt. In appearance the whole place resembles a very inferior chromo-lithograph ; and I cannot help thinking that the saying, " *Vede Napoli e poi Mori*," has more reference to the asphyxiating nature of its smells than to any over-powering beauty about the place.

Leaving Naples, we passed through the Straits of Messina, and soon lost sight of land. The weather was glorious, and one morning observing the chief

officer laboriously employed in doing nothing, I sauntered
up to him with a view to engaging him in conversation.
With the originality that distinguishes the British traveller, I observed that it was a fine day.  If I had
had the foggiest idea of the effect that this remark
would have on him, I certainly should not have ventured
to make it.  He looked at the sky : it was blue.  He
looked at the sea : it was blue too ; and I then noticed
for the first time that the expression of his face was
infinitely more blue than either of them.  Shrugging
his shoulders with an emphasis that would have frac-
tured the collar-bone of anyone but a Frenchman, he
called the Deity to witness that although the weather
was indeed fine enough just now, neither he nor anyone
else could possibly foretell what it would be like in
twenty-four hours' time.  If it did come on to blow, he
said, we were in a very exposed part of the Mediterra-
nean, and, as our present course lay, over 400 miles
from land.  I left him, to meditate upon the extraordinary effect that being out of sight of land has on a
French sailor.  It is true they do not seem to come to
grief very often, but still I rather mistrust these French
sailors in a bad time.  The least thing puts them into
such a ludicrous state of fluster, one cannot help thinking that a good gale of wind would dishearten them
altogether.  They never seem to be quite at ease until
they get back to Marseilles, and even then religious
enthusiasm, or the prospect of another voyage, often
wrings a votive offering to the Virgin out of the dregs
of their past terror.  The Church of the Virgin and
Child at Marseilles absolutely bristles with these offer-
ings, many of which indicate a singularly bad taste on

the part of the donor. Among a host of paltry toys calculated to amuse none but the youngest children, I noticed one or two perambulators in a prominent position. Now, under certain circumstances, a perambulator might be a very neat and appropriate gift to the mother of a young child ; but when we consider to Whom they are in reality offered, such presents become shocking in the extreme. It is impossible that people can have any real veneration for a Deity Whom they like to imagine wheeled about in a perambulator, or amusing Himself with the mechanical movements of a woollen rabbit. Indeed, except on the supposition that they are entirely destitute of any sense of humour, it is difficult to acquit such people of wilful profanity.

Upon this occasion, however, nothing occurred that the most pious or pusillanimous Frenchmen could distort into a pretext for presenting his Maker with a toy, and three days after leaving Naples we reached Port Said. This town forms a receptacle for all the scum and dregs of every nation under the sun, and is undoubtedly one of the most villainous dens in existence. Composed almost entirely of casinos, gambling saloons, and houses sacred to the worship of blind Cupid, it is a sink of iniquity whose waters, like those of the Dead Sea, are so dense as to support numbers who would go to the bottom elsewhere. The light-house and the coal-sheds are probably the only buildings in the place that have not a professional tendency towards the subversion of morals and the encouragement of vice.

Leaving Port Said, we crawled through the Canal, and after calling at Suez, steamed away down the oily expanse of the Red Sea. Between October and May

the Red Sea is not often oppressively hot; but for the
rest of the year the heat is excessive, and deaths from
heat apoplexy not unfrequently occur.

How is it that one so very seldom meets any nice
people travelling at sea, and then never discovers them
until just before leaving the ship? It cannot be that
no nice people travel by sea. It must be that the sea
has a demoralising effect upon those who do. But it
would seem that a prolonged sojourn upon the ocean
has exactly the opposite effect of a temporary cruise, for
sailors are, as a rule, as conspicuous for those qualities
that make a man a pleasant companion as passengers
are the reverse. Assuredly a passenger-ship presents
humanity under a most unfavourable aspect. Sea-
sickness alone renders most people positively misanthro-
pic while it lasts, and excessively irritable for some time
after it has passed away. But besides this, and such
minor annoyances as having your cabin deluged with
salt water if you leave the port open, and being suffocated
with foul air if you keep it shut, the bare fact of being
boxed up in the same ship with a number of fellow-
sufferers is often very exasperating. Just as in hot
weather a man is never so thirsty as when he knows
that he can get nothing to drink; so on board ship a
wild yearning for solitude is apt to overtake him, all the
more violent that it cannot possibly be gratified. As to
the ordeal of being obliged to live in the same cabin
with one or more individuals for any length of time, it is
not only sufficient to cause unreasoning hatred between
strangers, but often to destroy a friendship of long
standing. I am convinced that if David and Jonathan
had been subjected to the disenchanting test of sharing

a small cabin in a gale of wind, they would have been famous to posterity, less for the great love that they bare one another than for a propensity to quarrel savagely over trifles.

Certainly the sea develops the worst qualities of human nature more rapidly and more surely than any other phase of existence. In particular, I remember one man in whose company it was once my misfortune to make a voyage. My previous experience of him as a fellow-traveller, on dry land, had led me to suppose he was rather a pleasant companion than otherwise. Beyond an insane habit of appearing on every possible occasion in a variety of hideous and fantastic caps, he appeared to be unusually free from the vices of travellers. That is to say, he was neither inordinately greedy nor passionately selfish. He had no particular taste either for sight-seeing or for grumbling, and when in the presence of strangers, he did not consider it necessary either to insult them with impertinent familiarity or to repel them with churlish incivility. When I say that he was capable of visiting the Alhambra, St. Marc's Cathedral, and the Pyramids, without displaying the slightest desire to engrave his name on the walls of any of them with a pen-knife, it will at once be seen that he had no ordinary claims to respect. Furthermore, his manners were those of a gentleman, and his language remarkable for the absence of anything like expletives. After he had been at sea a week, his own mother would not have recognised him.

For the first few days it was calm, and everything went well enough. My friend justified the sanguine expectations I had formed of him, by reclining all day

in a long chair, puffing at a pipe with a head as big as
his own, and with twice as much in it. This sort of
thing was too good to last. We dropped in for a spell
of bad weather. It did not last long, but from the
moment that it began he was an altered man. An expression dismal as the latter end of tea-time took permanent possession of his usually cheerful countenance,
and even the re-appearance of fine weather entirely
failed to restore him. He became exceedingly restless,
and would indulge for hours at a time in the reprehensible practice of pacing up and down the deck, which is
of all performances the most trying to the nerves of the
spectators. Suddenly he would flump down into a chair
with a violence extremely distracting to anyone who
happened to be seeking repose within a radius of five
yards. Just as one began to hope that he was settled
at last, he would bound up again out of his chair, upsetting it against someone's shins, and, without thinking
it necessary to apologise, resume his detestable pastime
of patrolling the deck.

But what astonished me more than anything was the
bad language that he took to using upon the most trivial
provocation. I lived in the next cabin to him, separated
only by a partition open at the top. One day, as I was
lying on my bunk reading, I heard him fossicking about
among the things in his cabin in that spasmodic way
which, even when a man is out of sight, never fails to
convey an idea of awful passion to the listener. For a
while his movements were only illuminated by smothered
execrations, which the partition rendered nearly in-
audible. Suddenly, however, he broke out into a torrent
of oaths so fluent, so comprehensive, and so ornamental,

that, shocked as I was at his profanity, I could not help admiring his genius. I have since reason to believe that be borrowed a great deal of it from the form of cursing employed by the Church of Rome against persons who happen to disagree with her doctrines. At the time, however, I thought it was quite original, and, of course, shouted to him to know what was the matter " Oh ! are you there ? " he replied. " Nothing ; only I cannot hang up my towel."

He grew rapidly worse, but it was not until about a week later that his downward career reached its Nadir of demoralisation. I hardly expect to be believed when I say that one day, without the slightest provocation, at a distance of over 1,500 miles from land, he appeared in broad daylight, on the ship's quarter-deck, in knickerbockers. The spectacle of such a self-constituted pariah of society was extremely depressing. I cannot help thinking that a man who wears knickerbockers on board ship in the tropics, must be capable of committing almost any crime. It was a painful occurrence altogether, and I should not have mentioned it, except with a view to showing how apparently harmless people frequently become exceedingly disagreeable at sea.

Six days out from Suez we got to Aden, a most magnificent cinder-heap, quite unlike anything else I have ever seen. The town of Aden lies at the foot of a range of most discouraging-looking mountains, so forlornly barren, so pitilessly rugged, they do not appear to be made of anything half so cheerful as rocks and stones. They have more the appearance of the material by means of which an inferior bird-stuffer endeavours to reproduce the handiwork of Nature in a rock-work at

the back of his specimens.   There is something genuine
and hearty about a good mass of rock very different to
the attenuated peaks of Aden, compared to which a
granite boulder is affability itself.

When lit up by the splendour of a tropical sunset,
however, the mountains of Aden assume a different
aspect.   They are usually of a pale mauve colour, which
deepens, as the sun sets, to a glorious purple, forming a
startling contrast to the green and golden expanse of the
surrounding sea.   Gradually the purple fades, the opal
light dies out of the sea, and a spectral gloom creeps
over everything but the highest peaks.   Round these
the rays of the departed sun linger with an unearthly
glare, till in the increasing darkness they seem to glow
like the ragged teeth of a red-hot saw.

On the whole, the scenery of the tropics can never
compare with that of higher latitudes.   The strength
of the sunlight is so great that objects are either defined
with unpleasant sharpness or blurred in a quivering
haze of heat.   There is none of that glorious depth of
colouring and softness of outline, one distance fading
into another, softer and softer yet still distinct, that the
moist atmosphere of the west coast of Scotland or of
the fen countries produces in such perfection.   For my
own part, I do not believe the scenery of the west coast
of Scotland has a rival in the world.   Of course it is
easy to find places constructed on a far larger scale, but
it is not altogether upon this that the beauty of scenery
depends.   It is very doubtful whether a mountain
derives much additional beauty from its summit being
invisible ; and certainly a river so broad that no one
can see across it, is less picturesque than one which

affords a view of both its banks at the same time. For a few minutes at sunrise, and at sunset, it is difficult to imagine anything more gorgeous than the colouring of the tropics. But it quickly fades, and even while it lasts it is more calculated to dazzle than to please. There is too much of the patchwork counterpane and the circus-poster about it. Of course a tropical sunset is a sight that it does not happen to everyone to witness, but any-one can get a very fair idea of what it is like by eating a quantity of cold pork-pie and unripe apples just before going to bed.

Leaving Aden, we passed one night to the northward of the island of Socotra, and were fortunate enough to come across the phenomenon known as a "milky sea." It was a wonderfully beautiful sight. The sea was deadly calm, and all round as far as the eye could reach it was as white and as transparent as London milk. Out of this the mountains of Socotra, distant eight miles, rose up clear and distinct in the brilliant star-light, and black as ink by contrast with the whiteness of the sea. Several ambitious passengers ladled up some of the water, to try and discover its component parts, but I don't think they found out much, except that if it was allowed to stand some time, a thick sediment was precipitated, leaving the water quite clear again.

Crossing the Indian Ocean, the weather was so mono-tonously calm that one day the captain was encouraged to give the order for fire and boat station practice. If intended to display the smart discipline and efficiency of the ship's company, this exhibition had better have been suppressed; but if merely to warn passengers against the incautious use of matches, and the danger of falling overboard, it was invaluable. Whether the crew had been expecting the order or not, I cannot say; but I will do them the justice to affirm that the ringing of the fire-bell was followed by no sort of confusion or hurry. It was only after an interval had elapsed sufficient to allow the strongest swimmer to drown, and the smallest spark to become a conflagration, that they began to saunter leisurely aft, dragging after them coils of hose, with the dejected air of men who have seen the same thing done a dozen times before and never known any good to come of it. Far more activity was displayed by a vast army of stewards who swarmed up the companion at the first sound of the bell, headed by the chief steward, or *maître d'hôtel*, with a drawn sword in his hand. As these worthies took no part in the subsequent proceedings, they probably only came up to be saved.

After some consultation, it was agreed that an attempt should be made to lower one of the quarter-boats, and to this the crew turned their attention. But an unforeseen difficulty presented itself. Who was to undertake the arduous task of climbing into the boat, and removing the canvas cover? An animated discussion took place, the result of which was that one man was singled out, apparently much against his inclination, for the enterprise in hand. With a vast effort he collected his energies, and, scattering a glance of melancholy defiance at his recreant companions, he ascended the bulwarks and climbed cautiously on to the boat. It soon became evident that there was far more cause for his alarm than at first appeared. As, long as he was engaged in unlashing the boat's cover, the crew amused themselves by rolling up cigarettes and smoking them. But he had no sooner finished than the men stationed at the after " fall " of the boat suddenly awoke to an enthusiastic sense of duty, and lowered away. Those at the other " fall " were not so alert, and the consequence was the stern of the boat went down with a run, sending oars, stretchers, planks, and everything movable in her except the man, flying into the sea. Fortunately for himself, this hero got mixed up round one of the thwarts and remained there until the boat was once more raised to a horizontal position, when he was extricated positively gibbering with terror and rage. It having been conclusively proved that in case of emergency one end of the boat, at any rate, could be lowered, this was considered sufficient, and the fire-hose became the next object of interest to the company. After some minutes of patient toil, one end of this ingenious contrivance was connected with the machinery, and the order to start pumping was given. An ominous pause followed, during which not a drop of water appeared. The men began to look grave and to whisper hurriedly and excitedly together. But a breathless silence fell upon all present when the second lieutenant advanced to the business end of the hose, with the air of a man who knows his duty and is prepared to perform it at all risks. The excitement now became so intense as to be quite painful, but still silence prevailed. Suddenly a terrible gurgle was heard in the pipe, absolutely paralysing the lieutenant, who remained rooted to the spot with countenance transfigured by terror. In a moment a young Niagara burst from the pipe, discharging itself full upon the unfortunate officer, and hurling the hose in con-

vulsions about the deck.   The shock at once restored
the use of his limbs to the lieutenant.   With a loud
yell of anguish he turned and fled from a foe, with
whom, to judge by appearances, it was some time since
he had had an encounter.

This concluded the diversion of fire and boat-station
practice, and the ship's company returned once more to
their ordinary duties.   The captain resumed his occupation of walking up and down, spitting frequently and
emphatically upon his own quarter-deck.   The chief
engineer took up his position by the rails of the engine-
room, and, with his watch in his hand, counted the
revolutions of the propeller.   The doctor and the first
lieutenant threw quoits into a bucket, and the remainder
of the crew, with the exception of a few who still retained
sufficient energy to smoke, went fast asleep.

# CHAPTER II.

## THE VOYAGE—(*cont.*)

AMONG the passengers on board, there were several newly-married couples, and their behaviour was sometimes rather interesting. Of all places to spend a honeymoon, I can conceive none more discouraging than the sea. We all know that some of the gilt must come off the gingerbread sooner or later, but there are many ways of removing it, and it is just as well to take care that the more solid material beneath it is not injured during the process.

It would be interesting to a psychologist who was also a good sailor, to study the appalling effects of sea-sickness upon the soul, no less remarkable in the case of a subject who does not actually suffer, but is merely compelled to witness the misery of others. Cervantes, we are told, smiled away the chivalry of Spain. Fortunate for Spain that he did so. Had he lived in an age when globe-trotting and going down to the sea in ships was as fashionable as it is now, he would have been spared the effort of smiling. All the finer feelings of human nature are more or less in abeyance during the reign of sea-sickness, but when it has passed off, they, most of them, readily reassert their sway. Not

so with the feeling which we term chivalry, now rapidly
becoming an obsolete word in these days of social
progress. Its loss is the less felt, since its place has
been supplied by coxcombry, a feeling more nearly
allied to chivalry than might at first be imagined. Both
have a common end in view, which is to please. But
there is this distinction, that whereas chivalry arises
from a man's exalted ideas of the intrinsic perfections
of the opposite sex, coxcombry originates in an exaggerated notion of the perfections of his own. Chivalry
however, cannot exist without a profound and sincere
respect for woman; and when that is once destroyed,
or even severely shaken, chivalry receives its death-blow.
Sea-sickness is, of all iconoclasts, the most terrible, and
before its fell advances chivalry withers more quickly
and more surely than ever it did before the smile of
Cervantes, and it withers to anything but the tune of a
smile. If it were only for this reason alone, life at sea
would present matrimony under the most unfavourable
aspect it is possible to imagine. Can anything be more
terrible than to watch a countenance in which you take
the deepest interest, transfigured by sea-sickness into
the ghastly semblance of a frost-bitten turnip, and
every atom of self-respect crushed by this most levelling malady.

But there are other annoyances besides. Careful
and comparative observation leads me to believe that
a woman whose digestive organs have so far rallied
from sea-sickness as to allow her to eat, but whose
appearance still forbids her to leave her cabin, is the
most transcendently selfish of all God's creatures.
Under such circumstances I have seen offices of vica-

rions selfishness thrust upon the unfortunate husband, which the veriest egotist would shrink from negotiating for himself. He is expected to secure the undivided attention of the doctor, the purser, all the stewardesses, and half of the stewards, regardless of how many other passengers there may happen to be in exactly the same, or in a worse, predicament than his wife. He is further expected to ascertain from the captain (at intervals varying from five to fifteen minutes, according to the severity of the weather), the exact position of the ship, the amount of present danger, the prospect of fine weather, and the precise moment when the destination will be reached—distant, possibly, some two or three thousand miles. Most likely he will be sent to ask the quarter-master to prevent the crew from walking about overhead, and to induce the officer of the watch to moderate the noise made by the creaking of the ship's timbers and the working of the donkey-engine. Occasionally I have seen even severer tests applied to the devotion of man, but these have been amongst people who have been some time married. One day the vessel was rolling rather heavily, and though most of the passengers had got their sea-legs, some few remained below. Among the latter was the wife of a man whom I noticed staggering up the companion one morning, with the watery eye and uncertain gait of one just recovering from violent sickness. He reached the deck safely, however, and with a considerable slue to port, brought himself up in a deck-chair. I saw him scatter a glance round, possibly to discover the whereabouts of his better half. Finding himself quite alone, his eye brightened, and he blew his nose

in that triumphant manner which a man never adopts
except when he is quite at ease. He even pulled out
his cigar-case and looked at it, but discretion overcame
valour, and he put it back in his pocket, and prepared
for perfect repose. He was not destined to enjoy it
long. In a few minutes a whey-faced domestic appeared
at the door of the companion, shepherding two of the
most disagreeable-looking children I ever saw. They
had faces like badly-baked buns, and were dressed as
outrageously as only the offspring of British parents of
a certain class ever are. Their legs and feet were like
hockey-sticks, and looked so utterly incapable of supporting the distended waistcoats above them, that their
prudent mother had attached a long red ribbon to each
of their arms, to act as a sort of reins. These were
now entrusted to the hands of paterfamilias, with instructions to drive his progeny up and down the deck
for exercise. Of course he did so, and very ridiculous he
looked; but there was a pathetic side to the picture as
well. In his eye there was a piteous glance of retro-
spection, which seemed to recall the time when he
could take his ease or his exercise, as the spirit moved
him, without being required to make a greater fool of
himself than Nature intended him to be.

Eight days after leaving Aden we got to Galle, and
a greater contrast than the two places it would be difficult to find. At Aden, all the inhabitants who can
afford the luxury drive out daily a distance of four miles
to refresh their weary eyes with the sight of the Botanical Gardens, which consist of six weak-looking trees
and twelve blades of grass in a flower-pot. But at Galle
the sight is overpowered by the extraordinary luxuriance

of the vegetation, and the variety of shades of green displayed among the trees and bushes. Round the edges, of course, there is a decided preponderance of cocoa-nut trees, but a little distance from the shore the crowded way in which all sorts of trees and creepers are arranged is quite bewildering. There is a sort of show place, called Wak-Walleh, a few miles from Galle, to which everyone rushes directly they land, to get a view of the island. It is needless to say that there is a public-house and a tea-garden there; and as you approach it, the "spoor" of the British tourist, in the shape of orange-peel and beer-bottles, is very strongly marked. The view is glorious. A broad valley of green paddy-fields, fringed on each side with densely-wooded hills, lies stretched out below. It is mapped out almost into islands, so winding is the course of the river which runs through it, its waters shining like silver in the sunlight. In the distance rises the bold outline of Adam's Peak, supported by numerous other mountains of lesser pretensions. In the foreground are several marble tables with iron legs, chairs to match, and a party of tourists. Partly disguised by pith helmets and white trousers, nevertheless these last remind one forcibly of Greenwich Fair. They are shouting—positively shouting—and laughing in that aggressive way that only a Briton out for a holiday is master of. Several of them are drinking beer and throwing sticks at cocoa-nuts, and one or two, more utterly degraded than the rest, pick up little pieces of stone to carry away as relics of Wak-Walleh. The native jewellers do a very healthy trade in counterfeit stones, manufactured at Birmingham expressly for exportation to Ceylon. Sapphires are the

2

favourite importations offered to the verdant traveller. I saw one man beautifully let in. He was offered a sapphire about the size of a small tea-cup, of a brilliant hue that would have shamed the waters of the Mediterrauean. Two hundred pounds was the price demanded for this startling gem. The traveller to whom it was offered had heard something of the dishonest practices of the jewellers of Galle, and was anxious to display his capacity for dealing. He winked at an admiring crowd of fellow-passengers, and offered the man three pounds. Much to his disgust, the native instantly closed with his offer, and, securing the coins, left the ship with all possible speed. Of course the sapphire was glass, and, with the setting, might have been worth half-a-crown. There are some real sapphires but no very good ones to be had, as all that are worth anything go direct to the London market.

Five days after leaving Galle we got to Singapore, and had to wait there a week, which was a nuisance, as there is only one hotel in the place fit to live in, and even that one is certainly one of the vilest in the world. The food is simply filthy, and not much of it, the attendance wretched, and the manager gratuitously insulting to everyone. While I was there he was knocked down and shut up in his own coal-cellar by a resident in the town, to whom he had been impertinent, to the intense delight of everyone else in the place.

Singapore itself is a lovely place, with rather a disagreeable climate. The thermometer never varies above a few degrees, and stands at about 85° day and night, all the year round. The wealthier class of inhabitants live in bungalows scattered about over the ridges in the neighbourhood of the town, most of them surrounded by beautiful gardens. They all seem utterly depressed by the enervating climate, and do not aspire to any higher interest in life than a generous rivalry in the concoction of marvellous curries. An old resident of Singapore takes as much interest and pride in his curries as an Englishmen does in his race-horses or his hunters, and he always speaks of a rival connoisseur with deep feeling and respect. Both men and women look very faded and washed-out, and the only colour in their faces is yellow from a prolonged course of curry. I used to walk all round the place for miles every day, in the heat of the day, and never felt anything but better for it. Nothing will induce Indians to expose themselves to the sun, for fear of sunstroke, and nothing makes them so angry as to be told that if they drank less, led a more healthy life, and took more exercise, they would be able to stand the sun with impunity. And yet it is the case. Of course, a man who lies on his back drinking brandy and beer half the day, sleeps the other half, and sits up most of the night, cannot safely expose himself to the full power of an Indian sun without risk. There is something peculiarly treacherous in the sun all over India and the East Indies, but the medical profession know that nine-tenths of the cases of sunstroke that occur are the result of drink.

The only residents I ever saw, either in India, Ceylon, or Singapore, who enjoyed perfect health, and had not the slightest fear of exposing themselves to the sun, were invariably men who led most temperate lives, and who were out of doors all day long. In the bush of Australia, where men work all day long under a vertical sun, with little covering on their heads, sunstroke is absolutely unknown. But in the towns, where they drink all day, and take no exercise, it is not an uncommon thing at all for a man to be knocked over by the sun just in crossing the street.

A week's loafing around Singapore produced a wild longing to leave it, but I must say I was not exhilarated by the sight of the boat that was to carry me to Australia. She was called the *Somerset*, and was the property of the Eastern and Australian Company, and was about as depressing an old tub as I ever travelled in. In the best of weather she was not good for more than eight knots, and if it came on to blow ahead she went astern. The captain was in every respect worthy of the ship he commanded. He spent most of his time sulking in his cabin, and the remainder in entertaining the passengers with most gloomy forebodings. Three days after leaving Singapore the weather got very squally, and the rain came down in such torrents that, when standing on the bridge, it was sometimes impossible to see the foremast. After dark it grew worse, and the captain, who had been blowing an infernal fog-whistle at intervals of five minutes all through the day, informed the passengers that he had no idea where he was, but about three in the morning he ought to go through a winding passage two miles long and three-quarters of a mile wide, between two sunken reefs. After which, he turned the fog-whistle permanently on, and retired into his cabin.

Anything like the horrors of that voyage I never remember. The smell of bilge-water and cockroaches in the saloon was so overpowering that it was almost impossible to stay down long enough to swallow a meal. There were 320 Chinese emigrants forward, who not only smelt horribly themselves, but spent their whole time in cooking nauseous oily messes, the stench from which was wafted aft in a continuous stream from one day's end to another. For days at a time there was not a breath of air, and the heat was so intense that the pitch used to melt and bubble up in the seams of the deck. I used to lie on deck all day and smoke, with a saucer of chloride of lime under my nose as a disinfectant. It was beginning to make the whole crowd of us quite ill. The captain, the officers, and, I believe, everyone in the ship except myself, took to being sick as violently as if they had never been to sea before. Fortunately, when we got to the Arafura Sea we dropped in for a gale of wind. This, as Robinson Crusoe observed, was an amusement the other way. It delayed us three days, but I have not a doubt it saved some of our lives. In the middle of the night, when the gale was at its height, the boiler of the old *Somerset* burst. The man-hole plate flew clean off, and every particle of steam, of course, escaped. It took seventeen hours to repair it, during which time we lay like a log in the trough of the sea, with the waves breaking over us fore and aft. It cleaned us a little, though, which was very healthy.

Two nights afterwards we ran down a native boat, and drowned everyone in it. How many men there were in her I do not know, but we never picked up one. The next day we lost a man overboard ourselves. He was on the jibboom, where he had no business to have been sent, as there was a heavy sea on at the time.

The old *Somerset* put her nose right into a wave, and, of course, the man was washed away. In spite of the sea that was running, he swam like a duck for about twenty minutes, during which time the captain was busily engaged in turning his old craft round, to pick him up. I believe naval authorities are divided as to the advisability of going astern or turning the ship round to pick up a man overboard; but in the case of the *Somerset* I should certainly have preferred the former process, as she had at all times a natural inclination to go astern instead of ahead. However, the captain turned round, and I thought we should have got the poor fellow on board again all right. He was swimming beautifully, keeping his head and shoulders right out of the water, when suddenly he threw up his arms, rose half out of the water, and then sank like a stone. I expect a shark must have got him, as one had been prowling after us for some time. This incident brought the captain's ill-humour to a climax, and next day, when he found me throwing little pieces of stick over the side to see which way the vessel was going, he became quite uncivil.

# CHAPTER III.

## SOMERSET.

No one was sorry when, about sixteen days after leaving
Singapore, the coast of Australia hove in sight. We
passed through Torres Straits, which were adorned with
the remains of three recent wrecks, and anchored off
Somerset, the northernmost township in Australia. It
is merely a pearl-fishing station, and will never develop
into anything, as there is no back country to it. The
pearl fishers who live there are a rough-looking lot, not
encumbered with any superfluous clothing, and generally
without shoes or stockings. Their trade, which is an
exceedingly profitable one, is carried on by means of
black divers, who go down and bring up the mother-of-
pearl shells. These shells, which are about a foot or
sixteen inches across, and shaped like an oyster-shell,
were worth at that time nearly £250 per ton. The
pearls found in the shell were reckoned to pay all
expenses, and the profits were enormous. Even at the
present time, when pearl-shell has fallen in value to
£140 a ton, it pays well to get. There is another pearl
fishery on the western coast of Australia, and some of
the pearls obtained there fetch large prices. Though
they are never equal to the Oriental pearls in colour,

they make up for it in size, and I heard of one being
sold in London recently for £1,500. The West
Australian pearl-fisheries are liable to the most terrific
hurricanes. The signs which herald their approach are
perfectly well known, and give ample time to a vessel to
secure a good offing. But the pearl fishers are generally
much too recklessly intent on their occupation to take
any such precaution, and every now and then the whole
lot of them get swept right away, some of their boats
being sent to the bottom, and others blown clean out of
the water into the mangroves that fringe the shore.
The few that are not drowned in one of these visitations
do not seem to care or take any warning. *Mox reficit
rates*, the pearl-fisher picks up the pieces, sends off for
another schooner if his own is hopelessly damaged, and
goes on again as if such a thing as a hurricane was
unknown.

One or two white men, who have nothing to do with
the pearl-fishing, have taken up their permanent abode
at Somerset for no reason at all that I could see, except
to enjoy the society of black women, and to run an
imminent risk of being knocked on the head by black
men. The blacks in the neighbourhood of Somerset are
very bad. They are a fierce warlike race of athletic
savages, with a cross of the Malay in them. The
Government Resident at Somerset wages an endless war
with them, and from the intrepid bravery which he has
always displayed in his encounters with them he has
established a wonderful prestige. So recklessly daring,
and so successful have some of his raids against them
been, that he is firmly believed to be the Devil by all
the natives in the Somerset district. A mob of about

200 of them once came and camped on an island opposite to his residence. He knew that they would very shortly attack him, so he determined not to wait for them. As soon as it was dark, he stripped himself naked, and tying his rifle and his ammunition on to his head to keep them dry, he swam across to the island. The tide ran very strong, and the channel was a quarter of a mile wide, but he got across all right.

Without the slightest fear he attacked the whole camp of blacks single handed, and routed them utterly. So terrified were they at the fact of one white man daring to attack them alone, that they came to the conclusion that there must be something superhuman about him, and cleared out with all speed. It was months before he was troubled with them again. He has been there now for a good many years, and numerous are the hair-breadth escapes that he has had during that time. So far his courage has carried him safely through, and though he has often been wounded, he has never come to serious harm. But his enemies are numerous and implacable, and it is odd if a spear or a tomahawk does not finish him at last.

From Torres Straits right away to below Cape Capricorn, runs the great barrier reef of Australia. Inside this the navigation is very intricate; a perfect net-work of islands and reefs. We took a pilot on board at Somerset, but even then we had occasionally to anchor at night when there was no room. The scenery all down the coast of Queensland is very wild, and in some parts extremely beautiful. Endless masses of wooded mountain-ranges run all along the mainland, and some of the islands with their emerald slopes dotted over with patches of dark green firs are very picturesque.

Whit-sunday passage, just before coming to Bowen, is one of the prettiest bits of scenery on the whole coast of Australia. The ranges on the mainland here are very broken, and just off the shore is a large group of lovely islands, between which and the mainland the coasting-steamers' track passes. It looked very beautiful in the evening, when the mountains were turning to that soft clear smoky blue, peculiar to Australian scenery, and the crimson fire of sunset was still smouldering in the golden west.

The *Somerset* did not call off Mackay, which was my destination, so I had to go on to Keppel Bay, the port for Rockhampton, 200 miles further south, and wait for a boat back to Mackay.

I left the *Somerset* with feelings of unmixed joy, and with a hearty hope that she might go to the bottom when she got into Sydney harbour, and stay there. Since that time, to the great delight of everyone who ever travelled in any of their boats, the Eastern and Australian Company have abandoned the Queensland mail service, after losing nearly all their boats. The *Brisbane*, the best boat they had, was wrecked near Torres Straits. The *Normanby* shared her fate soon after. The *Singapore* ran ashore near Mackay and was totally lost, and the *Qneensland* was run into by the *Barrabool*, and sunk just off Sydney. They were altogether a most unfortunate company, and were very badly treated by the New South Wales Government, who induced them to start by the promise of a large subsidy, which promise was repudiated as soon as the company's ships began running. Their place has been taken by the British India Company, who run a service of very fine boats from London to Brisbane *viâ* Batavia, carrying the mails, and calling at Thursday Island, Cooktown, Townsville, Bowen, Mackay, and Keppel Bay on the Queensland coast. They do not run further south than Brisbane, and have no subsidy from any Government except that of Queensland.

My brother met me in Rockhampton, and we were fortunate enough to find a boat sailing for Mackay a few hours after I landed. We ran up to the entrance of the Pioneer river, on which Mackay is situated, in about twenty-four hours, and had to anchor there and wait for the tide to get in. We amused ourselves by fishing for sharks, and caught one about six feet long. About one o'clock in the morning the tide served, and we steamed up the Pioneer for a couple of miles, and lay alongside of a rather dilapidated wharf. No one appeared to take sufficient interest in the arrival of the steamer to be on the wharf, and, beyond a few sheds, I could not, at first, see any signs of a town at all. My brother knew the way, however, and, collaring as much of my luggage as we could carry, we set off to the hotel. Following his lead, I floundered through a mass of black mud, and several deep puddles of water, and emerged on to a road about three inches deep in dust. After going along this for a hundred yards, some buildings began to loom up against the starlit sky, and a little further on we turned a corner, and found ourselves in the main street of Mackay.

It might have been the city of the dead, for any signs of a population. Not a light was to be seen in the rows

of uneven low wooden buildings that ran along each
side of the street, and the only living creatures were
several dogs fast asleep in the middle of the road.
Turning another corner, we stumbled over the body of
a man with his heels on the pavement and his head in
the gutter.   His hat was off, and he was evidently in
the total collapse stage of drunkenness.   My brother
struck a match, and examined his features.

"Ah, I thought so," he observed, "it's the doctor.
He's been like that, off and on, for a fortnight.   Here,
lend a hand, and pull him out of the gutter.   He'll
have a fit if he lies like that much longer."

Having dragged him into a less apopletic position,
we turned into the hotel.   There was no one up, but it
was open; so we went upstairs and hunted about for a
couple of empty rooms.   After one or two bad shots,
which disclosed the prostrate forms of several sleepers,
most of whom had gone to bed in their boots, we found
what we wanted, and turned in.   It was pretty hot,
and the musquitoes made it rather lively, but we got a
few hours' sleep, and next morning turned out early,
to get ready for a start up to the station.   The first
thing we heard from my brother's black boy, who was
waiting about the town for him, was that the horses
had got out of the paddock.   They were certain to go
straight back to the station, so my brother borrowed a
horse, and sent the boy down the road to look for them.
He got them about ten miles away, and did not re-
appear till the middle of the day.

Meanwhile, I amused myself by examining the town
of Mackay.   Of all horrible places to live in, the worst
is a small coast town in Queensland.   They are all

alike. The streets are very broad, and almost all the houses built entirely of wood, with verandahs in front of them, extending over the pavement. There is not a green thing to be seen anywhere. Dust is everywhere, inches deep in the streets that are not macadamised, and trees, bushes, houses, and everything are powdered over with it. In summer it is sweltering hot, the glare is frightful, and before I had been half an hour in Mackay, I began to understand why my brother was in such a hurry to get out of it. When I first landed there, the white population of the whole district was under 2,000, and that of the actual township under 1,000, but I counted seventeen public-houses in the place. The first thing that struck me was that not a single man in the town had a coat or waistcoat on, and the next thing that struck me was what very sensible people they all were, for it was about the middle of March, and the weather was so hot that any superfluous clothing was unbearable.

There was a *table d'hôte* at the hotel at which we camped, and at dinner-time a crowd of men assembled for the feed. Squatters down from the country, bank-clerks, planters, and business men, not one of them had a coat on. Their invariable costume was a pair of moleskins or tweed trousers, fastened round the waist with a leather belt, a cotton shirt with the sleeves rolled up, and a silk handkerchief loosely tied round the neck. The Bushmen were easily distinguished by the mahogany brown to which constant exposure to the sun had turned their faces, necks, and arms.

The fashion of wearing no coats is peculiar to Mackay, and has been adopted by the planters, who consider themselves the *élite* of the place. At a dinner party on one of the plantations it is a most curious sight to see all the ladies, *en grande tenue,* dressed in the latest fashion, and the gentlemen sitting down with no coat or waistcoat, and their arms bare to the elbow.

It was one o'clock before we were ready for a start, and, as our station was forty-five miles away, we settled to go out and camp at a station about five-and-twenty miles up the Pioneer river, and go on home next day. The country round Mackay is a dead level alluvial plain for ten or twelve miles, and is all under cultivation for sugar-growing. Our road for the first mile and a half went through a sort of straggling township of small detached houses, each surrounded by a grass paddock; but after this we got among the cane-fields, and the sight of them was very refreshing after being shut up for weeks at sea. There are few prettier plants than sugar, and the panorama of the Mackay cane-fields is really beautiful. For miles the cane stretches away in a level sea of emerald green, here and there a tall brick chimney rising up to indicate the whereabouts of a mill. A broad belt of dark green forest marks the course of the Pioneer, winding through the plains, and beyond this again the cane-fields rise right away to the base of rugged mountains, thickly wooded to the very summit. All along the horizon the mountains of the coast range are piled one behind the other in dark blue masses, their outline rising here and there into sharp peaks against the western sky, and forty miles away towers the mighty form of Mount Dalrymple, over four thousand feet high, the second highest mountain in Queensland. On both banks of the Pioneer, at intervals of a few miles, are the resi-

THE HERMITAGE PADDOCK, - MACKAY.

dences of the planters, and certainly the lines have fallen to them in pleasant places. Their houses, as a rule, are extremely comfortable, and very well furnished, and the gardens of many of them are paradises of beauty. In good times, they make tremendous profits, and their occupation chiefly consists in watching other people work, in the intervals of which they recline in a shady verandah with a pipe and a novel, and drink rum-swizzles. Most of them keep a manager, so that they can always get away for a run down south, or a kangaroo hunt up the country. They are very hospitable and keep their houses always open to strangers visiting the place, and to their friends in the country, who come uninvited, and are welcome to stay as long as they please.

About fourteen miles from Mackay we passed the last plantation, and got among the gum-trees, and shortly afterwards the track struck the bank of the Pioneer. I have seldom seen a more beautiful river. As a rule Queensland rivers are muddy, sluggish streams, with low banks covered with mangroves, and many of them would not be called rivers at all in a country where water was more plentiful. But the scenery along the Pioneer is lovely. Its whole length is only about one hundred miles, but it drains a large extent of country, and for the last thirty miles the average width of its bed is from one to two hundred yards. It rises in the coast range, and its course lies through heavily-timbered country all the way to the sea. The banks, sometimes sloping, sometimes very steep, vary in height from fifty to a hundred feet, and are thickly covered with a dense forest of trees and creepers. The river itself is a succession of deep black pools of beautifully clear water, some of them nearly a mile in length, with long rocky rapids between them.

The track wound along the banks for some miles, and every now and then we pulled up to admire some more than usually beautiful reach, where the water was turned to gold in the evening sunlight, and the dim blue mountains showed up through the forest beyond. Swarms of ducks of every description were paddling about in the pools, and sunning themselves on the rocks and sandbanks.

At one bend of the river, just at the head of a deep pool, where the " scrub " on the banks was very thick, my brother said there was pretty sure to be an alligator, and if we went quietly we might get a sight of it; so we got off, hung our horses up to a tree, and crawled through the scrub down the bank to the water's edge. Peering cautiously through a tangled curtain of creepers that hung over the water, we were rewarded by the sight of a huge alligator, basking on a sankbank about sixty yards off, and apparently fast asleep. The instant we showed ourselves, however, he shuffled into the water with incredible speed. The upper waters of the Pioneer are inhabited by numbers of these brutes, and some of them grow to an enormous size. One was killed not long before I arrived, nineteen feet long, but even this was eclipsed by Big Ben of the Fitzroy, who measured twenty-three feet six inches, and who when last I saw him was in the possession of Mr. Jamrach in London. These alligators do not seem to increase much in numbers, and the same ones hang about the same pools for years. From October to March during the hot weather, they do not show themselves at all, but during the rest of the year, in the cool weather, they lie about on the sandbanks warming themselves all day.

The sun was getting low, so we climbed on to our horses again, and after a three-mile canter along a splendid level track winding through an endless forest of gums, under which the grass grew three feet high, our destination hove in sight.

"Sleepy Hollow," or, as it is always called, "The Hollow," the station at which we were going to camp that night, is about the prettiest place on the whole of the Pioneer. As we rode up we were greeted with a chorus of barking from a small army of cattle-dogs that were lying about the out-buildings, and Mr. Charles Rawson, the owner of the Hollow, came out to meet us. He gave a wild shout of delight when he saw who it was. He was an old friend of my brother, and, seizing me by the hand, he bade me welcome to Australia with a heartiness there was no mistaking.

"Hooray, boys!" he said, "this is just about the soundest day I've seen for a deuce of a time. If I'd known when your old dug-out was going to fetch the Mackay wharf, you bet I'd have been there to meet you. Here, George, take these horses and turn them into the big paddock."

"Hold on," said my brother. "Better put them in the small one, we want to get away early to-morrow."

"To-morrow! to-morrow be blowed; you'll stop here for a week any way. You'll surely never be so beastly mean as to come here for only one night?'

To his great disappointment my brother declared he

3

must be back at the station the next day, as there was a man coming up to pick fat cattle.

"Well, if it's business," he observed sadly, "I don't so much mind; but any way, come on inside now, and have a drop of something short. I was just going to make it sundown when you boys rode up, and I was suffering to look at somebody through the bottom of a glass."

We followed our host into a cool shady verandah, and he quickly produced the materials for a drink.

"Now, then," said he, "just let me mix you a swizzle. What's a swizzle! Oh! I forgot you'd only just landed. Well, I believe a swizzle is about the squarest drink that's yet been invented, and there's no one in the district can lay over me at mixing one. But hold on till you try it."

Never having heard of a swizzle, which is a drink peculiar to Mackay, I believe, I watched his proceedings with interest. First of all he put two inches of Jamaica rum into the bottom of a tumbler, into which he shook a few drops of Angostura bitters from a bottle, with a small hole in the cork. Next he added a small teaspoonful of brown sugar, and a squeeze of a lemon, and filled the tumbler two-thirds full of water. He then took a small stick with three prongs growing the reverse way up at the end, and whirled it round in the tumbler between his hands, with a dexterity only to be acquired by constant practice, till the decoction was foaming to the top of the glass.

Handing it to me quickly, with directions to "drink it while fizzing," he watched it going down, with one eye shut, and an expression of sympathetic interest on his face.

" How 's that for high ? " he asked as I set down the
glass with a sigh of satisfaction.

I acknowledged that he had not over-rated the
beauties of the drink, and asked him where he got the
peculiar little stick with which he stirred it up.

" Ah ! " he said, " that 's just it. That 's nothing
short of a swizzle-stick, and it grows on a tree that 's
peculiar to the Mackay district, and no doubt a bounti-
ful Providence placed it there on purpose for the inhabitants to stir up their liquor with. I discovered it myself, and it hadn't a name, so we christened it the
*Swizzlestickia Rawsoniensis* There 's two of them
growing down there in the paddock, alongside the
fence."

The owner of the Hollow is probably one of the most
popular men in the north of Queensland. He was one
of the earliest settlers in the district, has been
identified with its rise and progress, and has not an
enemy in the place. There were wild times in the early
days of Mackay, and most of his contemporaries have
been stretched out for the undertaker, or, if they still
live, are mere wrecks of their former selves. But sixteen years of hard work and hard living in the tropics
have made never a mark on the iron constitution of our
host. His head is marble, and perfectly proof against
the influence of Mackay rum, forty-five over proof, as
anyone who drinks alongside of him will find to their
cost. Many a reveller, waking after a heavy night to
repentance and a sick headache, has turned sicker still
to see him enter his room at five the next morning, with
a cheery smile on his face, a pipe of nigger-head between
his lips, and an invitation to come down and bathe in

the river. He is nearer fifty than forty now, and his
hair is not quite so thick as it was, and getting gray
in places. But to use his own words " he has still got
as bully a set of works as there are in the island, and,
bar accidents, is good for another ten years yet." A
kind heart and an inexhaustible fund of good spirits
made him as pleasant a mate as a man could wish for,
and if there 's any fun going, from an exploring expedition to a game of euchre, he is bound to be up to the
neck in it. Having finished our drinks and lit our
pipes, we sallied out to scatter a glance round the
place.

The forest has been cleared for a little distance round,
and the house and garden are surrounded by a paddock
of short green turf. The house itself is a large one-
storied building, with a fourteen-foot verandah all round
covered with masses of every sort of creeper. It stands
right on the river-bank, which rises to an elevation of
a hundred feet above the bed, and the view up the river
is magnificent. Right in front of the house the bed
of the river is full of rocky islands and rapids; but
above this there is a long stretch of still deep water up
to the next bend, three quarters of a mile away. The
opposite bank is covered with a most magnificent forest
of enormous trees, called in Australia a " scrub," to
distinguish it from open timbered country.

Nothing can be more beautiful in the way of a forest
than a Queensland scrub. Fig-trees, Leichardts, white
cedar, red cedar, beech, and a hundred other trees whose
names I never heard, are crowded together in wild confusion, their dense foliage mingled in masses of every
conceivable shade of green. Here and there a group

of feathery palms rear their heads above the surrounding forest, and giant creepers hang suspended in thick curtains from one huge tree to another.

In front of the house, just on the fall of the river-bank, is a gigantic bamboo, the father of all bamboos in the Mackay district, and round about the house are several smaller ones. But the garden running along the top of the bank is a sight worth going to Queensland to see. There is fifty feet of black soil here, and it must be a mean sort of plant that would not grow. Lemons, limes, guavas, custard-apples, grapes, mangoes, oranges, and grenadillas all flourish in a state of perfection that speaks equally well for the care of their owner and the excellence of the climate. Mangoes and oranges seem to do especially well, and the trees of the latter were absolutely weighed down with fruit, and Bananas and passion fruit grow like weeds. In the middle of the garden, on a patch of smooth green turf, stands the most magnificent Poinciana tree I ever saw, about sixty feet high, with huge spreading boughs sweeping right down to the ground. The foliage is light green, and exactly resembles the leaf of a sensitive plant, and in summer it is literally covered with huge spiral flowers of the most brilliant crimson. The roof and side verandah of the house are overrun with masses of Boganvillea creepers, of every shade from pink to purple, and the flower-beds around are full of roses and geraniums. Gardenias grow all about, in bushes five feet high, and flower most beautifully. The back of the garden is sheltered all along by an impenetrable row of bamboos, Leichardts, and fig-trees, and in front, just along the edge of the river-bank, runs

a low hedge of hybiscus, blazing with scarlet flowers.
The front verandah of the house has been extended into
a sort of conservatory, made of a lattice-work of battens
split from palm-trees, inside which is a rockery covered
with most beautiful ferns.

The mountains and creeks of northern Queensland are
full of every sort of fern, and in the fernery at the
Hollow I counted over thirty varieties which Mr. Rawson had picked up in his wanderings about his own
runs, and brought home and planted.

# CHAPTER IV.

## FIRST IMPRESSIONS OF THE BUSH.

NEXT morning, my brother and I saddled up early, and started off through the Bush for Mount Spencer, directly after breakfast. There is something very bewildering about one's first introduction to the Bush, especially in the coast country of Queensland, which is one vast stupendous forest of different sorts of trees. Mile after mile, day after day, you ride on through the forest, with a tree on an average every ten yards. If you keep in the valleys you see nothing but trees, and if you climb up a mountain you see nothing but more trees. Here and there you come upon a small open plain, a few hundred yards in extent; but until you get used to it the monotony of the endless timber is appalling, and it is easy to realise the terrible madness that so often comes over those who get lost in the Bush. The only change is from white gum-trees on the flats, to black iron-barks on the ridges, and one ridge and one flat is so like another, to an inexperienced eye, it seems incredible that anyone can ever find their way about, or know exactly where they are. Some people never can, and I have known natives of the country, who have lived for twenty years in the Bush, and who have still been helpless to get from one place to another without a guide, in country that they had ridden over for years. These are the exceptions, however, and, as a rule, a man with a moderate bump of locality soon learns the art of finding his way in the Bush. Very slight land-marks will serve to guide a good bushman, for no two places are really exactly alike, and on the coast country there is generally some mountain or other to get a sight of, which will enable anyone who knows the country he is in to take his bearings. Away on the open rolling plains of the West, or, worse still, in country covered with endless brigalow scrub, the bushman has often not a single mark to guide him for many miles, except the sun or stars. In such country, finding one's way about is reduced to an instinct, which is a natural gift by no means to be acquired; and unless a man be endowed with it, he had better never attempt to wander far alone in the trackless wilds of the Australian Bush. Many a man who has tried it, under the delusion that he was born to be an explorer, has paid the penalty of his rashness with his life. Witness the fate of Burke and Wills, whose miserable end was due not nearly so much to the force of circumstances, as to their being by nature utterly unfitted to find their way about the Bush ; for they perished within a few miles of their own plant of provisions, without having the slightest idea where they were.

The first thing that strikes one, is the lifeless solitude of the Bush. The fierce searching light of a vertical sun prevents it from being gloomy, and, indeed, the trees in the open timbered country give a very scanty shade, but everywhere there is a weird solemn stillness that is most impressive. In the middle of the day, birds and beasts retire to the cool shade of the scrubs on the banks of the creeks, and there is not a sound to be heard, nor a living thing to be seen. The accumulated silence of a thousand years seems to brood over some of the mountains and valleys of this vast land, where, perhaps, the sound of man's voice has never yet been heard. Now and then a light breeze rustles in the tops of the trees, which move softly, as if stirring in their sleep, but it quickly passes away, and sunshine and silence are everywhere again. But the sensation of loneliness very soon wears off, and in a little while even the endless trees come to look like friends in whose company it is no hardship to pass a day. There is a deep fascination about the freedom of the Bush, whose subtle influence very soon enslaves those who go to live there, and generally unsettles them for any other mode of living.

A " new chum," as a new arrival in Australia is called, is never very long in the country without getting some sort of fall off a horse, and I got my first one a few miles from the Hollow. Like nine out of every ten station horses, the animal I was riding had a sore back, and was girth-galled as well, so I was riding with the girths very loose. Now there is one thing in riding through the Bush which the sooner a man learns the better, and that is, however fast he is going, and however thick the timber is, never to attempt to guide his horse clear of the trees. As long as he gives him his head and does not attempt to interfere with him, his horse will never run him against a tree ; but he is certain only to have one side to his mouth, and any efforts to keep him clear of one tree will probably send him into another. The way in which an old stock-horse shaves the trees with just a couple of inches to spare, at racing pace, makes his rider's hair stand on end, and gives him a cold feeling down the back at first, but he soon drops down to sitting back and leaving his horse to steer clear of the timber by himself. These sorts of little peculiarities are so well known to everyone who has been a little while in the country, that they always forget to tell anyone of them who has not. As I followed my brother at a hard canter along the track winding through the timber, an ill-judged attempt to induce my horse to give rather a wider berth to a gigantic gum-tree produced exactly the opposite effect, and a collision was the result. The girths being quite loose, the cant which we got from the gum-tree, turned me and my saddle half round, and, as my intelligent animal at once redoubled its speed, it was not long before we parted. I landed on my shoulder, and the pace at which we were going sent me head over heels, my further advance being abruptly stopped by an iron-bark tree against which I brought up with considerable violence. My horse tore past my brother, who immediately set off after it, and they both disappeared in the Bush. The first impulse of anyone under the circumstance would have been to have a smoke, and my temper was by no means improved by finding that my pipe had been smashed to pieces between myself and the iron-bark tree. However, I set off down the track, and after about half a mile, met my brother coming back, leading my horse. He had hunted it for about a mile, and fortunately bailed it up between two gullies, and caught it; for, as a rule, it takes at least three men to surround a loose horse in the Bush, and even then, unless it is a very quiet one, they will not catch it. After about fifteen miles of low ridges and flats, we came to the foot of the main coast range.

A zigzag road cut through the scrub took us over the pass, and the moment that we got to the top the change in the atmosphere was quite extraordinary. Though the sun was just as hot, there was a delightfully fresh light feeling in the air, the horses ceased to sweat, and one felt the same sensation as when one comes out of a green-house into the open air. The top of the range was covered with spotted or scented gum, the perfume of which is very strong, and rather like that of a lemon-scented verbena.

About sixteen miles of monotonous stony ridges covered with endless black iron-barks brought us to a dense clump of wattles, a sort of mimosa—tall, feathery, graceful trees, with leaves like a willow, and sweet-scented yellow flowers. Through this the road passed, and we emerged on to a piece of level country covered with white poplar-gums and grass-trees. The latter are most comical-looking objects. They have a black bare stem, from one to eight feet high, surmounted by a tuft of a sort of half rushes and half grass, out of which, again, grows a long thing exactly like a huge bull-rush. A lot of them always grow together, and a little way off they are not unlike the illustrations of Red-Indian chiefs in Fenimore Cooper's novels. The tuft of grass at the top has a sort of core, white and soft, that tastes rather like a Spanish chestnut, and is good to eat, when there is nothing else to be had.  About a mile along the flat brought us to the Mount Spencer horse-paddock fence, through which we passed, and got to the station just at sundown.

Somehow or other, in Australia, no matter how long or how short one's journey is, one nearly always gets to the end of it about sundown, which seems to be the orthodox hour, especially for strangers, to arrive at a station.  As we emerged from the timber in the paddock into the large open space in which the station lay, it struck me as one of the most beautiful places I had ever seen.  As a rule, on the coast country the timber is so thick that the look-out is necessarily very limited, and although here and there there are very pretty spots, it is very seldom that there is a panorama of any extent worth looking at.  Of course on the downs you can see as far as the horizon in every direction, but the monotony of the rolling plains of grass is almost as bad as the Atlantic.  The view, however, from Mount Spencer, is magnificent, and certainly beats anything I ever saw in Australia.  The station stands on a low broad ridge, which was originally timbered like the surrounding Bush, but the trees have all been cleared away, the stumps burned out, and the holes filled in, so that the ground is now a smooth expanse of short green turf, sloping gently down to the edge of a large lagoon, about three hundred yards away. The lagoon itself is a mile and a half long, and about a mile across, the centre covered with water-lilies, and the edges fringed with a thick wide belt of rushes. On the far side from the station a forest of huge gum-trees follows the winding shores of the lagoon, its outline broken by one or two little promontories running out into the water, and above the forest, like an amphitheatre, rise the mountains of the coast, running back in broken rocky spurs to Blue Mountain, a vast densely-wooded range three thousand feet high and fourteen miles away.

The sun had just set when we arrived, and everything was deadly still. The shadow from the hills at the back of the station had fallen across the lagoon, in whose dark waters the forms of the white gum-trees around were perfectly reflected. The shades of evening had fallen upon the forest, but the mountain ranges beyond were still lit up with the rosy after-glow of sunset, and looked almost transparent against the deep pure blue of an autumn evening sky. Hundreds of water-fowl of every description were dotted over the expanse of the lagoon, the ducks now and then rising up in flights, and passing over the station to a swamp at the back. Rows of solemn-looking white egrets were sitting on the fences, running out into the water, or stalking about amongst the reeds, and high over head a solitary pelican was wheeling round in circles, with wings outstretched and motionless. Now and again a flock of whistlers would rise up with a tremendous clatter and excitement out of the rushes, as if they were frightened out of their wits, and then, after going for a fly round, settle again close to where they started from. The shores of the lagoon in front of the station, between the two fences of the small paddock, were always kept as a sanctuary for all the ducks and white fowl. Here they were never fired at. They knew it perfectly well, and, when inside the bounds, they were so tame that

they would let anyone walk up to within twenty yards
of them.

On the far side of the lagoon the smoke of a Black's
camp was rising up through the trees, and a mob of
cattle were standing up to their knees in the water,
taking their evening drink, and lazily nibbling at the
rushes round them.  The whole place looked wonderfully peaceful and quiet, altogether the kind of place that
it would be very easy to make a home of, and where it
would be very difficult to keep up the feelings of an
exile for very long.

The last feed on a station—dinner, tea, supper, or
whatever it may be called—is always just after dark,
and is the most solid meal in the day.  Bushmen smoke
so much, and drink so much tea, that they are rather
mean performers at breakfast, and in the middle of the
day they are generally out on the run, but there must be
something wrong if they cannot eat a square meal in
the evening.  After we had had supper, and a smoke, of
course, I was shown my camp, which was a slab hut
about a hundred yards away from the big house.  The
furniture consisted of a canvas stretcher for a bed, a fragment of looking-glass balanced on two nails driven into
a post, a table with a tin basin, and a bucket.  But
there were heaps of blankets, and a fire-place, which
is all that is wanted to make one perfectly comfortable.
The slabs which formed the sides of the hut were put
up vertically, and as I lay in bed the spaces between
them afforded a fine view of the surrounding country.
There was no door, and the roof was not as water-tight
as it might have been, so that when it rained, five little
streamlets of water descended on my bed ; but I subse-

quently diverted them on to the floor by means of a couple of sheets of corrugated iron, which I secured overhead.

Besides the light of a wood fire, the inside of the hut was illuminated by a fat-lamp, a simple contrivance in the form of a jam-tin full of fat, with a fragment of tweed trousers stuck through a hole in the top for a wick, which gives a very fair light. I was rather tired, and not sorry for the prospect of a camp; but when I dragged back the blankets to turn in, I discovered an enormous carpet-snake, about eleven feet long, comfortably coiled up in my bunk. It raised its head lazily, and after looking at me for a second or two with a want of interest that I was far from feeling myself, it coiled itself up again, and prepared for another sleep. My brother had just gone, but I shouted to him to bring a stick or something and help me kill it. He came back, and looked in.

" What's the matter ? Snake ? Oh, don't kill that one. That's a tame one, that belongs to Rice. He wouldn't have it killed for anything, and, besides, its only a carpet-snake, and they are perfectly harmless."

" H'm, it's all very well to say it's harmless," I observed; " I suppose you mean it's not poisonous. From the look of its head, it could bite a piece out of you about the size of a tea-cup, and anyhow it's not going to sleep in my bed."

" Oh no," said my brother, " it has no business here. It lives in a tub. Here, I'll take it away and put it to bed," and seizing it by the neck, he dragged it off, and dropped it into a barrel outside the store, about fifty yards away, from which I devoutly hoped that it would not be able to get out again that night.

I turned in, in hopes of a good sleep, but I soon discovered that I was very unlikely to get it. The station seemed peaceful enough at sundown, but no sooner had night fairly settled down than a combination of noises arose that would have awakened Rip Van Winkle himself. In the first place my camp was not far from the calf-pen, in which the six or seven calves belonging to the milkers were shut up every night. These little brutes bellow incessantly all night, and their mothers come and look over the railings, and answer them. Then my partner Rice was a great poultry fancier, and had a vast army of chickens. Cocks in Australia always begin to crow about twelve o'clock at night, and leave off at sunrise, so about twelve of these pests added their voices to the general clamour, supported by a dozen or so of call-ducks, which were certainly pure-bred, if the noise that they make has anything to do with their pedigree. But the din reached its climax when a native dog howled some-where away in the Bush. Instantly every dog on the station started up mad with excitement, and began barking with a fury that nothing but exhaustion could abate. Two Russian wolf-hounds, three Kangaroo-dogs, three cattle-dogs, four bull-dogs, and five fox-terriers, all started a volley of barking which was kept up inces-santly for a quarter of an hour, and then slackened down to a sort of platoon-fire of yaps and howls which lasted the rest of the night. In time one gets perfectly used to this sort of nocturnal concert, and can sleep through any amount of it, but at first it is simply maddening, not one wink of sleep did I get the first night, and I was glad when daylight came, and it was time to turn out.

No words can describe the glory of a morning in the Australian Bush. There is a pure soft freshness about the air, full of the peculiar scent of the gum-trees, of which no one ever tires, and a sparkling brilliancy in the morning sunlight that no other climate can produce. Surely this is the time of all others for a smoke. There is sure to be something left in your pipe from the night before. If not, fill it again, and light it with a fire-stick from the hearth; and years after, if you are a true lover of the weed, you will own that no smoke in the world comes up to the one before breakfast on a summer's morning in the Bush. There is something in the climate that brings out the flavour of tobacco, and a good deal in the way of living that encourages smoking; for Bushmen, as a race, are probably the heaviest smokers in existence. The tobacco they smoke is very good, and very strong, mostly manufactured in America, and known as fig-tobacco. When once a man takes to smoking it, it ruins him for any other sort of tobacco, but, as a general rule, about ten years is as long as a man can go on smoking it without finding that it is knocking his nerves to pieces. A fig a day, or just short of an ounce, is a common allowance, but a Bushman's pipe is never out of his mouth. He is always lighting it to have a few whiffs, which is a most poisonous form of smoking. The last thing he puts away at night, and the first thing he looks for in the morning, is his pipe; and if he wakes in the night, he has a smoke then.

4

I was not long in falling into the ways of the country in this respect, and, lighting a pipe, I sallied out to have a look round. A soft white curtain of mist was rising off the lagoon and rolling away before the sun, to gather for a little while on the sides of the deep blue mountains around before it finally disappeared. The sun rose over the range in a blaze of heat, turning the dark waters of the lagoon into a sheet of gold, and streaming through the forest in long bands of glittering light. The water-fowl on the lagoon awoke, uttering a hundred different cries, the ducks standing up on the lily leaves and flapping the dew from their wings. Close to the station one or two butcher-birds were piping their morning song, a strange little melody with not many notes, which no one who has heard it will ever forget. On a dead iron-bark tree, just outside the horse-yard, three or four black crows were sitting, talking to each other, and looking as wise as nothing but an Australian crow ever did. They are far the most interesting birds in the Bush, and the way in which they talk to each other is simply fascinating, for it really seems as if one could not help knowing exactly what they are saying.

Round the store-door a sound assortment of poultry were assembled waiting for their morning feed, most of them thoroughbred game, bred from imported birds, and on the roof were about a hundred pigeons of every conceivable breed. Rice was immensely fond of his chickens and pigeons, never went home to England without bringing back a fresh supply, and some of the birds which he raised on the station were very high-class specimens indeed. Besides all these he always

MOUNT SPENCER: HEAD STATION.

had a menagerie of tame birds and beast of all kinds. When I got there the collection contained an eagle-hawk, three crested falcons, seven wood-ducks, five whistlers, a magpie, three teal, a kangaroo, a walla-roo, a native bear, five flying squirrels, three spur-winged plovers, and a cage-full of parrots and small birds, and last, but not least, the infernal carpet-snake which I found in my bed. They were all quite tame, and, except the flying squirrels and parrots, which lived in cages, and the eagle-hawk, which had a string to its leg, they all used to hang about the place on the loose.

The station itself was quite a small village of houses. The big house stood a little way apart, in a garden with a paling fence round it, about eighty yards square. Unfortunately it was right on the top of a quartz ridge, where there was very little soil, so that it was difficult to get trees of any size to grow; but all sorts of creepers throve wonderfully. In front of the house were one or two Poincianas, and a very pretty bunya, a sort of fir-tree; and round every pile of the house grew masses of scarlet geraniums, which are supposed to possess the virtue of keeping away snakes. At the back there was a rock-work covered with beautiful ferns, and be-yond that a small pond with dwarf bamboos round it, where the tame wild-ducks lived.

The house itself was a very comfortable building, two stories high, about sixty feet long and thirty-five feet wide, built upon round piles seven feet high, with an eight-foot verandah all round. Down below was the dining room, with a huge brick fire-place, the pantry, a small store, an office and a bath-room. Over the

dining-room was the sitting-room, also with a large
fire-place, and with " French-lights " opening on to the
verandah, and, on the same floor, four very comfortable
bed-rooms. The house, with the exception of the
chimney, was built entirely of wood, the walls being
made of iron-bark slabs, dressed very smooth, and laid
horizontally; and the roof covered with shingles, which
are small pieces of wood, eighteen inches long and about
four inches wide, split out of iron-bark or stringy-bark
wood. If properly laid on, with sufficient pitch,
shingles make about the best roof possible for a hot
climate, they are perfectly water-tight, keep out the heat,
and last for many years. But there is a good deal of
art in laying them on, and unless it is done scientifically, they let the water through like a sieve. The
sitting-room was very well furnished, with any amount
of tables, pictures, book-shelves, arm-chairs, and above
all an excellent piano. Rice and my brother had been
there for some years, and had made the place very
comfortable, and altogether hardly what one would expect to find in the Bush.

Near the house stood the kitchen, with a cook's room
adjoining, and a little covered way all overgrown with
creepers, leading from it to the house.

About a hundred yards away were the rest of the
station buildings, consisting of two stockmen's houses,
a store, a meat-house, the spare hut in which I camped,
the men's kitchen, the blacksmith's forge, and the black
boys' hut, all slab buildings with shingle roofs, also a
large dove-cot and a row of fowl-houses, surrounded
by wire-netting yards, and beyond these again the
milking-yards, killing-yard, calf-pens, and horse-yards.

Having completed my round of the station, I had just arrived at the rails of the horse-yard, when I heard a sound like distant thunder away down the horse-paddock. In a few seconds a mob of about seventy horses came tearing down the track in a cloud of dust, with their tails in the air, and dashed into the big yard, of which the slip rails were down. Behind them came a black boy, cantering leisurely along, who proceeded to put up the rails, and then taking the saddle off the horse he was riding, he turned him out in hobbles into the small paddock. All the station-horses in use are run up every morning into the yards, and then turned out again, when the stockmen have picked out those that they require for the day.

Anyone would think that with seventy or eighty horses in the yard, and only three or four men to ride, there would be plenty for everyone. But a nearer inspection generally shows that at least half of them are unavailable from sore backs or want of condition. No one ever yet saw a cattle station that was not in a chronic state of being short of horses, and it is easier for a stranger to squeeze blood out of a stone than to borrow a horse from the manager.

Sore backs and girth-galls are the curse of Australian bush-riding, and are chiefly due to carelessness on the part of the riders. Of course, a horse fed entirely upon grass is much more liable to a sore back than one which is fed upon corn. Then, again, they are never groomed, and, therefore, their coats are very dirty. The colonial saddle, too, is a shapeless cumbersome fabric, made of rough leather, with a high pommel and cantle, and huge knee-pads, weighing on an average

20 lbs.  The greatest care is necessary to prevent such
a diabolical machine from giving a horse a sore back,
but still it can be done.  The chief points to attend to
are, always to brush a horse's back before putting the
saddle on, to wash it and rub it dry after taking the
saddle off, and to keep the saddle-cloth scrupulously
clean and soft.  Few bushmen ever take the trouble to
use these precautions, and the consequence is that it is
the rarest thing in the world to see a Bush horse over
three years old that has not got either a sore back or
the mark of an old sore.  An English saddle seldom
gives a horse a sore back, with decent care, and all the
time I was in the Colony I always used one, unless I
knew the horse I was going to ride was certain to buck,
in which case it is perfectly hopeless to try and stick
on in an English saddle.  I have seen men ride very
bad buck-jumpers bare-backed, and I have often *heard*
of men who could ride them in an English saddle, but I
never saw it done, and do not believe that it is possible.
As long as a horse bucks straight ahead it is all right
enough, being no worse than crossing a succession of
high fences; but when he takes to bucking sideways,
and turning round as he bucks, I never saw anyone that
could stay on in an English saddle.

The performance of buck-jumping is a most extraordinary one to watch, and still more extraordinary to
feel underneath one.  When seated on a bucking horse
the rider sees nothing whatever in front of him but the
pommel of the saddle, and feels rather as if he was
assisting at an earthquake or a railway accident.  The
performance is quite peculiar to Australian horses, and
no one who has not seen them at it would believe the

rapid contortions of which they are capable. In buck-ing, a horse tucks his head right between his fore-legs, sometimes striking his jaw with his hind feet. The back, meantime, is arched like a boiled prawn's; and in this position the animal makes a series of tremendous bounds, sometimes forwards, sometimes sideways and backwards, keeping it up for several minutes with in-tervals of a few seconds, and occasionally falling flat down and rolling over his rider if he fails to get rid of him in any other way. Of course a "new chum" succumbs at once to the movements of a buck-jumper, but, after a little practice, anyone who keeps his nerve and sits back can easily learn to stick on in a colonial saddle with big knee-pads to help him. With practice some men become extraordinary hands at sitting rough horses, and a favourite piece of "flashness" is to stick half-a-crown between each thigh and the saddle, and keep it there while the horse is bucking.

The great art consists in getting cleverly on to a rowdy horse; for it is before a man is fairly seated, just as he is swinging himself on, that a horse is likely to get the best of him. An old hand draws the reins tightly through his fingers, and takes hold of a piece of the mane with the same hand to keep his horse's head well in to his neck, and then, with his face to the horse's tail, he sneaks one foot into the stirrup, and swings himself into his seat with the rapidity of lightning. A great deal of practice is required to do this neatly, and to avoid touching the horse with either foot during the act of mounting, which would almost certainly start it bucking if it were that way inclined.

The ordinary run of Bush horses show a great deal of

breeding, but they are generally deficient in bone, and the worst point about them is the shoulder. You often come across a well-shaped one in every other point, but the whole time that I was in the Bush I never saw a really pretty pair of shoulders on a horse. They run about fifteen two in height, and are very low in the wither, which accounts for the extraordinary feat which I have several times witnessed, of a horse bucking its rider and saddle over its head, without breaking the girths. But whatever they may be to look at, horses raised in the Bush have generally a good heart inside them, and the amount of work that they will do upon nothing but grass is almost incredible.

A ride of a hundred miles from sunrise to sundown is no uncommon performance, and there is a well-authenticated instance of a man who, for a large bet, rode a pony a hundred miles in that time, and then carried it a hundred yards. The unfortunate animal died, and the man ought to have been knocked on the head for his cruelty, but the feat stands recorded as showing what an Australian horse can do.

A still more remarkable performance was that of a son of Panic, bred in Victoria, who carried his rider, Mr. Lord, 263 miles in three days, 88 miles on the first, 83 on the second, and 92 on the third. Mr. Lord rode 14 st. 3 lb., and the journey was accomplished without any bad effects upon the horse.

Considering the treatment that Bush horses get, it is wonderful how they live at all. After a long hard day they are turned out, dripping with sweat, into a cold winter's night, where, perhaps, in a few hours the temperature will be down to freezing point. They are ridden hard after cattle, over stony ridges and black-soil bogs, and yet filled legs and curbed hocks are unknown ; and the whole time that I was in Australia I never saw a broken-winded horse, or even a whistler. It is very rare indeed to find a really pleasant horse to ride in the Bush. They are all very badly broken in, and have nearly always had their tempers spoiled when quite young, so that they generally have some disagreeable tricks, and it is never safe to go near the heels of one of them. There are men who make a living by breaking in young horses, going round the stations and contracting to break in a mob at thirty shillings a head. Considering the way in which it is done, it is no wonder that Australian horses buck, and are generally vicious.

A lot of young ones are run into a yard, most of which have probably never seen a man within a quarter of a mile since they were foals, and have certainly never been in a yard more than once in their lives. The horse-breaker picks out one, and with the help of another man runs it into a small yard by itself. If the animal is not very nervous, with a little patience he will be able to go up and handle it, and get a bridle over its head. If all other ways fail, he has to lasso it. The next thing is to sneak a saddle on to it, the wretched animal standing shaking and shivering with fright the whole time. The horse-breaker is most likely a man that no living horse can throw by any means short of rolling on him ; so he blindfolds the horse, and gets straight on to its back. His mate removes the bandage from its eyes, and the rider sticks the spurs into the horse, and makes it buck, till it cannot buck any more.

He then leaves it for a few hours with the saddle on, and having repeated the process on two subsequent days, he hands it over to the owner as broken in, and it is probably turned out for six months into the Bush. It is real rough work breaking in young horses in this way, and very few men stick at it for more than a year or two. Undoubtedly the very worst man in the world to give a young horse to, to break in, is a " flash ",rider. He is not the least afraid of its bucking, and will probably make it do so on purpose, in order to display his powers of riding, or rather sticking on.

Bucking is a regular habit ; and when once a horse acquires it he never altogether loses it. The surest way to get a horse quietly and well broken in is to give it to the most nervous and arrant funk you can find, if he will undertake it. He will spend days in getting the horse used to the vicinity of a man, and sit for hours on the top of a rail alongside of it, to accustom it to seeing him above it, before ever he attempts to get on its back, and the odds are that he will have it so quiet by the time that he dares mount it, that it will never think of bucking, except under extraordinary provocation, for the rest of its life.

The proceedings of a " new chum," as a recent arrival in the Colony is called, are always a source of amusement to all old residents, and nothing is more entertaining than his early struggles to catch his horse in the yard. Having cornered it off, with the help of a black boy, he advances towards it, in a hesitating, doubtful sort of way, addressing it in soothing terms which are entirely thrown away upon a Bush horse. The animal detects him instantly as a novice, and prepares to take advantage of him by every trick that it knows. Jammed up against the rails, in a corner of the yard, it stands, looking at him as he approaches, with an expression in its eye and a droop of its quarters that no one could mistake. When he gets up to it he probably discovers that he has got the bridle over the wrong arm, and while he is changing it the brute gives a frightful snort, rushes past him, rolling him over in the dust, and gallops round and round the yard, with its tail in the air. Once more he pins it up in a corner, and has nearly got the bridle over its head when it gently turns its head away and sticks it over the rails, where he cannot possibly reach it, at the same time turning its quarters round, and lifting a hind foot, in a way that causes its future rider to get out of focus as quickly as possible.

After a few more vain attempts the "new chum" looks imploringly round, and one of the old hands gets down from the rails, where he has been sitting enjoying the fun. Hanging the bridle over his left arm, he walks straight up to the animal and addresses it with " Stand up, you crow-bait ! " in a tone that knocks all the folly out of it for the rest of the morning. Bush horses are as cunning as foxes, and, unless they are really rowdy, they never attempt to play the fool with men who are used to handling them, so it caves in at once, and allows him to put the bridle on without any further trouble.

# CHAPTER V.

MOUNT SPENCER country consisted of three runs adjoining each other, known respectively as Mount Spencer, Haslewood, and Blue Mountain. The whole area was nearly 400 square miles, capable of carrying over 20,000 head of cattle in any season; but when I first went there, there were not above 12,000. Though some parts of the run were very rough riding, it was all very good cattle country, and wonderfully well watered. Numbers of large creeks ran in every direction, and large water-holes were scattered all over the run, so that it hardly suffered at all in the severest drought. The cattle were a very well-bred herd, and the grass was first-rate, so they fattened splendidly. The head station was at Mount Spencer, and the adjoining run was kept principally for a breeding station. At Haslewood there was another station, with yards and paddocks, and the run was fenced off from Mount Spencer by a line of fence twelve miles long, and was used with Blue Mountain run for a fattening station for bullocks. At Blue Mountain there was a small hut, a horse paddock, and stock-yard, and at the far end of Mount

THE FARM,—MOUNT SPENCER.

Spencer run was another small hut, used for camping out, and a sapling yard for yarding cattle at night, when it was too late to take them to the head station.

At Mount Spencer there were two stockmen, Frank Boyle and Timothy Harris, and a couple of black boys. At Haslewood was another stockman, Billy Burgess, with a couple of boys, one white and the other black; and at Blue Mountain a half-caste named Yellow-Pat lived by himself, and looked after a mob of draught mares. Of course Rice and my brother worked amongst the cattle themselves just like the other stockmen, but this was all the "permanent staff" on the place, and quite sufficient to work the cattle.

In mustering, more hands are required, but at such times neighbouring stations always help each other, and send up a spare hand or two to help muster and brand, and to bring back their own cattle, of which there are sure to be some that have strayed on to their neighbours' country. The ordinary work of a stockman is rather monotonous. Every morning he gets on his horse, and goes out on the run, jogging along about five miles an hour the whole day, and returning in the afternoon. His business is to be constantly amongst the cattle, riding the boundaries to put his own cattle back, and his neighbour's away, hunting up stray calves and bringing them home and branding them.

It is impossible to do too much of this work. The more cattle are worked, and accustomed to the sight of men when they are young, the better they will fatten when they grow up; and, of course, it is of the greatest importance to get all the male calves branded before a certain age. In rough country where there

are few fences, numbers of calves escape the general
muster, and the more the stockmen scour the run, and
hunt them up, the better the station will pay. Sometimes the stockman takes a black boy with him, but
more frequently he is quite alone. Occasionally he goes
and camps out for a few days, to work some outlying
end of the run, rolling up sufficient beef and damper
in his blanket strapped across his saddle, to last him
until he returns. In rough country, such as the coast
of Queensland, no one ought ever to ride about the run
alone. While riding hard after cattle through the long
grass, it is impossible to avoid a nasty fall occasionally;
and if a man were to be crippled away in the Bush,
and unable to ride or walk home, it is a thousand to
one if he would ever be found before a miserable death
had overtaken him. Considering the number of men
who every day of their lives make a practice of riding
about the Bush quite alone, it is astonishing that more
of them do not come to grief. But the annals of the
country contain ghastly records of the horrible death of
solitary riders who have met with an accident, and been
rendered helpless, and many an unfortunate being has
disappeared entirely, without leaving a trace of his fate.
Years afterwards, perhaps, a skeleton is found somewhere near where he was supposed to have been lost,
and the few who have not forgotten all about him
connect the discovery with the unknown end of the
missing man. Not far from Mount Spencer run, a man
came to his end a few years ago, in a manner that is
almost unique in horror. He was away riding by himself in the Bush, and his horse threw him, injuring
his spine in the fall, so that he was quite powerless to

move. Close to where he fell was an enormous ants'-
nest, and when he was found three days afterwards
he was half eaten by millions of ants. He was still
conscious, but unable to speak, and died very shortly
afterwards. It is impossible to imagine a more terrible
death than to lie paralysed and helpless, to the agony
of intolerable thirst being added the torture of being
eaten alive by crawling insects.

If any parallel could be found for the awfulness of
such a fate, it would be in the case of a man who was
burned to death by a tree which fell on him. He was
working by himself, several miles away from anywhere,
and a burning tree fell on him, pinning him to the
ground, without doing him any serious injury. The
tree was alight at the butt-end, some thirty feet away
from where he lay; but it is a peculiarity of some sorts
of Australian trees that when once they are set on fire
they will smoulder entirely away, leaving nothing but a
track of white ashes in the grass. No efforts of the
unfortunate man could extricate him from his awful
position, and after a time he appears to have abandoned
himself to his fate, for he amused himself by scratching
a record of his sensations with a knife upon the bottom
of a tin dish that lay within reach. It took a day and
a half before the fire reached him, and it is shocking to
think of what his sufferings must have been. When
he was found he was nothing but a charred and blackened mass, which no one would have taken to have
been a man, had his fate not been recorded on the tin
dish that was found near him.

In the north of Queensland very few of the cattle-
runs have boundary fences. There are large paddocks,

of course, but the cattle roam at large over the greater portion of the run. All about the run, at intervals of five or six miles, are cattle-camps, and the cattle that belong to the surrounding districts are mustered on their respective camps.

The camp is generally a level place, as free from stones as possible, where there is water handy, and where the timber is not too thick. It is the stockman's business to ride round constantly, and put the cattle on to the different camps, so as to accustom them to running there. The same mobs of cattle frequent the same districts, and if they are properly broken in they will run right into the camp by themselves, when started with a few cracks of the stock-whip, and stay there till the middle of the day. In mustering, of course, it is essential that a stockman should know the country thoroughly, and be perfectly acquainted with the run of all the gullies and creeks, or he will never get all his cattle on to the camp.

Two mornings after I arrived at Mount Spencer, we all started out to muster the Water-hole camp, at the lower end of the run, twelve miles away. Frank and Billy had gone on the night before, and camped out, to work the country on the far side of the camp. Having had breakfast about five, Rice, my brother, Timothy, and I started off, soon after sunrise, with the man who had come up to buy cattle. He had been butchering on the Palmer diggings, and made a rise, and was hunting up a big mob of fat cattle to take back with him. He had a huge nugget of gold hanging on to his watch-chain, and always wore a waistcoat and no coat, a get-up which in the Bush somehow or other, imparts an air of blackguardism to a man which it is impossible to describe.

After going a few miles through the forest of endless gum-trees and blood-wood, we crossed a big creek, and came to a succession of low iron-bark ridges. Everywhere the country was heavily timbered, and it was impossible to see more than half a mile through the trees in any direction. Here we separated, Rice and the cattle-dealer going in one direction, and Timothy, my brother, and I in another. Presently a mob of about seventy cattle appeared ahead of us in the long grass. We rode up to them at a canter, shouting, and cracking our whips; and they set off at a gallop, apparently in the right direction, for my brother and Timothy pulled up and did not attempt to follow them.

A little farther on we came upon another small mob, which turned as soon as they saw us, and trotted off towards a creek on our left. Off went my brother after them, full gallop, through the grass, which was up to his knees as he rode, shouting out that "he knew that old devil of a white cow was off to the Island camp again." He disappeared after them over the creek, and we did not see him again until he turned up on the camp an hour later, driving the refractory mob in front of him. Timothy and I jogged along for some distance, and fell in with some more cattle, that looked lazily at us as we rode up. Timothy scared them up with a shout and a crack of his whip; but they did not seem in any great hurry, and rather inclined to stop, so he turned to me, and told me that "if I would keep behind them, that old yellow cow with a down-horn would take me right into the camp, a couple of miles away, while he went and tried

5

the ridges away to the right." I had not the least idea where the camp was, and only very vague ideas of where I was myself, and the idea of being shown the way about the Bush by a yellow cow with a down-horn seemed rather novel; but Timothy had already started, so I thought I had better do as I was told.

There was not a vestige of a track to be seen any-where, and, as I jogged along behind the mob, I could not help thinking to myself, " Supposing this flaming old cow takes it into her head to go to the wrong camp, like the other one did, or lies down, or gets sick, where the deuce will I be?" The sun was just about square overhead, so it was difficult to tell where the points of the compass lay, and I was by no means sure that if the cow did not take me to the camp I could find my way home again. However, she trotted along with a busi-ness kind of an air that was very encouraging, always keeping in the lead of the mob, while I brought up the rear. After crossing two more deep-running creeks, and struggling down several awful gullies and up the other side, clinging on to my horse's mane with rather a weak feeling about the inside during the final struggle that landed us on the top, I came on to a long black-soil flat, covered with big box-trees, at the far end of which I could see a big mob of cattle standing on a low ridge. My pilot had led me as straight as a die, and when I got up I found Frank and Billy were already on the camp with about six hundred head of cattle. There are few sights more picturesque than an Aus-tralian cattle-camp, and it is one that anyone who takes an interest in stock will never grow weary of.

The Water-hole camp lay on a broad low ridge, run-

ning down to a big creek full of flooded gums and
dark-green she-oaks, about three hundred yards away.
Close to the camp was a round water-hole, covered
with lilac water-lilies, from which the camp took its
name. The cattle were moving restlessly about on the
camp, the cows bellowing in search of their lost calves,
their red, roan, and white colours looking wonderfully
bright in the sunlight, among the trunks of the black
iron-bark trees. The two stockmen, and a couple of
black boys, were riding incessantly round the edges of
the camp to keep the cattle together, and prevent them
from straying away ; so my brother and I lit our pipes,
and rode in amongst the cattle to have a look at them.
The first thing that struck me was what a very well-bred
lot they were. Here and there was an old crow-bait of
a cow, a miserable relic of old times, crawling about to
save itself the annoyance of a funeral, but most of the
cattle showed a great deal of quality. Among the young
ones there was scarcely a hard skin to be seen, and some
of the heifers were perfect pictures. There were not
many bullocks on the camp, as most of them had been
cleared off Mount Spencer and put on to Haslewood,
but what there were left were very healthy sights. It
is astonishing to anyone who has been used to cram-
ming bullocks with oil-cake, hay, and mangolds, before
they are fit for the market, to see animals raised entirely on grass, with the fat laid on level all over them
wherever there is room for it. A mob of seventy bullocks
once left Mount Spencer that averaged over 1,000 lbs.
when they were killed, one of them weighing 1,430 lbs.
They were four and five year olds, and the weight was
taken as they hung up clean in the butcher's shop.

5 *

"Well, Sam," said my brother as we finished a round
of the camp, "what do you think of them? Not a bad
lot, are they?"

"Very sound," said I. "What are those bullocks
worth now?"

"Six pound ten delivered at the yard, and heaven
send they may stick at it. They've never been up to
that before, around these edges. Look there, at that
white one; he'll go over a thousand; and isn't he a
plum to look at?"

The animal referred to was a four-year-old bullock,
with the head of a heifer on him, and a soft white skin,
very deep in the girth, with a broad, level back, on
which the fat was laid on to admiration. It struck me
that I had seen many worse animals in the show-yards
of the old country, and there were several quite as good
as him on the camp.

Climbing off our horses, we sat down on a log, and
waited for the others to come up to camp with the rest
of the cattle. Our horses were standing lazily brushing
away the flies with their tails, with their heads down, and
their eyes half shut; but presently they pricked up their
ears and looked up. Following the direction in which
they were looking, we saw a long string of cattle in the
distance, winding along like a snake through the forest
towards the camp. Timothy had fallen in with Rice
and the cattle-dealer, and they all three appeared, bringing about 400 head of cattle with them. There
were now about 1,000 head on the camp, and Frank
and Billy declared it was pretty full, that is to say that
all the cattle belonging to the district in which it lay
were there.

Nothing is more extraordinary than the knowledge of cattle that those who work constantly among them acquire. A good stockman will go on to a camp where there are 1,000 head of cattle, and in ten minutes time will tell you if there are any missing that should be there. Very likely he has half-a-dozen similar camps in other parts of the run; but if he has been a year or two on the place, he knows most of the cattle by sight perfectly well. Although a great deal may be done by practice, no one who is not born in the country ever possesses this power to the same extent as a native, with some of whom it is really a remarkable gift. Billy Burgess was a native of Australia, and was generally allowed to be one of the best hands at working cattle in the north. His faculty for remembering cattle was simply astounding. I have seen him come on to a camp where he had not been for two years, and on which there were about 1,200 head of cattle at the time. After riding round the camp amongst the cattle for a little while, he began inquiring from the stockman who was working that part of the run at the time, why such and such a cow or steer was not there, and in every instance he was right. Animals that must have been almost calves when he was last there, he instantly recognised; in fact, if once he saw a beast, it seemed as if no alteration in its appearance could ever prevent him from identifying it afterwards.

Having scattered a glance round the Water-hole camp, he said all the bullocks were there that ought to be, and, as it was roasting hot, we left the black boys to mind the camp, and went down to the creek to have a feed, and to give the cattle a spell before we started drafting.

Dinner did not take long, none of us having brought
more than a piece of beef and a bit of damper, and most
of us had forgotten to bring any at all, and had an extra
smoke instead.    When we had finished we went back to
the camp, and Frank and my brother started drafting out
the bullocks, the cattle-dealer riding through the camp
and picking the ones that he wanted.    Drafting on the
camp, or "cutting out" as it is generally called, is a
very pretty performance to watch, if it is well done.
First of all a small mob is cut off from the main body
of the cattle, and driven gently away for a little distance,
and then allowed to stand.    This is the nucleus of the
draft mob; for no beast will stand still a moment by
itself, and one of the hands is told off to watch them.
One or two men then ride in among the cattle, and draft
out the ones they want, one at a time, while the rest of
the hands ride round the camp and keep the cattle from
breaking away.    Both my brother and Frank were very
sound hands at cutting out, and they were both riding
first-rate camp-horses, so I watched them at work with
the greatest interest.    A "camp-horse" is one used for
cutting out cattle on a camp, and very few horses are
good at it; but the performance of a really first-class
one is a sight worth seeing.    Each man picks his beast,
and edges him gently to the outside of the mob, on the
side of the camp nearest the draft-mob.    The instant
the animal finds itself cut off from the camp it makes
the most desperate efforts to rejoin the herd, and the
speed at which a bullock can travel, and the activity
with which he turns, are marvellous.

The timber was pretty thick round the camp, and
as I watched my brother it seemed as if he must

inevitably come to grief; but a good camp-horse is wonderfully smart upon his legs, and goes through the trees like an eel. Away went the bullock round the edge of the camp, my brother, with his reins loose, and his hat on the back of his head, going after it through the timber as if there was no futurity. As he ranges up alongside, the bullock wheels sharp round and gallops back again the way that he came. Toby, the camp-horse, stops dead short, with a violence that would have sent an inexperienced rider ten yards over its head, and is off after the beast again like lightning, following every twist and turn as if he was tied to the bullock's tail with a string. Toby's heart and soul are in the work, and without a word or a touch from his rider he hits out all he knows, to keep the animal from getting back into the camp. This time as he comes up alongside, the bullock lowers his head and charges; but Toby has had a horn in his ribs before now, and avoids the sweep of the bullock's head with marvellous dexterity. For a while the tables are turned, and for a hundred yards or so the bullock hunts Toby; and though the horse is as quick on his legs as a rabbit, a pair of sharp horns are kept quite as near his quarters as is pleasant. Finding that Toby is too quick for him, the bullock turns and gallops back towards the camp. Once more the horse is after him, and turns him back into the Bush; and this time the bullock gives in, and trots sulkily off to join the draft-mob.

The cattle-dealer knew his business, and picked out about forty grand-looking bullocks, which pretty well cleaned out the Water-hole camp. On a camp of mixed cattle, of course, it is not very difficult to pick the best

bullocks; but when there are nothing but bullocks, and perhaps eight or nine hundred of them, it takes a consummate
judge to go in and pick the cream of the camp, as he
rides through them on his horse.   It was past 3 o'clock
when we finished drafting, and, as we had twelve miles
to drive the cattle home, it looked like taking us all our
time to get them in the yard before dark.   Fat bullocks
are the worst kind of cattle to drive, as they are always
inclined to break away, and, of course, have to be driven
dreadfully slow, in order to take as little out of them as
possible.   A long drive home is very tedious after a hard
day's ride, and it takes a great deal of patience to prevent a man from hurrying the cattle.   The great thing
is never to push them too fast at first.   If cattle are
allowed to start very steady, they will walk quietly along,
and by-and-by get over the ground at a very fair pace ;
but if they are hustled when they first leave the camp
they will not settle down and are certain to be troublesome all the way home.   On the whole, about two or
two and a half miles an hour is quite fast enough to
drive cattle, and, of course, if they are going to be on the
road for some days or weeks they must not be driven
nearly so fast.   Droving, however—that is to say,
taking a mob of cattle on a journey extending, perhaps,
over three or four months, is a science of itself, and is
a very different thing from merely driving a mob home
from the camp to the yards.

Some of the bullocks had come a long distance to
camp in the morning ; so we took them home very
slowly, and it was dark before we got within two miles
of the station.   In a little while, however, the moon got
up ; not the sickly, dissipated-looking object that makes

night hideous in northern latitudes, but a good, useful, healthy sort of moon that rose suddenly, in a circle of ruddy gold, and threw a powerful light over the whole country.

We looked a very weird sort of procession, as we wound along through the thick, long grass. The huge gums rose up on all sides, giants of the forest, their towering tops meeting high overhead, and their stems, white and ghostly, throwing deep, clear shadows across the brilliant moonlight. Ahead of the cattle, to prevent them from going too fast, rode one of the black boys, perched on an old white horse, and looking as utterly disreputable as only a black boy can. Behind the mob rode the rest of the men, wild-looking objects begrimed with dust and sweat, their arms bare to the elbow, and each with the battered remains of a broad-brimmed felt hat jammed on the back of his head. Every now and then one of them would drop behind for a hundred yards, and the ruddy light that shortly afterwards illuminated the end of his nose proclaimed him to have stopped to light his pipe, which he dare not do in the vicinity of the cattle. No one spoke. The men rode silently behind the mob, checking instantly the slightest evidence of a wish to break on the part of any of the cattle. They were getting very nervous, and disinclined to go on, as they drew near the yard, and any mistake on the part of the men would have been disastrous. The yard stood on a slight rise about a quarter of a mile from the station, and on the side from which we were approaching them the fences of two paddocks ran out from the gates like wings.

Suddenly, as the cattle were going up the rise to the yard, three or four ducks got up with a loud clatter out of a small water-hole in one of the paddocks. With a sudden rush the bullocks turned and dashed down the hill, breaking through the line of horsemen, and tearing off into the Bush as if all the fiends were after them. Fortunately the country below the yard was a pretty level plain; but the timber was thick, and the grass three feet long, and full of fallen trees. To ride full gallop by moonlight over such country seems little short of madness; but his neck is the last thing that a stockman ever thinks of, and away we all went after them, as hard as ever our horses could go. A " new chum " on occasions like this is never of the slightest use, and generally very much in the way; but this time I was saved from doing any mischief by my horse going head over heels into the head of a dead tree in the long grass, before I had gone three hundred yards, and sending me flying. Luckily I was able to catch him before he got clear of the fallen timber. We were neither of us hurt, and in the distance I could hear the men shouting at the cattle, so I cleared out of the way as quickly as I could, to let them come up to the yard again. Fortunately the cattle kept together pretty well, and the men were able to round them up on the flat, about half a mile away, and brought them back to the yard with the loss of only three, which got clear away over the creek, where it was useless to follow them. This time they went into the yard without any trouble, and with a sigh of relief we secured the gates, and went down to the station and turned our horses out. Having forgotten to take out with me anything to eat, I was beginning to get hungry, as it was now about 9 o'clock, and I had breakfasted at five in the morning.

During the next few days we were out again every day, and collected about 100 fats ; and some men belonging to the cattle-dealer having come up in the meantime, he started off on the road to Cook-town, over 500 miles away to the north. We heard afterwards that he got the bullocks up all right, and made a big profit on them.

In Australia large mobs of mixed cattle are continually being moved about from one station to another, or to stock outlying country, and fat cattle are often obliged to travel an enormous distance to market. For the Barcoo, and central districts of Queensland and South Australia the best markets are Melbourne and Adelaide, each of them distant about 1,000 miles. Droving, in consequence, becomes a regular profession, and there are numbers of men who make a living, and a very good one too, by nothing else but taking charge of cattle that are travelling from one place to another. To take a mob of a thousand fat bullocks over a thousand miles of all sorts of country, and bring them into market in prime condition, is a business involving a great deal of responsibility and care, for although cattle are generally travelled at the owner's risks, of course the drover's reputation depends upon the order in which his cattle reach the end of the journey. A good drover is always in requisition, and the wages of the head man in charge of a mob are generally about £4 a week. It is a dog's life, too, a drover's. From daylight to dark he is on horseback, exposed to all kinds of weather, crawling along behind his cattle at the slowest possible rate that is consistent with moving at all. If he averages between four and five miles a day,

on a long journey, it is quite as fast as his cattle ought
to travel. Every day the man in charge rides on
ahead of the mob, to pick a place for them to camp
at night. Water, of course, is a *sine qua non,* and he
must have reliable information as to the state of road
for a hundred miles ahead of him, or he will get his
cattle in a terrible fix. Every night the cattle have to
be rounded up, and watched on the camp the whole night
long. A drover never gets more than four hours
sleep at a stretch, and he is lucky if he can get that
for the first month his cattle are on the road.

There is nothing better for a new arrival in the
country, who wishes to get colonial experience, than to
be sent on the road with a mob of cattle. He will
get an insight into the country and its ways, become
acquainted with the habits of cattle, get nothing but the
plainest possible food, and altogether he will have such
a disgustingly bad time, that he will afterwards accept
any other sort of work with cheerfulness.

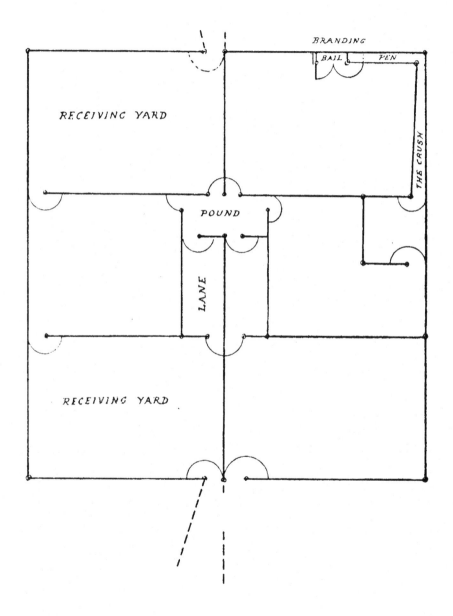

BRANDING

BAIL    PEN

RECEIVING YARD

THE CRUSH

POUND

LANE

RECEIVING YARD

GROUND PLAN OF A STOCK-YARD.

# CHAPTER VI.

LIFE ON THE STATION.

THREE times a year all the cattle on the run are mustered, and passed through the drafting-yards, that the young calves may be branded, and the older ones weaned.

The cattle belonging to each camp are brought in separately, drafted and turned out again to make room for the next lot, as the yards will only hold about a thousand head comfortably at a time. Mustering is pretty hard work, for, when once you start, you have to stick at it from daylight to dark, Sundays very often included, until it is finished. A general muster at Mount Spencer used to take us a month, and a fortnight after to " clean up." One or two hands from the neighbouring stations used generally to come up and help, and look after their own cattle, a good number of which were pretty certain to pass through the yards.

Drafting cattle in the yards is very good fun, especially if they are at all rowdy, but it is work that requires a good deal of nerve to start with, and long practice before a man becomes a good hand at it. The yards are very strong enclosures of posts and rails, the posts from a foot to sixteen inches thick, set in eight feet apart, and the rails not less than four inches thick and

ten inches wide, the top rail being about six feet from
the ground. For the purpose of drafting the various
classes of cattle, the yards are subdivided according to
the accompanying plan. The whole mob are first of
all run into one of the big " receiving yards," an enclosure about seventy yards long and forty yards broad.
The gate leading into " the lane " is then thrown open,
and five or six men, each armed with a sapling about
six feet long, and a couple of inches thick, go into the
receiving yard, and jam the cattle up into the corner
against the gate of " the lane," until seventy or eighty
have gone through, when the gate is shut. This is
called " yarding-up," and is about the most dangerous
part of the work ; for if a beast charges a man in the
middle of a big yard, he has a very poor chance of
getting out of its way. An old hand knows in a moment,
from the look of a beast that charges him, whether it
is safe for him to stand his ground and turn it with a
blow on the nose from his stick, or whether he ought
to clear out for the rails. But the instant the cattle
begin to move in the yard, the dust becomes something
awful. It rises in dense clouds sometimes entirely hiding
the cattle from view, getting into one's eyes, nose, and
mouth, and mixing with the sweat into a thick black
paste, which makes white men and niggers all pretty
much the same colour for the time being. I have
often seen the dust so bad that we have had to knock
off for half an hour to let it settle, as it was perfectly
impossible to see to work the cattle. Under cover of
the dust it is often hard to see a beast charging, until
it is too late to attempt to get out of the way, and then
the best thing to do is to lie flat down in front of it,

and in nine cases out of ten it will jump over you and pass on, unless it is a cow, when most likely it will stop, turn round, and horn you as you lie on the ground. When a beast comes tearing out of the mob in an awful hurry, its head down, its tail in the air, and its eye rolling, it is quite safe to stand still. It will pass you with a frightful snort, that gives a new chum rather a queer sensation under the ribs, but hardly makes an old hand smile. But when it comes out rather slowly, with its head in the air, its brisket shaking, and its eye fixed straight upon you, it is time to clear out. The animal means business, and, be it a cow or a bullock, you might as well hope to stop the charge of an express train. It will hunt you for your life, and if you are not up the rails before it can catch you, it will have its horns into you as sure as fate.

A man running for his life, pursued by an infuriated animal with horns two feet long and as sharp as needles, does not at first sight seem to be a particularly mirthful spectacle. Familiarity, however, breeds contempt, and a charge in the yard is always greeted with shouts of laughter from the lookers on, especially if the man who is hunted has a narrow escape. Provided he is not actually hurt, the nearer he is to being horned the funnier everyone thinks it, including the individual himself, who is always ready to join in the laugh the instant that he has got up the rails out of harm's way. Occasionally the best and most experienced hands get caught, and very few men have worked for any length of time amongst Bush cattle without getting a horn into them once or twice. The wound from a beast's horn is always a nasty one, and very bad to heal, and I have known several cases where it has ended fatally.

The "lane" leads into a small square enclosure called "the pound," from which gates open into five different yards. Behind each gate a man stands, ready to open it when a beast intended for his special yard comes into the pound. Two men work the cattle in the lane, running them into the pound according to their respective classes, calling out "stranger," "weaner," or "calf," as the case may be. The proper gate is open ready for it, before it gets into the pound, and a man stands ready to hurry it through, so that no time is lost.

In drafting cattle, everything, of course, depends upon the men working in the lane, and there are very few prettier sights than to see a good hand amongst cattle that are inclined to be rowdy. The least nervousness or flurry on the part of the man communicates itself in a marvellous way to the cattle, and makes them perfectly unmanageable; while, on the other hand, a man who keeps quite cool and collected, has an extraordinary influence over the animals which he is working.

One of our stockmen, Billy Burgess, was reckoned to be about the best hand in the yards in the north of Queensland, and, certainly, the whole time I was in the country, I never saw anyone who could hold a candle to him. No one ever saw him in a hurry, but he would draft more cattle in an hour than most men would in two. While other men were shouting, and swearing, and running for their lives, he would stand perfectly still, watching the cattle with an amused smile on his face, and seeming to know by instinct exactly how far he could trust them. To an outsider, the power he

THE BRANDING BAIL.

possessed over cattle seemed little short of mesmerism; but in reality it was only the result of years of experieuce and work amongst them, combined with an excellent temper and iron nerves.

In or out of the yards he knew every beast on the run by sight, and was never at a loss for a moment when he was drafting. A furious charge from an animal that would send most men flying up the rails, seldom elicited more than a gentle remonstrance of, " Steady, old man! where are you coming to now?" from Billy, and perhaps a tap on the nose from his stick if its horns went rather nearer to him than he considered good manners. But if a beast meant mischief, no one knew it sooner, and he took care to put himself out of harm's way. If the animal was more than usually vicious he would wait his opportunity, and give it a blow just behind the horns with infinite precision, which would bring it blundering on to its knees, and, without killing it, leave it sick and stupid for the rest of the day.

It does not require at all a heavy blow to stun a beast, if laid on in the right place, just on the " pith " of the neck, behind the horns. I have seen a full-grown bullock drop in its tracks, as dead as a herring, from a blow with a stick no thicker than a man's finger.

The rowdiest cattle, as a rule, are bullocks, and the quietest of all, in or out of the yards, are bulls; but a cow, if she *is* rowdy, is the worst of all. It is a curious thing, however, that the quietest of bullocks will become absolutely infuriated, and charge anything and everything he can see, if he is shut up alone in a yard for a little while. A bullock bred and raised in the Bush, though he may be as fat as a pig, is a very different animal to the sleepy creatures that one meets on their way to an English market, driven by a couple of small boys and a dog. He is as quick on his legs as a rabbit, and for a few furlongs it takes a good horse to get away from him, and, moreover, as a rule, he can jump like a deer.

One day my brother was drafting in " the lane," and I was working " the pound." I had just turned a beast back into the lane, and was going back through the gate, when my brother sang out, " Stranger ! clear out, or he 'll have you ! " Looking round I saw a great hard-skinned white bullock belonging to the next station, with horns about a yard long, just behind me. He was charging up the lane full gallop, and as I sprang through the gate-way and turned aside, he made a sweep at me which just grazed my ribs, but, fortunately, did no damage beyond tearing my shirt. Without the least hesitation, the brute went straight at the opposite fence of the pound, six feet high, and got over without a fall, though he hit the top rail hard with every leg he had. The performance was the more astonishing as he had not a very long run, and what there was of it up the lane was slightly up-hill. We ran him round again, and into the lane, as he had jumped into the wrong yard. The next time he came up we all let him alone to see what he would do. He came full tilt up the lane as usual, looking for someone to kill, and when he got into the pound, he turned sharp to the right, pulled himself together, and going straight for the gate at the far end of the pound, five feet six high, he cleared it

without a mistake. After this performance we concluded to leave him alone until we had finished drafting.

In some yards it is the fashion to leave a big post,
or the stump of a tree about four feet high in the middle
of the big yard, so as to afford a shelter for anyone
who is charged and has no time to get to the rails at
the side. We had nothing of the kind at Mount
Spencer; but I remember a most ludicrous scene at
Gracemere, a station near Rockhampton, where there
was one of these harbours of refuge in the middle of
the yard. Seven or eight men were yarding up a mob
of cattle, when suddenly an old cow came out and
charged in a most business-like manner. Five men all
ran for their lives for the post. The first who got there,
of course, was all right; but there was only room for
one, so the next man had to hang on to the belt of the
man in front, and so on, till the whole five were extended in a row. The cow charged, and, of course, no
one could tell which side of the post she would pass, so
it was not until she was within a few feet that the
human tail swung round out of her way, a yell of terror
escaping from the last two men, as the brute's horns
passed within an inch of them. Quick as lightning the
cow turned and charged again, and again the end of
the tail had a narrow escape. Four times the cow
charged, four times the tail swept round, their howls of
anguish mingling with shouts of laughter from the men
on the rails who were looking on. Anything more
ridiculous than the whole scene cannot possibly be
imagined. The last man at the end was very fat, and
very nervous, and had no business in a yard at all. He
was evidently getting weak with terror and exhaustion,

6 *

so a diversion was made by those on the rails, and, the cow having been induced to charge someone else, the men in the middle of the yard were enabled to leave their post and make for the rails.

When the cattle are run through the yards in a general muster, all the calves that are old enough to wean are picked out. They are then "tailed," as it is called, for several weeks; that is to say, they are let out in a mob in the day-time to feed, and carefully watched by one or two hands, to see that none get away, and that no strange cattle mix with them, and shut up in a small paddock every night. Of course, the object of every-one in working a cattle-station is to get all the cattle as quiet as possible, and nothing has such an excellent effect in quieting a whole herd as tailing the weaners when they are young. But of all occupations that fall to the Bushman's lot, it is probably the most irksome.

Shepherding sheep is bad enough, and the asylums are three parts full of idiot shepherds, whose reason has succumbed to the dreariness of their lives; but for a short time it is infinitely preferable to tailing a mob of weaners. A man who is looking after sheep can, at all events, enjoy long intervals of perfect repose, during which, if he likes, he can lie on his back and read a book. But a mob of weaners will never give him an instant's peace. Without being at all interesting, their habits are extremely irritating. They never know exactly where they want to go, or what they want to do, but the one thing they will not do is to keep still and feed sensibly. Out of a thousand weaners you may possibly induce nine hundred and ninety-nine to lie down round a water-hole for an hour in the middle of the day. But the remaining one is certain to keep on the move the whole time, walking off into the Bush, first one way and then another, so that you never have a spell. If you get off your horse for a drink, the whole mob will probably pretend they never saw a man on foot before in their lives, and make a wild stampede. Fortunately, it is an occupation that does not last long; for a continuance of it at the best of times would drive the most sane man out of his mind, and in wet, cold weather it is simply deadly. However, it is very necessary and very useful work, though everyone shirks it who can, and a "new chum," if one can be found, is invariably selected for the duty.

A great many young men who go out to the colony with the view of following stock-growing as a profession, make a grave error in not making themselves fully acquainted with all the details connected with the working of a station. Of course, before starting on their own account to work a station, they go into the Bush to gain colonial experience, during which process they are known in the colony as "Jackaroos." Especially on a cattle-station, the Jackaroo very soon discovers that a great deal of the work is very pleasant. He goes into the yard every morning and catches his horse, rides round the run with the stockman, camps out when required, and lends a hand to draft and brand at the general muster, and generally has a very good time. The consequence is, at the end of a couple of years he knows very little more about the management of a cattle-station than he did when he started, and probably labours under the additional disadvantage of imagining that he knows a great deal.

The efficiency of the manager of a cattle-station depends largely upon his being a good judge of other men's work ; and it is impossible for him to be this, unless he has actually performed the work himself. It is not enough to sit on a rail and watch another man breaking-in a horse or a milking-cow. However good a hand he may be, you will learn much more by helping him than by watching him. One of the largest items of expenditure on every station is always fencing, and the manager should be thoroughly able to form an estimate of how much it ought to cost. It is nearly always done by contract, and, of course, the price at which a contractor will put up fencing varies enormously according to the nature of the country. An old hand riding through the forest with a tomahawk, and cutting a chip out of a tree here and there to try if it will work freely, can tell to a nicety at what price it will pay him to split posts and rails and any other class of timber that may be required. But this experience is only gained by practical work, by felling trees and splitting them up with a maul and wedges oneself. The manager of a station ought always to be a thorough judge of timber-getting in all its branches, for it is a part of his yearly expenditure where experience and judgment will enable him to save largely. It is pretty hard work to pull a cross-cut saw and swing a heavy maul all day, with a vertical sun and the thermometer up to 110° in the shade, and it requires a good constitution to stand it. But if a man is thoroughly sound, the harder he works in Australia the better health he will have, and it is odd if he does not look back to the time when he was splitting rails for ten hours a day as one of the happiest

A BUSHMAN'S CAMP.

in his life. It is not a very intellectual employment, certainly. Still, it must be an unfortunate nature to which perfect health does not bring the keenest pleasure, in a climate like that of Australia.

It is pleasant to set out to work in the morning, after eight hours of such sleep as none but men who work hard ever enjoy. The sun is just rising, and there is not a breath of wind, but the air feels as cool and fresh as iced champagne. The tools have been "planted" under a sheet of bark by the big tree which you felled overnight; so you have nothing to carry but a pipe, and as the blue smoke curls round your lips, mingled with the fragrant scent of the gum-trees and blood-wood flowers, you decide that certainly the first pipe after breakfast is the most thoroughly enjoyable of any. By the time that you have got to your work you are wet through up to the knees, and it is just cold enough to make you very glad to roll up your sleeves and start in with a will to work yourself dry. This does not take long, and as the sun rises and makes himself felt, it does not take long to work yourself damp again. If you are wise you will not drink much in the morning, for if you once start you will be thirsty all day. With a cheery mate, and an occasional spell of five minutes for a smoke, the morning does not seem very long, and the sun fair overhead, combined with certain internal sensations, warns you that it is time to knock off and boil the "billy" for dinner. Every meal in the Bush is, if possible, accompanied by a brew of tea; and, though it may seem strange, when you have worked yourself up to boiling-point under a grilling sun, there is nothing in the world so refreshing as a pannikin of very hot tea, not too strong, with not too much sugar and without any milk. Refreshed with a square meal of salt beef and damper, which is of all forms of bread the sweetest and most easily digested if it is properly made, you start in again, with a firm determination to raise a good " tally" by the end of the day. As the sun gets low, a hundred sound rails nine feet long bear witness that your day's work has been an honest one. A pleasant feeling of languor, which cannot be called fatigue, makes you very glad to get home, and a wash in the creek brings a sensation of perfect strength and soundness into every fibre and muscle of your body, unknown to those who have not worked hard in the healthiest climate in the world. Supper ended, you pitch a fresh log on the fire to make a blaze, and, stretching your limbs full length on a 'possum-rug, prepare to devour the last number of the *Australasian*, a paper which, for general interest and information, was never surpassed. A fresh pipe lighted with a fire-stick, just as the stars are coming out, makes you forget the sweetness of the morning air; and for the hundredth time you tell yourself that tobacco never tastes so nice as in the cool of the evening, after a real sound day's work splitting rails.

# CHAPTER VII.

## PLAGUES AND PLEASURES OF THE BUSH.

EMUS are still plentiful in the downs country, and occasionally we used to come across a straggler that had wandered on to the timbered country of our run. Quite a young one appeared once, in a little open plain on the opposite side of the lagoon from the house. With the help of several blacks, after a tremendous chase, we ran it down, and brought it home intending to tame it.

It was only about two feet high, and could not have been more than six weeks old ; but the way it ran before we caught it made us think it must be tired, so we shut it up in a stable about twenty feet square. The instant that we put it down it began to run round and round the stable as hard as it could go. My brother suggested that this might be nervousness, and that perhaps it did not like strangers looking at it. So we left it for an hour quite alone. When we came back it was running round harder than ever, with its mouth open and its wings hanging down. Frank declared that young emus always acted like that when they were having a good time, but its appearance was anything but joyful. Three hours after it was still running round, and it never stopped till it fell down dead four hours and

a half after we first shut it up, during which time I am
certain it must have travelled over forty miles.

The speed and the endurance possessed by a full-
grown emu are perfectly incredible to anyone who has
not tried the experiment of running one down. The
only way is to make a dash at them, and try and come
up with them in the first spurt, for if they once get their
second wind very few horses will ever catch them. They
straggle along in the most ungainly fashion, looking all
the time as if they were dead-beat, and were going to
drop with exhaustion, but the way in which they get
over the ground is quite astonishing. I once rode a
very good horse five miles on end across the downs after
an emu as hard as we could go, but no efforts could
diminish the distance between us. The bird kept
about ten yards in front of me the whole way, and
finally escaped into a patch of scrub. Their bones
contain the celebrated oil very much in favour among
the blacks for curing swollen joints and sprained sinews.
None but full-grown men whose frames are thoroughly
set ever use it, for they declare that it has the effect of
softening anyone's bones who has not arrived at
maturity. The penetrating qualities of the oil are certainly very remarkable, for if it is placed in a glass
bottle a portion of it will always sweat through the
glass and escape.

The birds themselves are easily tamed if they are
caught quite young. In their wild state they are
mischievous where there is much fencing about, as
they seem to take a delight in breaking down the
wires.

Many people, whose ideas of Australia are chiefly

gathered from representations of the traditional bush-ranger in the illustrated periodicals, imagine that the inhabitants of the country are invariably arrayed in enormous long boots half way up their thighs, to protect them from the attacks of snakes and other deadly reptiles. There never was a greater delusion. The whole time that I was in the Bush I never in my life saw a man with long boots on, unless he was a very recent arrival in the country. The fact is that long boots in a country where you have often to camp out are the greatest mistake. In cold weather you cannot pull them off, and in wet weather if you pull them off you can never get them on again. As for taking the slightest precaution to guard against being bitten by a snake, I never knew anyone who did it after the first week in the Bush. It is impossible to live in a state of chronic apprehension. The feeling is bound to wear off, and, after riding about the Bush for some time, the most nervous man discovers that snakes, as a rule, are quite as anxious to avoid a *rencontre* as he is himself, and very soon he ceases to trouble his head about them until he happens to see one.

In some localities, as, for instance, the cane-fields of Mackay, or the reed-beds on the Murray river, snakes are so plentiful that it is necessary to be extremely cautious. But generally, all over the Bush, especially in Queensland, it is curious how seldom one stumbles upon one. In Queensland there are five deadly kinds, the black snake, the brown snake, the tiger snake, the diamond snake, and the death-adder. Of these the black and the brown are the commonest ; the latter sometimes reaching a length of eight or nine feet. The bite of any of these varieties is sufficient to cause death within a few hours, unless the proper remedies are applied at once, but by far the worst is the death-adder. It has this peculiarity, that, unlike all other snakes, it does not attempt to move out of anyone's way, but lies quite still until it is touched, when it fastens with a spring upon its victim. Its bite is by far the most deadly of all Australian snakes, and, with the exception of Underwood's celebrated performance, I never knew a well-authenticated instance of recovery from it.

Deaths from snake-bite are not uncommon, especially among the Kanakas who work in the cane-fields. The best known remedies are injection of ammonia, and large quantities of brandy taken internally.

Undoubtedly the man Underwood, above alluded to, was the possessor of a perfectly efficacious antidote to the bite of any Australian snake. He gave a series of performances in which he used to allow the most deadly snakes to bite him, afterwards applying some remedy, the nature of which was known only to himself. There can be no sort of doubt that the reptiles which he employed were perfectly healthy, and in full possession of their poisonous faculties.

The second bite of any snake is always less poisonous than the first, as some time is required to secrete a full supply of the venom which has been partially exhausted in the first bite. But dogs and rabbits which were bitten immediately after Underwood by the same snakes, died very shortly, which conclusively proves the genuine nature of his experiments. Indeed, the most convincing proof of all was the death of the unfortunate man himself. Having one day allowed a snake to bite him, while he was himself under the influence of liquor, he forgot where to find his own antidote, and died from the effects of the bite. He demanded £10,000 from the Victorian Government as the price of his discovery, which they refused to pay, so his secret perished with him.

Almost as deadly in its effects as any snake, and far more dangerous in its habits, is a small black spider, about the size of a large pea, with a brilliant crimson mark on its back. It lives mostly in old timber, but frequently it takes up its abode in an inhabited house, and, far from having any fear of man, it does not wait to be provoked before attacking him. Its bite, unlike that of a snake, causes the most intense agony, and the after effects are very bad. Death is by no means an uncommon result, but more frequently the victim becomes hopelessly insane, or paralysed. I killed several of them at odd times in my room, and once, while on the diggings, I was unfortunate enough to get a bite·from one. I was camped in front of the fire, and, just as it got light, I sat up and kicked the blanket off. As I did so I felt a sharp pain in the calf of my leg, and looking down I saw one of these little black devils on it. I killed it instantly, and reaching out my hand for a knife, I took up the piece of my leg where the bite was, between the finger and thumb of my left hand, and cut it clean out. I had always some ammonia with me, and I rubbed a quantity of that in. Certainly not more than ten seconds elapsed between the time I was bitten, and when I cut the piece out. But my leg got very bad. The pain for days afterwards was intense, and after that, the whole leg swelled and became soft like dough. The place itself turned into a running sore, about an inch deep, which did not heal for four months afterwards. Centipedes and scorpions are common enough, and the bite of either of them is painful, but not dangerous to anyone who is in a good state of health.

The real pests of the Bush are flies. Mosquitoes and sand-flies are bad enough, but after a time one gets used to them, and, after all, they do not come out much except at night, and are very local annoyances, some places being almost entirely free from them. But I defy the most philosophical of men to get used to flies. On the coast they are only troublesome for a few months in the year, during the autumn. But in the interior they are always bad, and really sometimes they make life almost intolerable. In the western country no one ever rides about in fly-time without wearing a veil. As I write now I can almost fancy I am in the middle of them again. One falls into the ink, crawls out again nearly drowned, tumbles with a flop on to the paper on which I am writing, and, rolling over on to its back, whirls round and round in a death-flurry, leaving an archipelago of ink-blots on the paper. A savage dip of the pen into the ink-pot, the result of suppressed irritation, harpoons the corpse of another one, and discloses the interesting fact that the bottom of the ink-pot is full of dead flies that have fallen in and never got out again. Four in each eye, three inside my shirt, two in each nostril, one glued firmly to my under lip, entirely unmoved by the language that is flying past it, thousands on my hands and arms, and several crawling pensively over the most sensitive portion of my ear,—oh! what on earth do they want? I would give them anything to eat or drink if they seemed to want it, but they do not. They simply come for the fun of crawling about, like people go to look at the wicket at a cricket-match between the innings, from conceited curiosity. Far from being a plague to which one grows accustomed, the annoyance of flies is one which gets worse and worse the longer that one has to endure it. It is a kind of cumulative irritant, which has the effect of making a man feel more entirely wicked than anything else in the world. Millions of flies are bad enough, but I am not at all sure that one fly which you cannot kill is not worse. The combined attack of a large number produces a sensation of general discomfort and irritation which is very hard to bear, but the deeper feelings of one's nature remain untouched. It is reserved for the solitary and persevering fly to call forth the wildest passion and the bitterest personal animosity of which the human breast is capable. There is no mistake about which fly it was that crawled up your nose and caused you to let fall your favourite pipe in a spasm of facial agony, and break it to pieces on the floor. There is only one. There is not another near you for miles. He is always bad at any time, but pray earnestly that the Solitary Fly may never attack you after dark, just when you have lit the lamp and are preparing for a quiet read and a smoke. If he does he will break everything in the room; at least, he will make you, which comes to the same thing. Having smashed your pipe, an injury which he knows you will resent deeply, he settles in a conspicuous position on the edge of the mantel-piece, not on the clock, but near it, and remains perfectly still. As you sit down again with a fresh pipe, the idea is certain to suggest itself that now he is so quiet, it is a splendid opportunity to finish him. There is sure to be a towel, or a coat, or something handy, left there by your evil genius to lure you on to ruin. Seizing the towel, and laying your pipe carefully down for fear of accidents, you rise cautiously up, keeping an eye on the fly all the time. If absolute immobility means anything, he does not see you coming. His indifference is, if anything, just a little overdone. You do not notice it at the time, in your excitement, but afterwards it occurs to you that no fly ever sat as still as that, except with some diabolical purpose.

Fury nerves your arm, and the towel descends upon the mantel-piece with a violence that throws a transient uncertainty over the fate of the fly, but leaves no sort of doubt about the clock, which is hurled into the fire-place, and lies there a hopeless wreck. The towel was longer than you thought it was, that is all, and two china ornaments, after rocking doubtfully backwards and forwards once or twice, roll suddenly over the edge, and commit suicide by the remains of the clock. The ruin is so complete, that you are encouraged to hope that your enemy has perished in the midst of it. Once more you sit down, and the few minutes of peace that succeed would be heaven, if it were not for the uncertainty that still surrounds the fate of the fly. Just as you are beginning to allow yourself to hope that your troubles are over, small cold damp feet planted on the back of your neck remind you that your adversary is not only not dead, but inclined to be quite as brutally

annoying as ever. You had better give in. He will
settle on the lamp next, and you will certainly smash
it to pieces in trying to kill him ; so you may just as
well put it out at once, and go to bed.

About the end of July, on the coast, bush-fires begin,
and go on all August and September. The grass grows
very rank and long in many places, and is much improved by being burnt off every year. It is a great
object to get the whole of one's run burnt every year,
but it is also very important to avoid getting the
whole of it swept at the same time. In order to
guard against this, the parts of it that will burn first
are set fire to as soon as they are ready. Directly the
first shower falls these parts are immediately covered
with beautiful young grass, " burnt feed " as it is called,
which grows with wonderful rapidity. When the whole
country is burning in patches for miles round, it is a
very pretty sight to see the fire at night creeping up the
sides of the mountains, the whole outline of a range
sometimes being marked by a long line of fire against
the steel blue of the sky. A considerable rise in the
normal temperature, of course, takes place in a district
where large bush-fires are burning, and the atmosphere
for weeks at a time is hazy with smoke. But to anyone
who has seen a bush-fire, at any rate in Queensland,
the wild stories of men on horseback, and herds of wild
animals, flying for their lives before the advancing
flames, become the merest fables.

I never saw a bush-fire, even when backed up by a
strong wind, that one could not walk away from, with
the greatest ease ; and even when the grass was three
or four feet long, I never saw one that one could not,

7

with equal ease, walk straight through on to the blackened country beyond. In Victoria and New South
Wales the danger of a bush-fire is much increased by
the fact that the tops of the trees burn as well as the
grass, and the flames are carried away from one to the
other with considerable rapidity, if there is a high wind
blowing at the time. But unless deprived of his senses
by terror, no one but the most stupid man could contrive
to be killed by a bush-fire.

In the dry weather, as the small lagoons and water-
holes scattered all over the country get low and dried
up, large numbers of every kind of wild ducks congregate on the big lagoon in front of Mount Spencer
station. In the evenings we used to have some very
good flight-shooting, one of us standing on each side
of the lagoon, at a point in the middle where it narrowed
down to a neck only about a hundred yards wide,
opening out again beyond into a second large lagoon,
or rather a swamp, between which and the main water
the ducks used to fly backwards and forwards just about
sundown. But by far the best duck-shooting, and
indeed the best shooting of any kind that I ever saw
in Australia, was down on the Pioneer river, which
literally swarmed with ducks from October to January.

One day, towards the end of November, eight of us set
off, with a gun apiece, and several niggers to drive, a
spring-cart keeping in our tracks to bring along the
ducks which we bagged. There are about ten duck-
drives on the river, each from a mile to a mile and a
half in length, and it takes two days to work it all
properly.

Arrived at the first station, we hung our horses up

some distance from the bank, and stationed ourselves
in a line across the bed of the river, which just there
was full of rocky islands covered with bushes. On
each side the banks rose up to a great height, so that
there was no fear of any ducks that the niggers might
put up leaving the river. They all came in twos and
threes, and small mobs, beautiful " rocketers " right
over our heads, as pretty shooting as one would wish
to see. I know nothing pleasanter, on a broiling hot
day, than to stand up to one's knees in the cool clear
running water, or sit down on a shady rock, with a
pipe of nigger-head in full swing, knocking over the
ducks as they come overhead. Let those who like
extol the pleasure of walking up your game. For
myself, I infinitely prefer the delights of driving, which
combines the joy of anticipation, the additional satisfaction of shooting a bird that is flying as fast as it
can instead of flapping, and the inestimable advantage
of sitting perfectly still oneself. There is no lack of
variety in the shooting on the Pioneer, and the bag
at the end of the day is certain to contain at least
five different kinds of ducks.

How many ducks eight good shots would bag in the
two days it is very difficult to say. My brother was
not with us on this occasion, and I can confidently
declare that I never saw seven worse shots. My own
was by no means a satisfactory performance, and I
do not think I got more shots than anyone else, but
out of one hundred and seventeen ducks which we
killed in one day, I myself shot sixty-three, and ought
to have shot a great many more. Of course, numbers
are lost. In the middle of a drive one cannot stop

7 *

to pick them up ; and besides the winged ones which escape, many which fall into the stream are carried out into the deep pools, where it is most unsafe to follow them, on account of the numerous alligators which haunt the river. These brutes breed on the banks, and I remember once coming upon a nest that had just hatched. The young ones had shuffled into the water for the first time, and were paddling about in the most awkward way, some on their sides, and some on their backs, learning how to swim. The old one was there, lying close to the bank, in about three feet of perfectly clear water. She never attempted to move until I got a long pole and jobbed her on the back with it, when she crawled sulkily off into the black depths of the pool.

In crossing the Fitzroy river at Yaamba I once had a narrow escape of being " scruffed " by an alligator. There was a fresh in the river at the time, and the water was very muddy and thick. The crossing was about a hundred yards wide, and the water just up to the saddle-flaps. When I got within about ten yards of the opposite bank, my horse made a roll and a plunge forward, sending his head right under water. I thought, of course, that he had stumbled over a log ; but a moment · after the head of an enormous alligator appeared close to my leg. His jaws were open, and he made a snap which took effect on my horse's belly, the two upper teeth of the brute leaving two clean deep cuts about four inches long. This had the effect of considerably hastening my horse's exit from the water, but it had exactly the opposite effect on the animal that a man was riding some twenty yards behind me.

Evidently it had caught sight of the alligator, for it remained rooted to the spot, shaking and snorting with terror, and absolutely refusing to move one way or the other. The apprehensions of its rider were, if anything, even more acute, and his appearance was a perfect study, as he knelt up on the highest point of his saddle, tucking his feet under him, and trying to make himself as small as possible. He had no whip, and would have died sooner than put one of his feet down to use his spurs ; so he did nothing but shout and swear at his horse, which had the effect of terrifying it more than ever. Every moment I expected, and so did he, to see the alligator's head alongside of him ; but, strange to say, though it was at least five minutes before his horse would move, it never appeared again until just as he was safe ashore.

The Fitzroy is the most southern water in Australia in which alligators are found, but from there up to Cape York the rivers and creeks are full of them. Why they are called alligators no one knows, for the formation of their jaws and the shape of their head distinctly prove them to be crocodiles. They have a great fancy for dogs in the way of food when they can get them ; but their diet extends over a varied range, from a full-grown cow to a paving-stone. On one of the plantations on the Pioneer an alligator was seen to perform a feat which gives some idea of the enormous strength which these brutes possess. The milking cows belonging to the plantation used to go down every morning to the river to drink. The bank was rather steep, and the water just there deepened very quickly. As one of the cows was

standing drinking, with her fore-legs in the water, an
alligator came up and caught her by the nose, and,
in spite of the animal's struggles, held firmly on, and
succeeded in dragging her down into the depths of the
pool. The incline of the bank was, of course, in the
reptile's favour, and no doubt terror deprived the cow
partly of her strength ; but, anyway, the pair of them
disappeared, and the cow never was seen again.

With regard to the paving-stones, no one knows
whether they are taken in for ballast, or to assist
digestion, or to fill a vacuum caused by hunger; but
it is a very common thing to find half-a-dozen stones,
each double the size of a man's fist, in the stomach of
an alligator.

Down at the end of the run, at a place called Blue
Mountain, about fourteen miles from Mount Spencer,
there were a quantity of wild pigs, and we had long been
meditating a pig-sticking excursion. No one had ever
tried to import this kind of sport into Australia before.
There are plenty of wild pigs in some parts ; but the
country in which they are found is so rough, it looks
almost like suicide to ride after them. However, one
has to ride after cattle in just the same country ; and
there is no more reason why one should break one's neck
riding after a pig than after a bullock, seeing one goes
just as fast as the other.

My brother had written home to me that he thought
there was some healthy fun to be got out of the pigs on
Blue Mountain flats, so I brought out three of Thorn-
hill's spears with me, and on my way through Singapore
I collected some bamboos for shafts. Armed with a
spear apiece, Rice and my brother and I set out one

day, towards the end of August, to try our luck. It was the wrong time of year, as the grass was fearfully long ; but we had been so busy, and had to put it off so often, we would not wait any more, and took the first spare time that we could get. We camped over-night at the hut at Blue Mountain, a small out-station with a horse-paddock and a yard, and early next morning we sallied out on to the neighbouring flats to look for the pigs

The country was heavily timbered, and the grass everywhere from two to three feet long, and in some places four or five. Any quantity of fallen trees and dead timber were scattered about, but there were no stones, and the country was pretty free from blind gullies, and, barring the long grass, it was not a bad place for galloping. We had not to look long for our game. Sneaking quietly across a small creek, as we emerged on the opposite bank, we came right upon a mob of eleven pigs, and amongst them two enormous boars. The instant they saw us, they tried to make for the bank of the creek, but with a wild yell we charged at them, and succeeded in cutting them off from the creek and turning them back on to the flat. Away we went after them, and, neglecting the small fry, my brother and I singled out one of the boars, and Rice pursued the other. For about half a mile the pace was excellent, and the fallen timber made it very lively.

My brother and I were rapidly coming up with our pig, when suddenly he disappeared into a gully. He was out the other side and away again in a moment ; but we had to make a slight round to cross the gully, which gave him a bit of a start again. The country was pretty open the other side, so we could hit out like anything, and once more we were close on to the boar, who was getting about played out, when in crossing a patch of long grass my horse went head over heels over a fallen tree, and sent me flying over his head. Neither of us were hurt, but, of course, my horse cleared out for home, with his tail in the air, as every Australian horse does the instant it parts with its rider ; so I picked up my spear, and set off after my brother as hard as I could to see the fun. A few hundred yards further on, he came alongside the boar and speared him in the neck. The brute turned sharp round and rushed between his horse's legs, almost upsetting it. My brother pulled up, and the boar promptly charged again ; whereupon his horse, which had never been at close quarters with a pig in its life, began to buck like mad. My brother hung on like wax, the natural disinclination of anyone to be slung from his horse being considerably enhanced in his case by the infuriated animal waiting to get a chance at him on the ground. But the blood was pouring in torrents from the wound in its neck ; and before I got up, it had lain down to die. We finished it off, and then examined my brother's horse, to see if it was damaged. Fortunately it had escaped with only a slight cut on the fetlock, which was lucky, as the old boar's tusks were over six inches long, and as sharp as knives.

A cooee from the ridges away to the right, about a quarter of a mile off, informed us of the whereabouts of Rice. We set off, and when we came up we found him standing with a broken spear in his hand, examining the carcase of a still more enormous boar than the one which my brother had killed. He had run him for about three-quarters of a mile, and in trying to spear him he had broken his spear, leaving only about five feet of a shaft. A little further on the boar "bailed up," on the top of a ridge, and stood with his legs wide apart, and the foam dropping from his huge tusks, and looking altogether such a discouraging sight, that nothing would induce Rice's horse to go anywhere near him. Whereupon he coolly got off, and, grasping the remains of his spear, walked straight at the boar, without, as he said afterwards, the slightest notion of what either he or the animal was going to do. Of course the boar charged, and as the brute came at him, Rice slung the spear at him with all his force, and with infinite precision. It entered the animal's chest, and he ran right on to it, driving it into his heart, and falling dead on the spot. It was a most miraculous escape for Rice; for if he had not killed the boar, it is pretty certain the boar would have killed him.

# CHAPTER VIII.

On the whole, Australia is one of the worst countries for sport that can be imagined. There is no big game of any kind, except kangaroos ; and after the novelty of a kangaroo hunt has worn off, it is very poor fun. Since the destruction of native dogs and eagle-hawks by the squatters who stocked the country with sheep, the kangaroos have not a single natural enemy left, and in some districts of Queensland they have increased to such an extent as to bring absolute ruin upon the runs which they infest. An Act known as the Marsupial Act was accordingly passed to encourage their destruction, a reward of so much a scalp being offered by the Government. In some places countless droves of them blacken the plains, eating up every vestige of grass, and literally starving the sheep off the country. Some of the squatters have gone to a vast expense in fencing in their runs with marsupial fencing, but it never pays.

The usual method adopted for slaughtering them is to build a yard with a very high fence in one of the " scrubs " on the plains. From this yard two fences run out through the " scrub," widening out and extending like wings for a long distance over the surrounding plain. A whole crowd of men on horse-back get together, with a mob of blacks to assist them, and drive the country for miles around up towards the wings of the fence. Once between the fences, the wretched animals are doomed. They make straight for the " scrub," and never know where they are till they find themselves inside the yard, with a mob of black devils yelling behind them. The rails are then put up, and the blacks go in and slaughter them with tomahawks and clubs. Hundreds and hundreds of kangaroos are often secured at a single " battue " of this kind ; but when once a good herd of them gets fairly started on a run, it is very difficult to get rid of them, or even to keep them down. This, however, is brutal work, though it is absolutely necessary it should be done, and no one could possibly describe it as sport. Even with good dogs and good horses, there is not much fun to be got out of hunting kangaroos singly. It is too much like coursing, which is of all bastard forms of sport the most detestable ; and though an " old-man " kangaroo will generally show fight when he is bailed up, there is very little difficulty in knocking him senseless with a stick.

Away up north an occasional raid after the wild Blacks enlivens the monotony of life, and there are some men who are brutal enough to enjoy hunting them down. But apart from the chance of getting a spear through his ribs, or a tomahawk in his skull, no one who has not lost every vestige of decent feeling could possibly look upon this as sport, or be induced to undertake it except in self-defence. Of the few kinds of sport which Australia does afford, undoubtedly the finest is hunting wild cattle. It is part of the legitimate business of a stockman, and a very necessary part too, for nothing is more injurious to a tame herd than the presence of wild cattle on a run. It ought, therefore, to be classed as work rather than sport; but anyone who has once been at it will own that it is a form of entertainment that is exceedingly bad to beat. Of course there are no wild cattle indigenous to the country, but in some places there are cattle that have been neglected, and that have bred wild for generations, and they are to all intents and purposes as wild, and twice as savage, as bisons. There was one corner of Mount Spencer run, on the coast-fall of the range, known as Black's Creek, the creek itself being one of the heads of the Pioneer river, and here the former owner of the station had allowed a mob of wild cattle to establish themselves. In reality it was the business of the neighbouring run, below the range, to get rid of them. The Black's Creek country belonged half to Mount Spencer and half to our neighbours, whose yards were very much nearer to it than ours, and very much more accessible from the part where the wild cattle were. But they neglected their business, and, as the wild cattle were a great nuisance to us, we had great sport for several years in hunting them down.

Black's Creek was about as wild a piece of country as it would be possible to find in Queensland. Its course lay right among the mountains, which towered on both sides, sending rocky spurs down in many places right up the banks of the creek. The grass was frightfully long, for it was not once in two years that we could get it to burn, and in many places it was up to one's elbows as one rode through it. There were a few little open flats along the course of the creek, but the rest of the country was very heavily timbered, the banks of the creek, and a good deal of the country being covered with dense scrub, for which the cattle made the instant they were disturbed. Once in the scrubs, one never saw them again that day, and the only chance was to corner them off, and hunt them out on to the more open country.

One day my brother and I settled we would make an expedition down Black's Creek, and hunt up some of the "clean-skins" as the wild cattle are called, in allusion to their never having been branded. We sent over to Haslewood for Billy Burgess, who appeared armed with an uncomfortable-looking sort of old musket, which he declared was a most reliable weapon if it was only held straight. My brother and I had a "Winchester" rifle each, and we provided Frank with an "Express," with which he was not half a bad shot. Rolling up our weapons in our blankets, which were strapped on to the saddle in front, we set off one afternoon in October, taking a black boy and some rations with us. The head of Black's Creek was about thirteen miles from the station; so we meant to camp out, and start early the next morning to look for the cattle.

There are various phases of camping-out in the Bush, some of them very pleasant, and some of them very much the reverse. On a warm dry summer night, with plenty of food and tobacco, and one or two good mates, there are few things more thoroughly enjoyable than to turn your horses out, light a fire and boil a "billy" of tea, and, after supper, to sit round smoking and yarning till it is time to roll yourself up in a blanket and sleep like a top under a tree. Occasionally, however, there are times when the camper-out does not have by any means a good time, and anyone who has knocked about the Bush for some time is sure to have spent more than one night of which the dismal recollection will not easily be wiped out of his mind. · When the rain is falling in torrents, and a cold winter's night overtakes the solitary wanderer who has lost his way and knocked-up his horse, it is by no means pleasant to find that he has got between two flooded creeks, and that the only thing to do is to wait for the morning's light before he attempts to go any farther. Soaked to the skin, and shivering with cold, without shelter and without food, he is lucky if he can find a rock, or the trunk of a big tree, to keep the piercing winter's wind from freezing the marrow in his back-bone. As he sits there huddled up, with his horse's bridle between his numbed fingers, the howl of the native dog, and the forlorn wail of the stone-curlew, strike with a mournful cadence upon his ears, about which the dead sticks from the trees overhead are flying. Mechanically he cuts up a pipe of tobacco, and fills his pipe, fumbling with shaking fingers in the recesses of his pouch for a dry match. Fortunate for him if he finds one dry enough to raise a smoke ; but if the hours before morning do not seem preternaturally long he must be of an exceedingly cheerful disposition.

Just before sundown we got to the place where we meant to camp, on the bank of the creek. The creek was not running ; but just here there was a small water-hole in the bed, full of clear water, with rocks all round covered with beautiful maiden-hair fern.

A little way back from the bank a huge mass of rock rose up, and between this and the creek we camped. Having unstrapped our blankets, we put our weapons together, and, taking off the saddles, we piled them against the rock, spreading the saddle-cloths over them to keep off the dew, and then, having hobbled the horses, we turned them out, with a small bell hung round the neck of one of them to tell us their whereabouts in the morning. In a few minutes the black boy had got a good fire going, with a couple of quart-pots set down to boil for making tea. "Quart-pot" tea, as tea made in the Bush is always called, is really the proper way to make it. A tin quart of water is set down by the fire, and when it is boiling hard a handful of tea is thrown in, and the pot instantly removed from the fire. Thus the tea is really made with boiling water, which brings out its full flavour, and it is drunk before it has time to draw too much.

Frank, meanwhile, went and chopped a piece of bark off a tree, and set about making some "Johnny cakes" for supper with a small bag of flour which he had brought with him. Emptying some of the flour into the sheet of bark, he poured some cold water into the middle of it, and stirred it quickly up into a paste. "Johnny cakes" are made with nothing but flour, but there is a great art in mixing them. If it is done properly, they are about the lightest and nicest sort of bread that can be made ; but the efforts of an amateur generally result in a wet heavy pulp, that sticks round one's teeth hke bird-lime. Frank, however, was quite a professor, and, having got his dough to his satisfaction, he pressed it out very thin, and tossed it on to the hot ashes in three-cornered pieces, which he kept turning over with a stick every few seconds. In a very few minutes a good supply of them were done, and as the tea was made, and a " Johnny cake " is nothing unless it is eaten red-hot, we produced the salt beef, and set to work at once.

After supper we all lit our pipes, except Frank, who did not smoke, and lay down round the fire with a sensation of absolute contentment and peace that one must go and camp-out in the Bush to understand. The only single drawback to my enjoyment was that Frank did not smoke. There is always something uncomfortable about a man who does not smoke ; but in the Bush, where one's pipe gets to be such a companion as it never does elsewhere, it was really quite painful to think of Frank setting off out on the run every day by himself without a pipe. He and Billy, not having seen each other for some weeks, began instantly to jaw about cattle, and the way in which they went at it laid over anything in the way of " shop " that I ever heard. Two fox-hunters fighting their battles over again are bad enough, and a couple of old University men recounting their college experiences will drive anyone who is obliged to listen nearly out of his mind. But for pure professional " shop-talking," unbroken by a single pause, and undiluted by a single digression, commend me to a pair of stockmen who take a hearty interest in the cattle that they are discussing, and who have not seen each other for a month.

Frank began it.

" I say, Billy," he said, " I was over at the head of Running Creek yesterday, and I saw that red bullock that we missed last time we mustered on Tommy's Camp."

" Ah ! " said Billy, " he runs about there now. Was that dying old crow-bait of a white cow along with him ? "

" Yes ; and that strawberry heifer too, whose mother died in the yard this time last year, when Stewart came up for fat cattle."

" I remember ; and a fine old bit of stuff her mother was, too. She was a calf of one of the last of old Lloyd's lot, that were here when I came."

" What! not that big roan cow that used to run down at the Gum Swamp, that broke away the time you and me and Fraser were yarding that mob down at the Hut ? "

" No, no, not that one at all. Do you remember a dark-red cow, branded AL on the cheek, that was always with that mob that used to be about the ridges behind the Black Swamp about five years ago ? "

" Of course I do. She was a milker."

" Well, *she* wasn't the mother of that strawberry heifer's mother, but her sister was. They were both of them milker's calves, and their mother was the mother of that big yellow bullock that went away down to Rockhampton with Kirwan's mob, five years ago."

" My word, what a rowdy brute he was ! Do you remember how nearly he horned Dick in the yard ? And when we let them out that white down-horned bullock hunted you half-way across the swamp. His mother 's alive yet, and got another calf, as like its mother as can be, only it 's got a white star. I saw them the other day down Back Creek, the time I fetched in that big roan calf belonging to that white cow, that was a calf of old ' Susan's.' "

8

And so they go on, discussing the appearance and the performance of one animal after another, and all its sisters and its cousins and its aunts, till one's brain reels in trying to follow them.

I had always heard Brahmins upheld as the possessors of the most marvellous memories in the world, but until a Brahmin gives some better proof of it than merely reciting five or six thousand lines of prose by heart, he must sink into insignificance compared to men who have twelve thousand cattle to look after, ranging over four hundred square miles of country, and increasing at the rate of three thousand every year, and who apparently know them every one by sight, and can remember most of the ones that they have seen during the preceding ten years, whereabouts they used to run, and how they were bred.

Hour after hour Frank and Billy went on, and when I lay down to sleep, with my feet to the fire and a big stone for a pillow, they were still hard at it, in the middle of a discussion as to whether the great-great-grandmother of a big roan bullock on the Main Camp had a black nose or not.

Next morning we all woke up just before day-break, while the stars were still shining, the straw-coloured light over the hills to the east showing that it would not be very long before the sun appeared. The ashes of last night's fire were still hot, and the addition of a few dry sticks soon raised a blaze again. After a wash in the creek we lit our pipes, and, leaving Billy to boil the tea for breakfast, we sallied out to look for our horses. The grass was up to our waists, and saturated with dew, so that before we had gone fifty yards we were soaked to the skin; but the weather was warm, so it did not matter. In winter, when the ground is covered with hoar frost, it is no joke to have to wade perhaps a couple of miles through the long grass to look for your horse, for it is hours before the sun has sufficient strength to dry your clothes. On such occasions I used to leave all my clothes at the camp-fire, and set out without a rag on, as I infinitely preferred a slight cut or two from the grass to sitting on my horse, shaking with cold and perfectly wet through, for four or five hours. This time our horses had not gone very far, and we were back in the camp by the time that the tea was made. Breakfast did not take long, and the instant we had done, we loaded our weapons, and, clambering on to our horses, we set off down the creek to look for the cattle.

Frank had been down some weeks before, and burnt as much of the grass as he could, but it was only in places that it would burn. In such a country it was perfectly hopeless to dream of getting any of the " clean skins " home to the yards, and all we wanted to do was to shoot as many of them as we could. Sneaking silently along for about a couple of miles, we came to a crossing of the creek, on the opposite side of which was a small plain. As we emerged on to this, we came suddenly upon a mob of about thirty wild cattle, among which were six or seven bulls, one of them about the biggest I ever saw. The instant they saw us the whole mob charged, and cleared us out in every direction. The black boy's bridle came off, and his horse tore wildly into the middle of a mob of raging bulls, with him yelling murder and absolutely white with funk.

8 *

Frank and my brother disappeared into the creek after the big bull and one or two others, and Billy and I tore across the plain after a small mob that were going like mad for the ridges beyond. As we came up with them, Billy discharged his weapon at a young bull that was a little behind the rest, the bullet breaking his shoulder, and bringing him bellowing on his head. Away we went after the rest; but a little further on Billy got a most awful buster over some rocks in the long grass, he and his horse rolling over each other in a most uncomfortable kind of way. Looking back over my shoulder as I galloped on, I saw him on his legs again, so I hit out like anything to get a shot at the rest of the mob before they got away into the ridges. Just on the edge of the plain I came up with them, and put a bullet behind the shoulder of a good-sized bull that was nearest me. He turned and charged, but my horse cleared out too quick for him, and after struggling on for about a hundred yards, he rolled over. The others were gone where it was hopeless to follow them, so I rode up and put another shot into him to finish him, and then turned back to see how Billy was getting on.

Fortunately he had landed clear of the rocks, in the long grass, but his saddle was smashed to pieces, and his horse's legs very much cut and knocked about. We rode back and finished off the bull that Billy had shot first, and then went over the creek to see what had become of the others. Following their tracks for about half a mile, we came upon my brother sitting upon a log all alone, smoking a pipe, and mopping the blood from his forehead.

"Hullo," I said, "are you hurt? had a buster? where's Frank? and what's happened to your horse?"

"Why, my horse has cleared out, and Frank has gone after him. He and I cornered off that big bull, and I rode up alongside and put a shot into him. I never saw anything turn as quick. He got me full on the ancle, and that kept his horn out of 'Darkie's' ribs; but the fool, instead of clearing, went into figures, and what with the cant I got from the bull, and the rifle, and one thing and another, down I went. It was all so mixed I thought the bull had upset me. 'Darkie' cleared out then, and left me on the ground five yards from the bull, on a dead level plain, without a bush for a hundred yards. I struggled on to my knees, and worked the rifle so as to load again; but before I could get it up the brute charged, and caught me full over the eye. Frank was yelling to me to lie down, but it's all gammon. I saw a bull the other day rooting up a daisy with perfect ease. I scrambled up again, and, the rifle being loaded, I put another shot into his shoulder, when he fortunately gave me best and left me. He's dead somewhere in the creek down there, I think. The 'Winchester' is good, and they always die of it, but the bullet is not stopping enough to prevent a charge. However, I've got off very well, with a sprained ancle from the first charge, and as to my eye, I think my head must be nearly as hard as the bull's, for, beyond cutting it open, it hasn't hurt me much."

"Well, hold on a minute," I said, "and I'll fetch you a pannikin of water out of the creek, if there is any here."

A little lower down I found a small pool of water, and having got my brother some, and washed his head for him, I set off down the creek to look for the bull. Sure enough, he was lying in the bed of the creek, stone dead, about a quarter of a mile below where my brother had last shot at him. Just then Frank reappeared leading " Darkie," whom he had managed to bail up amongst some big rocks lower down. Billy's horse was dead lame, and my brother's ancle so swollen that he could only just manage to ride; so we concluded to knock off and go home, and altogether, considering the frightful nature of the country, we had not done so badly to kill three of the bulls before they got away.

The next time we went down Black's Creek after the clean-skins we had a still more lively time. In the early part of the day my horse got badly horned in the belly, and not long after, while galloping after a beast, he went head over heels into a hole where the stump of a big tree had been burned out, and broke his shoulder. O'Donnell, the stockman from the neighbouring run, who came with us, came to fearful grief. He and his horse, and the bull that he was after, all went head foremost into a deep rocky gully. When we found them, the bull was lying in the bottom, among the rocks, with its neck broken, and O'Donnell on top of it, quite insensible. We got him out, and carried him home on a litter of saplings. For twenty-four hours he lay quite still, bleeding at the ears, and we thought he was away, but he came round, and eventually got all right again. The rest of us managed to get a mob of cattle, mostly clean-skins, into the yards; and about the gayest time that we had was drafting them. They exhibited shocking temper.

The worst of having wild cattle anywhere near one's run is that the tame ones go and join them, and become nearly as wild themselves. The country was so rough down Black's Creek that it was almost impossible to clean it up thoroughly, and we hardly ever went down there without crippling somebody. But there is no doubt that hunting wild cattle there was as healthy a form of sport as anyone could wish for.

# CHAPTER IX.

## COMPARISON OF CATTLE AND SHEEP STATIONS.

THE whole of the coast country of Queensland is un-
suited for sheep, chiefly owing to the prevalence of
grass-seed, but it fattens cattle admirably, and it is
along the coast-range that most of the cattle-stations in
the Colony are situated. Grass-seed is an abomination
which appears in autumn in all the grass on the coast.
It forms in bundles of hundreds of seeds, each of which
is a hard, black, little weapon, about a third of an inch
long, with a sharp barbed point at the business end.
When ripe, they shake off the instant anything touches
them, and attach themselves to it, and, the point being
as fine as a needle, they work their way into any soft
substance in a marvellous way, the barb preventing
them from ever going backwards. Anyone walking or
riding through the long grass in seed-time is certain to
get his clothes full of them, and the sharp pricks from
their points are most irritating. Life for a sheep in
such a country is an impossibility. Their wool becomes
so full of seeds that it is perfectly worthless, and eventually the seeds work their way right into the flesh of the
sheep, and, of course, when they reach the vital organs,
destroy its life. I have seen the unfortunate wretches
with their fleeces stuffed so full of grass-seed that they

are absolutely incapable of moving, and can only stand still, with their legs wide apart, looking more like a hedgehog on stilts than a sheep. Of course, grass-seed does not affect cattle, which do very well on the coast runs. But it is a remarkable thing that, although they lay on just as much fat upon the coast-country as they do upon the western downs, they will not travel without losing it. Cattle fattened upon the salt-bush and grasses of the west will, if driven carefully, carry their condition for hundreds of miles ; but the fat that they acquire on the coast-grass, and especially below the range, runs off them like melting butter when they travel.

Cattle-growing is not nearly so profitable as sheep, but, on the other hand, it requires far less capital to start with, and is attended with much less risk. The vast difference between a cattle-station and a sheep-station is this, that whereas the former can be made to pay its own way from the first, the latter requires a heavy outlay before it can be safely stocked at all.

Of course, in proportion as a man lays out money in improving a cattle-station at the first start, so his returns will be quicker, heavier, and more certain. But, if he is unable to do so, he will find that the expenses absolutely necessary to keep the place going are by no means heavy. We will suppose that a squatter puts 5,000 head of cattle on to a piece of entirely unimproved country. He ought to get the cattle, and sufficient country to carry 10,000 head, for £20,000. For about £400 he can put up yards, and a weaning-paddock for working the cattle, horse-yard, and paddock, and comfortable houses for himself and his men. Another £150 will start him with sufficient horses, and, if he is at all

inclined to work himself, two stockmen and a black boy
will be quite enough hands to work the cattle.˙ The
wages of the two former, at £75 a year, and the black
boy at 10s. a week, come to £176 per year, and another
£100 a year ought to find them all in rations.

We will suppose that the increase is allowed to
accumulate, nothing but fat cattle being sold off the run
for the first five years.

During that time the proceeds from sales of fat cattle
should be amply sufficient to cover all working expenses,
and to enable the squatter to keep on improving his run
by fencing, &c., to meet the increasing requirements of
his herd.

At the end of five years he should have at least 10,000
head of cattle, and have completed all the improvements
necessary for working them.

Allowing a liberal per-centage for deaths, his annual
increase from 10,000 head would be fully 2,500, of
which about 800 would be fat cattle.

Supposing him, for the future, to keep his herd at
10,000, and sell the whole of his annual increase, his
yearly profits would be as follows:—

|  | £ |
|---|---|
| By sale of 800 fat cattle, at £4 . | 3,200 |
| ,,   1,700 store cattle, at £1 10s. | 2,550 |
|  | £5,750 |

|  | £ |
|---|---|
| To working expenses    .    .    . | 1,700 |
| ,, Balance    .    .    .    . | 4,050 |
|  | £5,750 |

In the above calculation the price of fat cattle is taken

at the average price in Queensland for some years past, and the price of store cattle at the lowest possible figure, which is called " boiling-down " price ; for when store cattle are perfectly unsaleable, as they sometimes are, it is always possible to clear £1 10s. a head on them by boiling them down for tallow and hides.

The working expenses have been put rather high, and the increase below the average of fair seasons.

Thus, in five years the squatter's original capital of £20,000 will have increased to £40,000, for which he will get a return of £4,000.

Of course, in good times, when fat cattle are up to £5 or £6, and store cattle to £2 10s., his profits will be very much larger, but, at the same time, a squatter must always be prepared to spend a large sum of money upon the purchase of land, to secure his run against selectors. No allowance has been made for this in the above calculations, for legislation on the land question is continually assuming different phases, but a squatter may take it for granted that, sooner or later, he will have to lay out a great deal of money in securing his run, and he is generally quite willing to do so when the time comes.

The risks attending the working of a cattle-station are the possibility of an epidemic of pleuro-pneumonia breaking out in the herd, and, of course, the danger of a very severe drought. But the coast country, to which cattle are chiefly confined, is, as has been already said, not nearly so liable to drought as the interior where sheep-farming is carried on ; and although isolated cases of pleuro-pneumonia are nearly always to be met with in a big herd, it is extremely seldom that the disease assumes an epidemic form. On the whole, therefore, the risks of growing cattle may be considered as being very small. The disadvantages of a cattle-station from a business point of view are, that in the first place, although it will return a high and safe rate of interest if properly managed, still it will never afford a chance of making the rapid fortune that four or five consecutive good seasons on a sheep-station ensure. In the second place, a cattle-station requires very few hands, and not much capital to work it, and opens no connection with the banks and the business men in the towns. No one cares the least for the connection with a cattle-station, for it is worth nothing. The cattle are raised at a small expense, driven down to market by the station hands, sold to the butchers, and there is an end to them.

It is very often greatly to the interest of a squatter to be able to raise money on the security of his run, either to tide over bad times, to make improvements, or to secure his country by the purchase of freehold land. The indifference of the banks and of business men generally to the cattle industry makes it very much more difficult to raise money upon a cattle-station than upon a sheep-station. With the latter there is not the slightest difficulty. Wool is the staple product of the country, and represents an enormous proportion of the aggregate wealth of the community, and the bulk of the population are either directly or indirectly connected with its growth. Consequently " financing " is rendered very much easier upon the security of a sheep-station ; and if a man puts £20,000 of his own money into forming a sheep-station, if he knows anything at all of finance, he will easily get £40,000 of someone else's money to help him, at a rate of interest that will pay him remarkably well. All over the country a bale of wool is nearly as good security as the bank-note that represents its value; and it is no matter if a man's wool be in his wool-shed in the centre of Australia, under a tarpauling on the banks of a flooded creek, or in a vessel coming down the coast, he can always get an advance upon it from the bank.

Sheep-farming in Australia is now a very different thing to what it was twenty or even ten years ago. In those days a man had nothing to do but to go far enough into the interior, and he could take up as much new country as he pleased, paying nothing for it beyond the annual rent to the Crown. He put his sheep on to it, and in a few years, if he had good seasons, he made an enormous fortune, partly from his annual profits, but chiefly from the extraordinary rise in value of his country and stock. But if in the meantime he had two bad seasons, he was probably ruined; for the early settlers did not comprehend the vital importance of laying out capital in storing water upon their runs, to guard against the possibility of a long drought.

Long experience has now shown that every part of Australia that is fit for growing sheep is subject to occasional periods of very severe drought, at uncertain intervals, the occurrence of which it is quite impossible to foretell. Some of these droughts have been of extraordinary duration, and the early settlers were astonished to find that water-holes and creeks which they had been for years accustomed to regard as affording an inexhaustible supply of permanent water, suc-

cumbed at length to the severity of one of these
visitations, and left their country without a drop of
water upon it. Hundreds of men were ruined by
trusting to the natural water upon their runs, while
others, of course, who were fortunate enough to have
a run of good seasons, made tremendous profits.

But the lesson which has been learned is this, that
in order to provide against the possibility of a prolonged drought, the squatter must treat his country
as if practically there was no natural water upon it
at all, and expend a large amount of capital in making
dams and tanks, so as to have, if possible, a supply
of water stored in every part of his run that is
capable of holding out against any drought, however
severe. This entails vast expense, but it is the only
possible way of making a safe and profitable investment of sheep-farming in Australia. Of course there
are some lagoons and water-holes upon which the most
prolonged drought has little or no effect, and their
existence greatly enhances the value of any piece of
country upon which they may happen to be found.

An immense amount of loss was sustained in the
early days by over-stocking the country, and in some
parts the evil effects of so doing are still felt; for to
such extremities were the unfortunate sheep reduced
in a drought, that they not only ate up every blade
of grass, but tore out the roots and ate them as well,
so that it took years before any grass would grow
there again. It is by no means uncommon in such
districts as the Riverina, to be reduced to feeding the
sheep upon the leaves of gum-trees to keep them alive
during a dry season, when every vestige of grass has

disappeared. In most parts of Australia, however, water is the main thing, for, unless the country has been over-stocked, sheep will manage to eke out an existence in a most extraordinary way, provided they have a sufficient supply of water. A dozen years ago, if it had been represented to an English capitalist that the safest and most profitable investment that he could possibly find for his money would be to take up dry country in Queensland, and make a permanent supply of water on it, the idea would probably have struck him as eminently fantastic and unpractical. But it is probable that the world has never yet seen so certain and so quick a means of realising an enormous fortune. At that time an unlimited extent of country was to be had for next to nothing, which has since risen to a fabulous value, where money has been expended in storing water upon it.

At the present time, there is not the same amount of money to be made at it as there was in the old days, because every mile of country that is worth anything in Victoria, New South Wales, Queensland, and the greater portion of South Australia and the Northern Territory, has been taken up; so that instead of getting his country for nothing, the squatter has now to start by paying at least £10 a square mile, even in the back-blocks of Queensland, for, say, a twenty-one years' lease of perfectly bare country, without permanent water, stock, or improvements of any kind.

In Victoria the plundering and blundering of an ignorant radical legislature has considerably reduced the market value of every acre of pastoral land in the colony. In New South Wales the value of land is about stationary ; but in Queensland and South Australia its value is still increasing, though not at the same rate as formerly. The tremendous sums that have lately been paid for sheep-stations in Queensland might at first seem like fancy prices, but the profits subsequently derived forbid the application of any such term. Hitherto, most of the large fortunes that have been made in connection with sheep-farming have been made more from the rise in value of the country than from the annual profits derived from the industry itself, though these have been very great.

If we follow the career of the " leviathans " of Australia in the squatting line, we shall see that most of them made their fortunes by constantly taking up new country, stocking it and improving it, and selling it again as soon as possible, at an immense profit. Now, however, this can only be carried out in a very modified form. The value of country, whether dry or watered, stocked or unstocked, all over New South Wales and Queensland, has risen to such a point that, for the future, profit must be expected more from the annual proceeds of working the country than from any great subsequent rise in its value. Of course there are still districts, such as the northern territory of South Australia, and the Gulf of Carpentaria in Queensland, where a considerable rise in the value of bare country may be confidently looked for during the next few years. But in the central and southern districts the country itself may be considered to have attained a value at which it will remain steady for some years, and profits, as I have said, must be derived from increase of stock and sale of wool. What these profits amount to in fair seasons will be seen from the statistics appended below, and it must be acknowledged that they are in themselves sufficiently startling.

The following are the particulars of a station in the Barcoo district of Queensland, consisting of 800 square miles of country, of which only about 600 are available ·—

> Bought in 1882 for £200,000, with 135,000 sheep. Out of these there were 62,000 ewes in lamb, from which they got 54,000 lambs the first year.
>
> Clip of wool 1882 (135,000 sheep), 1,730 bales valued at £35,000. Sold since purchase 30,000 sheep off the run, at £15,000.
>
> In 1883 they shore 190,000 sheep, and including lambs there are now 210,000 sheep on the run. The value of this year's clip is £48,000, and the value of the increase is between £30,000 and £40,000.
>
> Taking the expenses at £15,000 per annum, this leaves a nett profit in two years of at least £113,000, besides which the station has risen greatly in value.

The following shows the rise in value and returns of another sheep-station in the Aramac district of Queensland. It consists of about one thousand square miles of country, and was bought in June 1881, for £70,000, together with 41,703 sheep, and 2,230 cattle on the run.

| | |
|---|---|
| Original number of sheep . . . | 41,708 |
| In all to date (Oct. 1883) they have had . | 77,327 lambs. |
| And bought . . . . . . | 86,014 sheep. |
| | 205,044 |

| | |
|---|---|
| Deaths and killed for rations to date | 12,996 |
| Lost travelling on road . . | 216 |
| Sold . . . . . | 34,830 |
| Number at present on the station | 157,002 |
| | 205,044 |

| | |
|---|---|
| Number of sheep at present on station . | 157,002 |
|     ,,     cattle     ,,     ,, | 5,610 |

In 1882 they shore 93,204 sheep, producing 383,174 pounds of wool, which brought £21,000 in London. Improvements since June 1881 have cost about £18,000. This year, 1883, they will shear 157,000 sheep, the wool from which will be worth £33,000, and the station is now valued at £200,000.

We will now consider the case of an outlying piece of country, which has never been stocked with anything but cattle, and which it is proposed to turn into a sheep-station.

The following tables of expenditure, income added to paid-up capital, and approximate increase and numbers of sheep, refer to an estimate made by the manager of a leading firm in Melbourne, for forming and stocking a piece of country in the Burke district of Queensland, about two hundred and fifty miles from Normanton, a township on the Gulf of Carpentaria. The run consisted of 500 miles of the best description of sheep country, and there were on it 2,000 head of cattle, and no improvements of any kind. It was proposed to form a company with a capital of £100,000 to purchase the run and stock it with sheep. The former owners agreed to take £5,000 in cash, and £20,000 in paid-up shares for the property.

The accompanying tables show the position of the

station at the end of four years. The run is capable, when fully improved, of carrying from 180,000 to 200,000 sheep, and would be worth at the end of four years, with the sheep, at least £150,000. In computing the cost of management £100 per annum has been allowed for every thousand sheep, whereas £70 per thousand is allowed to be the average cost; but the country being new, and labouring therefore under some disadvantage for the time being, so much more has been allowed for the cost of management.

The cost of everything has been put at the highest, and the selling price of wool and sheep at the lowest. The calculations have only been made for four years, showing the position of affairs, value of the station and stock ; and the returns, if the stock were allowed to increase, and improvements to carry the extra number of sheep were made, would increase wonderfully if allowed to go on. In computing the number of sheep at the end of four years, $2\frac{1}{2}$ per cent. which is usually allowed per annum for losses has not been taken into consideration, but at the same time the per-centage of lambs has been put at only 70 per cent., which is much under the mark in anything like a favourable season ; the expense of water to be made in the pad-docks has been put at a very high figure, and the fact of there being a good deal of natural water on the run has not been taken into consideration. If sheep were placed on the run at once, and improvements com-menced, there can be no doubt that within three years the cost of management, &c. would be at least 20 per cent. less than that computed. In allowing for the cost of water to be made the second and third years,

9 *

a great reduction has been made, as the cost of plant, &c. would not have to be calculated; and experience has shown that, after stocking a run, plenty of water that has not been permanent before becomes so, as the country is trodden in by the stock. Due allowance may, therefore, be made for a certain amount of natural water lasting permanently.

### ESTIMATE OF EXPENDITURE.

#### First Year.

| | | | |
|---|---:|---|---|
| Cost of 40,000 ewes, and driving them to station | £40,000 | 0 | 0 |
| Fencing four paddocks five miles square ; fencing to consist of five wires, at £50 per mile | 4,000 | 0 | 0 |
| Dams to be constructed in each paddock | 4,000 | 0 | 0 |
| Wool-sheds, hut and yards.      .      . | 3,000 | 0 | 0 |
| Management, at £100 per 1,000 sheep | 4,000 | 0 | 0 |
| Horses, plant, and contingencies      .      .      . | 2,000 | 0 | 0 |
| Rams      .      .      .      .      .      .      .      . | 1,200 | 0 | 0 |
| | £58,200 | 0 | 0 |

#### Second Year.

| | | | |
|---|---:|---|---|
| Cost of fencing paddocks for first year's lambs, say 70 per cent. on 28,000 sheep ; three paddocks as above      .      .      .      .      . | £3,000 | 0 | 0 |
| Dams made in paddocks      .      .      .      . | 2,000 | 0 | 0 |
| Management, £100 per 1,000, on 68,000 sheep      . | 6,800 | 0 | 0 |
| | £11,800 | 0 | 0 |

#### Third Year.

| | | | |
|---|---:|---|---|
| There would be 54,000 ewes to lamb, which at 70 per cent. would be 37,800 lambs, for which fencing would have to be put up, say at a cost of .      .      .      .      . | 4,000 | 0 | 0 |
| Expenditure for water      .      .      . | 2,000 | 0 | 0 |
| Management, 96,000 at £100 per 1,000 | 9,600 | 0 | 0 |
| | £15,600 | 0 | 0 |

*Fourth Year.*

There would be in all 132,000 sheep on the run by this time, and if it were intended to keep the numbers at this, the cost of management with that amount of sheep at £100 per 1,000 would be (*though it certainly would not be more than £80 per 1,000*) . . . . . £13,200 0 0

CAPITAL AND INCOME during four years expended on the Property.

After paying the original owners in shares, it was proposed to call up two-thirds of the remaining capital, which, after deducting £5,000 due to the original owners in cash, would leave £48,333 6s. 8d. to commence operations with, the balance to be called up as agreed on.

| | |
|---|---|
| Capital, two-thirds of £80,000, less £5,000 paid to original owners . . . . | £48,333 6 8 |
| Clip of 1st year, 40,000 sheep at 4s. nett . | 8,000 0 0 |
| ,, 2nd ,, 68,000 ,, ,, | 13,600 0 0 |
| ,, 3rd ,, 96,000 ,, ,, | 19,200 0 0 |
| ,, 4th ,, 132,000 ,, ,, . | 26,400 0 0 |
| Sale of increase, 14,000 wethers, half of first year's increase, at 5s. per head . . . | 3,500 0 0 |
| | £119,033 6 8 |

EXPENDITURE.

| | |
|---|---|
| First year . . . . . . . . | £58,200 0 0 |
| Second year . . . . . . . | 11,800 0 0 |
| Third year . . . . . . . | 15,600 0 0 |
| Fourth year . . . . . . . | 13,200 0 0 |
| | £98,800 0 0 |

At the end of four years, supposing the number of sheep to be kept at 132,000, the station would be worth at least £150,000, and should return an annual profit of fully £30,000.

In fair seasons, with good management, experience shows that the above figures are below rather than above what is certain to be realised from working a good piece of sheep country. Against this, there is always the danger of a drought such as the whole of New South Wales and Queensland are now suffering from. An ordinary drought can be provided against by the precaution of storing water, and by carefully avoiding over-stocking the country. But a period of such exceptional severity as the drought which has now (Dec. 1884) lasted for nearly two years in the above countries, cannot fail to do a certain amount of injury to everyone, and, of course, brings utter ruin to all who have not provided an artificial storage of water. A great deal of well-sinking has been done lately in Queensland, and so far with very satisfactory results. In many parts of the Burke district, round the Gulf, water has been struck at a few feet below the surface, which, of course, increases the value of the country considerably.

The effects of a drought in Australia at the present time are not nearly so disastrous as was the case formerly. In the first place, from the amount of artificial water that has been made, the country is far better fitted to withstand a severe season. In the second place, the extraordinary rallying powers of the country have been so conclusively proved, that a drought, even although the mortality among the stock at the time may be very heavy, does not produce the commercial crisis that invariably followed in the early days. The banks see that it is their interest to go on backing the squatters who are in their books, instead of selling them up, as they used to do ; and the squatters whose stations are free from debt simply lay themselves out to cut down expenses in every way, and wait for better times, instead of giving way to panic and putting their property in the market at a ruinous reduction in price. A run of bad seasons may make pastoral property almost unsaleable for the time, owing to the reduction it produces in the amount of floating capital throughout the country; but it has not the effect of materially lowering prices, except in the case of unstocked and outlying runs.

Civilisation is continually extending further inland from the coast, and as it advances the halcyon days of the squatter are swept away. It is in the early part of his tenure that he must look to realise vast profits; for when once his run is thrown open for selection, he must be prepared to secure the freehold of a great portion of it at a heavy outlay, and his subsequent profits will not exceed 10 per cent. on the money expended.

There is a fine opening at the present time for investing capital in developing the country in the Gulf district of Queensland. A great deal of it is allowed to be equal to any sheep country in Queensland, and in point of carriage—always a heavy item of expenditure on a sheep-station—it compares most favourably with the central and western districts, where sheep are now raised most profitably; for the distance to Normanton and Burketown, on the Gulf of Carpentaria, is not above 300 miles. It further possesses the incalculable advantage of being free for many years to come from all danger of selection, and, altogether, it is undoubtedly the " coming country " of Australia ; for eventually one of the chief outlets to the commerce of the continent must inevitably be a port on the Gulf of Carpentaria.

An English company has recently been formed, with a capital of £275,000, to work a large tract of country in this district; and with good management there is no doubt that they will get an excellent return for the money invested.

The new Land Bill in Queensland is not yet through Committee, but from the draft there is every reason to believe that it will be a most favourable one for the squatters, the main feature of it being that while half the squatter's run is taken from him and thrown open to selection, his tenure of the remaining half is rendered secure.    For the half which is thrown open he can, of course, compete on equal terms with any other selector.

It is an ill wind that blows no one any good, and there is no doubt that the severity of the recent drought has had an excellent effect in moderating the severity of the Land Bill.    Had the so-called reform been undertaken by the Legislature in the midst of good seasons, when the squatting industry was flourishing, there is no sort of doubt that we should have been plundered in the same ruthless manner that our neighbours in Victoria have been, who have escaped the drought.  " *Cantat vacuus coram latrone* " ; and the Queensland squatters have suffered so severely from natural causes, that even the Government realised that it would be unwise to rob them any further for the present.

# CHAPTER X.

THE BLACKS.

If you ask what sort of a race the Blacks of Australia are, nine people out of ten will immediately answer your question with that prompt assurance which no one ever ventures to bring to bear on any subject, except one about which he knows nothing and has thought less, and will tell you that they are physically and intellectually the most degraded race in the world.

There being no fixed standard to apply to the different races of the world for the purpose of gauging their physical and intellectual merits, we can only do so by comparing them with each other. When compared with those nations of the Old World who are universally admitted to have reached the highest point of civilisation as yet known, the Australian Black is, of course, a very low specimen of the human race indeed. But compared with the Digger Indians, the Bushmen of South Africa, and the inhabitants of not a few of the islands of the Pacific Ocean, he at once assumes a different aspect. I had thought of comparing him to some of those savages by no means extinct in the Old Country at the present day; but the comparison seems more than usually odious, and I will pass on.

From a physical point of view, many of the Australian Blacks are exceedingly fine specimens of humanity, and possess great muscular strength. In swimming, diving, climbing, picking up and following a trail, they are a match for any race under the sun; and in running and jumping many of them would give a good deal of trouble to a professional athlete. The extraordinary art of throwing a boomerang is peculiar to them, and with a spear they are not to be surpassed.

It will be objected that these are a very low class of accomplishments, displaying, with the exception of the boomerang, no inventive genius whatever. This is quite true, but it is equally true that they answer the end in view, which is more than can be said of many more elaborate contrivances; and, as a rule, the simplest means of obtaining an object are the best. Now the object of an Australian Black, in common with most of his fellow-creatures, is to provide himself with food; and it has been frequently brought forward as a proof of great want of intelligence, that he has never invented a bow and arrow for this purpose. But necessity, we all know, is the mother of invention, and so long as a Black can with perfect ease kill as many birds and beasts as he wants with sticks and spears, it is hardly fair to accuse him of want of intelligence for not employing the more complicated appliances which are necessary in countries where food is less plentiful and less easily obtained. We might with equal justice and discernment abuse the inhabitants of Upper Egypt, where it rains once in five years, for not having invented umbrellas; or the Esquimaux for not using refrigerators to preserve their meat. That the Blacks are by no means deficient in natural

BLACK-FELLOW PREPARING TO GO UP A TREE.

ingenuity is proved by the stone-headed tomahawks, heavy wooden swords, and bone-tipped spears which are in use amongst the wildest of the tribes. No doubt, when game becomes too wild or too scarce to be easily killed with sticks and stones, they will invent some more ingenious way of procuring it.

The countenances of these niggers, often very pleasing, are seldom devoid of a good deal of intelligence, and after a short intercourse with civilisation are highly susceptible of that expression of finished rascality which is usually supposed to be a peculiarity of the white man. Their sense of humour and perception of the ridiculous is exquisitely keen. A cow tumbling head over heels across a log in the long grass, a man looking for a pipe which he has got in his mouth, or a dog in search of food upsetting something on to its own head, and running away like the deuce, with nothing after it, will make a black fellow laugh for a week afterwards whenever he thinks of it. Nothing with the ghost of a joke in it escapes him, and finer shades of humour that are entirely lost upon many well-educated whites will be instantly and thoroughly appreciated by him.

We had a black fellow on the station, by name Wakarra, who was as pleasant a companion for a day's ride as could be wished. It is not too much to say his manners were those of a perfect gentleman. No amount of hurry ever made him forget himself for an instant, no scolding made him sulky, and no kindness made him disrespectful. The graceful ease with which he used to remove his battered hat to any ladies that happened to be staying on the station, was a sight that might have moved an Old Country swell to tears of admiration.

He learned to read with ease, and had a most surprising faculty for asking questions. One day he wanted to know how the sun set and rose. I explained to him that the earth went round, which he understood perfectly; but when I told him how fast it went, he thought for a bit, and asked why the trees and houses and things did not all fall off·? I told him that they were stuck on with a kind of invisible glue, which only partially allayed his thirst for information. He is certainly rather an extraordinary black, and perhaps hardly a fair specimen of his race. But I never saw one upon whose education so much pains had been bestowed; and most likely here, as elsewhere, there are just as good fish in the sea as ever came out of it.

In acquiring the rudiments of civilisation, such as drinking, lying, thieving, and twisting red handkerchiefs round their heads, the Blacks show themselves to be very apt pupils. But in all the higher branches of social science they are very backward. For instance, when their relations become incapacitated by age or disease from following the wanderings of the tribe, they have a nasty low habit of beating in their heads with a club, instead of gently assisting the course of nature by giving them little or nothing to eat, a method which I have occasionally seen pursued with the greatest success by the inhabitants of more civilised countries. Then, again, they are extremely particular about their wives, and resent any interference with them on the part of the rest of the tribe, with a violence which civilised society of modern times has branded as being in the worst possible taste.

any sort of religion to the Australian Blacks. I never heard of any great exertions being made in this direction; but undoubtedly the great obstacle to success would be not so much a black fellow's want of intelligence, as his unrestrained sense of the ridiculous. One of our poets has declared that

<blockquote>Life is a jest, and all things show it;</blockquote>

and seeing that it is impossible at the outset to impress a nigger with the solemnity of religion, there is great likelihood that he will fall in with the views of the poet, and laugh at it immoderately.

I remember once trying to give a fairly intelligent Black some idea of a future state. In the course of conversation he pointed up to the sky, and said:

"Big one Master stop up there? Where you been see Him that One?"

"Yowi" (yes), I replied, "you better believe it. By-and-bye you see Him that One too."

After a pause he again inquired, "That One got a store up there?"

Now the possession of a store implies unlimited power to a black fellow, so I promptly replied:

"My word! altogether big one store up there. Plenty flour, plenty tobacco; supposin' you good one nigger, by-and-bye you get plenty up there."

His next remark was, "I say! you go along o' that One by-and-bye?"

"Yowi," said I, "mine think it. By-and-bye go along o' that One, get wings, fly about close up like a bird."

This appeared to interest him immensely, without

striking him as the least odd. But when I told him that if he behaved well he would go there too, he had barely time to say " Gammon ! " with an amount of expression that no one but a nigger can put into that one word, before rolling on to the ground in perfect convulsions of laughter. That a white man should go to heaven seemed perfectly natural to him ; but the idea of a black fellow by any possibility getting there too, struck him as so utterly funny that he went on laughing for a week after whenever he saw me.

The Blacks that have received any religious instruction generally sneak up to you in the towns and offer to parade their knowledge for a consideration. " I say! you give it me one fellow sixpence, plenty mine yabber-yabber—belief! I say! Glass of whiskey—Our Father," and so on.

The most notable instance of anything like success attending the attempt to proselytise a Black, was that of an old nigger who once observed, in answer to some inquiry as to his views of a future state, that, " supposin' he was a bad nigger, altogether debbil-debbil come and take him off."

Their ordinary creed is very simple. " Directly me bung (die) me jump up white feller," and this seems to be the height of their ambition.

They have some sort of religion or superstition of their own. When a warrior of celebrity dies, or succumbs to a blow on the head from a nullah, they skin him with the greatest care, and, after eating as much of him as they feel inclined for, they pick his bones beautifully clean and wrap them up in his skin. Instances have been known where Blacks have carried these relics about with them in all the wanderings of their tribe for many years. Sometimes they embalm their chiefs, but very rarely one would suppose, as up to the present time very few of these mummies have ever fallen into the hands of white men. One of them is now in the Queensland Museum at Brisbane, and, according to the account of the tribe from which it came, it is over two hundred years old.

Whether it would be possible to teach Christianity to the Australian Blacks, or not, I do not pretend to say; but I am very certain that it would be far better to begin by teaching them to behave as respectable members of the community. By the time that they have learned to refrain from smashing the skulls of decrepit relations, from killing a man simply because he has some article about him which they wish for, and from eating him afterwards if they are hungry, it will be quite time enough to direct their attention to a future existence. The task of persuading an average nigger that punishment follows crime, and prosperity is the reward of virtue, will be found quite arduous enough to satisfy the most zealous of missionaries, even though it be the business of these admirable men to " turn black into white," after a fashion. Having, at any rate, got him to comprehend that there are certain rules that he cannot transgress with impunity, and certain enjoyments that he can only obtain by exertion, he will be more fit to be initiated into the mysteries of Christianity than when he had no idea of right and wrong.

A more lamentable example of misdirected zeal than is afforded by the South Sea Islanders cannot be imagined. If we may take as examples the large number of Kanakas who come over to Australia every year, we are obliged to conclude that any teaching that they get from the missionaries does them infinitely more harm than good.  No one will have anything to do with a " missionary boy," if he can by any means get another one.  We cannot for a moment allow the blame of this to rest on the religion taught, and we should be sorry to think that it was entirely the fault of those who teach it.  Experience proves that it has nothing whatever to do with the Kanakas themselves; for until they are persuaded to become Christians, they are an orderly, contented, and industrious race.  The fault, then, must lie in the manner of teaching.

Religion, someone says, makes an excellent roof, but a very bad floor; and it is the height of folly to try and teach Christianity to a savage before he has any idea of those fundamental laws which, quite independent of any revealed religion, govern the welfare of a community. It is not only teaching him to run before he can walk, but expecting him to jump over obstacles at every other step which, from the earliest ages, have brought the most eminent divines to grief.  More than this, it is putting an exceedingly dangerous weapon into the hands of an inexperienced and mischievous child.

For example, suppose that you make a savage understand that the God whom you are teaching him to serve has bade all the rich in this world to sell all that they have, and give it to the poor.  What will be the effect upon his mind ?  An earthly paradise of rum, blankets, and tobacco is at once opened up before him ; and having most probably gone to sleep the night before without even one of these luxuries, he must inevitably arrive at one of two conclusions, either that you are telling him a lie, or that there are a number of rich people around him sadly ignorant of their duties.

Most probably the latter is the view to which he will incline, and, fully persuaded that he is only promoting the gospel of peace on earth and good-will towards men, he will set off to the nearest plantation, and give the owner of it a lesson in practical Christianity by removing as many articles of value as he can, and retiring to distribute them amongst his friends. Be this as it may, one broad truth remains, that in attempting to convert a South Sea Islander into a Christian, the missionaries rarely fail to convert an innocent and industrious savage into an idle and worthless scoundrel.

Nearly every station in Queensland has one or two black boys employed on it as stock-riders, in which capacity they are very useful, as they soon learn to ride well, and are invaluable in tracking lost cattle and sheep. As a rule, however, they are not much use after they get about twenty years old. By that time they have begun to find out that they are useful; and as their idea of the value of their services seldom corresponds with that of their employer, they generally get sent away. Having once been employed by white men, they would instantly be killed if they tried to rejoin their tribe; so they generally take to loafing about the nearest town, and sooner or later die of drink.

There is a school now, down in Mackay, to teach Blacks to read and write, and get their living by some sort of work. It has hardly been started long enough to see how it will work. At present the only place where Blacks are employed in any numbers is upon the

Mackay tobacco-plantations, and their being so is a
most unqualified nuisance to the district. Of course
any effort to induce the Blacks to work for their living,
instead of spearing other people's cattle and picnicing
on their own relations, deserves the highest praise.
But we solemnly protest against their being turned
loose on society before their education is completed;
and we infinitely prefer having to deal with an entirely
wild Black, than with one who has imbibed a great
deal of mischief, and very little good, from a temporary
residence amongst white men. The services of these
Blacks are only required for a few months during the
year on the plantations, and they are then allowed to
wander off into the Bush, and amuse themselves until
the busy season comes round again. Familiarity having,
of course, bred contempt, and cunning taken the place
of timidity, they no longer scruple to turn the hitherto
sacred runs into their Happy Hunting-grounds. Pic-
nics on the cattle camps, and wild chases amongst if
not after the cattle, form the principal amusements
of these emancipated scholars. The results are appalling. We have all heard of swine urged by devils
running violently down a steep place and being lost
to their owners in the sea. Here in the Antipodes
we observe that our cattle, under similar circumstances, pursue an opposite but equally disastrous
course, and are lost to us in the mountain ranges.

It is annoying to go and muster a camp where a
few days before you had been gloating over thirty or
forty fat bullocks, and to find that the Blacks have
been scouring the whole country around, and fright-
euing the cattle iuto fits; so that instead of thirty fat

bullocks you probably only find half-a-dozen wretched crow-baits, with staring coats, and protruding ribs, and altogether such a played-out appearance, you can hardly believe they are the same animals that a few days before you watched swaggering up to camp, with that satisfied well-to-do air that so endears a fat bullock to the eye of his owner. In the more settled districts along the coast of southern Queensland, and in New South Wales and Victoria, the Blacks have given up spearing cattle, and, beyond frightening them occasionally, do not do much harm. But in the north and interior of Queensland they are still very trouble-some, and never lose a chance of killing cattle and horses, and spearing any unfortunate shepherd or traveller if they get a chance. They will follow a man for days, just keeping out of his sight, until they get an opportunity for killing him. Sometimes, when they feel more than usually cheerful, even the half tame Blacks in the settled districts cannot resist the tempta-tion of spearing a traveller. It is not long since they killed two South Sea Islanders on the range about fifteen miles from our head station. For the purpose of repressing this kind of joviality, there are native police-stations, at tolerably wide intervals, all over the country. At each of these are stationed a few black troopers, under the charge of a white man. These troopers become perfect devils for hunting down and killing the wild tribes from which they have them-selves been taken when young. The duty of the white man who commands them is a very unpleasant one. Whenever the wild Blacks in the neighbourhood become troublesome, and take to spearing cattle, or otherwise

10 *

misbehave themselves, it is his business to sally out with his mounted troopers, and "disperse" them, the meaning of which word is well known all through the colony. If it can be proved that in "dispersing" a mob of Blacks he has killed a single one except in self-defence, he is liable by the laws of the country to be hanged. On the other hand, he knows perfectly well that unless he manages to shoot down a decent number of them before they can escape, his services will soon be dispensed with. The Government will then replace him by a man who is better able to understand the peculiar form of justice which hangs a man for being detected in carrying out his recognised duty. It is very difficult to know what to do with the Blacks. It seems unjust to drive them out of a country to which they have at least as good a right as we have. On the other hand, we know that if they are allowed to remain, they take every opportunity of killing us and our cattle. It is impossible to tame them unless they are caught very young, and even then they are not always to be relied on. Whether the Blacks deserve any mercy at the hands of the pioneering squatters is an open question, but that they get none is certain. They are a doomed race, and before many years they will be completely wiped out of the land.

A gentleman who shall be nameless, but who once resided at a place well known as the Long Lagoon, in the interior of Queensland, is still famous for the tremendous "haul" of Blacks which he made in one day. They had been giving him a great deal of trouble, and had lately killed four of his shepherds in succession. This was past a joke, and he decided that the niggers required something really startling to keep them quiet, and he hit upon the following device, which everyone must admit was sufficiently startling. One day, when he knew that a large mob of Blacks were watching his movements, he packed a large dray with rations, and set off with it from the head station, as if he was going the rounds of the shepherds' huts. When he got opposite to the Long Lagoon, one of the wheels came off the dray, and down it went with a crash. This appeared to annoy him considerably; but after looking pensively at it for some time, he seemed to conclude that there was nothing to be done, so he unhitched the horses and led them back to the station. No sooner had he disappeared than, of course, all the Blacks came up to the dray to see what was in it. To their great delight, it contained a vast supply of flour, beef, and sugar. With appetites sharpened by a prolonged abstinence from such delicacies, they lost no time in carrying the rations down to the waterside, and forthwith devoured them as only a Black-fellow can.

Alas for the greediness of the savage! alas for the cruelty of his white brother! The rations contained about as much strychnine as anything else, and not one of the mob escaped. When they awoke in the morning they were all dead corpses. More than a hundred Blacks were stretched out by this ruse of the owner of the Long Lagoon. In a dry season, when the water sinks low, their skulls are occasionally to be found half buried in the mud.

As a rule, however, few people are ambitious of indulging in such wholesale slaughter, and, when the Blacks are troublesome, it is generally considered suffi-

cient punishment to go out and shoot one or two.
They are easily discouraged in their wild state, especially by anything that they cannot understand. Not
very long after this station was first taken up, while
the wild Blacks were still very bad round about, my
partner Rice was digging one day in the garden. Suddenly he became aware that half-a-dozen of these
"Myalls," as they are called, were creeping towards
him through the long grass. Armed with spears and
boomerangs, they were evidently on anything but hospitable thoughts intent. Rice waited until they got about
fifty yards off, and then, as they stood up ready to sling
their spears at him, he suddenly pointed his spade at
them like a gun. Two warriors fell flat down on the
spot from sheer fright, upsetting a third one who was
just about starting to flee. Two of the remaining three
tried to run away so fast that they hardly made any
progress at all, and the last one, while scattering a
Parthian glance at the object of terror in his rear, ran
with awful violence against a gigantic gum-tree. The
prevailing idea of all six of them seemed to be a wish
for seclusion, and in an incredibly short space of time
they had all picked themselves up and disappeared over
the horizon in a cloud of dust.

Some of the northern Blacks, however, are not so easily
frightened. They are a much finer race than those in
the interior and the south, and will stand up and fight
like anything.

There seems to be an inherent dislike in all Blacks
to anything like regular work. They will hit out like
Trojans for about a week, and then they cave in, and
declare they are sick. A few days' spell, and the diver-

sion of a kangaroo-hunt will sometimes induce them to
try another term of treadmill; but, as a rule, they
never stick long to any heavy work. Sometimes, when
they see any work going on in the Bush, the half-tame
ones come up and offer to help, and are quite content
with half a stick of tobacco and a good feed for a day's
work. Sometimes they content themselves with criti-
cising, without offering to assist.

There was a party (I use the word in its plural sense)
putting up a telegraph-line not far from here. One
day a Black-fellow sauntered up to them with the easy
air of an owner of the soil, the freedom of his movements being unhampered by anything but a red cotton
handkerchief twisted round his head. Securing the loan
of an atom of tobacco from the superintendent, he put
it in his mouth and sat down on a log. Presently he
glanced contemptuously at the telegraph-wire high overhead, and remarked :

" Altogether —— fool mine think it white-feller."

This did not look promising for an extended conversation The superintendent, however, had the
curiosity to ask why ; whereupon the child of Nature
pointed to the telegraph-posts and wires, and said ·

" You think it bullock stop along o' that one paddock ? My word ! you plenty stoopid ! "

And then, without listening to the infuriated official's
explanation that it was not a paddock that he was
putting up at all, the Black-man sauntered off again
into the Bush.

They are incurable nomads, these Blacks, and never
stay long in one place. They wander about the country
in mobs, invariably accompanied by a vast army of the

most wretched-looking mange-stricken dogs. They camp for a while where there is a good supply of food, and when that is done they move on. A couple of hours after they have camped they have completed as good a house as a Black-fellow ever wants, by stripping a few sheets of bark off the nearest trees and propping them up with saplings.

They are passionately fond of tobacco, and the children begin to smoke, when tobacco is plentiful, literally before they can walk. I have often seen a little object, not many months old, slung over its mother's shoulder, puffing away at a short pipe stuck in its mouth.

Away in the far north, round about the Herbert and the Cooktown district, numbers of white men are " put down " by the Blacks every year. A few months ago, the manager of Rocklands, a station on the Herbert water adjoining ours, was killed ; and many a solitary traveller who disappears in the lonely wilds of the Bush of northern Queensland doubtless owes his death to these black devils, who are always lurking in his tracks, waiting for a favourable chance to kill him. The traveller in the north carries his life in his hand. Any day he is liable to be attacked by the Blacks ; and at night when he lies down, he can never be sure that his awakening may not be a spear through his ribs, or a blow on the head from a tomahawk.

It is very seldom that the Blacks will attack a man on horseback. They will sooner follow him for days, until, perhaps, they get a chance at him when he is off his horse, stooping down to drink at a water-hole. Upon one occasion a traveller was riding quickly round the corner of a scrub, when he came suddenly on to a

A BLACK GIN AT HOME.

camp of wild Blacks. His horse propped short, and
sent him flying over its head right into the middle of
them. If he had displayed the slightest signs of alarm
he would most certainly have been instantly killed ;
instead of which he burst into wild shrieks of laughter,
as if he had done it for a joke, which so delighted the
Blacks that they all began to laugh too, and let him go
unmolested, after helping him to catch his horse.

# CHAPTER XI.

## SUGAR.

ALTHOUGH the cultivation of wheat is developing very rapidly, sugar-growing is at present the only agricultural industry of any importance that Queensland possesses. Her climate and soil are no doubt favourable to others, and, in small quantities, tobacco, coffee, and cotton have been grown successfully. But, so far, sugar alone has been cultivated to any great extent, and undoubtedly it is an industry that has a great future before it. It is only of late years that it has commanded much attention, and it is extremely interesting to see the rapid progress that has been made. For a long time sugar-growing languished. As is always the case in a new country, the pioneers were not altogether successful, and the losses which many of the early planters sustained deterred capitalists from investing their money until it was proved whether sugar could be successfully grown or not.

To Mackay belongs the honour of being the parent of all sugar-growing in Queensland. In 1866 Mr. John Spiller first made the experiment of growing cane in this district, and the end of the year saw twelve acres growing, which was increased to 140 acres the following year.

In 1868 the first mill was erected by Mr. John Ewen Davidson, and the output for the first season was 230 tons of sugar. From this date the progress was steady until 1875, when a serious visitation of "rust" took place. This disease for a long time puzzled all the efforts of scientific men and planters either to discover its cause or to arrest its progress, and its effects were so serious that at one time the sugar industry seemed about to entirely collapse. Many of the planters were working on borrowed capital, and the ravages of the rust were so great as to completely ruin some of them. Even now the real origin of the disease remains a mystery. All that is certain is that some varieties of cane are more liable to it than others, and the epidemic has so far been of service that it has enabled the planters to determine what varieties can be most profitably grown, and turned their attention to the economical working of their plantations—a consideration that had been too much effaced by the enormous profits made before the appearance of the disease.

In two years the district had pretty well recovered itself, and in 1879 the crop amounted to 10,000 tons. The following season was a bad one, and the yield fell off to 7,500 tons. In 1881 10,000 tons was again reached, and then a "rush" on sugar commenced among the southern capitalists. The success of sugar-growing was considered to be assured, and, after the manner of a new country, a perfect spasm of speculation set in. Many of the older planters of Mackay took advantage of the sugar mania that prevailed down south, and sold their plantations at high prices.

The profits made about this time were very great.

One of the oldest planters in Mackay in one year cleared £40,000 on his crop, and the next year sold one of his plantations for £95,000 and the other one for £85,000. The run on land anywhere within twenty miles of Mackay was astounding, and every acre, good, bad, and indifferent, was taken up. Land that had been for years considered barely worth paying rent for as a pastoral selection, and that nothing but the most vivid imagination could suppose capable of growing sugar, was readily disposed of to southern speculators at £10 per acre.

In the course of two years (1882, 1883) eleven new mills were erected, with a crushing capacity of 12,000 tons per season, bringing the total of the whole district to more than 30,000 tons. Taking the average price at £25 per ton, the annual output of the district has risen in fifteen years from £3,500 to £350,000, and the total value of the sugar grown during that time is fully two millions sterling. When we consider that this represents merely the probationary period of sugar-growing in the district, we may safely predict that its future is a great one ; and the impetus that the industry has received from the tremendous accession of capital invested during the last few years, makes it certain that the progress that has already been made will be trifling compared to the advance that will take place during the next ten years.

There are now thirty mills at work in the district, and others in course of construction. The white population has more than doubled during the past two years, and now amounts to 7,000

As soon as it was proved that sugar could be grown

successfully in Mackay, the rush for sugar-land extended to every other part of Queensland. To the north of Mackay, on the Burdekin, Johnson, and Herbert rivers, every acre of land was taken up, and a great deal of sugar is now being grown there. At present it seems doubtful whether the climate of any other part of Queensland is as favourable for growing sugar as that of Mackay. On the Burdekin the rainfall is too light; on the Johnson and northern rivers it is too heavy, amounting sometimes to 180 inches a year. In Mackay the average rainfall is 83 inches, which is distributed over a longer period than almost any other district, a circumstance which is extremely favourable to the growth of the young cane.

There is very little doubt that a great deal of money will be dropped in these northern sugar speculations. When the sugar mania set in, people who knew nothing about sugar, except the market price, rushed at it like a bull at a gate, quoting the enormous profits made in the Mackay district, and firmly believing that nothing but land and capital were necessary to grow sugar anywhere on the coast of Queensland. They quite forgot that not even the favourable climate of Mackay saved numbers of people from being ruined in the process of discovering what varieties of cane were best suited to that particular locality. It is probable that in the future the growing of sugar will develop into an enormous industry, and will include many other districts besides Mackay; but it is certain that numbers of people will be ruined in the process of developing it. The prices paid for land during the run on sugar-growing were far too high to allow of any profit, and in many cases, even supposing the climate to turn out favourable, the expense of clearing will be ruinous. By-and-bye the reaction will set in. Most of the pioneers will collapse, and a fresh lot of capitalists will come and buy up their improvements for next to nothing, and make a real good thing out of it.

Sugar has also been grown for some time at Maryborough and Bundaberg, to the south of Mackay; but the frosts to which these districts are liable make it an exceedingly risky speculation. On the whole, Mackay, as it was the first, so it is also the finest, sugar district in Queensland; and is likely always to hold a leading position, whatever may be the progress of the more northern parts. The great rock ahead of sugar-growing in Queensland at present is the difficulty of obtaining coloured labour, and it is astonishing that the planters do not display more enthusiasm on the subject. They are at present waiting with apparent indifference until their masters—the working-men—have made up their minds how to legislate in the matter.

No class in the colony is so entirely at the mercy of legislation as the planters. No class has shown itself more apathetic to its own interests until it is too late to protect them. The planters are a small community; but the absolute identity of their interests, and the fact that numbers of them live close together, makes it very easy for them to co-operate. Their trade is one involving an enormous outlay of capital, and a heavy current expenditure, so that any interruption in the work on the plantations is a matter which entails very serious loss. They are absolutely dependent for their existence upon being able to obtain a sufficient supply of coloured labour to do their work in the cane. It has been conclusively proved, in the first place, that white men cannot and will not do the work done by niggers in the field ; and, in the second place, that if white labour were available, it would only be at wages which the planter could never afford to pay. The sugar industry, therefore, is entirely dependent upon coloured labour.

Now in this matter the planter knows perfectly well that every man's hand is against him, and yet he takes no pains to protect himself. The conditions under which the existing labour traffic with the South Sea Islands is conducted, leave much to be desired. Though the frightful accounts which are constantly circulated by sensation-mongers and alarmists as to the cruelty practised towards the Islanders are very much exaggerated, still there is just enough truth in them to make it extremely dangerous for the planter that things should be allowed to continue as they are. The labour trade should not be in the hands of the planters and speculating captains of schooners. It should be conducted by the Government at the expense of the employers. I am taking the planter's view, of course. As far as the kanakas themselves are concerned, the fact of the Government of Queensland superintending the trade by no means implies that all abuses connected with it would cease, but rather the reverse. But it would take away one great weapon of attack from the working-man, which is the accusation of cruelty and slave-driving that is now so constantly urged against the planters.

The legislation of Queensland is entirely in the hands

of the working-men; and it is only in a new colony, where a six-months' residence suffrage gives full scope to ignorance and prejudice, that we can realise the suicidal mistakes which they are occasionally capable of making. A more extraordinary instance of inability on the part of working-men to understand their own interests than is afforded by the agitation against coloured labour in Queensland, cannot be imagined.

We will take the case of Mackay. Before sugar-growing was started there were not a hundred residents in the whole district, and there were never likely to be any more as long as it was merely used for pastoral purposes. It is now one of the most thriving and rapidly-increasing places in Queensland, with a population, as has been above stated, of 7,000 whites and 3,500 kanakas. Last year's sugar crop was worth over £300,000, and next year's will be very much larger. The amount of money annually expended in wages in the district is startling. The monthly pay-sheet of one of the plantations alone is £5,000. There is a very fair foundry in the town, and the demand for timber is so great as positively to have run the southern markets dry at times. Houses are being run up as fast as material can be procured, and are let before the piles to carry them are in the ground.

The whole of this progress is entirely due to the development of the sugar industry, which is, as has been said, dependent upon coloured labour. If this were withdrawn, the Mackay district would shut up like a match-box. And yet, so obstinate are the prejudices of the working-classes in the colony, that the very men in the district themselves, carpenters, sawyers, plough-

men, engineers, and all who get their living entirely
from the plantations, are foremost in the insane outcry
that has been raised against coloured labour.    The
planters are represented as slave-drivers, and as taking
the bread out of the mouths of white men to put it into
the mouths of niggers.   The fact is that the niggers do
work in the plantations that no white man could or
would do in such a climate, and by doing it they develop
an industry that supplies thousands of white workmen
with a means of living in clover.

In return the working-men of Queensland are doing
all they can to bring in a Bill for prohibiting the introduction of Black labour, which, if passed, would for
a time paralyse the growing of sugar throughout the
colony.   That so important an industry as the sugar-
growing of Queensland has now become could be permanently destroyed by any such false legislation, I do
not for a moment believe.

The result of any attempt on the part of the Brisbane
Government to stop Black labour would inevitably be
to make the north of Queensland, where the sugar is
grown, insist upon separation from the south.   But
in the meantime, before this could be done, the trade
would sustain a very serious shock, and the loss to the
planters would be enormous.   To many of them, who
work upon borrowed capital, it would mean utter ruin.
Seeing that the planters are perfectly well aware of
the feeling of the working-classes in the colony against
coloured labour, it is really surprising that they do not
take more pains to prevent its finding expression in
legislation.   Were the planters to form a sort of trades
union, and shut up their mills for a couple of months,

the white men would get a practical lesson that would
enable them to determine the exact source from which
their livelihood is derived, with an accuracy they never
would forget.

Up to the present time, the coloured labour market
of Queensland has been supplied by kanakas, as the
inhabitants of the South Sea Islands are called. The
word "kanaka" is really a Maori word, signifying a
man, but in Australia it has come to be applied exclusively to the inhabitants of the South Sea Islands. The
trade is carried on by means of schooners which run
between Queensland and the Islands. These vessels
are usually the joint property of one or two planters
and the captain, who share the risks and the profits of
the venture between them. At first there was not much
difficulty in inducing the kanakas to come to Queensland
and enter into an engagement for a term of years'
work there. But as the demand increased, greater
difficulty was experienced in obtaining a sufficient
supply ; and there is no doubt that in many cases the
captains of these vessels resorted to unlawful means
to induce the kanakas to leave their homes. Kidnap-
ping became frequent, and as a matter of course this
aroused the resentment of the natives, who in one or
two instances have retaliated by massacring the crews
of the schooners that visited their islands. The kanakas themselves, when well treated, are a cheerful, hard-
working, and rather intelligent race.

The inhabitants of some of the islands are very
much superior to those of the others, but all of them
are admirably qualified for the work that is required
of them in the cane-fields of Queensland. Their agree-

ment with the planters is for a term of three years, during which time they are fed, housed, and supplied with blankets, and receive £6 a year wages. At the expiration of their agreement the planter is bound to ship them back to their own country at his own expense, if it be their wish to return. But they can, if they like, remain in Queensland and enter into other engagements for such wages as may be agreed upon. Many 'of them remain as indoor servants, in which capacity they are very useful, and some of them make excellent cooks.

There is not the slightest doubt that as a general rule they are well treated on the plantations, and perfectly contented and happy. There are, of course, instances where they have been treated with injustice and cruelty, but they are the exception and not the rule; and a convincing proof of this is to be found in the fact that many kanakas elect to remain in the country of their own free will, and many others return a second time after having paid a visit to their native country. They are strong, sturdy men, as a rule, capable of doing a good day's work, but their constitutions seem to be perfectly incapable of standing against any sort of illness. Directly a kanaka gets ill he lies down, and apparently very often dies for no reason at all except pure funk and lack of the wish to get well. They are especially liable to consumption; and when an epidemic of measles breaks out, as it sometimes does, amongst them, its ravages are appalling. When they feel the fever upon them, nothing can keep them from going and plunging themselves into the water, and they die off like rotten sheep.

11 *

Not a shilling of their wages do they ever carry back to their own country, either in money or in money's value. The whole of their wages passes into the hands of the store-keepers of the nearest town, whose right to plunder them there is none to dispute. It is illegal to supply liquor to kanakas, so the store-keeper has no rival to fear in spoiling them of their hard-earned gains. The store-keepers of Mackay have earned an unenviable notoriety by the alacrity with which they have turned the ignorance of the unsuspecting savage to account. They import a special class of fancy goods, of the most utterly worthless description, and realise fabulous profits by selling them to the kanakas for about four hundred times what they are worth. There is no one to interfere with them, and it is difficult to see how it could be done, for, of course, at the end of his agreement the kanaka is entirely his own master, and if he likes to pay an exorbitant price for a worthless article, there is no way of preventing him.

Indirectly the planters could do a great deal if they chose, by intimating that their custom would be withdrawn from any store-keeper who continued the practice of fleecing kanakas. The store-keepers are entirely supported by the planters, and they would have to give in. Undoubtedly the temptation is a very great one. A cheerful and perfectly ignorant savage, who has just been long enough in the land to know that money will procure certain articles, but without the slightest idea of their relative value, exhilarated by the prospect of an immediate return to his native country, and with £18 in his possession, is a bait which, perhaps, it is too much to expect any tradesman to resist.

Certainly in Queensland they improve the occasion. Knives and tomahawks made of that peculiarly vile iron which combines the brittleness of glass with the softness of lead, muskets and pistols of a class unknown to modern warfare, handkerchiefs, hats, tobacco-pipes, and fancy rubbish of every description, fit only to hang upon a Christmas-tree, are palmed off upon these unfortunate savages for enormous prices. Many a time have I seen one of them returning from investing his wages in Mackay, with nothing on but a tomahawk and a tall hat, and perhaps a miniature lady's travelling bag on his arm, the delighted grin upon his countenance expressing perfect satisfaction and conscious pride in his recent purchases.

Of course the store-keepers justify their conduct by saying that as long as the kanaka is satisfied they fail to see what injury he sustains. That is all very well ; but to my mind there is something intensely melancholy in the spectacle of an industrious savage returning to his native country, after three years' toil in a foreign land, with nothing to show for it but a musket that would kill him if he tried to fire it off, and a cotton handkerchief that would fly to pieces if he blew his nose in it.

Intercourse with civilisation is producing its usual results among uneducated savages, and the kanakas in Mackay are beginning to get troublesome. The other day, at the Mackay races, a big mob of them attacked the whites, and a general scrimmage ensued. Had the kanakas only been armed with such weapons as the Mackay tradesman, might have supplied them with, they would have been quite harmless. But they had provided themselves with a supply of glass bottles, which they slung with infinite precision at the whites.

A glass bottle is by no means a contemptible weapon in the hands of athletic savages, trained to throw clubs and stones ever since they could walk. A lot of the white men climbed on to their horses and charged the kanakas, armed with their stirrup-irons, with which they knocked them over like nine-pins. The fight did not last long; but there were a good many broken heads even amongst the white men, and several of the kanakas were killed before they were finally driven off the race-course into the cane-fields. This is the only instance I ever knew of kanakas joining together to show fight away from their own country; but now that they have begun, no doubt this will not be the last disturbance of the kind.

The evening after the fight on the race-course a scare was got up that the kanakas were going to storm the town of Mackay. No one knows who started the report, and nobody cared; but it was quite sufficient to terrify the inhabitants. The peaceful town of Mackay presented a most ludicrous appearance; everyone having armed himself with some sort of weapon, a musket, a pistol, or a butcher's knife, with which he paraded the streets, giving all the corners a wide berth as he turned them, for fear of falling a prey to some bloodthirsty kanaka. The Mackay Volunteers, never having had an opportunity before of displaying their valour, except by shooting at each other with blank cartridge, showed the greatest enthusiasm and firmness upon this trying occasion.

Just after dark the most piercing shrieks from a woman's voice were heard, coming from the opposite

side of the river from the town. No one lived over
there except an old man and his wife, who kept a market
garden; and the idea at once seized the citizens of
Mackay that the man was away from home, and the
kanakas were murdering his wife. A wild rush was
made for the ferry, and four or five men, armed to the
teeth, jumped into a boat and pulled like mad for the
opposite bank. A volunteer who was with them assumed
the brevet rank of captain for the occasion, and directed
the movements of the attacking force. As they got
near the other bank the shrieks for help became perfectly
heart-rending; and the captain, wild with excitement,
exhorted his men to redouble their exertions.

"Pull, boys; pull like mad," he exclaimed, "or, by
Jove! we'll be too late. These treacherous devils of
niggers must have swum across here. Look out for
their heads in the water, or we'll be having some of
them in the boat. They swim like fish, and it's so
dark you can't see ten yards."

The instant the boat touched the shore they all sprang
out, and rushed up the track to the house. The cries
by this time had ceased, and it was feared that all was
over. When they got there a sad sight presented itself.
The hut was quite quiet, and the lights all out; but just
then the moon appeared from behind a cloud, and
revealed the figure of an old woman, with nothing on
but a night-gown, sitting on a log in front of the hut,
crying and sobbing in the most pitiable manner. In
answer to a hurried inquiry as to what was the matter,
and where the niggers were, she replied that "she
hadn't seen any niggers about the place, and the matter
was that her old devil of a husband had come home very

drunk, and given her the almightiest hammering she ever had in her life."

"Well, boys," said the captain, "this is the infernalest, meanest swindle I ever was amongst in my life. Never mind, we'll go back and have a drink. And I say, Missus, hadn't you better turn in again? That's rather an unhealthy get-up for a winter's night."

But the woman absolutely refused to go near her husband again that night, and was rowed across to the town by the disappointed warriors and taken to some of her friends. The whole town was assembled to see them return, and yells of laughter arose when it was discovered that the weird, white figure in the stern-sheets was nothing but the ill-used wife of one of the oldest inhabitants of Mackay, and that never a nigger had been seen. A vast procession escorted the poor old woman to her friends' house; after which all hands adjourned for a drink, and the scare of the kanaka invasion subsided.

In the meantime the present supply of labour from the South Sea Islands is rapidly becoming quite inadequate to meet the increasing demand. Not only has the cost of obtaining kanakas greatly increased, but much difficulty is experienced in inducing them to come to the country. In view of this state of affairs, the attention of the planters was naturally directed to India as a source of labour supply. Both from her enormous population and from her geographical position, this country seems to be most fitted to supply the requirements of Queensland in this respect. It is known that in India there are millions of coolies exactly suited for the class of employment that Queensland can supply, and to transfer some of them from the one country to the other would be to confer a benefit upon both. It would help, if ever so little, to relieve the great difficulty which is experienced in India in finding work for the enormous working population, and at the same time it would supply what is rapidly becoming a pressing want in Queensland.

The proposal to introduce coolies into the colony was met with a universal howl of rage. For electioneering purposes it was invaluable, and dismal pictures of the future of Queensland overrun by niggers, and her white population starving, formed the *pièce de résistance* in every idiot candidate's address.

About this time a change of Ministry took place. Sir Thomas McIlwraith retired after the collapse of the Transcontinental Railway Bill, and Mr. Griffith formed a new Ministry. Had Mr. Griffith and his party remained content with having defeated the iniquitous project of their predecessors, they would have been entitled to the undying gratitude of the colony. But they advanced under the anti-coolie flag, and must therefore be regarded either as enemies to the progress of Queensland or as strangers to common-sense. An attempt was made to pass regulations for the purpose of restricting coolies solely to the work of sugar-growing; but the present Ministry have refused to legislate on the subject at all, and its leader declares that he is incapable of devising any regulations that would be respected in this connection.

The very serious position in which the planters now find themselves, has induced them to try several experiments for the purpose of obtaining such low-class labour as they require to carry on their operations. So far, these experiments have all resulted in something worse than failure. A shipment of Cingalese was brought down. Anything less like agricultural labourers never was seen. They were arrayed in fine linen, with tortoise-shell combs stuck in their hair, and looked as if they had never done a harder day's work than stealing their own dinner, in their lives. Some of them were very well educated, and spoke three or four languages ; but evidently they had all been induced to come under false pretences, and had no notion of the sort of work that they were expected to perform. The majority of them absconded from service, taking with them as much of their employers' property as they could conveniently remove, as a souvenir of their visit to Mackay. A few Malays have been introduced, and a shipment of Maltese were tried, but with very discouraging results.

The remedy for which the working-man clamoured was then tried in an increased supply of white immigrants. The result followed which everyone who knew anything at all about the matter predicted. There was an immediate fall in wages, and it was discovered that the white men were entirely unable to compete with kanakas in the low-class labour on the plantations, and consequently took the first opportunity that occurred to break their engagements.

In the face of all this, it is still maintained by the working-classes in the Colony that the industry can be carried on by white men alone, and the problem seems as far off solution as ever. The capitalists who are engaged in the industry demand a large supply of coloured labour, and are perfectly willing that such labour should be so restricted as to make it impossible that it should ever come into competition with white men, and should be entirely confined to a class of labour that, from climatic reasons, white men have shown themselves quite unable to perform.

On the other hand, we have the insane outcry raised by the working-classes against every sort of coloured labour, backed up by the admission of the present Premier of his inability to frame any laws that would restrict the employment of coolies to sugar-growing. Unless some satisfactory solution of the difficulty can be found, there is undoubtedly a very bad time in store for the planters. But the importance of the sugar industry to Queensland is so manifest, and the amount of capital already invested in it so great, there is no doubt that eventually common-sense will triumph even over the prejudices of the working-classes in the colony, and coolie labour will be introduced. If this were done, the future success of sugar-growing would be assured, and there is no doubt that it is an industry which is capable of contributing largely towards placing Queensland in the position of the leading agricultural colony of Australia.

# CHAPTER XII.

## GOLD-MINING.

ONE day I heard that gold had been found in a creek on the western fall of the coast range, about forty miles from here, and that a "rush" had already set in, so I determined to go up and see what was going on. I was delayed for a few days by the flooded state of the creeks between here and the diggings. While I was waiting I was joined by Dick Absolon, formerly in our employ as stockman, and now on his way to the new rush.

Dick Absolon is the *beau idéal* of a colonist. Brave as a lion, which animal he somewhat resembles in appearance, gentle as a child, with a capacity for hard work that nothing can satisfy, and a cheerfulness that no run of bad luck can discourage, whatever he starts at he is a bad man to beat. His brother Jack, in every way as good a bit of stuff as himself, was already on the diggings waiting for him. They both came to the colony very young, and, through many ups and downs, have stuck together ever since. To use an Americanism, they have been pulled through all sorts of knot-holes; stock-riding, carrying on the road, contract-fencing, gold-mining, copper-mining, managing stations, they have worked hard at all of them, and finally, having made a rise, they went into sugar-growing in the Mackay district at a bad time, and lost all they had made.

Altogether they are sad examples of the fact that it is possible, even in Australia, for a shrewd sensible man to work hard and keep sober, and still to be pursued by a run of bad luck, that leaves him no richer in pocket than when he began, and poorer by the loss of the best years of his life. " Hope springs eternal," however, and here they are, ready to try again with undefeated ardour and cheerfulness, confident that this time at last fortune's wheel will give them a turn.

The weather, being the middle of our wet season, had been, as they say in the west of Scotland, " showery and rain atween whiles "; but the morning after his arrival Absolon went down to the first creek, half a mile from the station, to see if it was crossable, while I ran up the horses ready for a start. He came back and said he thought we could just do it without a swim, so we settled to go.

My swag was soon ready, consisting of a pick and shovel, a tin prospecting dish for washing gold, 20 lbs. flour, 12 lbs. beef, some tea and sugar, a couple of changes of clothes, and a blanket, unlimited tobacco and matches, a revolver, a quart pot, a calico fly of a small tent, a Shakespear, a pack of cards, a piece of soap, two towels, and a tooth-brush. Having planted these scientifically on the back of a pack-horse, we climbed on to our own horses, and, lighting the inevitable pipe, sallied down to the first creek.

It was coming down very strong, muddy and thick,

but from the marks on the banks we thought it was good enough, and, sousing in, we just managed to sneak across without absolutely swimming, a performance to be carefully avoided in Queensland creeks. The banks are always very steep and high, and the bed of the creek heavily timbered, and full of snags and fallen trees. The current is usually very strong, and the crossing-place, where the trees in the bed and on the banks of the creek have been cleared away, very narrow ; so that if you happen to be swept down below the opposite crossing, the chance of ever getting out again is very small. Your horse is certain to be drowned, and the strongest swimmer when swept by a furious current into a forest of big trees and saplings, and tangled masses of creepers along the banks, has no more chance than a fly in a cobweb. Numbers of travellers are drowned every year in this way.

Having crossed this creek we had the satisfaction of seeing it get up rapidly behind us, effectually barring our return. The next creek was seven miles ahead, and if that happened to be up too, we should have the pleasure of finding ourselves between two flooded creeks, with the cheerful prospect of sitting on the bank of one of them until it subsided. Of course, as a rule, we should not have thought anything of having to swim, but when you have got all your belongings with you on a pack-horse, and are on your way to a place where you cannot replace them, you are rather shy of risking a swim.

Some horses swim most beautifully, and will carry their rider in the saddle across almost any creek or river. Others lose all heart, and go down like a stone or roll over on their backs. The best way is, just as your horse gets into deep water and begins swimming, to slide quietly off, hang on to his tail, and let him tow you across in his wake. This time we were fortunate, and we managed to cross the eight creeks between us and the open country without any delay, and without wetting the pack.

We camped the first night at an old bark hut, the remains of a deserted station, about fourteen miles from the diggings.

Next morning we made a fresh start. Neither of us knew exactly where the diggings lay, beyond a vague idea that they were in the western fall of the main range, somewhere to the north of us; but after jogging along for a few miles we came across a new mark-tree line, made by the first prospectors of the diggings, which took us right away into them. As we got near the place, we began to overtake a few straggling swagsmen, pounding along through the black soil as if the devil was behind them instead of in front of them.

To the initiated it did not require the pick and shovel slung on their backs to tell where they were bound for. The pace at which they were going, so different from the languid dawdle habitual to men who are merely wandering about in search of work, betrayed at once that the "gold fever" was upon them. Once smitten by this malady, a man seldom or never thoroughly recovers, and the exertions he will make while under its influence are perfectly incredible.

All the evils that humanity naturally shrinks from at once assume a cheerful aspect. When the Palmer rush broke out on the Gulf of Carpentaria, it is a

positive fact that a man walked the whole way from
Melbourne to get to it, a distance of nearly two thousand miles.

While I was on Mount Britten diggings, a man came
in, wheeling his Lares and Penates before him in a
wheel-barrow. The whole certainly weighed over one
hundred and fifty pounds, and he had wheeled it through
two hundred miles of heavy black-soil country, in pouring rain, in just a fortnight's time.

The true professional digger passes his life in wandering about from one new rush to another. Any regular
employment he considers beneath him; and except for
the purpose of raising sufficient money to carry him on
to the next diggings, he will never work for wages.
No class of men work so hard; as soon as it is light
in the morning, he is off, and seldom knocks off
before dark. That a man should work so hard to get
gold is not in the least odd, but it is odd that the
value he sets on it should be in exactly inverse proportion to the trouble it costs him to get it. And
yet such is the case. As long as he is at work, no
miser could be more careful than a real digger in the
actual process of collecting gold. When he has got it,
no spendthrift could be more reckless in flinging it away.
Whether up to his knees in the freezing waters of the
Snowy river, or grilling under the fires of a Queensland
sun, no day is too long for him while he is on gold.
Not a crevice of his claim is unexplored, not a particle
of dirt likely to contain gold is wasted; and he will
spend as much time and trouble in collecting the finest
particles of gold in his dish, as if he were an analytical chemist making an experiment in weights and

measures. He toils patiently on, day after day, week after week, undismayed by failure, and quite unelated by success, until the moment comes when something impels him irrresistibly to squander all that he has collected.

The instant this happens, he knocks off work, and his fetische at once assumes a different aspect. Not only does the gold he has taken such pains to get become worthless, but apparently it becomes an incumbrance that some hidden law of his being obliges him to get rid of without delay. The only variation in the method of this madness, is in the time allotted respectively to collecting and to spending. This varies with the individual. Some men will never work more than a week at a time before spending all they have made; others will go on for several weeks, even for months, before going on the spree, but invariably with the same purpose, which seems to be simply that of collecting sufficient to make fools of themselves. At least ninety per cent. of their earnings goes in drink, of course; and the rest in good living when it is to be had. Whilst working, a digger generally keeps sober, but he lives on the best of food he can get. His drinking is reserved for when he knocks off work. As a rule, if he is getting gold, from Monday to Friday is about as long as a digger can stand without a spree; he then flings down his tools, leaves his claim, though he knows perfectly well that by so doing he is liable to have it taken from him by the first comer, and retires to the nearest public-house, to spend what plunder he has amassed in getting hopelessly drunk till Monday morning. He then creeps back, dejected in appearance, and shaking in every limb from the effects of the poisonous liquor he has swallowed, probably to find that some less fortunate individual, who had not raised sufficient for a spree by Friday, and so had to go on working, has "jumped" his claim. A row ensues, which is referred for immediate settlement to the arbitration of a couple of shovels, or whatever weapons are handiest, and subsequently to the decision of the Warden of the gold-field.

The idea of saving any money, and settling down anywhere to live comfortably, never enters a digger's head. He goes on at the same old game, sometimes for twenty or thirty years, exactly as eager to get to a new field and peg out the best claim, as the first day he started, until drink, exposure, and disease put an end to his wanderings. It is only the new chum who occasionally has sense enough to let well alone, and clear out on his first rise. I remember a man who had only been a few months in the colony, who used to dig in our garden at the station. He went up to the diggings, with no more notion of a digger's craft than of astronomy. He had not been above a week or two at it when he stumbled across a nugget of pure gold weighing seventy ounces. The very same day he set off down to the coast, climbed on to the first boat that started, and went back to the old country. I never saw anyone in such a hurry to get anywhere. But he was a very rare instance of an uneducated man who did not get more harm than good by finding gold. Although gold-digging is a profession requiring the exercise of some of the best qualities of human nature—enterprise, perseverance, a disregard of hardships, accompanied by unceasing toil—still there is something about the acquisition of the raw material direct from the ground that has anything but an elevating effect upon the lives of those who make it their business. This is probably accounted for by the enormous element of pure chance that enters into it. When employed in any other profession, a man knows that, with fair abilities and advantages, hard work is likely to be followed by the acquisition of money in direct proportion to the amount of energy and perseverance displayed. Profit follows labour to a greater or less extent, as regularly as day follows night in summer or winter.

But it is quite otherwise with the profession of mining, which is, in fact, the rankest gambling. Not only does a digger know that it is quite possible he may find a great deal of gold with very little trouble, but, worse still, he knows he may work very hard without getting any gold at all. He may toil for ten hours a day, and not " raise the colour," while his neighbour in the next claim, with half the exertion, is getting an ounce of gold to the dish. He therefore very justly ceases to connect the idea of profit and labour in any way, and comes to regard his profession as one of pure chance. Both wealth and labour lose their true value in his estimation, the one from its being occasionally unmerited, the other from its being frequently unrewarded.

The history of a new colony teems with examples in every profession and occupation of money quickly made and lightly lost; of men, on the one hand, who have squandered vast fortunes in the attempt to increase them, and, on the other hand, of men who have started with nothing at all, and by their own exertions and perseverance amassed colossal wealth.

The subsequent career of many of the latter has shown

12 *

them to be capable of employing their riches to the
credit of themselves and for the benefit of mankind.  It
is reserved for the profession of mining to deal destruction to its followers with the two-edged sword of profit
and loss ; and it would seem that the only worse thing
that can happen to a man than losing money at it, is
that he should make any.

Numerous as are the instances of enormous fortunes
made in mining, I doubt if the history of the Australian
Colonies affords a score of examples where money so
made has not done more harm than good.  As a rule
its possessor becomes bitten with an incurable mania for
wild speculation, if for nothing worse ; and whether he
makes a few ounces out of a pot-hole in a creek and
spends it at the nearest shanty, or makes a rise of
£100,000 out of a good reef and fools it away trying
to get more, it seems to be an inevitable law that
money made by mining should be provided with something worse than wings.

Innumerable are the cases where it has brought utter
ruin ; a whole legion of the lost rises before me when
I think of it.

I remember four men on Gympie, who in a short time
took £25,000 a-piece out of a claim.  Previous to their
striking gold they had been sober, industrious men; but
in two years three out of the four, and one of their
wives, were dead from drink, and the fourth had lost
all he was worth in prospecting other claims.

Another sad case I remember, of a man on Charters
Towers.  He was a blacksmith by trade, but he dabbled
a little in mining, and by degrees got so much in debt
to the bank that they would not allow him to leave the

field and go to the Palmer, a new rush which broke out a few hundred miles away. He stuck to his claim, and one day struck gold. In a short time he was in receipt of £500 a day, and continued at that for a very long while. I do not think anyone, not even himself, ever knew exactly how much he was worth. If he had simply sat down, and stuck to his money as fast as it came in, he would have been one of the richest men in the colony. But he never did any good. He taught himself to read and write ; took to wild speculation in other mines, in race-horses, in wheat, in everything; drank like a fish ; and finally completed his downward career by becoming a member of the Legislative Assembly in Brisbane, and his bankruptcy appeared a short time ago in the London *Times*.

Besides the fatality that apparently attends all profits made from mining, the statistics show that it is the least profitable of all professions. The average value of an ounce of gold is £3 10s., but every ounce of gold raised costs nearly £5 to get. In Victoria, where mining is more economically and profitably worked than in any of the other colonies, the average earnings of every man connected with it in 1873 was only £98 per head, considerably less than he could have made at the lowest wages' work in the colony. When we consider that every year some few individuals make enormous fortunes at it, the balance of loss to be distributed amongst the remainder is considerable.

Still, it is an industry most necessary to the world at large, and especially conducive to the prosperity of a young colony, and it is well that there are men found willing to carry it on. The *auri sacra fames* is a very pretty subject for a moral essayist to decry, but it would be extremely awkward if that particular form of it which impels men to seek gold in the earth were eliminated from a community. It is to that same hunger that no surfeit can satisfy, and no defeat blunt the edge of, that we owe the constant supply of victims, eager to embark in an industry which all must allow is a very necessary one, but which is clearly proved to be anything but profitable to those actually employed in it. Besides the race of veteran diggers, a new rush, of course, always attracts a heterogeneous crowd of outsiders, many of whom have never handled a pick and shovel in their lives, and whose pale faces and dissipated appearance proclaim them town-loafers, and strangers to the bush and hard work.

When I first arrived on Mount Britten gold-field there were seventy men on it, all living in tents. The only building that had any appearance of permanence about it was a butcher's shop and store, made out of a few sheets of bark and saplings. Flour had run out, the drays having all stuck in the mud half way from port to the diggings; but there were tea, sugar, and tobacco, and a few tools to be had, and any amount of beef, supplied by fat cattle from the neighbouring run, two or three of which were run in every week into a sapling yard near the butcher's shop, and killed. For some time beef was all we had to eat; but it was very good, and there was plenty of it, so we were glad enough to get it.

The diggings are very prettily situated in the centre of a horse-shoe formed by a spur running out from the main range on to the plains. A heavily-timbered creek running up the centre of the valley was where the gold was found first. Vast ranges of mountains rise up all round, the slopes of which are covered with forests of gigantic trees, and patches of dense scrub. The summit of the range is formed by a crown of cliffs, which rise sheer from the slopes below to a height varying from 400 to 1,000 feet, the red and yellow tints of their rocks contrasting beautifully with the sombre mass of dark-green woods below them.

Three very startling peaks, known as the Marling-spikes, guard the entrance to the valley; bare sugar-loaves of weather-beaten grey rock, quite detached from the main range, which rise right out of the surrounding country to a height of 1,700 feet, and form a glorious landmark over miles and miles of the adjacent plains.

The first time I saw the valley of Mount Britten was about sundown, and I never remember a more beautiful sight. To the dwellers in the valley the sun sets early behind the false range that lies between them and the west. But just at the head of the valley there is a narrow dip in the range, and through this the sunlight streams long after the sun himself has disappeared. As I surveyed the scene, seated on a rock at a considerable elevation above the valley, the effect was most startling.

Below my feet was stretched out a vast forest of every conceivable shade of green, from black to emerald; here and there the stem of some gigantic tree showing white and ghostly against the surrounding mass of foliage.

Along through the forest the creek wound its way, its course distinctly marked by the darker green of the trees that fringed its banks. A soft blue mist, the smoke of many a camp-fire, was rising and creeping gently up the valley, lingering just above the tops of the trees, as if unwilling to leave their shelter.   In the centre of the valley rose a stupendous mass of rock, the rugged off-spring of some awful convulsion of nature, towering like a ruined castle over the woods below, shadowy, vast, and indistinct in the deepening shades of evening.

Away to the head of the valley, through the gap in the range, there swept across the forest a flood of amber light, the dying glory of a setting sun, turning rocks and trees, where it touched them, into figures of molten gold, and lighting up the face of the opposite cliffs with a ruddy glow, made all the more startling by the gloom of the valley beneath.   To the east, above the cliffs, the soft azure of an autumn sky was hardening into the pure steel-blue of a night such as only Queensland knows.

Not a cloud marred the purity of the expanse above, not a sound broke the stillness of the valley below. One by one the stars blazed out in the deepening blue of their eternal home, the green shades of the valley sank to rest in the obscurity of advancing night, and still the amethyst light lingered on the face of the cliffs above. The effect was so weird I was spell-bound as I watched it, and began to experience an uncomfortable feeling of unreality, which was fortunately dispelled by a *deus ex machina*, in the shape of a green-head ant, which just then bit the back of my neck.   The bite of this insect is well calculated to dispel any momentary illusions as to the reality of existence.   For some minutes the pain is excruciating, and by the time I had recovered my temper the last rays of sunlight had departed, leaving me to stumble down the steep side of a mountain covered with long grass and rocks the best way I could.

Most of the men who were on the ground when I arrived were getting fair gold, though nothing heavy had as yet been discovered. Alluvial digging in Queensland is never worth very much ; in fact, with the exception of the Palmer, on the Gulf of Carpentaria, nothing worth calling an alluvial diggings has as yet been discovered. In Victoria the alluvial diggings are of enormous extent and great richness. They are worked on a scale requiring a large capital, and go on for years and years yielding tremendous profits.

The underground workings of many of them are on a gigantic scale. But in Queensland the run of gold is very irregular, and never of any great extent.

Seldom at any depth, it is generally confined to " potholing " and " crevicing " in the banks and bed of the creeks. This was the case at Mount Britten. The alluvial digging never extended above a few yards from the banks of the creek, and all the heavy gold was found in the bed of the creek itself, and cost little or no trouble to get, beyond the bare labour of shifting and washing the soil. No sinking or timbering was required, and what gold was got paid those well who got it.

Taking into account the comparative worthlessness of alluvial in Queensland, and the richness of many of the reefs, Jack Absolon had not thought it worth while to peg out a claim in the creek, but was spending his time prospecting the ranges at the head of it, in search of a reef.

From the appearance of the gold found in the creek, which was very little water-worn, and mostly in the form known as " specimen," that is, quartz and gold mixed, and from the formation of the surrounding country, it seemed certain it must have come from a reef somewhere in the ranges to the head of the creek. As yet nothing in the shape of a reef carrying payable gold had been found ; but a prospector, Charley Gibbard by name, had got on to a leader carrying nice gold, at the head of the valley.

Jack Absolon and I had a consultation, and it was determined that he and I, and his brother Dick, should go on looking for a reef, without troubling about the alluvial. Henceforth we were what is known on a diggings as " dividing mates." No written agreement is necessary. The fact of two or more men working together on a diggings constitutes a partnership in colonial law, which enables either party to claim his share of anything found by the others, and which can only be dissolved by the parties forming it declaring before witnesses that they are no longer mates.

The process of searching for a golden reef is often one requiring unlimited patience, and a great deal of hard work. The first thing to do is to apply to the Warden of the gold-field you are on for a Protection Area. You can get one four hundred yards square for a month. In this piece of ground the prospector has the exclusive right of hunting for a reef. No one else can come on to it, provided he works eight hours a day on it. Having secured his ground, the prospector sets to work to see if he can find gold on the surface, by washing prospects of surface dirt in a tin dish. Often he has to carry the dirt a long distance to water, and to wash hundreds of dishes before he gets a colour of gold.

Once let him get on a trail of gold, however, if he

GOLD DIGGING: CRADLING AND PANNING-OFF.

knows his trade he will never lose it. He will follow it up with the instinct and patience of a hound, and it is a hundred to one, unless the country is very broken, he will find the reef it came from.

Having followed the gold as far as he can trace it on the surface, he then knows the reef is not below him, and begins to look for it above. The usual course of true reefs is nearly due north and south; sometimes they crop out of the surface of the ground, with what is called a big " blow " of quartz.

Generally, however, the cap of the reef is a little distance below the surface, and it is necessary to dig for it, which is done by cutting narrow trenches, a foot or two deep, east and west, so as to cut across the course of the reef you are looking for.

Sometimes the reef or leader is merely a thread of pipe-clay, or rotten quartz, no thicker than a sheet of paper, but there is no mistaking the formation when once you know it.

Having hit on the reef, if it is what is known as " mullocky "—that is, soft and rotten—the next thing is to take out a prospect from between the walls, and wash it to see if it carries gold. If the reef is well defined, and the quartz hard, it requires to be crushed in an iron mortar before the prospect is washed.

Day after day the Absolons and I used to scour the ranges, opening up and prospecting numerous reefs and leaders, without coming upon anything that looked at all payable. Meanwhile, every hour brought news of richer alluvial finds in the creek below.

A real rush had now set in. Men poured in by hundreds, and the whole creek was pegged out in claims from the lowest point where gold had been found right up to the head in the ranges where we were working. In two months from the time I came there were nearly two thousand men on the field. Hundreds came from the adjacent colonies, and many even from New Zealand, attracted by the fabulous reports that never fail to be circulated about a new rush, and never fail to be believed.

These mad stampedes to a new rush are occasionally attended with very serious consequences. Thousands flock from all sides, each anxious to get first on to the field, without the slightest idea of how he is going to support life when he gets there, and usually entirely destitute of means to carry him away from it should the new field prove a failure.

Rockhampton, the second largest town in Queensland owes its existence to a " duffer rush." Gold was discovered at a place called Canoona, thirty miles higher up the Fitzroy river. In a short time there were about fifty thousand men deposited by steamers on the bare banks of the Fitzroy, with no means of procuring food, or of getting away again.

The Government was obliged to supply them with means of getting away ; but before this was done, many of them were reduced to absolute starvation. The township of Rockhampton was formed to supply the diggings.

The rush to Mount Britten was stopped before it assumed a serious phase, but at no time was the field capable of supporting more than two hundred men on payable gold. Most of those who came were rank new-chums at digging. Instead of setting to work to look for a new run of gold, they generally confined themselves to the melancholy pastime of sitting down and watching others getting it, and by-and-bye, finding that, with a few exceptions, gold is no more to be picked up without hard work on a diggings than anywhere else, they cleared out, leaving the fortunate ones who had secured good claims to work them out.

It is always difficult to estimate the amout of alluvial gold taken from a field, owing to the unwillingness of all old hands to tell anyone how much they have got or are getting. But I reckon that at least ten thousand ounces must have been taken from the two miles of the creek to which the diggings were confined, and, from the inexperience of many of those who worked the ground, it is certain that as much gold was wasted as was got.

By-and-bye a mob of Chinamen, the most patient, persevering, hard-working of all races under the sun, will start and systematically " ground-sluice " the whole course of the creek, from one end of the workings to the other, and make a real good thing of it.

A dead set has been made at this unfortunate race by the inhabitants of Queensland. A poll-tax of £10 a head has been imposed upon them on entering the colony, and they are not allowed upon any gold-field until it has been open two years.

Very heavy gold was now being got in the creek below where we were working, and the finding of nuggets ranging from ten to twenty ounces was no unusual occurrence. Occasionally a wild shout would come ringing up the valley, hailing the appearance of one of these " welcome strangers." A knot of men would immediately congregate round the finder, whose

joy betrayed him a novice at the trade, and the whole
lot would probably adjourn incontinently to the pub.,
and, handing the plunder over the counter, never
cease drinking as long as the publican's conscience impelled him to supply them with liquor, which would
probably be to about one-fourth of the value of the gold
he had received from them.

These repeated cries of joy were getting too much
for Dick Absolon. The gold fever attacked him with
a violence not to be allayed by wandering about the
ranges looking for a reef. It was with difficulty that
Jack and I dissuaded him from going to try his luck
at the alluvial. But the more gold they found in the
creek, the more certain we were that there must be a
good reef somewhere near us.

Meanwhile Gibbard was opening up his reef, which
looked very promising ; so when he offered to sell me an
eighth share in the claim, I closed with him. He had
christened his reef the " Little Wanderer."

One day soon after this, Jack, who had been patiently
following a trail of gold up a little gulley in our Protection Area, discovered the cap of a reef from which it
seemed likely the gold had come. A few hours' work
exposed the reef clearly defined between two walls
about two feet thick. The cap was of hard, hungry-
looking spar ; but when we had removed that, a vein of
very healthy-looking blueish quartz was opened up. We
broke up a few pieces, and in almost every one gold
was plainly visible.

It is very rich stone that shows gold when you break
it ; usually it has to be crushed to powder and washed
before gold shows, and many reefs pay well to work in

which you never see a colour of gold in breaking
down.

Jack and I looked at each other, and our countenances expanded into a smile of satisfied delight.
Dick was called up from where he was working a bit
down the side of the mountain, and we all sat down and
had a smoke, a solemn rite never neglected by an
Australian when entering upon a new phase of his career.

Alas! *Aurum irrepertum et sic melius situm!* Perhaps
it would have been better for me if we had never found
it at all. No such misgivings crossed our minds at the
time, however, and we hit out with a will to see what
our new reef was worth.

A few days' sinking on the underlie of the reef opened
up such a fine-looking body of stone, carrying splendid
gold, that we decided to give notice to the Warden of the
finding of a payable reef, and get him to come and lay
off our claim.

Anyone finding a reef that in the opinion of the
Warden of the field is a payable one, can take up as
much ground along the line of reef as he pleases; but
he is bound by the Government regulations to keep one
man at work on it for every hundred feet he takes up,
until there is machinery on the ground, and after that,
one man for every fifty feet. The breadth of a reef-
claim is always four hundred feet.

A few feet to the north of where we first found the
reef, its course was intersected by what is known as a
cross-course; that is, a belt of foreign country cutting
diagonally right through the reef, and shifting the
course of it away towards the east. Beyond this cross-
course we found the reef again, carrying still richer

gold than below, and it was here we finally decided to commence operations.

We applied for six men's ground; that is, three hundred feet along the reef, which, with a reward claim of one hundred feet which is always given to the first prospectors of a new reef, would give us a claim four hundred feet square. Nothing can be done without the sanction of the Warden of the gold-field, whose business it is to see that the Government regulations are carried out, and who has full power to settle any disputes about claims that may arise, in the most arbitrary manner.

Mount Britten was not yet of sufficient importance to be honoured with a Warden of its own, so the Warden for Clermont had his jurisdiction extended to take in our field. Clermont is 180 miles from Mount Britten, and often we had to wait a couple of months before getting the decision of the Warden as to some point in dispute.

The first thing to do upon finding a new reef is to christen it. After some discussion we decided to call ours the "Erratic Star"; its subsequent behaviour fully testified to the justice of the first part of the title. I do not suppose there ever was a reef whose wanderings so entirely mystified those who attempted to follow them.

This time the Warden was not long coming; but by the time he came we had already driven a tunnel in along the course of the reef for some distance, opening up magnificent stone as we went along. Our claim was situated on the fall of a very steep spur of the range, down the centre of which the course of the reef ran.

The Warden climbed up the hill to inspect our

workings, and we invited him to scratch a prospect out
of the reef for himself. He took a few pieces of stone
from different parts of the reef, and we all retired down
to the creek to crush them and wash out the gold. A
mob of at least a hundred idlers, attracted by the smell
of gold, sat round, like crows round a killing-yard, to
watch the proceedings.

When the prospects were washed out, the excitement
amongst the crowd was immense. As the last particles
of dirt were deftly washed out of the dish by Jack
Absolon, leaving the gold exposed, the Warden's jaw
dropped, and his eyes started out of his head with
surprise. Even Jack and I began to stare at each
other. We had expected to get a good show; half a
pennyweight, or a pennyweight at most, which would
have been a tremendously rich prospect. Instead of
which, though the stone was by no means carefully
crushed, we got at least a quarter of an ounce of gold
out of about a pound and a half of stone. As soon as
he had recovered from his astonishment the Warden
congratulated us upon our discovery, and laid off our
claim on the spot.

In anticipation of this auspicious moment I had
armed myself with a couple of bottles of rum, with
which we proceeded to celebrate the occasion.

# CHAPTER XIII.

## GOLD-DIGGING.

WHEN I first came to the diggings, I pitched my camp on the bank of the creek about two miles below the reefs. It never was much of a camp at the best of times. A piece of calico stretched over a pole supported by two forked saplings formed the roof, and the sides were made of a few sheets of bark knocked off the nearest trees. It rained incessantly for weeks after I got there, and, the calico roof being no more use for turning water than a hair-sieve, everything I had was always wet through, and the floor of my camp a morass of black mud.

Besides having to walk two miles up a steep rocky path to get to my work every morning, and the same distance home at night, the increasing population of the place made my camp a most undesirable one. A rowdy township was springing up all round it. Two stores, a post-office, a tobacconist and bookseller's shop, and no less than five public-houses, surrounded my peaceful abode.

Besides all these buildings, which were constructed at considerable trouble and expense out of sheets of box-tree bark and saplings, a perfect forest of tents grew up like mushrooms all round. One of these infernal public-houses was put up a few yards from my tent, and sleep at night became out of the question.

An army of drunken revellers made night hideous with their yells. They used to start drinking about sundown, and pass successively through the convivial, uproarious, and quarrelsome stages of drunkenness during the night, ending with total collapse about five in the morning. No early-closing interfered with the even tenour of their enjoyment, and there were no police to damp the geniality of their proceedings. As a rule, the fun did not begin much before one in the morning, by which time they had drunk sufficient to make them quarrelsome, and fighting took the place of singing for the remainder of the night.

This sort of programme was no doubt infinitely entertaining to those who assisted at it, most of whom slept solidly through the hours of sunlight, only waking up in time to begin the next night's orgie; but to anyone who had to work in the day, and wanted to rest at night, it was simply maddening. Nearly every night one or more of these Bacchanalians would stagger into my tent, and either collapse in a shapeless heap on the floor or begin shouting for liquor in language that made the whole place smell of sulphur. It was difficult to know what to do with them. Threatening to shoot them never had the slightest effect, and one has naturally a great disinclination to hammer a man when he is drunk, even though he does wake one out of a comfortable sleep at three o'clock on a cold winter's morning. If they were very drunk, I used to drag them out and roll them down the bank of the creek into the bushes that grew below.

13 *

One bitter cold night I was woke up by one of these worthies hammering at the sheet of bark I had stuck in the doorway of my tent to keep out intruders. He was demanding a drink in a whining voice of abject distress that would have done credit to a professional beggar. A happy thought occurred to me, and instead of replying in the language I was in the habit of using to my nocturnal visitors, I very civilly begged him to wait one moment while I got him a drink. A bucket of ice-cold water from the creek was standing by the doorway of my tent. Rising softly, I crept to the door and peered over the sheet of bark, which was barely five feet high, to ascertain his exact whereabouts. He was crouching close to the foot of it, so I seized the bucket of water and emptied it gently but firmly all over him. A galvanic shock could not have cleared him out quicker. He disappeared into the distance, too much surprised to say anything but " Oh dear! oh dear!" which he kept on repeating as long as I could hear him. He even forgot to swear. The night was so cold, and his voice sounded so utterly dreary as he went off, not even my fury at having been woke up prevented my being sorry for him, and my heart smote me at the thoughts of the miserable night he must have passed.

However, I had something better to do than shepherd drunken men all night, and I settled to shift my camp up the creek. I fixed on a place about a mile and a half above the township, on the bank of the creek, about half a mile below the reefs, for my new camp. I had sent a man out, some time before, to strip me seventy sheets of box-tree bark, on the plains a few miles away. He made an attempt to draw them right up to my camp

BULLOCK-TEAM CROSSING A LOG BRIDGE.

with a bullock-waggon, but the country was too rough and too heavily timbered. He got his waggon stuck in a short gully, and his team of sixteen bullocks so beautifully mixed up round the trees on the opposite bank, it took him a clear half-day to get out again.

When I found him he had been stuck about three hours. He was then perfectly exhausted with swearing, and as no team of bullocks will ever move without the incentive of most awful language on the part of the driver, he was obliged to hire a man to help him swear at them for the rest of the afternoon. So universal is this habit amongst bullock-drivers, and so well do their bullocks know the words that precede the application of the whip, they will not attempt to exert themselves until they hear them. I knew a man who once bought an admirable team of bullocks that were perfectly useless to him, from his disinclination to address them in the language they were used to hearing.

The driver had unloaded my sheets of bark about a mile below my camp, so I hired a mob of blacks to carry them the rest of the way. This is the sort of work at which a black-fellow shines, and which no white man I ever saw could do. Each sheet of bark was from six to eight feet long, and four or five feet wide. Many of them weighed considerably over a hundredweight each, and it is difficult to imagine more awkward things to handle. And yet some miserable, half-starved looking " gin," whose spindle legs look barely equal to supporting her own weight, will get under one of these enormous sheets of bark, and, balancing it on her head, walk off with it up a steep rocky path, for half a mile at a stretch, with perfect ease.

In a couple of days my new hut was finished. Of all buildings a bark hut is the quickest and easiest to put up, and the most comfortable to live in in a climate like Queensland. The framework is made of round saplings, on which the sheets of bark are laid and secured by strips of green hide. If the bark is carefully put on, and plenty of lap allowed for each sheet over the next one, it is perfectly proof against wind and rain, and in summer the thickness of the bark keeps the heat out admirably.

One of the chief elements of amusement on the field was an old German doctor who came and settled there. Although he was one of the cleverest men in his profession I ever saw, and a wonderful surgeon besides, he never made any money in Queensland because he was a homœopath.

The Queensland Government, not contented with figuring before the civilised world as sordid and immoral politicians, never lose an opportunity of proving themselves benighted barbarians as well. Accordingly, they refuse to recognise a homœopathic physician's diploma; and he is, therefore, not legally able to recover his fees. The world is not slow to take advantage of this, as the poor old doctor found to his cost. He was far too kind-hearted ever to refuse his services to those who were really in need of them; but it speaks ill for humanity that, out of the many patients I knew who called him in, and were perfectly well able to pay him, very few ever did so. Had he been paid one half of what he justly earned, he would have made a very good living on the field.

But I have known him keep sick men for weeks in

his own hut, sitting up with them at night, and feeding them on the best of everything he could procure for them, only to see them clear out without paying him a farthing. Often I knew for a fact that the scoundrels who did this had quantities of gold in their possession, and they generally proved it by celebrating their recovery at the adjacent pub. with a tremendous spree.

Later on, when the reefs were in full swing, and I had nearly a hundred men in my employ, I used to help him all I could by threatening to sack any men working for me who availed themselves of his services without paying him. But I could not do him much good, and finally he was starved out and had to leave the field.

I was very sorry when he went. He had a claim in the creek. I do not think there was ever anything in it, but it was close to his tent, and it used to amuse him to go and imagine he was working tremendously hard in it.

One day the doctor was subpœnaed to attend an inquiry on the death of a man at Nebo, a township about twenty-seven miles off. While he was away a party of men jumped his claim, and on his return he found them hard at work in it. They had not the slightest right to do it, as he was called away on Government work ; but what annoyed the doctor more than anything was, that they absolutely refused to stop working until the dispute was settled.

The rule is, that, if there is any dispute about a claim, it is to be referred at once to the Warden of the field. Pending his decision neither party has any right to work in the claim, and anyone who works a disputed claim at once forfeits any right in it.

The three men who had jumped the doctor's claim had done about as much work in the forty-eight hours he had been away as he had done himself in the six weeks he had been there; and from the rapidity with which they progressed, it became perfectly apparent that long before the Warden could arrive, the biggest part of his claim would be worked out.

The doctor's fury knew no bounds. He stormed and swore, and threatened and raved, but without the slightest effect in stopping the plundering of his claim.

Before two days were over, there was not a man in the field who did not know all about it, and the Doctor's Claim became the sort of theatre of the diggings, to which anyone, who had nothing better to do, adjourned to see what was going on. A more amusing scene than it occasionally presented it is impossible to imagine.

The old doctor was very short, very fat, and quite bald. His usual get-up was the most entirely disreputable one I ever saw, consisting of a pair of untanned leather slippers, no socks, a pair of flannel pajamas, a thin jersey with as many holes to the square foot as a herring net, finished off with a red cotton night-cap balanced on one ear. Thus attired, he was generally to be found executing a frantic war-dance on the edge of his claim, hurling the most awful language at his enemies below, three murderous-looking Italian scoundrels, who continued grubbing away, perfectly indifferent to everything but their one object of looking for gold. A fair-sized audience of loafers was generally seated around, encouraging the doctor, and trying to wind him up to the point of dropping a stone on his foes' heads below.

The poor old doctor was far too good-natured ever willingly to hurt a flea, but to hear him talk when excited would make anyone feel quite weak who did not know him. He was absolute master of the English language, and displayed a knowledge of its back premises I had not the slightest idea a foreigner could ever attain. Under the influence of passion, he would run down a chromatic scale of declamation, with an ornamental fluency that never failed to excite admiration, even from those at whom it was levelled.

I remember one day, after a more than usually severe attack of what he called " Choleric nervousness," the old doctor turned suddenly round, and found he had been overheard by a clergyman. The countenance of this worthy man, I am grieved to say, indicated more admiration, and less regret, than the occasion called for.

" My dear doctor," he observed, " I suppose it is my duty to tell you it is very wrong to use such language ; but I am going to do nothing of the kind. I am simply going to ask you how, when, and where on earth did you learn to swear like that ? "

"Learn ? " said the doctor; "learn ! my good sir, you *can't* learn it. It is a gift ! "

About this time the Government thought fit to honour the field with the presence of a policeman. He was a poor miserable crow-bait of an Irishman, and, like most of his compatriots, an arrant coward when alone.

I have often noticed that if half a dozen Irishmen can manage to set upon two or three men, they are all as brave as lions. But get one by himself, and he is a wretched funk.

The specimen sent up to keep the peace on the diggings was no exception to the rule. He used to creep about under the shade of a pith helmet, with a huge revolver dangling in front of him, like a Scotchman's sporran. He never ventured beyond the most crowded parts of the field, and, if called upon to act in an official capacity, his face used to turn the colour of cigarash with terror.

The doctor, however, hailed his arrival with delight, as he thought he saw his way to bringing the arm of the law to bear upon the plunderers of his claim. Off he started and called upon the constable to interfere at once, and stop the work. So far from doing this, it was with the greatest difficulty the constable could be persuaded to visit the claim at all, and, when there, he absolutely refused to interfere.

The doctor, whose last hope had now departed, became perfectly beside himself. The foam flew in spray from his lips, but for the first time in his life language failed him, and he became inarticulate from fury. Suddenly a horrible sort of spurious calm came over him, and he retired into his tent. In a minute he reappeared armed with the fossil remains of an aged pistol. One glance at it was sufficient to show that it was fearfully dangerous everywhere except at the business end, and that if it ever did go off, the safest place to stand would be straight in front of it.

No such reassuring considerations entered the mind of the constable. He remained rooted to the spot with terror, while the doctor's shaking fingers accomplished the task of loading.

An enormous audience had by this time assembled,

most of whom were stretched on the ground in convulsions of laughter. Even the three ruffians in the claim became interested, and ceased their monotonous occupation of baling water and cradling to watch the proceedings. *Stetit urna paullum sicca*, while the doctor delivered his harangue at the constable, for whom flight had now become impossible. He was trembling so that he certainly could not have walked, besides which, the doctor had edged round, and pinned him against a bank from which there was no escape. Drawing gradually nearer towards him, and brandishing his weapon all the while, the doctor swore all he knew that he was going to kill him on the spot.

The wretched man's terror now almost overcame him. His jaw dropped, he half-shut his eyes, and threw back his head in a mute appeal, which ought to have softened the doctor's heart, but which merely excited him afresh.

"Call yourself a policeman!" he screamed; "why do you hold your head back like a fowl drinking water? I kill five better men than you on the Lachlan before breakfast, for nothing at all! So help me three men and a boy, I shoot you now like one damn dog!"

The few of us who were not too weak from laughing began to think it was time to interfere, when suddenly the doctor's attention was caught by a parrot seated in a tree over his head.

"Look!" he shouted in a voice that would have frightened anything but a parrot into the next colony. "Look! you say I can't shoot! I soon show you. Watch me knock the stuffing out of that parrot, then you know what I do to you next time I catch you loafing round my side of the creek!"

A breathless silence ensued, while the doctor levelled his weapon at the now interested parrot. After aiming for about two minutes and a half, he pulled the trigger. The cap exploded and the parrot flew screaming away, leaving one of its tail feathers, in its hurry, to float gently down at the doctor's feet.

Nothing could exceed his pride and delight, and none of us were cruel enough to mar it by suggesting he could not have hit the parrot because his pistol had never gone off. Brandishing the feather as a trophy, he scattered a glance of withering contempt at the reviving constable, and retired to his tent to spend the afternoon in trying to give electric shocks to a mob of blacks, by the bait of a shilling placed in a basin of water connected with a small battery.

The inside of his hut presented the climax of disorder and untidiness. Rows of medicine-bottles were littered along the shelves, some with corks, some with none, mixed up with tins of pepper, boxes of ointment, jars of pickles, old clothes, and carpenter's tools. Surgical instruments used for cutting up tobacco or spreading butter, frying-pans, telescopes, boots, books, photographs, tobacco-pipes, the remains of a damper, and several packs of cards, were generally strewed about the floor, in a way suggestive of nothing short of an earthquake in a curiosity shop. Here he was generally to be found, when not dancing around his claim, bending over the fire, in the agonies of concocting some vile stew, which none but a German is capable of eating. I have seen him put tea, rum, milk, colonial wine, mustard, lime-juice, vinegar, and ginger into a sauce for some hideous mess which he afterwards ate.

The capacity of his internal economy was enormous. One Sunday I invited a party of seven, including the doctor, to dinner. I made two plum puddings in honour of the occasion, each about the size of my head. Seven of us ate one, and the doctor ate the other. He had already stowed away two vast mountains of salt beef, so no one was surprised when, after attending the funeral of a whole pudding, he patted his distended waistcoat, and observed that he " felt as if he had one schnake coiled up there ! " After which he became partially torpid for some hours.

The Little Wanderer reef, at which Gibbard was working, soon began to show heavy gold. He had three mates in the claim, two of whom drank themselves out, and I bought their shares at the same figure which I had paid Gibbard for his.

The third, a young fellow called S——, formerly an officer in the navy, was killed in a very sad manner. A drunken man came into his tent one night, and S—— got up and turned him out. The man closed with him and threw him, and, in falling, a stake of poison-wood entered S——'s leg, inflicting a shocking wound. His hut was not far from mine, and after his accident I used to go down and sit with him in the evenings after work. For a few days he seemed to be going on all right, and I believe, if it had been possible to have kept him quite quiet and away from everyone, he might have recovered. But he had been drinking heavily for some time past, and now he drank more than ever; for the whole day long, and well into the night, his hut was besieged by a succession of visitors anxious to show their sympathy for his misfortune. Unfortunately their invariable method of doing so was to insist upon his having a drink with them; and his wound, which was a serious one in any case, soon began to assume a dangerous appearance.

On the fifth night the old doctor came and told me that he thought very badly of him, so I immediately went round to his hut. A sadder sight than the interior of it presented I never saw. There was no furniture of any kind, of course, and the floor was a thick paste of black mud. Seated on packing-cases or buckets turned upside down, were five or six of the rowdiest men on the diggings. On the floor was a tin prospecting dish half-full of rum, and a bucket of water, and each man helped him with a pannikin when he wanted a drink.

The place was so thick with tobacco smoke that at first I could hardly see across it, though the hut was not above twelve feet long. By degrees, as my eyes got accustomed to it, the light of a fat-lamp at the far end showed me poor S—— lying on a rough sort of bed made of a sheet of bark laid upon a heap of grass.

A great change had come over him since I had last seen him, not very many hours before, and I felt certain, directly I looked at him, that he was dying. His cheery features had a drawn and haggard look, and already there was that unmistakable far-off look in his eyes that too surely announces the speedy approach of death. Evidently his companions had not the slightest idea of the state he was in. To do them justice they were all half drunk, and doing their best to become quite so; but when I came in they were all shouting and laughing and blaspheming, with the most uproarious

cheerfulness, and one of them had just called on S——
to give them a song.

S—— himself was perfectly sober, and, I am certain,
knew that he had only a few hours to live. But he
came of the sort that die very hard, and, calling for a
pannikin of rum, he raised himself on his elbow to
comply with his mates' request. The hardened and
reckless countenances of those revellers, drinking in the
presence of death, the unearthly look upon S——'s face,
rendered doubly ghastly by the miserable flickering light
over his head, formed a scene which I shall never forget.
His voice rang out clear in the weird, solemn silence
of a winter's night, and the words of his last song are
indelibly impressed upon my memory. They contain
only too true a history of his own ruined life, and of
hundreds of others who have fallen victims to the terrible
curse of drink.

> Who cares for nothing alone is free:
> Sit down good fellow and drink with me.
> With a careless heart and a merry eye
> He will laugh at the world as the world goes by.
> He laughs at power, and wealth, and fame;
> He laughs at virtue, he laughs at shame;
> He laughs at hope, and he laughs at fear,
> And at memory's dead leaves, crisp and seer;
>
> He laughs at the future, cold and dim,
> Nor earth nor heaven is dear to him:
> Oh! that is the comrade fit for me,
> He cares for nothing, his soul is free,
> Free as the soul of the fragrant wine!
> Sit down, good fellow, my heart is thine;
> For I heed not custom, creed, nor law,—
> I care for nothing that ever I saw.
>
> In every city my cup I quaff,
> And over my liquor I riot and laugh.

I laugh like the cruel and turbulent wave,
I laugh at the church, and I laugh at the grave;
I laugh at joy, and right well I know
That I merrily, merrily laugh at woe.
I terribly laugh, with an oath and a sneer,
When I think that the hour of death is near;

For I know that Death is a guest divine
Who will drink my blood as I drink this wine.
Ah! he cares for nothing, a king is he!
Come on, old fellow, and drink with me.
With you I will drink to the solemn past,
Though the cup that I drain should be my last;
I will drink to the Phantoms of Love and Truth,
To ruined manhood and wasted youth.

I will drink to the woman that wrought my woe,
In the diamond morning of long ago;
To a heavenly face in sweet repose,
To the lily's snow and the blood of the rose.
To the splendour caught from southern skies,
That shone in the depths of her glorious eyes;
Her large eyes wild with the fire of the South,
And the dewy wine of her warm, red mouth.

I will drink to the thought of a better time,
To innocence gone like a death-bell chime;
I will drink to the shadow of coming doom,
To the phantoms that wait in my lonely tomb.
I will drink to my soul in its terrible mood,
Dimly and solemnly understood.
And lastly I drink to the monarch of Sin,
Who has conquered that fortress and reigns within.

My sight is fading, it dies away;
I cannot tell, is it night or day?
My heart is burnt and blackened with pain,
And a horrible darkness crushes my brain;
I cannot see you—the end is nigh,
But we'll drink together before I die.
Through awful chasms I plunge and fall,
Your hand, good fellow; I die—that's all.

Exhausted by the exertion, S—— sank down again on the couch, and a deadly look came over his face. Even the drunkards began to see that there was something wrong, and obeyed a not very civil recommendation to clear out of the hut with unexpected readiness. I got the doctor to come as soon as I could, and he at once pronounced S——'s case to be hopeless. Mortification set in, and he died not many hours after.

He was a great favourite with all who knew him, and much regretted, especially by his mates, as he used to do all the work in their claim in the creek, while they got drunk at the public-houses. His share in the Wanderer Reef was sold by auction, and knocked down to me at the reserve price, without a bid.

I and Gibbard were now sole owners of the Wanderer, I holding seven-eighths and he one-eighth.

Meanwhile the Absolons and I had got down with our shaft on the Erratic Star to a depth of sixty feet, and the prospects on both reefs were so good that I determined to put up machinery for crushing the stone. For this purpose I went down to Gympie, one of the chief gold-fields of Queensland, and got the estimate of a first-rate engineer for the cost and erection of a battery of ten head of stampers, and a seventeen horse-power stationary engine. His estimate was £1,500 for the cost of the machinery in Melbourne, and £1,000 for the cost of erection on the field.

I mentally doubled his estimate on the spot; but, for the benefit of anyone who is ever tempted to go in for putting up a quartz-mill on a new field, I may here observe that before I had completed the work it cost £9,000. It is almost impossible to estimate beforehand

14

the cost of such an undertaking in new country, a hundred miles from anywhere where you can buy a nail or a piece of string. The natural difficulties incidental to the work are great enough, but in my case the unnatural ones I had to contend against were greater still.

As a rule, anyone who starts putting up machinery on a new gold-field, or who does anything towards developing any sort of mining, is hailed as a public benefactor by the neighbouring towns. The inhabitants, especially of the nearest seaport towns, hasten to display their appreciation of the good gifts of Providence by putting the roads between themselves and the new diggings in good order, and vie with each other in offering every assistance to the prospectors and promoters of the mines.

The reason of this is not far to seek. Nothing gives such an impulse to the trade of a seaport as the vicinity of a diggings. Many large towns have been called into existence by nothing else. The town of Melbourne itself, one of the greatest wonders of the world, with its 300,000 inhabitants, its broad streets, its magnificent public buildings, and its almost unlimited wealth, owes its rise, its very existence, to the Ballarat diggings.

It is a very common thing for the storekeepers of a town to supply parties of men with tools and rations gratis, for months at a time, to prospect the adjacent country in hopes of discovering a gold-field.

The Mount Britten diggings, upon which I was at work, was most unfortunately situated. The only possible means of communication with the coast was through the port of Mackay, from which it was distant 100 miles by road. Now the distance was nothing, and the road, fairly good at all times, might easily have been made an excellent one. But the township of Mackay is a very peculiar one. It is the saccharopolis of Queensland, and in point of intelligence may safely be described as the Bœotia of Australia.

The planters of the district have long been a byword for meanness and stupidity. Entirely absorbed in the process of growing and making sugar, they absolutely refuse to acknowledge the importance of any other industry, and have always entertained an unreasoning aversion to any kind of mining in the neighbourhood, only to be accounted for by the supposition that a prolonged course of sugar-boiling has turned their heads into vacuum-pans, and raised the density of their wits to the level of that of their most prolific cane-juice.

Nothing is of more vital importance to the prosperity of a coast town in Australia than to keep open its communication with the interior. If the outside roads are allowed to fall into bad repair, the wool and other traffic is rapidly diverted to some other port; and, once lost, it is extremely difficult to regain.

The difference of fifty or sixty miles more or less is nothing to a carrier, compared with the difference between a bad and a good road. When in the interior he will infallibly choose the best road to the coast, though it may be very much the longest.

And yet I have heard one of the leading planters, at a meeting of the Mackay Road Board, openly declare that Mackay had nothing to do with the interior, that she did not want the wool, or the copper, or the gold, or the squatters; and that there was no necessity to spend a shilling in keeping up the road to the interior.

14 *

Now I should be the last person to under-rate the value of the sugar industry to Mackay. It has raised a population of seven thousand people, where formerly there were not thirty, and brought some millions of capital into the district. But I cannot conceive why Mackay, because it is blessed with one most prosperous industry, should close its doors to every other.

The dislike of the planters to any sort of mining being started in the district I can, to a certain extent, understand. They are ignorant and short-sighted, and no doubt imagine that the proximity of a diggings would raise the price of labour on their plantations. It would do nothing of the kind. The class of men who follow mining as a profession are quite distinct from the sort of hands required on a plantation.

Besides this, a diggings always attracts a large number of men who go there with a vague idea they are going to get gold, but are destitute of either the knowledge or the means to set about it. They dig for a while, and, finding the work very hard and gold very scarce, they clear out, and are glad to find employment elsewhere.

Our station, which lay half-way between Mackay and the diggings, was inundated with men returning from the field in search of work. So that it is probable that the immediate effect of a diggings in the neighbourhood would be to lower, rather than to raise, the price of labour on the plantations; while the indirect benefit that the planters would derive from the increased trade of the town would be considerable.

Whatever the planters views might be, I should have thought that the store-keepers in Mackay would have held but one opinion as to the advantages they would be likely to derive from a diggings. And yet so saturated were they with the prevailing sugar mania, and so servilely dependent upon the planters had they become, I soon found out that any exertions upon their part would be directed more towards retarding than assisting the progress of the diggings.

The whole district unanimously refused to spend a penny on repairing the road to the Mount Britten field. My orders for goods were persistently unattended to or delayed. The manager of one of the principal banks took the trouble to ride up to the field, for the sole purpose of returning to spread false reports as to the poverty of the reefs which I was engaged in working. My own agents left my machinery lying for weeks on the wharf, and sent empty away the carriers whom I myself had taken the trouble to hunt up and send down for loading. The inconvenience and loss which I suffered in consequence was incalculable. After hanging about Mackay for some days, vainly endeavouring to induce my agents to give them my machinery, the carriers loaded up for elsewhere, and went off up the country.

It was months before I could get hold of them again. Meantime the wet season set in, and the roads became perfectly impassable. I had soon a vast army of men at work on the diggings, sawyers, carpenters, boiler-makers, brick-makers, and others, whom I was very unwilling to leave to themselves for any length of time.

But after I discovered that the whole district of Mackay had deliberately laid themselves out to block my endeavours to develop the Mount Britten diggings, and were prepared to resort to foul means to accomplish their object, I resolved not to trust to any agents, but always to personally superintend the loading of any of my machinery or stores that might arrive in Mackay.

Many a hundred miles of travelling it cost me. It was eighty-six miles to ride from the diggings to Mackay, and sometimes I had to ride up and down twice in a week. I soon found that this kind of business, combined with superintending the working of the two reefs, was more than could be done effectually by one man.

But the engineer I had engaged in Gympie to put up the mill turned out an invaluable acquisition. His name was William Holliman ; and a smarter man at his trade never existed. From morning till night he worked as I never saw a man work for wages before. The erection of a quartz-mill, at any time, is an undertaking that involves very heavy work, and no little engineering skill. But in an out-of-the-way place like Mount Britten the difficulties are increased a hundred-fold, and can only be overcome by infinite patience and skill. Holliman, however, proved himself equal to any emergency, and finally accomplished the work, in a way that has earned for the obscure field of Mount Britten the reputation of possessing the most perfectly erected mill in Queensland. It is impossible to do justice to the admirable qualities he displayed during the time he was with me. Machinery stuck in the mud, broken castings, drunken contractors going on the spree with their contract uncompleted, thunder-storms sweeping away work half finished, the wrong goods sent up by a mistake which takes months to rectify ; these and many other annoyances await the enthusiastic individual who is rash enough to start putting up a mill on a new field.

Holliman was equal to them all; and, though his professional reputation was at stake, and I believe he felt any hindrance to the work far more than I did, I never saw him discouraged for a minute, or otherwise than cheerful.

For anyone who lives in the midst of civilisation, and who has nothing to do but walk into a shop and buy what he wants, it is impossible to realise the situation. What words can depict the helpless fury of a man in the mountains of Northern Queensland, who has ordered a keg of a peculiar kind of nails from Sydney, and who, after an interval of four months, receives a barrel of rock-sulphur instead? This actually happened, without, however, in the least disturbing the equanimity of Holliman. He merely remarked, with an expression of countenance it is impossible to describe, that " he hoped my dog was not going to have the distemper." Though not a teetotaller, he was strictly sober, and a keen sense of humour, combined with an inexhaustible fund of anecdotes, made him an exceedingly pleasant companion. He was with me for eighteen months; and when at last I handed over the concern to a company, who sent up their own manager, I parted with him with the greatest regret.

A most absurd accident happened one day at a shaft on the " Star " line of reef. The shaft was down about thirty feet, and, as usual, one man was working below, and his mate on top, winding up the stuff in an old oil-drum instead of a bucket. Somehow or other the man on top let fall the drum right on his mate's head below. Fortunately, though made entirely of iron, the bottom was very nearly worn out, and the man's head went fair through it. He was naturally very angry, but his rage redoubled when he discovered that all attempts to get his head out again were perfectly useless. Though bashed in, none of the bottom was actually knocked out, and the jagged edges had closed round his neck again, like a spring trap, causing him excruciating pain.

He was wound up the shaft, perfectly helpless and swearing fearfully, and led down the hill to the black-smith's, to get his helmet knocked off.

Anything more ridiculous than he looked I never saw in my life. He kept up a perfect hurricane of blasphemy, rendered absolutely awesome by the unearthly metallic ring which the oil-drum gave to his voice.

We were, most of us, too weak from laughing to be of the slightest assistance to him. Had the rim of the drum caught him, instead of the bottom, of course it would have killed him on the spot. Accidents of this kind are very frequent.

The greatest care is required on the part of those working at the mouth of a shaft to see that nothing, however small, is allowed to fall down below. A very small stone, falling from a great height on to a man's head, is sufficient to cause instant death.

It is extraordinary what escapes some men have, and what a slight thing will kill sometimes. I remember a man being killed on the spot by a pound of candles being dropped from a height of sixty feet on to his head. On the other hand, Jack Absolon was once working at the bottom of a shaft seventy feet deep, when the whole windlass up above carried bodily away. It came right down the shaft, together with a hundredweight of copper ore that was being wound up. He heard it coming, squeezed himself into a corner of the shaft, and never got a scratch.

No one on a diggings ever seems to possess a surname. But there is generally some epithet attached to their Christian names, whereby they may be distinguished. " Red Pat," " Maori Bob," " Little Dave," " Ironstone George," " Long Mick," and " Deaf Harry "—a host of them rises before me. Their faces were better known to me than my own, seeing that the back of a sardine-box was the only looking-glass I had for months ; but if they ever had any surname it was known only to themselves.

" Deaf Harry " had certainly the best right to his name of any man I ever knew. The immoderate use of quinine had made him so deaf that no combination of sounds, however appalling, could attract his attention.

I used to work with him for a long while, sinking a shaft, and soon gave up attempting to make him hear. If he was below and I wanted him, I used to carefully drop a small pebble on his head.

One day Deaf Harry was at the windlass, and another man working below. They had arranged a series of signals between themselves. Two jerks on the rope meant " heave up," one meant " steady," and three meant " lower away."

I was working a little higher up the hill, when all of a sudden I heard most awful noises echoing out of the shaft. Looking down the hill I saw Harry peacefully winding away at the windlass, quite unconscious of the yells and oaths that were flying up the shaft past his ear. I knew something must be wrong, so I ran down the hill, and arrived just in time to see Harry's mate being wound slowly up to the mouth of the shaft head-downwards, with his foot noosed in the rope. He was struggling fearfully, and still trying to swear, but was rapidly becoming speechless from having been wound up a distance of seventy feet in that position.

For once in his life Harry's rugged countenance relaxed into an expression of delighted surprise. Instead of making the slightest attempt to extricate the unfortunate man, he remained looking critically at him for several seconds, with the windlass handle in his hand. Then turning towards me, he said, quite quietly :

" Well ! I 've been twenty-two years digging, and I never saw a man come up the shaft like that before ! "

I made a dive at the wretched man's leg, dragged him out of the shaft, and laid him out to dry. He was perfectly exhausted, and purple in the face, but, having been revived by a bucket of water poured over his head, he explained that he had been standing in the bottom of the shaft, and, he supposed, had unintentionally jerked the rope twice with his foot. Harry, of course, began to wind up, and knew no more about it till his mate appeared at the top. He lost all interest in him as soon as he found he had not come up head downwards on purpose.

## CHAPTER XIV.

### DRINK.

ONE day a man known as Ironstone George died at one of the public-houses on the field, entirely from the effects of drink. It is really infamous that no one has any power to interfere in such cases. I had seen the man hopelessly drunk, day after day, at the same public-house, and had warned the owner that I should take the first opportunity of taking away his licence.

Being the only resident magistrate on the field, I held an inquest on the body. In the inquiry it appeared that the publican had supplied him during a fortnight with as much liquor as he could drink, but had never given him anything to eat. A nearer approach to wilful murder it is not easy to imagine. I took the opportunity of repeating my assurance to the publican that he need never expect a licence again, coupled with an expression of my unfeigned regret that the law of the land did not allow me to hang him.

I was unfortunately unable to attend the first licensing board for the diggings, and the rascally local magistrates granted no less than six licences for the Mount Britten field.

These public-houses are a perfect curse all through

the Bush of Australia, and no finer field was ever open to a philanthropist than a crusade against the iniquity that goes on in them.

In touching upon this subject, I wish very clearly to state the ground that I take up, which is not so much reduction of drunkenness as the prevention of murder. In spite of the most specious attempts on the part of such fanatical optimists as Mr. Gladstone, Mr. Mundella, and others, to cook the returns of drunkenness and liquor consumed, statistics show that the amount varies very little. Wherever a certain number of the British race are gathered together, there a certain amount of liquor will be consumed, and my own conviction is that legislation can do little or nothing to prevent drunkenness. It can, if it please, force men to get drunk in their own homes instead of in public-houses, but here its power ends.

There is no truer picture of humanity than John Leech's cartoon of the British workman arriving home on Saturday night, laden with an enormous jar of liquor, to provide against the inconvenience of a Sunday Closing Act.

But legislation can and ought to do a great deal towards the prevention of such monstrous crimes as are universally prevalent throughout the Bush public-houses in Australia. The most violent poisons are habitually used to adulterate the liquor sold, and to an extent which renders a very moderate consumption sufficient to destroy life. Bluestone and tobacco are the most favourite drugs in use, the effect of them being to cause temporary insanity, accompanied by raging thirst.

I have seen a strong sober man driven perfectly mad

for the time being, by two glasses of so-called rum, supplied to him at one of these shanties. He had not the slightest appearance of being drunk about him, but every appearance of having been poisoned, and he did not recover from the effects for a fortnight.

There is not a shadow of a doubt that scores of perfectly healthy men die every year from the immediate effects of being poisoned at these infernal dens. It is a very common occurrence for a man to be found dead within a short distance of one of them. Possibly he has retained sufficient vitality to drag himself a few hundred yards on his journey, after exhausting his credit with the publican. Possibly he has actually died in the house, and been dragged a little way down the road by the publican, to avoid the unpleasantness which an inquiry into a death in his house might entail. Fear of any such unpleasantness, however, must be purely sentimental, for I never heard of a single case where any death of the kind brought serious consequences to the publican.

It is by no means necessary that a man should be a drunkard for him to fall a victim to this system of secret murder.

After a twenty-mile tramp, or a fifty-mile ride along a scorching road, the traveller arrives at the public-house, possibly the only building that lies between him and a similar journey in front. There is no earthly reason he should not have a drink. He is tired and thirsty, and the water is probably very bad. And yet it is possible that the very first glass he swallows may entirely deprive him of his reason.

The object of every Bush publican is to make anyone

with money, who visits his house, as quickly as possible drunk, in order that he may either voluntarily hand over all he has got to the publican, and drink it out, or become so helpless as to allow himself to be robbed.

A system known as " knocking down one's cheque " prevails all over the unsettled parts of Australia. That is to say, a man with a cheque, or a sum of money in his possession, hands it over to the publican, and calls for drinks for himself and his friends, until the publican tells him he has drunk out his cheque. Of course he never gets a tithe of his money's worth in any shape or way—indeed, the kindest thing a publican can possibly do, is to refuse him any more liquor at a very early stage of the proceedings ; for cheques for enormous amounts are frequently " knocked down " in this way. A quarter of the worth of them, if honestly drunk out in Bush liquor, would inevitably kill a whole regiment.

I remember a man who, for years, had been a hard drinker. He went on the square—that is, he kept perfectly sober—for five years, during which time he raised a cheque of £600. With this he started down to the coast, intending to go home to the old country. On the way he was persuaded to have a drink. The old madness came over him, and in three weeks he had drunk out every penny of his cheque.

At one of the public-houses at which he stayed he had champagne at a guinea a bottle, in a bath in front of the house, with a pannikin by the side for all comers to help themselves.

As if by instinct, crowds of loafers assemble at a Bush pub. where a good cheque is going, like flies round a honey-pot, and the wildest orgies prevail.

The scene is generally pretty much the same. A crowd of noisy blasphemers, enveloped in a haze of tobacco-smoke, elbowing each other to get near the counter where drinks are served.

Behind this stands the barman and the landlord, the obsequious expression on the latter's face indicating to the initiated that the time has not yet arrived when his conscience will allow him to declare the cheque drunk out. He is still anxious to supply everyone with everything they want.

In one corner of the room lies huddled a shapeless mass, which few would suppose to be the hospitable individual at whose expense the company are drinking. An inarticulate moan bursts from the sufferer on the ground. Possibly he has been in the same position for some twenty-four hours. The landlord, who is civility itself, springs to attention at once, and hastening to him bends over him.

" Beg pardon, Sir—what did you please to say ? "

Another groan.

" Certainly, Sir. All right, Jim," (to the barman,) " drinks for thirteen."

And so it goes on. Half the men drinking at the unfortunate wretch's expense probably never saw him before, and the other half do not care if they never see him again—until he has raised another cheque.

The prevalence of drinking throughout the Bush, and in all the big towns of Queensland especially, is one of the most extraordinary features of the country. If it were possible to obtain any accurate returns, it would be very interesting to ascertain the exact proportion of the whole amount of wages earned in the colony, that

passes into the hands of the publicans. The amount
of liquor consumed in no way represents it, owing to
the system to which I have just alluded, which enables
the publican to get possession of a man's money, without
supplying him with anything like the value of it in return.
It is no exaggeration to say it is the universal custom
of most of the working classes of Queensland, whether
stockmen, miners, sawyers, carpenters, fencers, or shepherds, to spend the whole of their earnings in drink.

Their method of doing so is peculiar, and not many
of them are what could fairly be called habitual drunkards. That is to say, they do not, as a rule, drink
while they are at work, and they make a practice of
working steadily and industriously for long spells at a
time. But, in working, the object of nine out of every
ten of them is simply to raise enough money for a spree.
A periodical spree seems a necessity in the life of a
Bushman. It is, to him, what an annual excursion to
the seaside is to an over-worked London tradesman.
It brings him into contact with fresh faces and scenes,
empties his pocket, restores him to cheerfulness, and
sends him back with renewed ardour to work.

Now, if a Bushman were sure of being supplied with
good liquor, instead of poison, it is doubtful whether
this mode of living would ever do him any harm at all.
It is notorious that a man who gets occasionally drunk,
and drinks nothing between whiles, suffers far less than
a man who is continually drinking without ever getting
drunk at all. Further than this, a Bushman, while at
work, is of necessity restricted to the simplest possible
fare. Vegetables, or luxuries of any kind, he can seldom
procure. A prolonged course of nothing but tea, beef,

and damper, renders a change of living indispensable, to ward off scurvy and similar diseases.

Under these circumstances, though it is extremely to be regretted that he should carry it to the length of the orgies that prevail amongst his class, it is certain that an occasional drinking-bout does a Bushman more good than harm.

In considering the question, and the best means of dealing with it, it is better at once to relegate to a visionary Utopia the hope of universal thrift and sobriety; we may take it for granted that as long as men retain their individual freedom of action, they will drink just exactly as much as they want to. Of course, it admits of argument whether you cannot educate men up to the point of wanting to drink less. But the votaries of any such scheme would derive little encouragement from studying the subject in Queensland. So far from drunkenness being confined to the uneducated, it is, if anything, more prevalent among the upper and middle classes than any other. They drink incessantly, while the lower classes can only afford to drink occasionally. Preventive legislation, in the shape of early closing, or penalties for drunkenness, will never do the slightest good. Early closing only makes men drink at home, and drunkenness is not a vice upon which the fear of consequences will ever exert any great restraint, for the simple reason that few men, when they start drinking, do so with the deliberate intention of getting drunk, and when they are under the influence of liquor they are, of course, utterly indifferent to consequences of any kind.

What legislation can, and ought to do, is to interfere

15

to prevent a man being made to get drunk when he does not want to, and to save him from being poisoned after he has lost all command of his senses.

The conduct of the Queensland Government with regard to the adulteration of liquor in public-houses is perfectly scandalous. The penalties for its detection are by no means such as the gravity of the offence calls for, and are rarely enforced. The excise is most inefficient, and its duties are discharged in a way that no one acquainted with the morality of Colonial Government would credit. It is not long since the Queensland Government sent the excise round some public-houses in the neighbourhood of Brisbane. They had no difficulty in collecting a quantity of sixteen different sorts of deadly poisons, used for the adulteration of liquor. Instead of destroying them, the Government had the shameless effrontery to sell these poisons by public auction.

A great deal might be done by the local magistrates, if they chose. They have discretionary power to grant or refuse licences to holders of public-houses, and there is no appeal from their decision. If it were known that a man's licence was certain to be refused him if he were in the habit of adulterating his liquor, it would undoubtedly act as a check upon the practice.

If, in addition to this, a man were liable to be hanged, if convicted of causing the death of a fellow-creature by supplying him with poisonous liquor, it would go a long way towards stopping it altogether.

The extreme difficulty of obtaining any such conviction, the isolated position of these Bush publics, which makes supervision next to impossible, renders some extreme legislation on the subject imperative. Owing to the scarcity of population, and the consequent facilities afforded to crime, rape is punishable in Queensland by hanging. I cannot conceive that the crime of wilfully taking a man's life by poison calls for a less severe sentence. As a matter of fact little or nothing is ever done towards the prevention of this most dastardly of all forms of murder.

The reformation of Bush public-houses in Queensland would be a difficult task, even supposing that any large section of the community were interested in its accomplishment. It is rendered hopeless by the universal indifference on the subject that, to a certain extent, pervades every class in the colony.

The sympathies of the whole of society are largely with the publican. The squatters themselves, of whom the licensing board is usually composed, will always uphold him. They may regret that he sells poisonous liquor to stray travellers, but they have no fear of being treated in the same way themselves—at least, by the publicans in the neighbourhood of their own station. In return for the assurance of his licence, the publican has always the wisdom to keep a supply of decent liquor on hand for his supporters when they pay him a call.

A visit to the seat of power in Brisbane would be the reverse of encouraging to anyone interested in this subject.

A crusade against publicans is not likely to find much favour with an executive composed of men who spend half their time loafing around the drinking-bars in the town, and whose ranks generally contain one or two notorious drunkards, who are not in the least ashamed

to take their seat in the House, or to be seen in the
streets while in a state of intoxication.   It is no uncommon thing to see a telegram in a Queensland paper to
the effect that at such and such an hour " Mr. So-and-
so, who was intoxicated, rose to move the adjournment
of the House."

Our neighbours in New South Wales and Victoria
are not behind us in this respect.   If anything, the
Queensland Assembly is the most sober of the three.
The drunkenness of the judges throughout Australia
has become such a by-word as to entirely deprive the
time-honoured proverb of any but a sarcastic meaning.

I read, the other day, in the *Sydney Bulletin*, the
following interesting comment on the subject :—

" We have all of us heard the expressions ' as drunk
as a lord,' and ' as sober as a judge.'   Can anything
be more ridiculous ?   Who ever heard of a lord being
drunk, or a judge being——(ED.—There is no occasion
to continue this subject any further)."

It is by no means an uncommon occurrence for a
magistrate or a judge to take his seat on the bench in
a state of intoxication.   Not long ago a most absurd
scene took place at the petty sessions at a township
which shall be nameless, but which is not a hundred
miles from Bowen.   One magistrate, as not unfrequently
happens, was sitting in solitary state on the bench.
His features wore that expression of ludicrous solemnity by the adoption of which a man who knows himself
to be drunk endeavours to disguise the fact from his
neighbours.

A prisoner was brought in, charged with having
removed goods to the value of 1s. 4d. from a store.

Before the evidence was half finished, a terrible frown gathered on the magistrate's brow. Jamming his battered cabbage-tree hat well over his eyes, in imitation of the awful ceremony of putting on the black cap, he rose slowly up, and, pointing a shaking finger at the culprit, said : " Take'imawayand'ang'im ! "

" Beg pardon, your Worship," said the constable, " this is only a case of——"

" Take'im-'way—and 'ang 'im ! " repeated his Worship, more slowly and impressively than before.

" But, your Worship," expostulated the bewildered official, " you have no power——"

" No power ! Just aint I, though," shouted the now thoroughly infuriated magistrate. " 'Ear what I shay ? Take 'im away and 'ang 'im ! " And, subsiding into his seat, he was heard to add, in a voice of maudlin pathos : " An' Lor' a mercy on his soul ! "

Seeing that remonstrance was useless, the constable removed the prisoner, and shortly afterwards returned.

" Taken'imawayand'ung'im ? " asked the magistrate, cheerfully.

" Yes, your Worship."

" All right. I 'shmis shcase."

As long as the supervision of Bush public-houses remains in the hands of such men as these, no reform is possible. And no reform will ever come until a healthier tone as regards the subject of drunkenness pervades every class in the Colony. Throughout the whole country the reputation of being mighty to mingle strong drink carries no little admiration along with it, while the fact of getting occasionally drunk entails little or no reproach.

Of course, in and near the big towns the possibility of a visit from the excise makes the adulteration of liquor rather more difficult than in the Bush. Away in the back blocks it is done openly and shamelessly, and looked on, by everyone concerned, in the light of rather a good joke.

A friend of mine went into a Bush pub. near Hungerford, on the borders of New South Wales and Queensland, accompanied by three or four other men, for whom he was going to " shout." The usual invitation, " Give it a name, boys," was followed by requests on the part of his friends for various sorts of drinks. One called for rum, another for beer, and a third was just remarking that gin-and-bitters was what the doctor had ordered, when a cynical smile was observed on the landlord's face.

" Hold on," he said, " it 's no use going on like that. We 've run out of every drop of liquor, and been drinking ' Pain-killer ' for a week. So you can take that or leave it alone."

On another occasion, I remember hearing a man ask for a glass of gin, at a very out-of-the-way Bush shanty. He was supplied with a glass of bluish-white-looking stuff, which, after the fashion of dwellers in the Bush, he swallowed raw, intending to help himself to water afterwards. No sooner had he swallowed it than an expression of awful rage and terror came over his face.

" Why, damn everything an inch high," he exclaimed, as soon as he got his breath, " that ain't gin—that 's kerosene ! "

" Well," said the woman who had served him, " and what if it is ? There 's no call to make any flaming fuss. There's three gentlemen in the parlour drinking Farmer's Friend for rum, and they don't say anything."

On the next annual licensing day after my arrival on the diggings, I took the opportunity of refusing licences to every single publican on the field except one.

# CHAPTER XV.

MEANWHILE the work of putting up the mill got on very slowly. The A. S. N. Co.,* whose idea of handling machinery is to raise it to as great a height as possible, and then suddenly drop it, contrived to smash some of my heaviest castings in landing them on the wharf at Mackay. I had to send to Melbourne to get them replaced, and this caused a delay of several months.

Water was so scarce in the creek on which the diggings lay that I was obliged to put up the mill a mile and a half below the reef, at the junction of another creek. Even here there was so little water that I thought it was advisable to throw a dam across the creek.

Damming a Queensland mountain-creek is no joke. The violent storms which occur, and the heavy freshes that they cause in the creeks, make it necessary that any sort of dam should be remarkably solid.

The creek here was about 120 feet wide, and there was about ten feet of drift in the bottom. Of course it was necessary to cut a trench through this, right down to the bed rock, and fill it with clay, for the puddle-wall. The trench was three feet wide, and in it I sunk a

* The Australasian Steam Navigation Company, always known throughout the Colonies as the A.S.N.

double row of piles a foot thick, to support the frame of the dam above. Horizontal logs were laid against these and in between them, and this formed the centre wall of the dam. The amount of labour connected with this work was very great.

We used to keep three shifts going, night and day, at the pumps, to keep the work in the trench clear of water, and the clay for the puddle-wall had to be carted from a considerable distance. Several small freshes came down while the work was going on, and did a good deal of damage; but we managed to repair it, and at last the dam looked like being finished. I faced the front wall entirely with stone, and gave it a very big batter, to allow for the heavy floods that I knew the creek was subject to.

Had twenty-four hours more been given me to finish the work, I believe the dam would have been there to-day, and for twenty years to come. The by-wash was almost finished, and there were only a few feet more of the stone facing to be done. Those few feet, however, settled the fate of the dam. There came one of the most brilliant storms I ever saw. Queensland, at all times, can be relied upon to crowd more thunder and lightning into a minute than most countries can into an hour, and no better place for a display of the kind can be imagined than the valley of Mount Britten. It is a perfect funnel for collecting rain, about five miles across the centre, narrowing down to a few hundred yards at the mouth, where the dam across the creek was situated.

The row that a storm makes there is appalling. When once a clap of thunder is loosed off into the valley it can never get out. It slams round, cannoning up against the cliffs that surround the place, till its echoes are drowned in a fresh discharge, and so it goes on, till anyone who happens to be out in it feels as if the thunder was being manufactured in his own hat.

In ordinary countries, forked lightning descends from a storm one flash at a time, and its home invariably seems to be the earth. In Queensland lightning is slathered about as if it was of no value at all. Two or three flashes set off at the same time, and, after hunting each other about the firmament for some time, either part company and go off opposite ways, or twist themselves into a tangled knot, and discharge smaller flashes in every direction. In the background a perfectly incessant supply of sheet-lightning is kept up, which is constantly changing colour; sometimes it is white, sometimes a golden yellow, and sometimes a beautiful pale lilac, and the effect is most lovely.

The rain that accompanies these storms is sometimes terrific. I have seen as much as five inches fall in an hour. When this particular storm broke over the valley I was up at the reefs, a mile and a half above the mill.

It was about ten o'clock at night, and deadly dark; but I started off down the track at once to see how the dam would stand. Fortunately I knew every inch of the road, for a more disagreeable place for a stranger to find his way along in the dark it would be difficult to imagine. Besides the natural pit-falls in the way of rocks, logs, and gullies all down the track, the whole place was a perfect warren of old shafts that had been sunk in prospecting for gold. The mouths of them were quite open, and several of them were sunk right in the middle of the old track ; so that anyone who did not know them, and remember them, was certain to come to grief.

The track crossed the creek twice between the reefs and the mill, and when I started up in the afternoon the creek was not running at all. At the first crossing on my way back it was only ankle-deep. The next crossing was half a mile lower down ; and, though I ran all the way, by the time that I got there there was ten feet of water in the creek, running like a mill-race.

The lightning made the whole place as light as day now, and, as the crossing seemed to be clear, I soused in and got out all right at the other side. As soon as I got down to the dam, I saw at once that it was doomed. The by-wash was of no use at all to take the overflow. It had never been intended to do more than relieve the pressure, as the dam was an overshot one. But it was the few feet where the stone facing was still incomplete that ruined it. The water got a start there, and gradually ate away the whole concern like cheese ; and in six hours there was nothing left but a few piles sticking up to mark where the puddle-wall had been.

Holliman was standing watching the destruction of the work, looking the image of despair. The rain was coming down in sheets, but nothing could get him away. He looked so utterly miserable, standing on the edge of a foaming creek, with the water running in streams down his back and out of his boots, lit up every now and then by a purple streak of lightning, that I went into shrieks of laughter at him.

After a time a melancholy sort of smile stole over his face, and he allowed himself to be taken away. The water came down while some of the men were at work, and so suddenly that two of them, who attempted to save their tools, uncommonly nearly got drowned. They managed to hold on to some trees that had been left growing in the face of the dam, and stayed there till Holliman helped them out with a rope.

This settled the Mount Britten dam. It cost over £350, and would never have been any use, as from some subsequent working we found that there was an old underground course of the creek in one of the banks, through which all the water would have escaped. At the end of about eight months' patient toil, and after innumerable breakdowns and delays, the mill looked like being completed ; so I called for tenders for carting the quartz down from the reefs ready for a start. Plenty of carriers were willing to contract for the " Wanderer " stone, as there was no difficulty about the road, except in wet weather, when it was very greasy. But the " Erratic Star " was a different matter altogether.

The quartz-paddock was on the side of a mountain, and the last three hundred feet up to it was a "pinch" so steep that no one who did not know what a team of bullocks can do, would ever imagine it was possible to get to it with a waggon. At last a man called George Tucker, well known as one of the best drivers in the district, offered to try. His team of fourteen bullocks were a perfect picture. He was always very quiet with them, and very seldom used his whip, but his bullocks were marvellously obedient to the least word, and would follow him about like children. I believe they would have gone up two pair of stairs and down again without getting mixed up.

There is something wonderfully impressive about a good team of bullocks. In all their movements there is a solemn deliberation that it is most entertaining to watch. Nothing can hurry them. If you were going for the doctor you could not get three miles an hour out of a bullock team.

When the waggon gets stuck, they never plunge about, and snort, and struggle, as a team of horses do when they are called upon to do some extra pulling. They just lay themselves quietly down to their work, looking back occasionally at their driver out of their great, wise, patient eyes, as much as to say, " We're hitting out all we can, and if you swear till you burst, you can't make us pull any harder."

Each bullock has a name, which it knows perfectly. The driver gives his directions to each one separately, keeping up a running commentary of blasphemy the whole time ; and according to the amount of bad lan-guage that accompanies the use of its name, each animal knows the exact amount of exertion that is required of it. It is a beautiful sight to see a good driver straighten out a team of eighteen bullocks to fetch a waggon and five ton of a load out of a bad place. Apparently without the slightest effort, his animals just lean gently forward on the yoke ; but when once they get the pres-sure on, it is perfectly irresistible, and something is certain to happen. Either the waggon will shift, or the chains must break.

The bullock-whip with which the driver is armed is a terrible weapon in the hands of a man who knows how to use it. The lash is made of plaited greenhide about nine feet long, and is hung square on the end of a six-foot stick by way of a handle. A good·driver very seldom touches his bullocks with the whip at all, the crack of it, which is as loud as a pistol-shot, being quite sufficient to induce a well-broken team to pull their hardest.

Occasionally, however, the best driver finds it necessary to let a bullock feel the whip, and then he will do it in a way that the animal will never forget. A well-laid-on cut of the whip from the hand of a workman will lay six inches of a bullock's ribs open as clean as if it had been done with a knife. I have seen a bullock lie down and begin to bellow with terror when it got to the exact spot in a road where, months before, it had been flogged for not pulling.

Many drivers are brutally cruel to their bullocks, and are continually laying the whip into them merely to vent their own savage temper. But a good driver will always be known by the hides of his team. The marks of the whip will be scarce, but what there are will be deep and laid on in the right place. From constantly associating with his team, a bullock-driver imbibes a great deal of the lethargic nature of the animals themselves.

After crawling along the road for years beside his bullocks at the rate of a mile and a half an hour, anything approaching to hurry becomes eliminated from his nature.

There is an incurable dilatory dawdle about every movement of a man who has been a few years on the road, that will always proclaim his profession, and will stick to him ever after, whatever other line he may take up.

If you speak to a bullock-driver he will take as long

to turn his head round to look at you, as a horse-driver would to answer you, and nothing will ever induce him to get his bullocks yoked up before about ten o'clock in the day. When on the road, if he knocks eight or nine miles a day out of his team, he reckons that is very fair travelling.

George Tucker was a model specimen of his class. He was wonderfully patient with his bullocks, but he could get more work out of them than almost anyone I ever saw, and, I believe, was as fond of them as if they had been his own children. The first day that he started up to the reefs to bring the quartz down, I went with him, to see how he got on.

He got up to the "Star" paddock all right, having hitched his team on to the back of the waggon, and drawn it up backwards, as there was no room to turn at the top. Having loaded up, he prepared to start down the steep pinch again, and, in order to save the necks of his "polers," he tried to get the waggon as near the edge of the paddock as possible before locking the wheels. Relying upon the handiness and obedience of his team, he made a strange mistake for so old a hand, and had not even the brake on. In drawing on to the edge he just went a yard too far, and away went the waggon down the hill, with four ton and a half of quartz on it.

Tucker rushed after it, trying in vain to get the brake on, while the "off-sider," who was helping him, made futile attempts to keep the team straight out in front of the waggon. It was no use. For a few yards it went slowly enough, and it looked as if it might get safely to the bottom. But gradually the pace increased, the

leading bullocks stumbled and fell, bringing the others
down on top of them, and the waggon went with irresistible force right over the struggling mass of bullocks,
forging its way down the hill, till their carcases blocked
it from going any farther.

When we got down there, the team was a most heart-
rending sight. Horns, hair, and blood were strewed
about in all directions, and at first it looked as if every
bullock was dead. They were all jammed up in a dense
mass, with chains wound round them in such confusion
it was difficult to know where to begin taking them out
of winding.

By degrees we got them all clear, and found that
three were killed outright, another had its back broken,
and the two others were terribly knocked about. Nearly
every one had lost a horn, and some of them both. The
waggon, strange to say, had never even upset, and, of
course, was quite uninjured. Fortunately, Tucker had
only taken six of his bullocks up the hill, and left the
rest down below.

He took it quite quietly. The occasion was far too
solemn for any swearing ; so he helped us to light a
funeral pyre over the carcases of his dead favourites, and,
climbing on to his horse, he turned the rest of his team
out into the Bush, and went off to Grosvenor Downs,
some sixty miles away, to hunt up some fresh bullocks.
In a week he had his team in working order again, and
finished the job of drawing down the quartz without any
further misfortune.

Anyone would have thought that such an event as the
sudden death of four of his best bullocks would have
called forth a paroxysm of fury from such a habitual

DOWN-HILL WITHOUT A BRAKE

blasphemer as a bullock-driver, and made him exhaust every possible combination of oaths in his vocabulary. But in reality a great deal of the bad language which he is in the habit of using is what may be called professional swearing, and does not in the least imply loss of temper. A bullock-driver knows that his bullocks are so accustomed to hearing disgraceful language that certain words and a certain tone of voice are absolutely necessary to make them pull, and when they get in a fix he has to work himself up to a pitch of simulated fury, and use most awful expressions to induce them to exert themselves.

But while the rocks around are still resounding with oaths that make one shiver to hear, he will turn round with a cheery smile on his face to greet anyone who happens to be passing, and wipe the foam from his mouth to answer a question with the utmost good-humour. It is astonishing how a man who is apparently in the habit of getting into a violent passion upon the slightest provocation will sometimes command his temper when one would think it was impossible.

I remember perfectly well the disappointment of a large audience at finding that like causes do not always produce like results in matters pertaining to temper. A carrier was drawing sand up a very long steep hill, at the top of which there were a lot of men at work. He was a most notorious blasphemer, and his power of language was so extraordinary that everyone used to put down their tools and listen when he had a bad attack. Upon one occasion, as he was coming up the hill, the tail-board of his dray fell out without his knowing it, and, of course, all the sand ran out.

16

One of the men who was working near the top saw what had happened, and instantly attracted the attention of his mates to the impending scene. As the dray drew near the top all the men knocked off work and gradually collected around, in sure and certain hope of a more than usually lively display of profanity from the carrier.

When he got to the top he stopped and looked round. · A breathless silence prevailed whilst it gradually soaked into him what had happened. He looked at the empty dray, and at the weary long pull up the hill which he had just accomplished. Then he looked sadly and half apologetically at the expectant crowd around him, and in a tone of deep feeling observed, "Boys, I ain't equal to the occasion," and went straight off for another load.

While I was putting up the mill I had a bullock-team of my own to draw in the logs for sawing and do the work about the place. Whenever there was a slack time I used to send it down to Port Mackay for a load, but it was a horrid fraud. The bullocks were good enough, but it was impossible to get a decent man to drive them.

A man who drives his own bullocks is lazy enough, but a man who drives someone else's is simply the incarnation of idleness. I had several drivers one after the other, but it was always the same old game. When they were at home they used to swear they had lost the bullocks, having, of course, "planted" them up some obscure creek, and if they were sent on the road they always got on the spree.

I was very glad when Dick Absolon offered to take

the team off my hands, and to contract for the work about the place. I had a lot of trouble in getting sound trees for the bed-logs of my machinery. There was any amount of timber about the place, but it takes a good tree to square twenty-four inches for a length of twenty feet, because most Queensland trees, when they get to a certain size, get a pipe in the middle, and I would not stand anything that was not perfectly solid. In putting up a battery for crushing quartz it is impossible to be too careful about getting the foundations solid. Upon this everything depends. You may have the best mill, and all the most recent appliances and improvements for saving gold, but if your foundations shake you will lose a lot of gold.

Many a promising gold-field has been ruined by having bad machinery put up on it. Reefs that would have paid handsomely with good machinery are abandoned as unpayable, and the field is deserted.

In laying the foundations of my stamper-boxes, I went right down to the bed rock, with a trench twenty feet long and four feet six inches wide. In the bottom of this I laid three feet of concrete cement for the foundation of the bed-logs. The bed-logs themselves were two splendid sticks of curly red-gum, nineteen feet long, sawn square twenty-four inches by twenty-one, and bolted together with two-inch iron bolts. These were laid horizontally in the trench. Three upright piles, five feet high and twenty-four inches square, standing on the bed-logs, formed the foundation of each stamper-box. These piles were very strongly bolted together, fitted with the utmost nicety, and levelled with the accuracy of a billiard table.

Each stamper-box was a solid casting, weighing nearly a ton, about four feet long, four feet high, and fifteen inches in width.

In each box five stampers work. The stampers are raised about ten inches, and then allowed to fall, by means of a shaft which revolves overhead, which is fitted with " cams " or " wipers," which give two drops of the stamper for every revolution of the shaft. The weight of each stamper with the shank, head, shoe, and disc complete, is about eight hundredweight. They work close together in the box, and underneath each is placed a die of hematite iron, and between the bottom of this and the floor of the box itself a layer of quartz is always placed, to prevent the shock of the stamper's fall from breaking the box.

Round the boxes is placed a frame of heavy cross-logs to support the columns upon which the cam-shaft works. These logs are kept quite clear of any contact with the foundation of the boxes, so that the inevitable jar of the constant fall of the stampers may not injure the rest of the machinery. The shaft is worked by belting connected with a stationary engine, which can be instantly disconnected on to a loose pulley-wheel.

At the back of the boxes are the quartz-shoots into which the quartz is tipped out of the drays from the reefs, and broken up into pieces about the size of a man's fist. The feeder stands here with a long-handled shovel, and slings the quartz into an opening at the back of the box.

There is a good deal of art in feeding the stampers properly, and a good man will run a ton a shift more through the boxes than a duffer, with the same number of revolutions to the minute. If he feeds too slow, of course there is waste of power, and he is liable to break the dies by letting the stampers fall on to them too clean. On the other hand, if he feeds too fast he chokes them, and wastes any amount of time that way. A feeder takes a twelve hours' shift right on end, and a very monotonous occupation it is.

In the front of the box is an opening about two feet long and a foot high, fitted with gratings. The fineness of the gratings used varies according to the coarseness of the gold in the stone crushed, but from a hundred and eighty to two hundred and forty holes to the square inch are the ordinary ones. A constant stream of water is kept flowing through the boxes while the stampers are at work, and the stone is pounded up inside till it can only escape in the form of fine mud through the gratings.

From time to time a little quicksilver is thrown into the boxes, and all the coarse gold collects in the form of amalgam.

Below the boxes are the tables upon which the fine gold that escapes from the boxes is collected. These tables are sheets of copper on wooden frames, and have a slope of about half an inch to the foot. There are three sets of them, and at the end of each is what is called a quicksilver ripple, which is a solid piece of wood with three troughs cut along it, about two inches deep, each a little lower than the other, and filled nearly full of quicksilver. The copper tables themselves are faced with quicksilver, which is kept constantly bright by the use of nitric acid or cyanide of potass.

Keeping the tables and quicksilver in good order is

a science of itself, for, unless the quicksilver is lively, quantities of gold are lost.

The water flows from the boxes along the whole length of the tables, carrying with it the tailings from the boxes, and the fine gold. This last is caught by the quicksilver, and hardens on to the plates in amalgam. From time to time this is scraped off as the crushing goes on, and the tables faced again with fresh quicksilver.

The man who attends to the tables, and to the retorting and smelting of the gold, is called the " amalgamator." Good men at this trade are scarce, and will easily earn from four to six pounds a week, on a Queensland diggings. Even with the greatest care, and first-rate tables, a good deal of gold always contrives to get away. The tailings, as they are called, that have passed over the tables and run away into the waste drain, are analysed from time to time to test the waste of gold that is going on.

This process, above described, is the simplest form of crushing quartz, and is only fit for stone which contains gold in a pure form, unmixed with pyrites, galena, and other abominations that drive an amalgamator out of his mind. Where these exist, the tailings have to be separately treated, with more elaborate contrivances.

The tables lie close under the stamper-boxes, but great care is taken to keep them from actually coming into contact, for fear the jar of the stampers should interfere with them.

Holliman certainly did his work to admiration, and the mill is now reckoned to be about the best set up of any in Queensland.

Having got everything ready for a start, we fixed on a day for christening the mill, and my brother's wife came up from the station, forty miles away, to perform the ceremony. After some consideration I determined to call the mill the "Sabbath Calm." Anyone who has ever lived near a quartz mill, will see at once that the name was not altogether inappropriate. The row made by the stampers is perfectly deafening. They go on, when quartz is available, from six o'clock on Monday morning till six o'clock on Saturday night, and no one who has not been maddened by the incessant din for a whole week can thoroughly appreciate the repose that Sunday's quiet brings with it.

The christening morning broke fair over the valley of Mount Britten, and, if the sun thought anything about it at all, he must have been startled at the change which a few months had made in the wilderness. The mill itself was a most imposing sight, with its vast expanse of galvanised iron roof, and tall brick stack; and anyone who scattered a glance over the tremendously heavy machinery, fitted with all the most recent improvements, and faultlessly erected, would have found it difficult to realise that he was in the heart of the lonely mountains of Queensland, where, eighteen months before, the kangaroos and wallabies had had it all to themselves.

All the men who were working for me had a holiday in honour of the occasion, and all who were not gave themselves one, so that the whole population of the diggings assembled to see the start. They had all treated themselves to a wash in the creek, and everyone who could had fossicked out a clean shirt and a flash-

coloured silk handkerchief as a tribute of respect to the
important day.

The old doctor was in splendid form.  He had been
saving himself up for the occasion for ever so long, and,
I believe, had drunk nothing for a week on purpose to
enjoy himself all the more.  In his excitement he had
forgotten the wash in the creek, but he had climbed into
an old pith helmet and a faded blue coat, which made
him look far more disreputable than he did in his working clothes.  He drank enough for four without ever
turning a hair, and never stopped talking and laughing
from sunrise to sundown.

Holliman surveyed his own completed work with perfect satisfaction, and without a particle of anxiety as to
the working of the machinery in the approaching trial.
He had the confidence of a real artist in his own performance, and, knowing that it had all been done in the
best possible way, he had not a doubt about the result.
The amalgamating table was turned into a bar, and one
of the men told off as barman, with orders to give everyone anything they wanted as long as the liquor held out.
He had a couple of buckets full of rum, with a pannikin
to ladle it out, and an enormous army of bottles of beer,
porter, brandy, and whisky.

A bottle of brandy decorated with streamers of red,
white, and blue ribbon was hung from the roof, opposite
the fly-wheel.  Punctually, at 12 o'clock, my brother's
wife advanced, amid a solemn silence, and grasped the
bottle.  Holliman looked at me as much as to say,
" I 've done my part of the business, now you can start
yours."

The steam was on, so I jammed down the lever.

Slowly and smoothly the vast fly-wheel began to revolve ; the bottle, discharged with unerring precision, was dashed to pieces against it ; and the " Sabbath Calm " was fairly started, amid wild cheers from the assembled crowd. The old doctor nearly went mad with delight. He flung his old helmet into the air, and, waving his third pannikin of rum round his head, was about to give vent to the discordant bellow by which a German endeavours to imitate a British cheer, when he overbalanced himself and fell backwards into an enormous tailing-tub full of water. Far from discouraging him, this catastrophe seemed to delight him immensely. He was extricated, perfectly good-humoured and cheerful, and, having called for another pannikin of rum, he insisted on making a speech, to which no one listened, all hands being busily engaged in drinking success to the new mill.

# CHAPTER XVI

We had 98 tons of quartz to go through from the Erratic Star, and 185 tons from the Wanderer; and there was great excitement all over the field to know the result of the first crushing; for upon the success of a first crushing depends, in a great measure, the fate of a gold-field.

Until you get used to the appearance of the stone you are working, it is very difficult to form an estimate beforehand of the yield. There was the greatest divergence of opinion as to the Wanderer stone, in which coarse gold showed freely, and wagers were laid that it would go anything up to twenty ounces to the ton.

Gibbard and I knew better, and we decided that we should be very pleased if it went four ounces. After the stampers had been at work a few hours the amalgam began to show on the distributing plate, as the table next below the boxes is called. This was a good sign, as we had not expected to find very much fine gold in the stone.

There was no particular hurry, so we put the stone through slowly, in order to give it every chance. If the stone is pretty clean, ten head of stamps will crush about a ton an hour; but we only put through about sixteen hundredweight. I used to take the night shift of twelve hours, driving the engine and firing-up. This last is pretty hard work, when round logs with the bark on are used for fire-wood. Iron-bark wood burns perfectly well when quite green, and a log a foot through and five feet long requires a little handling to plant it scientifically in a furnace without wasting any heat. The share-holders in a claim always take turns to watch the boxes and tables when a good crushing is going through, and never leave their post for an instant. Nothing is easier than for anyone working about the tables to remove some of the amalgam, and retort it at his leisure; and in order to prevent this there is always a shareholder on guard. Charlie Gibbard used to watch all night, armed with a revolver, and in the intervals of firing-up I used to sit and yarn and smoke with him, and speculate on the result of the crushing.

We went on crushing for eighteen days and nights, with Sundays interval, and at the end of that time the whole of the stone was through. We had collected about one hundred ounces of amalgam off the plates, which would yield about thirty-five ounces of gold; but the important part of the plunder was, of course, inside the boxes.

When we opened them a very healthy sight was there. In the corners of the boxes the amalgam was piled like snow collects in the corners of a window-pane, and we saw at once that the crushing was fully as good as we had expected. The whole contents of the boxes were raked carefully out, and run through a sluice-box, to separate the amalgam from the quartz.

The amalgam thus collected was mixed with that

already taken from the tables, and with the quicksilver from the ripples, and the whole of it strained through a piece of strong brown-holland. The free quicksilver passes through this, leaving the amalgam behind, which is then retorted. The process of retorting is very simple. The amalgam is placed in an iron pot, fitted with a lid which is wedged on very tight, the joint being made up with a compound of ashes and clay. On the top of the lid is a long curved iron pipe. The retort is placed over a fire, and as it gets hot the quicksilver ascends in fumes into the iron pipe, over the lower portion of which a stream of cold water is kept constantly flowing. The quicksilver is condensed again, and flows down the pipe into a bucket placed at the end to receive it.

Quicksilver can be used over and over again in this way, and not above seven or eight per cent. is lost in the retorting. Just after it has been retorted it is in the best possible order for amalgamating purposes. We got 1,650 ounces of amalgam from the 185 tons of stone.

As a rule, amalgam does not retort more than a third of its own weight in gold, but the Wanderer gold was so coarse that we hoped for a much higher percentage. The event proved we were right, for the amalgam gave us 870 ounces of retorted gold. We had used two retorts, in order that the gold might be more conveniently packed for travelling, and it was turned out in two cakes about the size and shape of a beef-steak pudding. Retorted gold is curious-looking stuff, all porous and honeycombed where the quicksilver has left it.

This gave an average yield of 4 oz. 14 dwt. to the ton, which was very satisfactory, as it paid all the back expenses of the reef, and, after paying the mill 30s. a ton for crushing, left a very good dividend.

My brother, who was half shares with me in the mill and the reef too, came up just before the end of the crushing to help me bring the gold down to the bank in Mackay. Towards the last we had been running the stone from the Erratic Star through one of the batteries, and we cleaned up shortly after the Wanderer. The Erratic Star turned out a fraud. We had only run the pick of the stone through, and 98 tons only gave us 102 ounces of gold.

It was midday when we finished retorting, and my brother and I lost no time in getting ready for a start. We wrapped the gold up carefully in canvas, and then put it into two boxes, one of which we stowed away on each side of a pack-horse in leathern pack-bags.

Gibbard came with us, and the three of us formed the first gold escort that ever left Mount Britten. We had a revolver apiece, in case of being stuck up on the road. Our own horses were good enough, but we had rather misgivings about the pack-horse, which was an old crow-bait my brother had chartered from the station for the purpose of bringing down the gold.

The station was forty miles away, and we intended to get a feed and a change of horses there, and go on to Mackay the same night. For the first eighteen miles out of the diggings it was lovely travelling, over the downs country, without a stone or a ridge to stop one. But we made the pace rather too rough for the old pack-horse, and when we got to Nebo Creek, twenty-two miles from Mount Spencer, he knocked up. My brother was a little way on ahead, and I sung out to him to stop.

"Hi, Sammy! this dying old hair-trunk is about bust. We'll have to go steady or he'll camp altogether."

"Camp!" said my brother; "no fear. He's only blown; he was all right when we started, and he simply *can't* have bust on seventeen miles. Here, let me get behind him with a stick, and see if we can't scare a trot out of him."

So far from raising a trot, neither threats nor persuasion could induce him to walk, and it was evident we should have to leave him.

"Deuce take the old brute for going back on us like this," I said; "what are we going to do?"

"Why, walk, of course," said my brother. "We can't sling the plunder, and we certainly ain't going to camp here."

Walk! The day was sweltering hot, we were twenty-two miles from home, and the way lay over a succession of fiendish dry stony bare ridges. No one who has not been in the country can form any conception of the violent aversion which an Australian has to walking a yard, if he can help it. It is an old saying that an Australian will walk a mile to catch a horse to ride half a mile, and there is a great deal of truth in it. In this instance there was nothing else for it. We were particularly anxious to get to Mackay the following morning early, and, of course, could not dream of parting with the gold for an instant.

Charlie offered to lend us his horse to pack the gold on, and walk home, but we would not hear of it, so we decided to pack the gold on one of our horses and take turns to run alongside. My brother took the first spell on foot, and accomplished three miles and a half over the ridges in excellent time. We managed to do the twenty-two miles in three hours and a half, which was very fair travelling considering the road and the weather.

When we got to the station it was dark, but the moon got up soon after, and we sent the black boy out to run up some fresh horses. Having had a feed and a smoke, we lay down and had a sleep, and about 1 o'clock in the morning started again on our journey down to Mackay, forty-five miles away. This time we took care to select a reliable pack-horse, and we got safely to Mackay about 8 in the morning. As soon as the bank opened, we took the gold round there. Great was the astonishment of everyone in Mackay when they saw the quantity of gold that we had brought down. The townspeople had never taken any interest in Mount Britten beyond trying to put me to all the inconvenience that they could in connection with my work there, and the first crushing had been such a long while coming they had all come to the conclusion that Mount Britten was a "duffer," and that there was no gold there at all.

The manager of the bank especially had always had a great edge on the diggings, and been very active in circulating reports that it was a failure. His jaw dropped like a motherless calf's when he saw nearly one thousand ounces of gold produced at the first start, and he barely retained sufficient presence of mind to offer me his congratulations, which I accepted for what they were worth, as I had not forgotten his flying visit to Mount Britten, and his subsequent report of the field. My brother and I finished what we had to do as quickly as possible, and got back to the station the same night.

I was back again at Mount Britten the next day at midday, and started to get down another crushing from the reefs as quickly as possible.

From the "Wanderer" the next crushing turned out over six ounces to the ton, and the one after that between seven and eight ounces; and still the reef looked splendid. But another hundred tons from the Star only gave a hundred ounces, and the reef got so poor after that, that it was no longer payable.

As a speculation the mill itself did not pay, as there was not nearly enough stone to keep it going.

There were some other very nice reefs opened up, but there was no capital available to work them, and they remained idle. I soon saw that to look after the mines properly I should have to give up my whole time to it, and make a profession of mining. This I was unwilling to do, so my brother and I agreed to try and float the whole property, comprising the Wanderer and Star Reefs and Sabbath Calm Mill into a company down in Melbourne.

Having obtained offers of the other shareholders' shares for a certain time, I left Holliman in charge of the whole swim, and, armed with specimens from the different reefs, and authentic reports of the crushings, I set off down to Melbourne.

I was very sorry to leave Mount Britten. Certainly the two happiest years of my life were spent there, and I knew very well that if I ever revisited it, it would not be to live there. In the intervals of working, and on Sundays, I had contrived to finish a very comfortable little house for myself on the opposite side of the creek from the mill, and there I had been living for some months. It was all built of Bush stuff; but I dressed it all myself, and put it up very carefully. The slabs were adzed as smooth as glass inside, laid horizontal, and bevilled and fitted with the utmost nicety. I bestowed infinite pains upon the roof, which was shingles; and the whole, when finished, was as weathertight as a bottle.

It was twenty-four feet long and twelve feet wide, the whole of one end being blocked up by an enormous fire-place seven feet square inside. I always believe in a big fire-place. On a cold winter's night you can get right in and sit at the side of the fire, and it is a first-rate place to hang clothes up to dry, and also to smoke beef in.

There was plenty of waste timber of all sorts from the mill, so I had no lack of material for doors, windows tables, shelves, and other fixings. The floor was tongue and groove pine, which is a great luxury in the Bush, as it is always dry, and easily kept clean. In one corner was a bed; but I always kept it for visitors, as I infinitely prefer the floor to sleep on. Anyone who has once acquired the habit of sleeping on the floor or on hard ground will always wake up much fresher, and feeling more rested, than if he takes to sleeping in a bed again.

17

A well-lined book-shelf and an enormous clock adorned the walls on one side; on the other were rows of shelves filled with pickles, jam, soap, matches, and other stores. The corner opposite the bed was turned into an office, fitted up with innumerable pigeon-holes, shelves of account-books, and a table with a copying-press, and writing material of every description.

One or two butter-tubs to sit on, a huge arm-chair near the fire-place, a meat-safe, and a cupboard full of tobacco, completed the furniture of the establishment.

All the time that I was in the Bush I made it my boast that although I might occasionally be found very indifferently clad, and sometimes very short of rations, I never was without a supply of excellent tobacco.

I had gone over the creek for a site for my hut, in the first place, to be away from the clatter of the mill, and, in the second place, because it was the most perfect situation for a house that could be imagined. Just at the junction of two running creeks, there was a never-failing supply of excellent water; and the soil, being the old bed of the creek, was all made ground, and admirably suited for a garden, which I intended to have had, if I had remained there any time. The bed of the creek was full of timber, she-oaks, fig-trees, and Leichardt; and just opposite to my hut was a gigantic old flooded gum, with huge, spreading branches and a trunk at least forty feet round.

She-oaks are scraggy-looking poles of trees, rather like fir-trees; but both fig-trees and Leichardt are very handsome, and give a splendid shade. The latter is a very symmetrical tree, that grows to a height of about sixty feet, and has leaves rather like a big laurel.

Behind my hut towered the three mountains known as the Marling-Spikes; and a gap which I cut in the timber on the banks of the creek, gave me a beautiful view right up to the head of the valley of Mount Britten.

At the back of my hut I put up a bark building, which served for a carpenter's shop, and a kitchen, and beyond that was a small paddock with a sapling fence, into which I could turn my horses for the night. This was a great convenience. There was no paddock within four miles of Mount Britten, and, for some reason or other, no horse, even in hobbles, would ever stay a moment near the place. It is said that the grass in localities where minerals are found is always sour. Anyway, no cattle or horses would ever stay near the diggings, though the grass looked good enough.

I often used to get home in the middle of the night, and was always losing my horses, until I put up a paddock. When I first got to the diggings I brought four horses with me, and a black boy to look after them. They all cleared out the first night. I sent the black boy after them, but he was frightened of the other blacks, and went and planted instead of looking for them. I was lame myself, at the time, and could not go out after them, but I got two of them back at the end of a fortnight. The other two broke their hobbles, and I never saw them again for nearly a year, when they turned up on a station about a hundred miles off, as fat as pigs.

On Sundays I used generally to have a good many visitors after my hut was finished. It is said that there is no Sunday in the Bush, and certainly it does not

17 *

mean much of a day of rest to a man who lives quite by himself, and works hard all the week. Sunday is always the day for a general overhaul and repairs. Clothes are washed and mended, the hut cleared and swept out, and a supply of firewood laid in for the coming week; and a man who is away at work every day of the week, from sunrise to sundown, will always find that a dozen little jobs will accumulate in the week, which can only be done on Sunday. I had very little time for cooking in the week, and it was always an occupation I disliked, so I used to do most of the week's cooking on Sunday.

After the diggings had been open some time, the butcher used to kill a bullock nearly every day, and there was always fresh meat to be had. But the butcher's shop was nearly a mile away from my house, and, besides, I never would touch fresh meat as long as I could get salt. So on Sunday I used to boil twelve or fourteen pounds of salt beef, and bake a damper about the size of a small cart-wheel; and this used to last me, unless the beef went bad, until about Thursday. After which I used to get some fresh meat, or boil some more salt if I had time, until the next Sunday. Salt beef wants a lot of attention when it is boiling, for if the water boils too fast it turns as hard as a stone, and if it stops boiling it gets sodden.

My hut, being three quarters of a mile away from the township, possessed the great advantage of being perfectly quiet, and free from any disturbance of nocturnal revellers. From sundown to sunrise I never used to see a soul, or hear a sound except when the mill was at work. It was rather a lonely place, too, at night, when the wind was howling among the mountains, and the rain coming down in sheets, and the creek foaming and roaring bank-high before the door. Often I have gone up to the township after dark to get a supply of food, and had to swim the creek on the way home, with my supper in the form of a beef-steak in my mouth ; and when I got home found the fire out, and nothing but a poisonous black spider sitting on the table to welcome me. But anyone who knocks about the Bush for a time, ceases to care a farthing whether he is wet or dry as long as the weather is warm ; and as for being lonely, he soon comes to regard his own company, with a fire and a pipe, as quite sufficient.

As a speculation my mining had not been a success.

During the time that I was working the Mount Britten reefs, the receipts and expenditure were as follows :—

" Little Wanderer."

| | | |
|---|---|---|
| Gross expenses . | . | £4,967 18 5 |
| Gold sold . | . | £8,689 1 2 |

This left a balance of £3,721 2s. 9d. in favour of the claim.

" Erratic Star."

| | |
|---|---|
| Gross expenses | £2,275 5 10 |
| Gold sold . | £688 19 1 |
| | ———————— |
| Leaving a deficit of . | £1,586 6 9 |

The " Sabbath Calm " machine cost about £9,000, against which it received £1,050 from the reefs for crushing stone.

The first cost of opening up a reef is always very great, and it is doubly so, of course, upon a new field.

Wages at Mount Britten were very high, ordinary miners getting £3 a week; carpenters, sawyers and bricklayers from £4 10s. to £6.

The cost of carriage to Mackay was £15 per ton at first, but it afterwards fell to £8, at which figure it remained. My bill for carriage alone was over £600.

Had either the " Star " or the " Wanderer " continued for a year longer as good as they proved at first, we should have made a small fortune out of either of them, and the mill would have paid well as a separate speculation. On a new field where crushing is charged for at the rate of 30s. or £2 a ton, the profits from a mill that can get sufficient stone to keep it constantly going are enormous.

Ten head of stampers will put through 120 tons a week with ease. At 30s. per ton this gives a return of £180 a week. The whole cost of driving a mill, including wages, fire-wood, quicksilver and repairs, and allowing 7 per cent. per annum for depreciation in value of the plant, should not exceed £55 a week, even on a new field where wages and carriage are high. This leaves a clear profit of £125 a week, or £6,500 a year.

When we decided to try and float a company to work the reef the Wanderer was in full swing, and turning out seven ounces to the ton. But I know very well that all Queensland reefs are what is called " patchy." The gold runs in " levels " and " shoots," and is seldom evenly distributed throughout the whole line of reef, as is the case in Victoria. Consequently, anyone working a Queensland reef is liable at any moment to come upon a perfectly blank patch of stone; and the expenses of working through this, and looking for another level of gold are far too heavy to be borne by a single individual.

The " Wanderer " was what is called a first-rate show; that is to say, the surrounding country, the formation of the reef, the work done and the yields already obtained, gave every indication of its being permanent reef carrying heavy gold. More than this no one can ever say. The extraordinary vagaries of gold, especially in Queensland reefs, make mining the purest gambling, and any practical miner who has been long at his trade comes to disbelieve entirely in the " nostrums " of theoretical geologists and scientific miners for discovering gold, and subscribes to the Cornishman's maxim of " Where it be, there it be."

When a man has been working a particular reef for a length of time, he may come to know from certain indications in the stone that he is in the neighbourhood of a heavy patch of gold ; but on a new field, where the character of the country remains still untried, no man can see further than the point of his own pick. Indications that on one field point with almost an absolute certainty to the vicinity of gold, may mean nothing at all on a field fifty miles away.

For instance, on Gympie the presence of black slate is invariably accompanied by rich deposits of gold in the adjacent reef. When a claim strikes black slate, the shareholders go about the streets brandishing samples of it, and the shares go up just as if they had struck gold.

There is certainly some mysterious affinity between gold and black slate on Gympie. I have seen a reef there, in black-slate country, carrying heavy gold all

along, until a thin vein of grey rock came between the
reef and the slate. At the exact spot where this happened the reef became perfectly blank, and not a colour
of gold was seen until the grey rock was cut out, and
the reef touched the slate again, when it carried as
heavy gold as ever.

On Mount Britten the presence of black slate meant
apparently nothing at all. There was no slate in the
vicinity of the " Wanderer " at all, and the " Star " lost
her gold at a depth of ninety feet, just when she got
into the most magnificent black-slate country I ever saw.

Again, on Charters Towers, when mundic is struck
in a claim, the fortune of everyone connected with it
is considered to be made ; but on Ravenswood, sixty
miles away, if they strike mundic they shut up the claim
at once, for the Ravenswood mundic has hitherto proved
too much for any appliances available in Australia for
extracting the gold from it.

The Gympie reefs are very patchy, and some of them
are marvellously rich. I never saw a more wonderful
sight than a " patch " in No. 2 North Lady Mary claim.
The reef, which was about eight inches thick, was of
milk-white quartz, in slate country as black as coal ; and
as I stood back and held a candle over my head, the
whole face of the reef, eight feet high, was literally
blazing with gold. It was sticking out in bright, glittering masses, and even the slate walls of the reef were
thickly spotted over with the precious metal.

Gold, when it is first broken down in a reef, bears no
sort of resemblance to the dull-coloured compound that
is worked up into jewellery and the coin of the realm.
It is about the colour of brass, or rock sulphur, and

breaks into crystal cubes which glitter and shine with dazzling brilliancy.

This patch in the Lady Mary yielded 1,470 ounces from twenty tons of quartz. About the best paying claim on Gympie, when I was there, was the No. 1 North Phœnix. A party of men had bought it about ten months before, for £100, and were considered to be perfect fools for their pains. However, they set to work and sunk a shaft 320 feet, and struck the reef carrying heavy gold.

While I was there they crushed 700 tons for an average yield of over eleven ounces to the ton. In eighteen months the claim had paid over £100,000 in dividends, and the share-holders refused an offer of £150,000 for the claim from a Sydney syndicate. The shares, of which there were 24,000 in the original company, were selling at £7 10s. and £8.

In Victoria some of the big reefs there can pay a dividend with a yield of four pennyweights to the ton; but in Queensland the reefs are smaller as a rule, and it is seldom that anything less than one ounce to the ton pays well. Were more capital available, this would not be the case; and there is no doubt that in the future great numbers of Queensland reefs that have been abandoued will be taken up and worked again profitably.

Gold-mining in Queensland is still in its infancy. The best geologists declared that no gold would ever be found on Gympie below the second bed of slate, but a few enthusiasts persisted in going down to see for themselves, and experience proved that the surface-gold that had been obtained was insignificant compared with the yield below the second and third beds of slate.

So far, the rule seems to be that the deeper you go the more gold you get; but the deepest working in Queensland is only 600 feet, which is mere scratching compared to some of the southern workings, which are down nearly 3,000 feet  The ordinary history of a Queensland gold-field is this, and it is repeated with monotonous regularity :—First of all, alluvial gold is discovered, which brings a rush to the place.  Reefs are discovered, the surface of some of them proves tremendously rich; a second reefing rush sets in, and the surface levels of gold are worked out, with a very small outlay of capital.  The place is then declared to be a "duffer," and abandoned, except by a few fanatics, who stick there for months and years, and by incredible patience and perseverance manage to strike a fresh level of gold at a greater depth.  This brings capital to the field, the reefs are opened up and worked systematically, and the place becomes a permanent gold-field.

Up to the present time Gympie, Charters Towers, the Etheridge, and the Hodgkinson are the only diggings that have passed through the transition changes, and assumed a permanent aspect.  Of these Charters Towers is far the best, and Gympie the next, but the other two are developing quickly.  But all through Queensland, inside the coast range, runs a vast belt of gold-bearing quartz, and innumerable diggings have been discovered, from which heavy surface yields were obtained, but which have been partly deserted for want of capital to develop them.

Mount Wheeler, Clermont, the Cape River, the Normanby, the Mulgrave, Ravenswood, Cloncurry, and the Palmer have all as good prospects as ever Gympie or

THE END OF A GOLD RUSH.

Charters Towers had, but they are at present in a state of suspended animation, waiting for capital to work their lower levels. Of these Ravenswood and the Palmer are the most promising. On the Palmer the richness of the reefs is beyond dispute, and it is simply the heavy expense of keeping down the water in the claims that prevents their being worked. On Ravenswood the prospects are still better. The only difficulty to contend with there is the complicated nature of the mundic in which the gold is found. The richness of the stone is surprising, and the samples of mundic which have been sent home to Swansea to be treated yield as high as twenty ounces to the ton.

Undoubtedly in the future the gold-mining of Queensland will develop into vast dimensions, and already it has contributed largely to the prosperity of the colony. Gympie broke out at a time when the Queensland exchequer was nearly empty, and the revival that took place was undoubtedly due entirely to the discovery of gold.

The annual yield of Gympie is now nearly 100,000 ounces, and that of Charters Towers is considerably over. In 1879 the estimated value of gold produced throughout the colony was £1,010,000, but since then a large increase has taken place. The Day Dawn claim on Charters Towers is about the best claim in Queensland at the present time. Four or five separate companies were ruined in trying to make her pay, but in 1881 a party of four or five Germans struck gold there. In eighteen months they had taken £135,000 out of the claim, and apparently were only just beginning to find out what it was worth, for when last I heard of them, in July 1883, they had a reef nineteen feet thick crushing regularly three ounces to the ton.

By far the greater portion of gold raised in Queensland up to the present time has been got by parties of working men, who have just gone down as deep as they could without winding machinery, and then slung the claim, having perhaps been flooded out, or come upon a blank patch of stone.  Scores of reefs are now lying idle in Queensland from which tremendous yields were obtained near the surface, but which have been abandoned for want of capital.  It is only very lately that it has been considered worth while to erect winding gear, and work the reefs at a depth, but the results have been so eminently satisfactory that a vast increase in the annual yield of gold may be looked for during the next few years.

Besides this, fresh fields are constantly being discovered.  The Government offers a reward of £1,000 to anyone who discovers a gold-field upon which, six months after it is opened, there shall be upwards of two hundred men at work ; and though experience shows that they avail themselves of every possible technical or legal quibble to cheat the prospector out of his reward, the pursuit of gold is quite sufficient to keep up a constant supply of prospectors, without any other inducement.  Money may be the root of all evil, but, if so, it is like the root of a potato, the best part of it, and the Government need not trouble themselves to offer rewards for the discovery of gold.

They would do very much more to advance the good of the colony if they were to prospect the lower levels of the fields already discovered, by means of a diamond drill, at the public expense. Gold is of all mistresses the most exacting, and as long as it maintains its market value there will always be plenty of people to look for it. Experience proves that gold-mining, as a rule, does not pay, but the pursuit of gold is indeed the triumph of hope over experience. When once a man takes to it he is unfit for anything else, and, whether it make or mar him, he will pursue it to the end of the chapter. The noble army of mining martyrs stick steadily to their post, and the gaps that time and ruin make in their ranks are quickly filled up by an ever-increasing supply of recruits.

> Servitus crescit nova, nec priores
> Impiæ tectum dominæ relinquunt
> Sæpe minati.

# CHAPTER XVII.

QUEENSLAND dates her existence from the year 1859, when she was separated from New South Wales, and she is, therefore, the youngest of the Australian group of colonies. But her vast area, almost the whole of which is available, her varied climate, and the lavish manner in which Nature has bestowed upon her all the resources that go to make a country great, foretell, with certainty, that she will before long assume the leading position among her sisters, and eventually develop into one of the finest countries in the world.

The area of Queensland is 668,224 square miles, rather more than five and a half times the area of the United Kingdom, and the whole population in 1882 was only 248,255

All along the coast runs a broad belt of mountainous country, entirely covered with forest. The timber becomes thicker and thicker towards the tops of the mountains, the higher ones being overgrown with dense impenetrable "scrub," while the slopes and valleys between are open timber, with long grass growing everywhere amongst the trees.

Between the foot of the coast range and the sea is a

tract of level country, varying from sixty to a few miles in width, in which are situated large areas of the finest alluvial soil, suitable, in the southern parts of the colony, for the growth of all the fruits and cereals of a temperate climate, and, in the central and northern districts, for the cultivation of cotton, coffee, tobacco, sugar, and all the products of the tropics.

The whole of the coast country is well watered, and is not subject to the severe droughts which occasionally visit the interior. The mountains, of course, attract rain, and the valleys between form natural reservoirs, in the shape of chains of water-holes and big lagoons and, especially on the eastern slopes, innumerable creeks rise in the ranges, and find their way down to the sea.

One of the most extraordinary features of the coast country is the vast quantity of timber that grows everywhere. It is positively bewildering to think of the thousands of square miles that are covered with endless trees. The most common varieties are the blue, red, and spotted gum, iron-bark, stringy-bark, and blood-wood, all of which are admirably adapted for fencing and building purposes, as they are easily split and sawn, possess a very high breaking strain, and, when protected from the weather and the attacks of white ants, are perfectly imperishable. Even when standing in the ground, and exposed to the weather, they are good for fifteen or twenty years.

Of course, away in the Bush, the ravages of bush-fires and white ants make havoc among the fences ; but I have seen a stringy-bark sap-paling that had been twelve years in the ground, and when I took it up it was so sound that I made it into axe-handles.

Besides these varieties, on the eastern face of the coast range are pine, red cedar, and beech, and, on the western slopes, rose-wood, myall, dead-finish, plum-tree, iron-wood, and sandal-wood, all woods with a fine grain suitable for cabinet-making and fancy work. With the exception of cedar and pine, large quantities of which are exported every year, these woods are of little value at present, and on the Queensland lines of railway sandal-wood is used as fuel, the quantity of heat which it gives out being greater than that of any other wood in the colony. It is an inferior kind of sandal-wood, but still it contains a great quantity of oil.

The scrubs of Northern Queensland are full of different sorts of hard-wood, with most beautiful variegated grains, admirable for veneering; but at present their inaccessible position prevents their attracting the attention that they undoubtedly will when the country is more opened up. A visit to the Queensland gallery in the South Kensington Museum will give some idea of the beautiful quality of her different woods, but nothing but a visit to the colony can give any idea of the quantity.

The extent and richness of the mineral districts of Queensland are almost fabulous; and although the accounts of experts and others of what they have seen may, at first, appear incredible, experience proves every day that they fall short of the reality, and that the extraordinary wealth of the colony in metals is comparatively unexplored.

The recent crushings on Gympie gold-field read more like a fairy-tale than anything else, and when the report of them appeared in the papers everyone in the colony thought it was a misprint. One line of reef there lately took 500 tons of quartz out of a shaft that they were sinking, which averaged 20 ozs. of gold to the ton, and, on another line, a crushing of 53 tons gave the astounding yield of 2,534 ozs. In nine months, over £82,000 in dividends was paid by the latter claim.

Startling, however, as these returns undoubtedly are, they are entirely thrown into the shade by the recent discovery of gold at Mount Morgan, in the neigbourhood of Rockhampton.

The following is an account of the mine, taken from· the Charters Towers *Mining Journal* for September 1884.

" Situated about twenty-five miles south-east of Rockhampton, on one of the branches of the Dee river, it seems to be a portion of a large basin in the hills. It rises out of granite, and is from 400 to 500 feet high from the site of the crushing mill, half a mile distant on the creek, where an abundance of water may be conserved. The property consists of 640 acres of freehold.

" The gold-bearing stone is composed of ferrugineous quartz and ironstone, some of it having the appearance of 'clinkers' from a blacksmith's forge. The lodes, which seem to be parallel, run north and south. They are from 40 to 100 feet wide, and are very puzzling to most visitors. In some places they are quartz, in others porous ironstone, and in others there are cavities containing stalactites of black oxidised iron. Some portions are very much richer than others. Gold of a very fine grain is easily seen in the quartz, where it is not much oxidised, and, when prospected, it is apparently free.

18

"One lode now working is 40 feet wide, and another 100 feet wide in the face, and about 70 or 80 feet from the crown of the hill, and about 100 feet below this there is another face of similar stone, on the same quarry-like lodes.

"In these faces gold is always obtained from the drillings. By the present appliances, which are totally inadequate, the yield of gold is from 10 dwts. to 3 ozs. to the ton. Owing to the heavy nature of the ironstone quartz there is great loss in the 'tailings,' all of which and the sludge are being saved. Five assays from the 'tailings' give over 4 ozs. to the ton, and the 'blanketings,' after being put through the wheeler's pan, and the Berdan, and concentrated in the shoot, assay as high as 90 ozs. of gold to the ton. Taking it for granted that this statement is correct about the tailings, if the gold can be got out of the stone it will yield 5 ozs. of gold to the ton, and the top lode alone is estimated to contain 450,000 tons.

"According to Dr. Liebius, M.A., F.C.S., the gold from this mine is worth £4 4s. 8d. per ounce, assaying as high as 99·7 per cent. of gold, and is free from silver. The cost of production is remarkably low. It is said that 3 dwts. of gold to the ton pays for breaking, carting, and crushing. The formation cannot be called a reef. The whole hill-top seems to be of richly auriferous stone. It is merely cut away to suit the convenience of the miners, so that a broad quarry, or terrace, has been formed. The cutting is 20 feet deep and about 100 feet long ; the stone is of the same character the whole distance, and extends to the summit of the mountain, several chains higher.

" With reference to the statement that only one half
of the gold is extracted in the ordinary quartz-crushing
and amalgamating machinery, Dr. Liebius says :—

" ' Having the small quartz-crushing machinery in the
Sydney mint under my charge, I had an opportunity
of testing this fact. In November last we received
458 lbs. of this ferrugineous quartz, part of it consisting
of picked stone. It was carefully crushed, and amalga-
mated in the Chilian mill with 240 lbs. of mercury.
Thus 7·41 ozs. of gold were extracted. Another lot,
weighing 174 lbs., was similarly treated, and from this
12·12 ozs. of gold were extracted. Thus Lot 1 gave
at the rate of over 39 ozs. of gold to the ton of quartz,
while Lot 2 gave gold at the rate of over 169 ozs. of
gold to the ton of quartz. In Lot 1 gold at the rate of
46 ozs. 2 dwts. 12 grs. was left in the tailings, while in
Lot 2 the tailings averaged 46 ozs. 5 dwts. 18 grs. of
gold to the ton.'

" This discovery of gold is the largest, and richest in
quality, ever yet made in any part of the world. A
ninth share in the property lately sold for £31,000 (the
purchaser being one of the remaining shareholders), a
price very much below its value. Provided the owners of
the mine can extract the gold from the stone, and there
is no reasonable doubt of their being able to do so, the
top lode alone should yield over £9,000,000 of profit.

" It may be that this mine is unique of its kind, but
there is always a very great likelihood that where there
is one there are others. Its development will give a
great stimulus to prospecting, not only in the neighbourhood of Rockhampton, but throughout the whole
of Queensland. It discloses what prizes this colony,

almost unknown as yet, offers. It is barely two years
since the property was purchased from the Morgans ;
and had they held on to their interests, they would soon
have become millionaires. As it is, they have in a very
short space of time retired with large fortunes. It is
left for their successors to draw in the future wealth
from the mine beyond the wildest dreams of avarice."

Besides gold, the country is wonderfully rich in other
metals ; the chief of which are copper, iron, tin, silver,
cinnabar, lead, and antimony. The deposits of copper
are especially remarkable. The mines are but little
worked at present, since the price of copper fell to £60
per ton, and the total amount exported in 1882 was
only £650.

But formerly, when copper was worth £90 per ton,
the profits from the mines were very great. Peak Downs
copper-mine, the principal one in the colony, has paid
over £1,000,000 in dividends, and, so far from its being
worked out, it is the opinion of experts, and those who
worked in the mines, that there is as much copper there
as ever came out. The mines are not working at
present—a circumstance due principally to the greediness of the share-holders, who thought of nothing but
their dividends, and omitted to open up the mines ahead
of the work.

As an instance of how the work has been mis-
managed, an engine shaft twelve feet square was sunk
to a depth of 150 feet, which cut the lode they were
looking for, eighteen feet from the surface, without
the manager ever detecting it.

The reports of experts who have visited the copper-
lodes of the north, show that the resources of the colony

in this respect are unlimited. The following account, by Mr. Sheaffe, of the Mackinlay ranges, and the Cloncurry copper-mines, in the *Queenslander* of August 9th 1880, is well worthy of notice. He writes:

" The Mackinlay ranges, teeming with an extraordinary wealth of minerals, are flanked for nearly 200 miles by high undulating downs of exceeding fertility; so that on the one hand you have almost boundless pasture, and upon the other almost inexhaustible mines. That I am justified in speaking of these mines as almost inexhaustible, I shall proceed to show. The first known copper-mines approached by this route are the Mountain Home, the Rio Grande, and the West Briton, of which Mr. W. Wellington, who was sent to England by Messrs. Bolitho and Sons, reported as follows:

" ' The principal lode is at Mount Norma, a well-defined lode, varying from three to six feet wide, running north and south, and dipping to the east. It stands in the face of an almost perpendicular mountain, showing from 400 to 500 yards. The ore is principally grey, of the following per-centage, namely, thirty-four. The Rio Grand lodes consist of two, running parallel, with a distance of 250 yards between them. The out-crops show very distinctly on both these lodes for about 300 or 400 yards in length, consisting of red oxide and grey ores, of the following per-centage, namely, forty-four. The West Briton, also running north and south, is about a mile north-east of the Mountain Home, showing a large lode from six feet to eight feet wide, chiefly red oxide and grey ore, of the following per-centage, namely, thirty-eight. These lodes appear to be well defined and regular, all running north and south, and dipping to the east. The cost of working these lodes would be very little for some time to come, in consequence of the ore being so near the surface.'

" The line, after leaving these mines, should then pass near the gold reefs of Bishop's and Fisher's creeks. Near this are situated the Homeward Bound and Flying Dutchman copper-mines, from the former of which 250 tons of ore have been sent to Sydney, all of which have yielded over 40 per cent. of pure copper.

" Twelve miles further on the Cloncurry copper-mines are reached, the richness and magnitude of which it is difficult to conceive without having seen them; and though I have known many skilled miners who have worked at, and several mining engineers of note (Mr. H. A. Thompson, the Chairman of the Mining Board being one) who have inspected these mines, I have never known one who was not at first sight astonished at the almost incredible amount of rich ore lying on the surface of the ground. Half a mile to the south-west extremely rich and extensive lodes occur, while thirty miles to the north-west unnumbered lodes and copper-bearing veins appear. I myself know of nearly 100, only eight or ten of which are secured, and none worked. Eight miles to the north-west, on the Leichardt river, are two lodes, containing ores of red oxide, grey, and malachite. These lodes are from twenty to thirty feet wide, immense deposits of copper. Big boulders of grey are lying loose on the surface, of tons' weight."

Some very fine copper-lodes are situated at Mount Flora and Mount Orange, ninety miles from Mackay. The horse-shoe formed by the two mountains and the ridge that connects them is one mass of copper-lodes, some of them extremely rich, and consisting principally of red oxide and malachite. An attempt was made to work them, by some local men, and some Sydney capitalists, who put up smelting works on the field, and obtained very fair results. But the company collapsed, from no fault of the mines, but from the grossest mismanagement on the part of the share-holders, backed up by swindling on the part of the mining manager.

Men who used to work in the mines have since told me that they have known the manager to put a shot or two into the wall, and entirely conceal the face of the lode. He then reported to the share-holders that the lode had " duffered out," and that it was useless to continue working ; and one of the latter, who was " in the swim " with the manager, obtained the whole claim from the rest, for a trifling sum, and the lode was opened up again.

The peculiar natural advantages of the Mount Flora and Mount Orange mines should make them pay well, if properly managed, even when the price of copper is as low as it is now. Not only are they within a short distance of the coast, with a good road all the way to port, but they are in the centre of a district which is full of large deposits of coal. It is the opinion of geologists that the western plains will be found to overlie large beds of this mineral, which has already been found in nearly every part of the colony where it has been searched for.

In wandering about the runs in the neighbourhood of Mount Flora copper-mines, and Mount Britten gold-mines, I have come across many splendid seams of coal, cropping out in the gullies, and banks of the creeks,

some of the seams being eight feet wide, and all of them
a very good sample of coal. In the neighbourhood of
Bowen, one hundred miles farther north, there is a
seam of coal fifty feet thick, but it is not of quite such
good quality as that farther south.

The principal coal districts that have as yet been
tried are near Brisbane, in West Moreton, on Darling
Downs, at Maryborough, at Bowen, and at Cooktown
in the far north. But I believe, myself, that the coal
beds in the neighbourhood of Grosvenor Downs, and
Lake Elphinstone, runs lying between Clermont and
Bowen, will prove equal to any yet discovered in the
colony, both for quantity and for quality.

The tin-mines of Queensland are remarkably rich,
and the value of the amount of that metal exported in
1882 was £269,904. The chief mines are those at
Stanthorpe on the southern boundary of the colony,
from which tin to the value of nearly a million sterling
has been taken. Hitherto, all through the colony the
metal found has been chiefly in the form of stream-tin ;
but recently what was thought to be a valuable discovery
of lode-tin was made at Herberton, in the far north.

A tremendous rush set in, and boat-loads of speculators started up from Melbourne and Sydney to secure
the ground. Not a man came down from the north in
the steamers but had a sample of Herberton lode-tin
in his pocket, and glowing descriptions of the enormous
quantity of it that was sticking out of the ground excited
the southern capitalists to the verge of madness.

Certainly the samples sent down were of extraordinary
richness, but at present it seems doubtful whether the
lodes will prove permanent, and I think the people who

did best out of the Herberton tin-rush were the working men who originally took up the ground, some of whom sold their claims to maniacs from the south for as much as £20,000, without having done twenty pounds worth of work in them.

Extraordinary as is the mineral wealth of Queensland, however, it is not in this that her real greatness lies. Gold is all-powerful in most things, and its acquisition will, for a time, outweigh all other considerations, but its presence can never make a barren land fertile, or turn a bad climate into a good one; and although immense deposits of this, and other metals, will always attract a large floating population, they will never support a permanent one, unless backed up by other conditions. The real greatness of Queensland lies in the fact, that while she has been exceptionally endowed with what may be called ready-made wealth in the form of minerals, she possesses at the same time one of the healthiest climates in the world, and an enormous area fit for cultivation and stock-rearing, capable of supporting a vast population, under conditions of life the most favourable. She is, in fact, a self-contained country, having within herself all the elements of a powerful nation, the germs almost of that chimerical greatness that has been described by Prince Bismarck as "une puissance finie."

The term was applied to England; and whether it was intended to mean that she is strong enough to maintain her position unassisted either by an alliance with foreign Powers, or by her Colonies, or whether the double meaning of the last word was meant to imply that the greatness of England has departed, in either case most

Englishmen will be inclined to question the fitness of its application. The phrase is a trebly unfortunate one.

In the first place, the greatness of England has not yet departed ; in the second place, no Power that has ever existed has proved itself strong enough to entirely disregard an alliance with others ; and in the third place, the only thing in the history of the world that has ever pointed to the possibility of such a Power arising, is the present question of a permanent union of all British territories throughout the world. The British Empire, so united, would be by far the most powerful one that the world has ever seen, and would, indeed, be independent of any possible combination against it. But as regards England herself, now that Imperial Federation is attracting the universal attention that it deserves, it is apparent that she depends quite as much upon her Colonies for retaining her present position in the world, as her Colonies depend upon her for retaining theirs ; and Queensland, with a territory of over half a million square miles, and a population of less than one for every two square miles, must be an important factor in the future history of a country so over-populated as Great Britain.

To the west of the coast-range lie the prairies of Queensland, an almost boundless extent of rolling downs and plains, covered with grass and herbage that for rearing sheep and cattle is unsurpassed in any country of the world. Every mile of available country is now taken up, and held by the squatters, who are, of course, the chief producers of the colony, and to get new country a man must go into the northern territory of South

Australia and into Western Australia. The number of sheep in Queensland in 1882 was over twelve millions, and the number of cattle about four millions ; the value of the wool exported in the same year being £1,329,019. In the future, sheep will increase very much faster than cattle, for no one who can afford the expense of forming a sheep-station will continue to rear cattle upon country that is fit to carry sheep. For many years to come, from climatic reasons if for no others, it is certain that the interior of Queensland will continue to be what it is now, essentially a wool-producing country ; and its capabilities in this respect are incalculable.

The rainfall is unreliable, and the absence of natural water renders even the squatter's industry at all times rather a precarious-one, and obliges him to spend large sums of money in making permanent water upon his runs. The danger of drought is lessened by the largeness of the areas held by the squatter, and is further reduced by the precaution of storing water, but in a drought such as has recently visited the southern portion of Queensland, and New South Wales, nothing can save him from serious loss, and it is in reality only the enormous profits which he makes in good seasons that enable him to face an occasional bad one with cheerfulness.

In the chapter devoted to a comparison of the relative advantages of a sheep-station and a cattle-station, will be found statistics which show what the profits of the former amount to in fair seasons ; but anyone who is acquainted with the Western country would see at once the absurdity of supposing that it could be profitably held except in large areas, for pastoral purposes, until a great change has taken place in the civilisation of the colony.

It is impossible, of course, to imagine that such a country can remain permanently in the hands of a few hundred graziers, whose object is to keep away any population from their runs beyond the few hands necessary to work their flocks and herds. The Western Downs are supposed by geologists to overlie large underground reservoirs of water, and certainly wherever wells have been sunk to any depth success has attended the experiments, so that in time it is probable that some system of irrigation will be developed, which will turn the country into something more profitable to the community than sheep-runs ; and the opening up of the country by railways will transform the interior of Queensland from a purely pastoral into an agricultural country. That cheap carriage to the coast is the one thing needful to make wheat-growing pay, has been conclusively proved by the large quantities grown in the Allora and Roma districts, since the opening of the railway from Brisbane to the latter town. Five quarters to the acre is not an uncommon crop, and in 1880 250,000 bushels were raised in the colony. The quality of the wheat is excellent, the weight being as high as sixty-seven pounds to the bushel, and the flour fully equal to Adelaide. Land is being rapidly laid down under wheat in the Darling Downs and Maranoa districts, and it is expected that before long Queensland will produce sufficient to make her independent of any foreign supply.

With such resources as these at her command, it is evident that the colony requires nothing but an extended system of railway communication from the interior to the coast, to bring population and prosperity in its wake. The transformation that has been wrought in those districts where railways have already been constructed, shows what progress might be expected if the colony were to put forth her whole strength in this direction. With a good Government the thing would be done at once ; for no sane man disputes the advisability of doing it, but, unfortunately, Queensland, like her neighbours New South Wales and Victoria, suffers in this respect from a succession of selfish, sordid adventurers, whose proceedings it is impossible to watch, without forgetting the impurity of their principles in the imbecility of their policy. It is as absurd to distinguish the members of either party as Conservatives or Radicals, as it is to call any of them politicians ; since the transparent motive of all of them is to plunder their colony. The Ins and Outs of Legislation would be a more appropriate term. The party who are in go straight for whatever they want ; and the only security of the country lies in the certainty that the party who are out will do their best to prevent them from getting it, not from any consideration for the public weal, but because they want it themselves.

The great natural want of Queensland is navigable rivers and deep-water harbours. In all her sea-board of 2,000 miles there are hardly any good harbours for vessels of large draught, and not a single decent navigable river. By a sort of practical joke of nature every one is adorned with a sand-bar at the mouth, and a mud-flat a little way up. These efforts of nature are a thorn in the side of every coasting skipper, and a perfect god-send to the rascally *employés* and *pro-tégés* of the Department of Public Works, who derive a regular annuity from misdirected attempts to deepen the rivers. More or less illegitimate plunder is made out of every public work in Australia by all concerned in it, from the Ministry downwards; the most notable instances being the adoption of Wood's brake by the Victorian railways, the Steel Rails Inquiry in Queensland, and the Transcontinental Railway scheme in the same colony, which will be more fully described hereafter. These are official swindles, and require the active co-operation of those at the head of affairs, and a great deal of tact on the part of all concerned, to carry them through. Even then they do not always succeed. The Transcontinental Railway scheme was the downfall of the Ministry whose Premier was its chief instigator and promoter.

But in a small way nothing is so profitable and so popular with Government engineers as deepening a river, because it is work that can be indefinitely prolonged. At any other work they are bound to show some sort of progress, be it ever so miraculously slow, or else show some reasonable cause for delay. But in deepening a river, the engineer has it all his own way. No one can tell what he is about under water, and, by combining a studious neglect of the most elementary principles of engineering with a slight knowledge of the bottom of the river, he can extend his work over any period of time. The amount of public money that goes in this way is enormous.

The Fitzroy river, on which lies the town of Rockhampton, affords a striking example of Queensland

Government engineering. Seven miles below the town are situated the Flats, on which there was naturally about three feet of water at low tide. It was decided to remove these flats, so as to allow vessels drawing nine feet of water to get up at any tide. The estimated cost of the undertaking was £25,000. Time not specified, being, as the advertisements say, "not so much an object as a comfortable home" for the engineer to whom the work was entrusted.

After fooling around dredging for some time, this worthy hit upon a notable scheme. Starting a little above the flats, he built a training wall slantwise down the river, so as to leave a narrow passage near the opposite bank. He calculated that the rush of the tide through this narrow channel would very soon deepen it.

He was perfectly right. It very soon did, and, by the simple process known as robbing Peter to pay Paul, the sand so washed away formed a fresh flat a little lower down, with only eighteen inches of water on it, instead of three feet!

Finally, after expending £110,000 during a period extending over ten years, they have at last succeeded in getting a depth of about five feet at low tide. Less than half the money wasted in tinkering the bottom of the Fitzroy would have given Rockhampton a deep-water port in Keppel Bay, at which ships drawing thirty feet of water could lie at any tide, and a railway from thence to the town.

There is not a single town on the coast of Queensland that has the natural advantage of deep-water communication with the sea, either by means of a harbour or a navigable river, except Bowen and Gladstone. These two townships are situated on the coast itself, and have good deep-water harbours; but there is no back country to either of them, so it will be long before they are of much importance. All the other ports are only accessible to boats of very light draught, and generally these have to wait for the tide.

Townsville lies right on the coast, but the neighbouring bay is so shallow that no vessel of any size can get within a mile and a half of the town.

Mackay lies two miles up a river, with flats upon which there is not more than a foot of water at low tide. At the mouth of the river is a sand-bar, and outside nothing but an open roadstead.

Rockhampton is forty-five miles from the coast, up the Fitzroy river, the flats in which have just been described.

Bundaberg and Maryborough are each of them some distance up a narrow, muddy, shallow river.

The coasting-trade of Queensland is increasing so enormously, there is no doubt that in time these difficulties will be overcome, and some, at least, of the coast towns will be provided with good artificial harbours.

In 1841 the whole trade of the colony of Queensland was carried on by a small cutter trading between Brisbane and Sydney. In 1879 the entrances inwards to Brisbane were 1,261 vessels, with a tonnage of 637,695 tons, and the clearance about the same. Since then the increase in the coast trade has been even more surprising.

In 1883 Townsville alone, the most northern town

of any importance in Queensland, was importing about 4,000 tons of goods a week.

The production of sugar alone in the colony has risen from 12,300 cwt. in 1868, to over 400,000 cwt. in 1883. Very soon good sea-ports will be an absolute necessity ; but, in the meantime, with the exception of the work done in the Brisbane river, all the money spent has been so much thrown away

Mackay, the great sugar-growing district of Queensland, is about the worst off for a port of any town on the coast. It has, as I have said, a river with shallow flats and a bar at the mouth, and nothing but an open roadstead outside.

There are, however, two small islands, known as "Flat-top" and "Round-top," just off the mouth of the river ; and it was thought that something might be done in the way of a breakwater. The genius of the Fitzroy flats was accordingly consulted on the subject.

He assured the delighted inhabitants of Mackay that it would be the simplest thing in the world to make an excellent harbour. Nothing to do but connect one of the islands with the mainland, throw out a breakwater on the far side, and run a railway right away from the end of the breakwater into the town.

After an interval of four years, during which time they had been driven nearly out of their minds by the patriotic agitation on the subject by the member for Mackay, the Government proceeded to vote some money for the furtherance of this scheme. The breakwater was to be about a mile long, and tenders were called for in sections. The first section was the only one ever completed, and the only one ever likely to be, until some very much more able men take it in hand. The contractor's only notion of a breakwater seemed to be to blast rock out of an adjacent cliff, break it up small so as to be convenient for handling, and barrow it into the sea, leaving it to form its own batter. He never got further than high-water mark. His work, about forty yards long, remains, another monument of Government stupidity, and the Mackay breakwater ends where most breakwaters begin.

But the most notable attempt of modern times to rob the public exchequer was the Trans-continental Railway scheme. The responsible position of those whose names were connected with it, the magnitude of the undertaking, and the great care with which the real conditions under which it was to be carried out were concealed, for a long time saved this gigantic fraud from detection. At length, however, it was exposed, the public realised the amount of which it was intended the colony should be robbed, and the result was that the Ministry who brought in the Bill were defeated, and obliged to resign.

The proposed scheme is really worth some consideration, in order to show the enormous vitality of a colony that can still make rapid progress, even under the incubus of a Government that endeavours to plunder instead of fostering its resources.

The Trans-continental Railway was to run from the inland head of the Brisbane-Roma line (a Government line) to Point Parker, in the Gulf of Carpentaria, a distance, roughly, of 1,000 miles.

There is no doubt that such a line would be of inestimable benefit to Australia at large, and especially to

Queensland ; but it is certain that the latter colony individually would benefit much more from an extension of her existing lines of railway further into the interior.

The whole colony being fully alive to the importance of extending her railway system in some shape or way, the Government made it their business to try and persuade the inhabitants of Queensland that her credit was already strained to the utmost, and that it would be inadvisable, even if it were possible, to borrow sufficient to perform the proposed work.

We were told by the Premier that because we owed £58 per head of our population, which would be increased to £70 when the loans authorised were issued, we were on the verge of ruin, and could not possibly borrow any more.

Now it may be very sound to estimate the gravity of a public debt in this manner, when the money has been borrowed for unproductive purposes, such as war, or construction of national defences. But in a colony like Queensland, almost the whole of the money so borrowed has, with a due allowance, of course, for official plunder, been expended on developing the national estate, so that the debt is represented to a great extent by valuable assets which bring in a revenue far in excess of the interest on the capital borrowed. Thus, in New South Wales, a colony that owes £18,000,000, the railways alone are valued at £25,000,000, and pay 5 per cent. on the cost of construction.

The estimate of Sir Thomas McIlwraith, the Premier of Queensland, for the construction of the Transcontinental Railway, was £3,260 per mile.

In his reply of 22nd February 1882, to General

19 *

Fielding, the agent for the Syndicate that was formed in Europe for taking up this scheme, Sir Thomas McIlwraith declared most positively that the cost of a railway from Charleville to the Gulf, including every item, surveying, supervision, rolling stock, construction, stations, and all other outlay, should not exceed the above sum. Sir Thomas is himself an expert, and had besides the benefit of Mr. Watson's survey and estimate to help him. The whole cost for the 1,000 miles, therefore, should not exceed £3,260,000.

The Syndicate were to be allowed seven years and a half to complete their line. This gives £434,666 as the sum required to be spent every year to complete the line within contract time. Queensland can borrow at the rate of 4 per cent. interest; we therefore find that had Queensland herself undertaken the work—

Amount required to be spent annually on construction, £434,666.

| | |
|---|---:|
| 1st year's interest at 4 per cent. | £17,387 |
| 2nd      ..              ,, | 34,774 |
| 3rd | 52,161 |
| 4th | 69,548 |
| 5th | 86,935 |
| 6th | 104,322 |
| 7th | 121,709 |
| half 8th | 65,202 |
| | £552,038 |

So that in seven years and a half Queensland would have completed the 1,000 miles of railway, at a cost of £3,260,000 of loan funds, on which she would have paid interest during that time £552,038. The total cost to the colony therefore would be £3,812,038, and at the end of the time she would herself be the owner of the line.

Later on we shall see what it was proposed the colony should pay the Syndicate for the railway, before it eventually passed into her hands. Having partly succeeded in persuading the colony that it would be impossible for her to borrow sufficient to accomplish the work, the Premier drew our attention to a body of philanthropists in the shape of a European Syndicate, who were ready to do it for us.

The fact of a joint-stock company being able to do what a colony like Queensland cannot do, is sufficiently startling. But no matter; we were told that although our credit was run dry, Providence had provided us with the means of accomplishing our object in the shape of land-grants. Nothing could be more simple than to use the enormous area of comparatively unremunerative land to pay for the railway.

It is a most fortunate thing that the colony came to its senses, and realised the merits of the case before it was too late. At one time there was a danger that the Government might snatch a victory, and rush their nefarious project through Parliament, before the colony understood what was taking place. Had this happened, there is no doubt it would have had a lasting and most injurious effect on the prospects of Queensland.

There is not space here to transcribe the full terms of the agreement between the Queensland Government and the Trans-continental Syndicate, but what it amounted to was this: the Syndicate in the first place were to receive eleven million acres of land, freehold. This land was stated by the Premier to be worth at least 10s. an acre, and Government have been repeatedly solicited to offer it at auction at that upset price.

Not allowing therefore for the prospective rise in the value of the land upon the completion of the railway, this gives the value of the land-grant to be given to the Syndicate at £5,500,000. But in exchange for the inferior portion of land adjacent to the railway on the Gulf watershed, the Syndicate were allowed to select 1,200,000 acres on the Batavia river. This is grand agricultural land, which cannot be valued at less than £1 per acre. This brings the total thus:

1,200,000 acres on the Batavia at £1   £1,200,000

10,000,000 acres along the line at 10s.  5,000,000

                          £6,200,000

In making this valuation, no account has been taken of the extra value of the land in the various townships along the line, and of the port on the Gulf, half of all which was to belong to the Syndicate.

Having induced the Syndicate to make the railway for us by the above enormous bribe, the agreement further provided for the purchase of the railway from the Syndicate when it was completed, by the following remarkable clause.

"13. In the event of the Governor-in-Council exercising the right of purchase of the said railway and rolling stock and appurtenances, given by the 26th clause of the said Act, the basis of valuation upon which the fair and reasonable value thereof shall be ascertained as therein mentioned shall be twenty-five years' purchase of the average net earnings of the railway during the three previous years with 15 per cent. added thereto for forced sale, but not being less in total than £100 for every £100 of capital paid by and expended on the said railway, rolling-stock, and appurtenances."

In order to give an idea of the probable amount that the colony would be required to pay under this clause, I cannot do better than quote from a pamphlet which appeared at the time the Bill was before the country. It was called *The latest Political Device for partitioning Queensland amongst Speculative Rings, and its Exposure.* It was written, I believe, by Mr. R. Newton, and was of immense service in showing up the gigantic fraud that the colony was very nearly swallowing. He says :—

" From the above clause it may be inferred that the Government cannot exercise the right to purchase the line till the expiration of three years from its comple-tion. By those most competent to form a correct esti-mate, it is computed that this colony will possess not less than 30,000,000 sheep in its central districts by the expiration of the time to be allowed to the Syndi-cate for the completion of their line to the Gulf. For it must be remembered that the country through which this Syndicate line is proposed to be taken, is not a useless unoccupied territory, only to be made of any value by this railway. With the exception of a barren strip at the Point Parker end, the country is occupied as grazing-runs along the whole length of the proposed line, and for hundreds of miles to the west of it. Some of the country through which the line would pass is highly improved, and the whole is now being developed in an extraordinarily rapid manner. Few people under-stand or realise the vast traffic this increase in sheep will bring to our railways.

" We will take, as a basis for calculation, that only the produce and requirement for working one half of these 30,000,000 sheep can be influenced on to the Syndicate lines; and considering the enormous power they will possess, with the facilities they would be able to give at their port, Point Parker, by lines of steamers of their own, carrying at low freights, to allow the Syndicate line only one half the traffic is a moderate calculation.

" This, then, would give the Syndicate the traffic for 15,000,000 sheep. The wool from these, at 4 lbs. all round for clean and greasy wool, gives 26,786 tons. We will put the average freight on this at £8 per ton, a rate much below what is at present charged on our lines, the freight on clean wool from Roma to Brisbane, a distance of only 317 miles, being now £8 per ton.

"Allowing only double the weight of up-carriage to wool down, which is considerably under what is found in practice (as *vide* the traffic returns of the Central Railway, a line supplying almost solely pastoral country), and calculating the average charge on up-freight at the same rate as wool down—viz. £8 per ton—and allowing for passenger fares, together with the large traffic which may be expected from live stock, meat, &c. (without taking into account the mineral traffic from the Clon-curry, which may be immense), we give the same amount as wool freights bring in, we have the following result :—

26,786 tons wool down at £8 per ton average
    freight . . . . . . £214,288
53,572 tons up loading at £8 . 428,576
Passenger fares, live stock, meat, &c. . 214,288

           Total gross earnings    £857,152

" Taking the working expenses at 50 per cent. on gross earnings, which is an ample allowance over such an extremely easy and level country, we have £428,576 per annum nett earnings, which, at twenty-five years' purchase, with 15 per. cent added, comes to the enormous total of £12,321,560. This amount, if not considerably more, is the sum we should have to borrow in a few years, to purchase a railway, for the construction of which the country will have already given away £6,200,000 of its lands, besides vast unknown values in sites of towns, &c., and which line the country could have constructed itself, including interest on loans, and every possible charge, for a sum not exceeding £3,812,038. It is simply utter nonsense to spread abroad the idea that this great colony, with its vast undeveloped resources, with the great future which is undoubtedly its inheritance, is unable to borrow for the making of its main trunk lines of railway (which would represent so grand an asset) a sum scarcely exceeding £3,000,000, extended over a period of eight years."

Such was the great Trans-continental Railway scheme, which occasioned the downfall of Sir Thomas McIlwraith's Ministry. It is deeply to be regretted that they ever took such a proposal in hand. They were the best Government Queensland has ever had, and, had they chosen to do so, they were in a position to pass measures that would have been of inestimable service to the colony, such as the Coolie Bill to introduce coloured labour from India to the sugar plantations. Instead of which, they took advantage of the security of their position to tamper with the interests of the colony.

Allusion has been made above to the Steel Rail Inquiry.
This was an attack made by Mr. Griffiths, the leader
of the Opposition, upon Sir Thomas McIlwraith's conduct in the purchase of some £60,000 of steel rails for
the Queensland railways.

Mr. Griffiths directly impugned the honesty of the
Premier's conduct in the transaction, and, although he
was unable to establish his charge, the extremely un-
satisfactory circumstances that appeared in the inquiry
greatly weakened the confidence of the country in the
Ministry. When this further scheme for wholesale
plunder was exposed, of course the country could stand
it-no longer, and turned them out.

Headed by Mr. Griffiths, their successors advanced,
and, having elected a congenial spirit in the shape of a
thrice-convicted felon to the Speaker's chair, they laid
themselves down to try by every means in their power
to retard the progress of the colony, and feather their
own nests.

The conduct of the Queensland Parliament in select-
ing such a man to fill the position of Speaker was
severely censured by the neighbouring colonies, and
deeply resented throughout Queensland herself. The
tone of our Parliament has never been very high, but
compared with the Houses in New South Wales and
Victoria we always felt ourselves to be eminently respectable. All claim to such distinction is now gone. Whatever elements a House may be composed of, it cannot fail
to lose caste by assigning the position of Speaker to such
a man as now holds it.

But although the Queensland Assembly may be deficient in a sense of dignity, it certainly does not lack wit.

Some years ago the present Speaker (Mr. Groom) was very desirous of obtaining a Government appointment. In the course of debate, one of his friends declared that Mr. Groom's long services under Government most distinctly entitled him to hold some office. Whereupon someone on the other side got up and observed, with more truth than feeling, that "considering what the nature of Mr. Groom's services to the country had been, the only appointment he was qualified to hold was that of Groom of the Stole."

It is deeply to be regretted that a more healthy tone does not pervade the legislature of the colonies. But as long as all respectable people hold aloof, and excuse themselves from attempting to take part in the Government of their country, on the plea that they do not care to be mixed up in such disreputable society, there is not much hope of improvement. Such idle seclusion and selfish apathy deserves to be afflicted, as it is, by the worst of government.

Throughout the whole of Australia a feeling obtains that Parliament is a profession which it is just as well for all decent people to keep clear of. In a book of advice to those visiting the colony of Victoria, I read the following interesting warning :—

"If you enter into conversation with a respectable-looking individual to whom you are a stranger, on no account ask him if he is a member of the Legislative Assembly. You cannot offer him a greater insult."

As a class the squatters are marvellously indifferent to the legislation of the colony they live in, and they have greatly their own selfishness to thank for the losses that they suffer in consequence. The squatters are, of course, the backbone of a pastoral country like Australia, and represent the greater portion of its wealth. But anything like co-operation amongst them for the purpose of protecting their interests in Parliament is unknown. Each one thinks he can do best for himself by attending to nothing but the management of his station, and letting legislation take care of itself. They are by far the most poorly represented class in Parliament throughout Australia, and the consequence is that their seclusion in the Bush is subject to periodical interruptions of a most disagreeable kind.

While busily employed in making money in the back country, they awake too late, to find that literally the ground has been cut from under their feet at headquarters, and perhaps half their run taken away by some empirical piece of legislation on the part of the town-loafers to whom they have abandoned the reins of government without a struggle

Of course, in a new country, the most difficult question that any Government has to deal with is a satisfactory adjustment of the question as to how the land shall be occupied. So far the problem has not been treated in the manner most likely to conduce to the welfare of the community, for at first, in the older colonies, immense freeholds were allowed to accumulate, the evil effects of which have found vent in measures of retaliation against the class that owned them.

The difficulty in a colony like Queensland lies in the fact that while the great want is felt to be an increase of population, it is almost impossible to find a class of people who can occupy the country profitably in small areas. The squatter knows, of course, that he only occupies his run upon sufferance, and that, unless he chooses to spend large sums in securing it as a free-hold, he must· expect to surrender his country when it is required for other purposes. When the time comes he succumbs to the inevitable, and moves farther away in search of fresh country ; but his sorrow at being forced to give up the whole or half of his run is by no means diminished by the discovery that it is not of the slightest use to those who have taken it from him.

Of course, if a squatter holds land that is fit for culti-vation either of sugar or of wheat, it is only right that he should hand it over to those who are able and willing to turn it to a use which is obviously more remunera-tive to the colony at large than the growing of stock. But when he holds country that is out of the scope of agriculture for the present, it is annoying to have to surrender it prematurely to people to whom it is no sort of good. Even in Queensland, land without capital is more of a curse than a blessing to those who are forced to hold it, and there is no more wretched class in the colony than the holders of pastoral selections.

It is perfectly impossible that a man can make any-thing more than a bare living out of one, and generally it is impossible for him to do even that honestly. When he has complied with the conditions of occupa-tion, by completing the necessary improvements in the shape of fencing-in his selection, there is no more work for him to do, and he simmers down into growing pumpkins and sweet potatoes for his own consumption, and generally ekes out a living by stealing his neigh-bour's cattle. A more utterly useless class of men to the colony cannot be imagined. The fact is that, for a

long time to come, the most profitable way in which
the greater portion of Australia, and certainly of Queensland, could possibly be held, would be in the form of
large pastoral leaseholds, paying a fair rent to the
crown, but having a security of tenure that would
encourage their holders to invest their capital largely
in improvements. To throw open the runs of the
squatters to selection wholesale is merely to try and
drive civilisation at high pressure, which always means
waste of power, and to foster a mushroom growth of
population that will weaken rather than develop the
natural resources of the country.

The population required for a country like Queensland consists mainly of two classes, large capitalists and
skilled workmen of all trades. The former will find an
ample field for profitable investments upon any scale
that they may desire, and the latter will readily find
employment at a high rate of wages.

But to the man of small capital, who is master of
no trade, the colony is indeed a delusion and a snare.
The days are over when large fortunes were rapidly
made out of nothing at all, and anyone who makes
money there has to work for it, and to work hard too.
The possessor of a few hundreds, or even a few thousands of pounds, who goes to Queensland with the idea
that he is likely to make his fortune, will find himself
wofully mistaken; for the odds are a hundred to one
on his losing every penny of his money.

If he goes out there to friends whom he can
thoroughly trust, and who will take care of his money
for him, of course he will get a higher rate of interest
than he could get in England, and as he gains expe-

rience of the country he will see opportunities of increasing his capital safely. But unless he has good introductions to thoroughly sound men of business, he had far better stay at home.

The standard of honesty is no higher in the colony than it is elsewhere, and there are always crowds of sharpers on the look-out for men with money to invest. A form of partnership is often entered into, in which the new arrival in the colony provides the money, and the old hand the experience. These partnerships seldom last long, and at the end of them the respective commodities have generally changed hands : the unfortunate " new chum " has got the experience, and his rascally partner has got the money.

But Queensland is certainly the Utopia of the working-man who is not afraid of work, and numerous are the ways of making a living that are open to him.

On the gold-fields, ordinary miners' wages run from £2 10s. on the old-established field to £4 on new diggings in the back country. Amongst the trades, carpenters, joiners, masons, and workers in iron are the most in demand, and at any of them a good tradesman will, in the towns, earn at least fifteen shillings a day. In the Bush, the wages for ordinary station-hands employed for shepherding or stock-riding are from £1 to £1 15s. a week, with rations, running up to £2 5s. for shearers in shearing time. Nearly all the fencing and putting up of station-buildings, yards, &c., in the Bush, is done by contract, and contractors always reckon to make at least £2 10s. a week.

After he has been six months in the colony, the working man is endowed with the inestimable boon of the franchise, an advantage for which he has at all times, and in all parts of the world, shown himself willing to barter every other consideration.

A great deal has been said about the climate of Queensland, and it is often described as being a "trying" one. The only possible way in which it can be justly so described, is in the sense of its being a climate in which people are constantly trying to kill themselves without succeeding. Probably there is no other country in the world in which men habitually take such frightful liberties with their constitutions with impunity.

The ordinary mode of living pursued by the inhabitants both of the town and the Bush is such that, if the climate were not an extraordinarily healthy one, they would die like rotten sheep. We will take the average Bushman's life, say a stockman, or a hard-working squatter, who helps to work his own cattle. His food consists of beef and damper, and jam if he is luxurious. Vegetables he often does not see for weeks and weeks together, except in the form of pickles, and he is very lucky if he can always get them.

An occasional piece of pumpkin, or a sweet potato, forms a red-letter day in the calendar of his diet, and every meal is washed down with floods of strong scalding hot tea without any milk. Breakfast is the only regular meal that he gets in the day, and he has that soon after he gets up, but not before he has had a smoke. If he happens to be at home in the middle of the day he has dinner; if not, he has nothing from breakfast to supper, which is a movable feast, somewhere about sundown.

All day he is riding about under a broiling sun, and smokes an ounce of the strongest tobacco in the world every twenty-four hours. For days and nights together, sometimes, he is wet through, when camped out away from home ; sleeping at night under a tree, with no covering but a blanket in winter, and in summer not even that, and awakening in the morning, perhaps to find himself lying in a puddle of rain-water that has fallen in the night, perhaps to find his hair stuck to his hat with hoar frost.

The only diversion in his *régime* is an occasional visit to a neighbouring town, where he probably gets half poisoned by the extraordinary quantity and the infamous quality of the liquor that he drinks. If after ten years of this he should find his digestion not as good as it was, or feel symptoms of the approach of rheumatism, he is certain to put it down to the climate instead of to his own imprudence.

With the townsmen, the case is still worse. Their climate is certainly not as healthy as that of the Bush, and in summer it is rather depressing ; but they take little or no exercise, which is the only way to counteract its effects, and drink quantities of spirits from morning till night, every day of their lives, and even then it seems to take years and years to do them much harm.

All below the coast range of Queensland cannot be described as a pleasant climate, though it certainly is not an unhealthy one. But in summer it is rather a sticky, damp sort of heat, and both men and animals perspire far more than they do over the range on the table-lands.

In the Bush, though the thermometer is very high

20

all through the summer from October to April, there is
nothing whatever depressing or enervating about the
heat; and the harder a man works, even though he be
out in the sun all day, the better he will feel.

It is only the habitual loafers and the constitutionally
weak who feel any bad effects from the heat of Queensland.   The thermometer runs to about 90° in the shade
in the middle of the day in the summer months, though
on some few days it is much higher.   I have seen it up
to 120° in the shade of a back verandah, and 176° in
the sun ; but I never felt the slightest ill effects from
going out and working all day in the sun, with no more
covering for my head than an old felt hat.

Sunstroke in the Bush is unknown, though I have
seen men working all day in a brick-kiln, when there
was not a breath of air, with a vertical sun over their
heads, and no protection but a workman's linen cap.
Even in summer, in the Bush, when the sun goes down,
the air always gets nice and cool.   Hot nights are unknown, and there are very few all through the summer
in which a man is not glad of a blanket just before
dawn.

If the climate of Queensland were a perpetual summer,
it might, indeed, be rather trying to such people as are
constitutionally unfitted to stand heat ; but, for seven
months in the year, it is impossible to imagine a more
delightful climate, even for those who object to hot
weather.   From the middle of March to the middle of
October is an unbroken series of bright, warm, sunny
days, with a blue sky over which soft, fat white clouds
sail on the wings of a fresh, cool breeze, the mornings
and evenings being quite chilly, and the thermometer

at night, during the months of June and July, falling sometimes to ten degrees below freezing, even in latitudes well within the tropics.

As is always the case with new countries, ague prevails in Queensland, but chiefly in the districts that have been recently taken up, and it disappears almost entirely in places that have been settled for some time.

In the interior a form of blood-poisoning, known as slow-fever, is not uncommon, and is entirely due to the effects of drinking impure water.

The only really unhealthy district of Queensland is on the shores of the Gulf of Carpentaria, where several obscure sorts of fever prevail, one of which very closely resembles the terrible Yellow-Jack, if indeed it is not the real article itself.

The rest of the colony may be considered as extraordinarily free from all the maladies incidental to hot climates, and it must be greatly a man's own fault if he does not enjoy as good health in Queensland as he could in any other country in the world. I have tried the climates of New South Wales and Victoria, and certainly prefer that of Queensland to either of them; for during the seven years that I was knocking about the latter colony, at all sorts of work, exposed to all kinds of weather, I not only never had a day's illness that I could by any ingenuity attribute to the effects of the climate, but I feel that I laid in a stock of good health, of which the beneficial effects will last during the remainder of my lifetime.

# CHAPTER XVIII.

BRISBANE, the capital of Queensland, lies about twenty-five miles from the coast, on the river of the same name. The town is rather prettily situated on some high ridges sloping down to the river. Except in point of size, all coast-towns of Queensland are pretty much alike, and are certainly not pleasant places to live at. They have all the disagreeables of town as compared with country life, and none of the advantages which are to be found in the older-established towns of Sydney and Melbourne. I never knew anyone who was obliged to live in a Queensland coast-town who did not complain of his lot, and wish himself elsewhere; and no Bushman will ever stay a day longer in one of them than he can help. This is not to be wondered at, for the heat and dust in summer are intolerable, and flies and mosquitoes abound. There are hardly any places of amusement of any kind, and the consequence is that in order to kill time, and to counteract the depressing effects of the climate, most of the inhabitants drink a great deal more than is good for them.

The greatest misconception prevails in the old country as to the mode of living generally in Australia; but especially as to the relative advantages of life in the towns and in the Bush. Even amongst the inhabitants of Australia themselves there is no subject upon which I have heard more nonsense talked. The dwellers in the Bush are constantly represented as dirty and degraded ruffians who, from their very manner of living, cannot possibly continue to be decent members of the community, while the inhabitants of the towns are up-held as orderly, industrious, and useful citizens. Comparisons are always odious, and I should never have dreamed of making one so especially obnoxious as this. But it is so constantly done that I believe from mere reiteration it passes for truth.

Were any such idea to gain credence, it would un-doubtedly deter numbers of people from going into the Bush, or allowing any of their belongings to do so.

Now, to a country like Australia, at present the development of her back-country is of infinitely greater importance than the growth of her towns, and it should be the object of everyone who is interested in her future to import as much capital and population into the Bush as possible.

In order to give a fair idea of the relative advantages of town and Bush life in Queensland, it may be as well to make a few remarks on the subject. The manners and morals of those who habitually reside in the Bush are undoubtedly not all that can be desired; but to represent them as a class with whom it is impossible to associate without being defiled is unjust.

It is true that a great many people are unable to do

so, for there are some in whom the struggle after cleanliness and morality is so feebly maintained that a
feather suffices to turn the scale, and these, of course,
avail themselves only too readily of the seclusion of the
Bush to give full swing to their degrading propensities.
By all means let such people keep out of the Bush, if
they feel themselves unequal to retaining their self-
respect without such assistance as the external influences
of a town life afford them.

The importance of such external influences it is impossible to exaggerate, but it is very doubtful whether
they are not of infinitely greater value to a man's
neighbours than to himself, if he be such a man as is
above described. " A fig for virtue ! 'Tis in ourselves
that we are thus or thus," and the man who only washes
under compulsion is not likely to derive much moral
benefit from his enforced ablutions, though it is of para-
mount importance to all his associates that he should
not be allowed entirely to abstain from the use of soap
and water.

But writers on the subject would have us believe
that he who journeys into the Bush must leave his
religion and his tooth-brush behind, and were there a
turnpike to mark the entrance to this awful abode, they
would no doubt place over it the inscription with which
Dante has adorned the gate of inner Hell. We are
further given to understand that a short residence
in this remarkable region destroys both youth and
abilities.

Now youth is such a perishable commodity, and its
decay such a fixed law of nature, that no means have as
yet been discovered of arresting its departure. It seems

rather unfair, therefore, to tax the Bush in particular with promoting it ; and as for a man's abilities, it must be his own fault if he finds them impaired by an open-air life of hard work in what we conceive to be the healthiest country in the world.

Nothing is more common than to hear a charge of drunkenness brought against Bushmen, as if they as a class possessed a monopoly of this vice.   That there are drunkards in the Bush is beyond all question, but that they are as numerous in proportion to the population as they are in the towns is very doubtful.   Neither is their method of drinking, though equally deplorable, by any means as destructive to health as that pursued by the inhabitants of the towns.

In the first place, a man working hard in the open air can consume with perfect impunity an amount of alcohol that would soon finish off a man leading a less healthy life.

In the second place, the Bush drunkard works hard for his cheque, adjourns to the nearest public-house, and, having drunk it out, returns to work again, to recruit his health and refill his pocket.   " Though this be madness, there is method in it."

Now the town drunkard, and many who would be inexpressibly shocked to hear themselves described as such, indulge in a series of " nips," the frequency of which increases to such an alarming extent, that at last the fleeting remnant of their brain is barely equal to the effort of elaborating an excuse for swallowing another nobbler.

It is the undivided opinion of medical men that this habit of soaking is far more injurious to the system than getting occasionally drunk. Either is bad enough, of course. Like Cassio, "we could well wish that courtesy would devise some other custom of entertainment." It is only the fallacy of upholding the sobriety of the towns in Australia against that of the Bush, that I wish to draw attention to.

In the columns of the *Queenslander* I read not long ago a most deplorable description of life in the Bush by an old colonist who signed himself "Musca." Anyone who read it would come to the conclusion that Bushmen are the only men alive who really know how to drink and to swear.

After drawing a most romantic picture of the benign influence of a "fair and virtuous woman" upon the destiny of man, and deploring her absence in the Bush, "Musca" next proceeded to lay down the extraordinary doctrine that the hardships and privations which the pursuit of duty in the Bush entails, must end in "moral degradation."

This prepares us for his no less startling theory that the "comforts, luxuries, and enjoyments of a town life" are more conducive to health than working in the Bush. The first of these fallacies is so ridiculous as to need no answer. If the second required one, it would assuredly be found in a glance at the relative physiques of the inhabitants of the Bush and of the towns. Health is as conspicuous by its presence in the one, as it is by its absence in the other.

How many men have I seen who, having exchanged a life of roughing it in the Bush for the "comforts, luxuries, and enjoyments of a town," have exchanged with it the exterior of an athlete for that of an anatomical specimen creeping about to save the expense of a funeral. Really I should be ashamed to quote such rubbish, but for the fact that "Musca" is unfortunately only a type of a large class who endeavour to represent the Bush as a place entirely unfit to live in.

The fact is that many men go into the Bush and fulfil their destiny by making fools of themselves there as they would anywhere else. They then return to loaf away the remainder of their existence in a town, and amuse themselves by giving the world a history of their experiences, distorted by the recollection of disappointed hopes, for which they have only their own folly to thank.

The custom of using profane language cannot be too severely censured. But to maintain, as "Musca" and his class do, that the residents in the Bush monopolise, or even excel in this bad habit, argues a very limited experience. Deplorable as is the language of an excited bullock-driver to a refractory steer, it pales before my recollections of the daily conversation of a number of young gentlemen at Woolwich, qualifying to serve in the highest branches of Her Majesty's Service. While before me rises a vision of more than one "fine old English gentleman" full of strange oaths, which not even the presence of ladies prevents him from using.

In extolling the influence of à "fair and virtuous woman," we must all sympathise with "Musca," and with him regret that her presence in the Bush is not more frequent than it is. But we must also remember that all women are not fair, neither are all women virtuous.

Woman's influence, equally potent for either, is more frequently exerted for evil than for good. Were we to compare the instances where a man's downward career has been arrested, with those where his progress to the dogs has been assisted by the fair sex, numerous as are the former, we fear the latter would greatly preponderate. We must conclude, therefore, that the extreme scarcity of muslin in the Bush is not a matter for unconditional regret.

It is as ridiculous to say that everyone living in the Bush is degraded, as it would be to say that everyone with red hair is a ruffian. The inhabitants of the Bush are no doubt worse in some ways than their neighbours, but certainly a great deal superior to them in others ; and I am heartily sorry for anyone who has lived amongst them and has been unable to detect anything of good beneath the rough exterior and somewhat battered appearance that are, to a certain extent, the necessary effects of roughing it. I have seen as kind and generous dispositions and as excellent qualities in a rugged and toil-worn Bushman as I ever expect to see again.

It is the tendency of nearly everyone to hold their circumstances, their surroundings, and their neighbours responsible for failures and mishaps for which they have only themselves to thank. There are temptations in every line of life which no one can avoid. To try and escape from them altogether is as foolish as it is cowardly. But to select a line of life as free from them as possible is open to most people, and, after dispassionate consideration, the Bush would seen to offer as few temptations to go wrong as any line of life that could be chosen. Certainly it offers far fewer than the towns—I am talking, of course, of ordinary mortals. It is impossible to legislate for persons so peculiarly constituted as to feel " morally degraded " by sleeping under a tree and breakfasting off beef and damper. It is not of such choice spirits that I am talking, for whom it would be necessary to construct a Utopia upon a plan hitherto undreamed of, but of the ordinary young man of sound constitution and fair abilities, whom I maintain to have as fair a chance of keeping straight in the Bush as anywhere else, and an infinitely better chance of preserving his health. But both his constitution and his resolution must be of no ordinary strength, if he can sojourn for any length of time in a Queensland town without being the worse for it.

The climate of the coast towns especially is, to say the least of it, a thirsty one. He will be assailed from morning till night with invitations to " step round and have a liquor," which we all know it is considered the height of churlishness to refuse. Even supposing society in the Bush to be worse than that in the towns, still its existence is necessary to the welfare of the country ; and the desire of " Musca " and his friends to keep all respectable and well-educated people out of it, is the strangest scheme for the improvement of a community that ever was heard of. It would surely be better if as many respectable members of society as possible were to go there and exert what influence they have for good.

The amount of hard steady drinking that goes on in all the towns of Queensland is astonishing. Brisbane is no exception to the rule. Bankers and business men, legislators and lawyers, doctors and tradesmen, they all make a practice of every now and then deserting their business and sallying forth to the nearest bar for a drink. Brandy and whisky are the favourite drinks, and the amount a man consumes in the twenty-four hours by this habit of " nipping," without ever getting quite drunk, is surprising.

No *habitué* of a Queensland town who wishes to find a business man ever goes to look for him first in his office. If he knows the run of the town, he will start the reverse way round the various public-houses, and if he fails to run the man he is looking for to ground, he will then go to his office, in hopes of catching him before he starts round for another series of drinks.

At whatever hour of the day a man meets another whom he has not seen for say twelve hours, etiquette requires that he shall incontinently invite him to come and drink. This is a custom that pervades every class in the colony, and cannot be departed from without something more than a breach of good manners.

Now, there is no harm whatever in inviting a man to have a drink. The invitation would seem to be prompted by nothing but a feeling of generous hospitality, and as such there is nothing to be said against it. But it assumes a different aspect when a refusal on the part of the man invited is regarded as little short of an insult. And yet such is the case. No matter whether a man is thirsty or not, no matter if he has just swallowed a drink, a refusal to swallow another cannot be tolerated for a moment. A more insane custom cannot be conceived ; and there is no doubt that numbers of men who have naturally no taste for drinking acquire the habit, and entirely ruin their health, from reluctance to give offence by refusing to drink when invited.

All through Australia, in every class, it is not considered good form for a man to drink by himself. Very few even of the most hopeless drunkards ever do so. The consequence is, that when a man feels inclined˙ for a drink he immediately looks out for someone to drink with him. This accounts in a great measure for the annoyance that is aroused by a refusal.

In America an "Anti-shouting Society" has been formed, the members of which bind themselves never to drink at anyone else's expense. This is a move in the right direction. Without going the length of forming any society, which always argues a conscious weakness on the part of its members, it would be an excellent thing for Queensland, and for Australia generally, if the etiquette of drinking were so far relaxed as to enable a man to refuse to drink when he does not want to, without risk of giving offence.

The great want of Brisbane is a really good hotel. There is a population of over thirty thousand residents, besides a considerable floating population of travellers on their way up and down the coast, and squatters down from the country for a few days at a time on business. This is just the sort of population to make hotel-keeping pay. And yet in all the numerous hotels in Brisbane there is not one that can fairly be ranked as third rate.

The attendance and the food are both very bad, and the bed-rooms wretchedly small and stuffy. The summer nights in Brisbane are often very hot, and sleep is out of the question in a wooden box no bigger than the cabin of a steamer, so constructed as to allow the snoring of anyone within twenty-five yards to be perfectly audible, but with the worst possible provision for ventilation from the outer air.

There is no doubt that anyone who put up a really first-rate hotel in Brisbane, and ran it upon sound principles, would soon make an enormous fortune. In the meantime, however, the want of hotels in Brisbane is greatly made up for by the hospitality of the people who live there. For several miles up and down the river, the northern bank is dotted with the country houses of those who have business in the town.

Many of these houses are delightfully situated, with lovely gardens sloping down to the river. The cool shade of these gardens is a heavenly change from the blinding glare and dust in the town. Bamboos, orange trees, lime trees, bananas, and other fruit trees abound, and their dark green foliage is illuminated by the masses of gorgeous colouring from the Boganvillea and other creepers which grow here in perfection.

Brisbane possesses a fair club, and supports a theatre; which is visited by a succession of travelling companies. The chief recreations of the inhabitants are standing on the wharf to see the steamers arrive and depart, or going for a walk with the musquitoes in the Botanical Gardens.

The most entertaining thing I ever saw in Brisbane was a small detachment of the Salvation Army. They were parading the streets in search of truth, and I had the curiosity to go up and examine them closely. Their soul-saving apparatus consisted only of four blasphemous hymn-books, a cracked concertina, and a very faded banner that I think had once seen better days in the form of a kite.

But although their technical appliances were rather defective, fate had been kind in lavishing on them a profusion of those higher gifts that are indispensable to their calling. They all possessed in perfection the whining voice, the vicious droop of the eyelid, and the peculiar expression of petrified rascality about the corners of the mouth, that neither vice nor sickness, drink nor toil are capable of implanting there, without the assistance of a course of open-air piety. I sincerely hope that I did not misjudge them. Appearances are very deceitful, and from a short distance I defy anyone to tell whether the *prima donna* was shouting " Glory," or had just sat down on a tin-tack.

In a few years there will be a railway right through from Brisbane to Sydney. At present (1884) it only extends from Brisbane to Stanthorpe, on the borders of Queensland, leaving a distance of one hundred and sixty miles to be done by coach to Armadale, in New South Wales. From there the railway runs to Newcastle, a town on the coast sixty miles north of Sydney. Between Armadale and Stanthorpe, and between New-castle and Sydney, the line is in course of construction. The latter section crosses some very rough country.

In the meantime anyone who wishes to see a marvel-lous performance in the way of four-in-hand driving cannot do better than travel by one of Cobb and Co.'s coaches from Stanthorpe to Armadale. This firm run a perfect network of coaches all over Queensland, New South Wales, and Victoria; and their drivers, for a rough country, are probably the finest in the world.

It is perfectly extraordinary how these men will remember every bad place, and hole, and stump over a stretch of perhaps fifty miles, so as to be able to avoid them on a dark night, while going ten or a dozen miles an hour.   It is not as if the road always kept the same. Violent storms and floods are constantly washing out fresh holes, and blowing down fresh trees, so that the driver has to remember the road from day to day and from night to night.   It is possible that something fresh may have happened in the few hours that have elapsed since he last went down the road, but he runs the chance of this with perfect complacency.

On a pitch-dark night there is something awesome in the way these mail-drivers slam through the forest, along what is by courtesy called a road, but which in places is more like a rocky water-course than anything else.   An occasional log, or a fallen tree across the track, prevent the road from being at all monotonous. If a passenger has time to do anything but hold on he will be greatly interested.   At every turn of the road the glare of a lamp on each side of him will reveal some obstacle or pitfall, which his pilot contrives to avoid with marvellous dexterity.   Sometimes he comes to grief, but not half so often as would seem inevitable to anyone who did not know the capabilities of an Australian mail-driver.   An axe and a coil of green hide make him independent of any catastrophe short of smashing a wheel, and when this occurs there is nothing to do but to sit down and wait patiently for the arrival of the coach coming the opposite way.   They change horses about every ten miles, and, barring accidents, they keep excellent time.

The voyage down the coast from Brisbane to Sydney is a very unpleasant one. There is a break here in the lines of ocean-going steamers which call at all other ports of any importance on the coast of Australia. From Cape York to Brisbane the British India Company run the Queensland mails with a service of very fine boats, averaging nearly 3,000 tons, which call off all the Queensland ports.

From Sydney to Melbourne and Adelaide the vessels of the P. & O., Orient, and Messageries are constantly running. But the run from Brisbane to Sydney has to be negotiated in the little coasting steamers of the Australasian Steam Navigation Company, better known as the A. S. N. This Company are the possessors of a flotilla of the most villainous boats in the world. For a long time they waxed fat upon a monopoly of the whole coasting trade of Australia ; and had they chosen to keep pace with the advancing times by improving the class of their vessels, they would now be in possession of as fine a trade as the world ever saw. But want of competition produced its usual effect ; and instead they preferred to go on running a class of vessels which never go to sea on a coast like that of Australia without endangering the lives of all on board, and occasionally go to the bottom incontinently.

Up to the present time they have still an enormous trade, as there are many ports in Queensland into which their vessels are the only ones small enough to go. But, if they continue their present extortionate tariff, their trade will be taken away by some more enterprising company better able to understand the spirit of the age. In all their arrangements the A. S. N. display

21

the most profound indifference to the comfort and convenience of passengers.

For example, at Port Mackay or Keppel Bay, where their steamers do not go up the rivers, it is a constant occurrence to be kept waiting out at sea in the tender for sixteen or twenty hours, simply because the Company will not expend a shilling in telegraphing the steamer's departure from the last port of call.

The distance from Brisbane to Sydney is about five hundred miles, and ought to be a fourty-four hours' run. I have lively recollections of the indefinite way in which it can be prolonged by a bad boat in bad weather.

One Tuesday morning I got on board an old eggshell fitted with paddle-boxes, described by the advertisements of the A. S. N. as "the magnificent fullpowered steam-ship *City of Brisbane*, 450 tons, to sail for Sydney at 10 A.M." My heart sank as I observed the stormy appearance of the sky, and noticed the steam escaping in every direction but the right one from the boilers, the authorised pressure on which had been reduced from 60 lbs. to 15 lbs. to the square inch.

Quivering like a leaf, the old tub set off down the river at the rate of a well-conducted funeral, and in the course of a few hours, assisted by the tide, we got outside. The only other passengers besides myself were a Roman Catholic priest, nearly dead with consumption, and a man who went into violent delirium tremens a few hours after we left Brisbane. Anything so utterly depressing as that voyage I never wish to see again. The weather, for the first day, was not bad, and with the help of the great Australian current we got on capitally, and found ourselves nearing Smokey Cape.

Then it came on to blow, and got worse and worse till the sea and wind were something startling.

At a very early stage of the gale a big sea smashed the saloon skylight, and left us with about a foot of water on the main deck. The priest was sick with monotonous regularity about twice every three minutes, and with a violence that made itself heard above the howling of the storm. The man with D. T. wandered about yelling and howling horribly, and tumbling up against all the fixtures until he had cut his face out of all resemblance to anything human. With his eyes fixed with horror, and the blood streaming down his face and neck, he presented the most dreary spectacle I ever saw. We could do nothing for him, for it was impossible to hold him, and we were at last obliged to put him in irons.

Meanwhile the old boat had managed, in the course of three days and a half, to get down opposite Sydney, but there was such an awful sea on that the captain dared not alter her course to enter the harbour, for fear of foundering. It now came on to blow worse than ever, and it is a positive fact that by next morning we had been blown fifty miles back, and found we were nearly opposite Newcastle. Here we lay for thirty hours, without going either backward or forward. Had the wind been a few points more on shore nothing could have saved us, as we were never more that a few miles distant from land. Fortunately there came a lull of a few hours, and we managed to sneak down and run into Sydney, just as it came on to blow as badly as ever. We had been five days and a half out from Brisbane, and were running rapidly short of coal.

21 *

The man with **D. T.** expired just as we got into harbour.

Two years afterwards I found the old *City of Brisbane* still running the same track, the only change in her being a further reduction of 5 lbs. pressure on the boilers. This time it did not blow so hard, and we reached Sydney in three days and three quarters.

# CHAPTER XIX.

## SYDNEY.

WHERE Sydney harbour got its reputation for beauty I am quite at a loss to imagine. I never saw anything more forlornly ugly in the way of scenery. Undoubtedly it is one of the finest harbours from a naval point of view in the world, but there is nothing whatever picturesque about it. It is surrounded by low rocky ridges about two hundred feet high, covered all over with stunted trees.

At the far end lies the town itself, which has not a single feature to recommend it. All over the ridges to the south, and on a part of those to the north, are scattered staring white villa residences. Many of these have lovely gardens and grounds, and when you get near them are very pretty spots. But the general panorama of Sydney Harbour, whether viewed from the sea or from the land, is positively ugly.

There is no distance to be seen anywhere, and nothing pretty in the way of a foreground. The sea is never a healthy blue, and the colouring of the land is a dull, dirty, monotonous green, that looks as if it had been dredged over with sand. There is invariably a sickly glare in the atmosphere, except just at sunrise and sunset, that would effectually destroy far greater pretensions to beauty than any that Sydney can boast of. I have lived in Sydney for months. I have sailed all over the harbour in a boat, and have walked round about it on land. I have seen it in every weather, under every sort of sky, but I never for a moment saw it look pretty.

The town of Sydney is by no means a pleasant one. The streets are winding and cramped, the pavement in many places being only five or six feet wide, and George Street, the main street, follows exactly the winding of an old track that went through a Blacks' camp that originally occupied the present site of the town. There are many very fine buildings in the town, but they do not show to advantage, and their position prevents any possibility of widening or improving the streets. The first thing that strikes anyone who goes to Sydney is the extraordinary number of people that there seem to be there who have nothing to do.

Crowds of loafers block up the main streets, standing in mobs at the corners, or sauntering along the *trottoir*, with their hands in their pockets, a pipe in their mouth, and their hat tipped well over the eyes. They never get out of anyone's way, and are a source of infinite inconvenience to anyone who is in a hurry.

The town and suburbs are built on a series of steep hills and valleys round the harbour, and it is impossible to go a hundred yards anywhere without going up or down hill. The best thing about the place is the

GOVERNMENT HOUSE SYDNEY

Botanical Gardens, and grounds of the late Exhibition, which are really quite beautifully kept.

The Exhibition itself was unfortunately burnt to the ground in 1883. It would have been an eye-sore any-where else, but was quite an ornament to Sydney, and its loss was deeply felt by the inhabitants, who entertain feelings of superstitious reverence for the supposed beauty of the place. Land in the town and suburbs has risen to such a fabulous value, that, although it is never likely to be worth less than it is at present, it cannot rise much higher for some time.

The wealth of Sydney is enormous. For miles to the north-east of the town, away towards the south head, the suburbs are a mass of villa residences overlooking the harbour. Many of them are extremely pretty, and an immense deal of money has been laid out on them. But the inhabitants of Sydney never know what to do with their money, and seem incapable of having a really good time.

In the first place, society is split up into cliques, the members of which regard anyone who is not in their own set with the most unreasoning hatred and con-tempt. Besides this, the climate is a most depressing one, which accounts in a great measure for the pre-vailing listlessness of everyone in the place.

In spite of the climate, I have most pleasant recollec-tions of many very happy days spent at a house on the shores of the harbour, beyond Rose Bay. A son of the owner, whom I had known five years before, found me staying at a hotel in the town. I was in bad health at the time, and he took me away to stay at his home. He was the only member of the family with whom I was acquainted, but had I been their oldest friend I could not have been made more heartily welcome.

Since then I have stayed there very often, and a friendship of many years has given me ample opportunity of appreciating the real kindness that has made the hospitality of Carrara a household word, even in Australia, where kindness to strangers is the universal rule. I am bound to say that the pleasure with which I look back upon the time that I spent there has no reference to the proximity of Sydney. The attractions of the place itself, beautifully situated on the shore of the harbour, were sufficient to prevent any great wish to wander far away, and the powers of entertainment possessed by its inmates made their visitors quite independent of any other society, and rendered a moment's dullness impossible.

The climate of Sydney, always a detestable one, is never the same for more than a few hours. I have often seen a day there open with a hot scorching wind, which lasts perhaps until 1 o'clock ; suddenly a fierce, cold wind, a " southerly buster " as it is called, sweeps up from the ice-fields of the southern sea, and blows, perhaps, for two days, perhaps only for a few hours, to be succeeded either by a dead calm or a " black north-easter," accompanied by torrents of rain. But whether it is hot or cold, whether it blows from the north, south, east, or west, or not at all, there is always a sickly, enervating feeling about the air, which the inhabitants themselves complain very much of, and which a stranger at first feels unbearable. Most of the inhabitants, who can afford it, always go away for a few weeks in the summer, either to Tasmania, or to the Blue Mountains, which is the sanatorium of Sydney, and where there are townships at an elevation of from 2,000 to 3,000 feet.

Sydney is, if possible, worse off than Brisbane for hotels. I have tried half-a-dozen of the best of them, and everywhere the dirt, discomfort, and bad attendance are the same. The Sydney waiter is an entirely distinct species, of which fact he is himself quite unconscious, and treats all visitors who will allow him to do so as his equals.

At the fashionable *table d'hôtes*, where hundreds of business-men and visitors in the town assemble every day for luncheon, the flippant behaviour of the waiters is perfectly bewildering to a stranger. His call for "waiter" will probably be answered, after an interval, by an inquiry of "Did I hear your lovely voice?" from a patronising individual, who leans on the table and begins to talk on the merits of the Harbour. I have seen the astonished look on a visitor's face, who was explaining to a waiter that he had brought the wrong wine, when that functionary suddenly offered to bet him five pounds that he had done nothing of the kind. His neighbour, a stranger to Sydney too, was so interested in the discussion, that he paused in his occupation of helping himself to the greens, and remained motionless, with the spoon in his hand, and an expression of blank amazement on his countenance. From this trance he was rudely awakened by another waiter laying his hand on his shoulder and remarking "After you with the cabbage."

The first time I went to Sydney I camped at what was supposed to be the best hotel in the town. The walls between the bed-rooms were not particularly thick, and the morning after I arrived, as I was lying in bed, I overheard the following dialogue in the next bed-room to mine.

" I say, old man, lend me a shirt."

" Can't, old man. I 've only got one."

" Never mind, lend it me. I want to go out for an hour now, but I 'll bring it back before you want to get up."

The town of Sydney suffers from an odious nuisance in the shape of steam tram-cars, which run along several of the main streets. The shares of the company that works them are about the best paying thing, next to the telephone, that has been started for a long while in the colony. But the cars themselves are a perfect infliction. They rush down the most crowded thorough-fares, terrifying the horses, and killing, on an average, about two foot-passengers a week, besides maiming numerous other ones. There are omnibuses and han-soms all over the place, and, of course, any number of private carriages to be seen. But although many of the latter are well-appointed, and the quality of some of the horses undeniable, it is remarkable that one never by any chance sees a coachman decently got-up. There is something quite pitiable in seeing the effect of a really good turn-out entirely marred by an apparition on the box with check trousers, an acre of green tie, and a moustache.

Altogether Sydney strikes one as a steady-going, sleepy old town, thickly covered with blue mould, with-out any of the rowdyism of the north, and with little of the vigorous life of Melbourne.

Nowhere in Australia are there to be found pleasanter people than in Sydney, in their own homes. But they do not care to go much out of them, and take life very quietly. Money comes to them more by accumulation than by speculation, and they spend it lavishly in beautifying their residences by the shores of their beloved harbour. The lower orders in Sydney drink heavily, but the middle and upper classes drink less than any community in Australia, and the ascending scale of sobriety attains its zenith in the present head of society, who, when he gives a ball, regales his guests with nothing more potent than raspberry vinegar and lemon syrup.

Sydney keeps several newspapers going, the chief of which is the *Sydney Morning Herald*. Except to the readers of advertisements, it is impossible to imagine a more dreary publication. It contains the " latest intelligence " only in the sense of its being a week later than anywhere else, and most of the space allotted to news is occupied with hypothetical accounts of what would have happened if something else had taken place that never occurred.

For instance, its readers are informed that H.M.S. *Wolverene* has left Fiji for Sydney. After following the Editor in an intricate calculation as to the different dates on which she may be expected, supposing the wind to be favourable or not, and supposing her to steam seven knots or eight, they are next informed that it is quite uncertain whether the destination of H.M.S. *Wolverene* be Sydney or not. This involves more calculations, as to how long she will take to arrive, if she goes round by New Zealand, Hobart, or Melbourne. Finally those who have had patience to read to the end find a telegram to say that H.M.S. *Wolverene* entered Sydney harbour from Fiji that morning.

But the *Sydney Bulletin*, a weekly publication, is probably the wittiest and most amusing social paper in the world. It sticks at nothing, and never troubles its readers with asterisks instead of names. The Editor is constantly in hot water, and has more than once been heavily fined for libel; but he is far too valuable an institution to be parted with, and his supporters subscribe freely to see him through a bad time, and the fire of sarcasm, raillery, and scandal, never ceases. Of its kind, the *Sydney Bulletin* is perfect, and all the wretched wit of *The World, Truth*, and all the London social papers put together, might be clipped from it without being missed.

The harbour always presents a most animated appearance. Vessels of every description, from a yawl to a 4,000-ton steamer, are constantly passing in and out, and endless little steamers ply between the different bays all round. Yachting is a very favourite pastime with the inhabitants, and sometimes the whole harbour is alive with a flotilla of small craft. The largest vessels can come right up and lay alongside the quays right against the town.

The line of railway is completed now from Sydney to Melbourne, but, of course, the jealousy of the two colonies has impelled them to adopt different gauges, so that through traffic is at present impossible. The population of Sydney is 237,000, and that of the whole colony of New South Wales, 840,000.

The first discovery of gold made in Australia was at Summer Hill, in 1851. Since then gold has been found occasionally in very large quantities in various parts of New South Wales, and several of the alluvial diggings have proved both rich and permanent. But so far, strange to say, there has never been a true reef discovered in this colony. Some immensely rich veins of quartz have been found, but they have all run out, or proved barren at a depth.

The chief produce of the country is stock of all kinds, and a considerable quantity of wheat and Indian corn is also grown. The number of sheep in the colony in 1883 was 31,796,308, and in the previous year no less than 153,351,354 lbs. of wool were exported. New South Wales, however, has suffered most terribly during the recent drought, which has been the most severe ever known in the colony.

The whole of the northern and western portions were described by one who had recently visited them as one vast corpse-dotted desert, and the description is hardly exaggerated. No returns have as yet been made of the total losses, and, indeed, in Riverina and Southern Queensland the drought still continues (October '84), but I hear of one station alone that has lost 160,000 sheep, and another where every single hoof of cattle on the run, in number over twenty thousand, have perished.

New South Wales and Southern Queensland have suffered by far the most severely during the recent drought. Victoria and Northern Queensland having had, if anything, more than usually favourable seasons. But the depression caused by the enormous losses in stock, has made itself felt in every branch of industry, in every part of Australia; and although the price of stations has not gone down, very few are changing hands.

In New South Wales the feud against the squatters among the lower classes, which obtains all through Australia, is very violent. Following the example of Victoria, the Government have dealt with the land question in a manner that has brought the transfer of leasehold land throughout the colony to a dead-lock, and a Bill is now before Parliament by which all squatters holding leases will be deprived of half their runs ; but the squatting element in New South Wales is still very powerful, and it is probable that they will obtain compensation for improvements.

There is a railway from Sydney to Melbourne, and the journey across takes about twenty-three hours. It is very comfortable travelling, the berths in the sleeping-cars being certainly above the average in point of size and cleanliness. There is nothing that could by courtesy be called an express train, and on the Victorian line all the trains stop at every station, and at about every third one there is an extra pause for refreshment.

On the New South Wales line the sale of liquor is everywhere prohibited, and the consequence is that both the guards and the drivers lay in a store of liquor to take with them, and consequently drink a great deal more than they would if there were a bar at every other station, which is shown by their being much more frequently drunk than the *employés* on the Victorian lines, who can get liquor whenever they want it.

The mail-train leaves Sydney every night at 8.30. Passengers for Melbourne change carriages at Wodonga, a station on the border of Victoria. On the Sydney line the trains travel a fair pace ; but from Wodonga to Melbourne, a distance of about 190 miles, they absolutely crawl, and take nearly eight hours over the journey.

# CHAPTER XX.

## MELBOURNE.

MELBOURNE is one of the cleanest, best laid-out, and most pleasantly situated towns in the world. It lies on a succession of gently undulating rises, about three miles from the sea, and, with the suburbs, some of which extend down to the sea itself, has a population of 290,000. The town itself is all laid out in rectangular blocks, and the streets are very broad and well-paved.

Everywhere there is a look of permanent solidity and accumulated wealth most extraordinary in so young a town. It would be difficult to pick out a street in London where, in the same space, there are as many fine buildings as there are in Collins Street, one of the main streets in Melbourne. The banks especially are most of them very handsome buildings, both inside and out, and an enormous amount of money has been spent on their construction.

The interior of the Bank of Victoria is modelled from that of the hall of one of the palaces at Venice, and is most elaborately laid out with marble floors and pillars, and cedar fittings. Evidently the banks have more money than they know what to do with, for the amount of dead capital that they have sunk in building is astonishing. There are two very good hotels, Menzies and the Oriental, one at each end of the town, which is more than can be said of any other town in Australia, except, perhaps, Townsville, the northernmost port of any importance in Queensland, which, strange to say, possesses the next best hotel to Melbourne of any town in the island.

The most conspicuous building in Melbourne is the Scotch Presbyterian church, which stands in the highest part of the town, and has a handsome tower and spire about 200 feet high. Besides this there are the English and Roman Catholic cathedrals, and endless smaller churches of every size and denomination.

In spite of water being laid on everywhere and freely used, the dust in the streets is very often appalling. It is not like ordinary dust either; for the streets are all macadamised with a basalt rock, which breaks up into a most detestably sharp, three-cornered, irritating sort of dust, extremely trying to the eyes. At present the streets are free from the Sydney abomination of tram-cars; but endless omnibuses and hansoms pervade the town and suburbs, the fares being about half as much again as those in London. There are open gutters along all the streets, with little bridges over them at the crossings.

A good shower of rain floods the lower parts of Melbourne in a few minutes, and sets these gutters running like a mill-race, three feet deep, and I once saw a man nearly drowned in one of them. A crowd of passengers were waiting patiently at the crossing, till the river in

22

the street subsided ; but this particular man seemed in a hurry.   He was going to be very smart, and leap over the deep gutter ; but he made a bad shot and soused right into the middle of it.   He was swept down like a straw for a little distance, and then jammed under a low bridge, from which position he was fortunately pulled out by the heels before he was quite drowned.

The Public Library and Institute of Fine Arts is a very handsome building in the Grecian style, open to the public every day of the week except Sunday.   The picture-gallery contains a good deal of rubbish, and one or two good pictures, the best of which are Long's " Esther " and " Question of Propriety."

In the middle of the town is a splendid tennis-court, reckoned by lovers of the game to be one of the best in existence, and at one of the clubs there is an excellent raquet court.

The extraordinary proficiency of Australians in cricket, which enables the representative eleven of a population of three millions to hold its own against a country with thirty, is less wonderful when one sees how universally popular the game is in the colony.   There is not a spare piece of ground fit for a pitch anywhere round Melbourne that is not covered with " larrikins " from six years old upwards, every evening for nine months in the year.   Their soul is in the game, and one and all of them display a precocious talent for round-hand bowling, very different to the sneaking underhand affected by the uneducated youth of great Britain.   There are two or three excellent cricket-grounds in Melbourne and the suburbs, the principal one in North Melbourne being as good a ground as anyone could wish to play on, and the pavilions and arrangements connected with it first rate.

Much as I admire the indomitable pluck of the Australian cricketers who have met the English teams both at home and in their own country; beyond their skill in handling the weapons of their trade, there is little to be said in praise of their conduct. While arrogating to themselves the title of amateurs, they make it perfectly plain that they follow cricket as a lucrative profession, and do not care to play except for sufficient plunder, and they seldom lose an opportunity of taking an unfair advantage of their opponents.

All round the suburbs of Melbourne, there are local railways worked by the Government. They run a frequent service of trains, and occasionally have a smash. The inhabitants of Melbourne must be exceedingly nervous upon wheels, for whenever there is an accident every single soul in the train at the time goes straight for the public exchequer, and collects heavy damages for a " shock to the nervous system." An accident which occurred recently on one of the suburban lines cost the Government, or rather the Colony, £140,000 in damages to the survivors.

The chances of an accident are infinitely increased by the Government having insisted upon adopting an utterly worthless description of brake for all the railways. Of course, like every other contract of the kind, it was made a rank political job. While I was in Melbourne the papers were full of it, and a furious discussion was raging in Parliament as to the rival merits of the Westinghouse and Wood's brake, and some of the scenes in the House were most amusing.

A Commission was appointed to inquire into the practical working of the two brakes, and their relative advantages, and an overwhelming weight of evidence was brought to show that the Westinghouse brake was infinitely the superior one of the two. But Mr. Straight, the Commissioner of Railways at the time, whose legitimate business was keeping a market garden, inclined to the adoption of Wood's brake, and, entirely unassisted either by evidence or by common-sense, succeeded in carrying his point.

Seeing that the experiments of the Commission proved conclusively that whereas the Westinghouse brake was one of the most perfect ever invented, Wood's brake was only automatic in the sense of its being frequently impossible either to put it on or to take it off when it was wanted, cynical critics were ill-natured enough to attribute Mr. Straight's support of the latter contrivance to a personal intimacy with the inventor. Indeed, in the heat of a discussion on the subject in the House, one of his opponents went so far as to challenge Mr. Straight to finish the controversy by personal combat, and in delicate allusion to his professional calling, wound up by shouting out, "Come outside! come outside! and I'll put a head on you like one of your own —— cauliflowers!"

In spite of such heroic attempts to block Mr. Straight's Bill, jobbery finally triumphed over justice, and the inferior and more costly brake was adopted on the local lines.

The port of Melbourne is Williamstown, six miles away, and here all the big steamers and sailing vessels lie. But the river Yarra runs up through the town, and vessels of 1,500 tons can get up, and lie alongside of the wharves in the middle of the town.

The Yarra is a foul sluggish stream, brown in repose, and the colour of ink when stirred up, and smelling horribly all the time. On the opposite side of it from the town, on a slight eminence, is situated Government House, a large building with no pretensions to architectural beauty of any kind ; but the Botanical Gardens adjoining its grounds are very prettily laid out, and nicely kept. St. Kilda and Brighton, the two watering-places of Melbourne, are suburbs situated on the shores of Hobson's Bay, and their piers are a Sunday lounge for the inhabitants. At both places there is excellent sea-bathing, and at St. Kilda an extremely comfortable hotel.

The busy life in the town of Melbourne is a striking contrast to sleepy Sydney, whose streets are thronged with crowds of loafing idlers. An experienced eye can always pick out a Sydney man in a Melbourne crowd, as easily as it would detect a weevil in a beehive ; and though in point of wealth there is not much to choose between the two places, it is easy to see that in Melbourne money is made, while in Sydney it grows.

The telephone is in use all over Melbourne, and the shares of the Company that work it pay wonderfully well. In Collins Street is situated the Melbourne Exchange and all the business-men, brokers, and mining-men assemble there about noon every day to exchange notes ; and outside, in the racing season, there is always a whole crowd of book-makers, with their hats over their eyes, and pencil and note-books in their hands.

I soon found out that as far as floating a company on the Mount Britten mines was concerned, I had come to

Melbourne at a very bad time. In the first place, money was getting rapidly very tight, and the banks instead of being anxious to cram money down people's throats at 6 per cent., suddenly refused to advance any more, and ran the rate of interest on deposit up to 9 per cent.

Between them the banks of Australia at that time had lent eighty-three millions, and speculation was getting so furious that they determined to put a stop to it. In the second place the Melbourne mining men had just dropped £80,000 in a fearful swindle in New South Wales, and this, coupled with the tightness of the money market, had for the time pretty well stopped all speculation. The mining market was as flat as a postage-stamp in the dust; and here is where the luck of gold-mining comes in, for the men to whom I subsequently disposed of the mines, told me themselves that had I offered them for sale six months earlier they would willingly have given me the same money for them that they dropped in the New South Wales venture, for that mine was by far the best show of the two.

With some trouble I succeeded in getting together a Syndicate to consider my proposals as to the Mount Britten mines, and they sent up an expert from Sandhurst to inspect the property. I had always heard that the mining men of Melbourne were as great a lot of scoundrels as there are in existence, but I was surprised to find that in addition to this they were most of them perfectly ignorant of anything connected with the practical or theoretical working of a mine. Most of them would not know a gold-mine from a blue gum-tree, and the object of everyone of them seemed to be to puff up the shares of the companies whose scrip they held by lying reports, and to sell out at a profit.

So low had the morality of mining in Victoria sunk, that it was almost impossible to float a company involving the share-holders in any liability, and the industry suffered severely in consequence. To remedy the evil, the Legislature has legalised an anomalous form of swindle called a No-Liability Company, the shareholders in which can at any moment abandon their interest in the concern.

The very title of a No-Liability Company is a contradiction in terms, for I cannot conceive how there can be a company formed without liability, nor how any body of men working without liability can obtain credit for so much as a box of lucifer-matches. Yet in the whole colony of Victoria there is not a single gold-mining company that is not registered as a No-Liability one.

But, as I told the votaries of the scheme, who pointed out triumphantly that this system had revived the mining industry of Victoria, it only shows that mining in Victoria is more mining in people's pockets than in the ground, and my subsequent acquaintance with the Melbourne mining market tended most materially to strengthen my opinion. I at once informed the Syndicate that if they did not choose to float a Limited Liability Company on Mount Britten they could leave it alone, as I had no idea of being connected with such a no-nation piece of rascality as a company without any liability.

A fierce discussion ensued, for nothing terrifies a Melbourne mining man so much as the prospect of having to pay calls. As long as a mine pays dividends he is all there ; but a call of threepence is generally suffi-cient to make him sling up every share he holds. It is impossible to conceive mining enterprise at a lower ebb than is represented by a community whose mutual faith is so severely shaken as to make it impossible to induce them to incur a joint liability for the purpose of pro-specting a mine.

In Queensland mining is conducted on very different principles, and the dogged persistence with which comparatively poor men will go on paying call after call into a mine that never returns them anything for years, in the hope of striking gold, is as remarkable as is the impulse of Victorians to throw up really valuable property the moment it ceases to pay dividends, and, of course, does infinitely more to develop the gold-bearing resources of the country.

The Syndicate, however, having received an excellent report of the Mount Britten mines from the expert who went up to inspect them, and from one of their own number who accompanied him, finally agreed to my conditions, and a Limited Liability Company was formed to work the properties. The price paid to my brother and myself was £11,000, and a fourth share of the com-pany in fully paid-up shares. After paying the remain-ing original share-holders for their shares, and deducting the cost of the mill, this did not leave a farthing of profit, and our only chance of making any lay in the shares we still held in the new company.

The gold-mines of Victoria, both alluvial and quartz, are of great extent, and some of them of extraordinary richness. The reefs as a rule are larger, and carry their gold more regularly throughout than do the reefs in Queensland. Many of them are worked on a gigantic scale, and will pay a dividend with a yield of 4 dwt. to the ton. The chief alluvial diggings is Ballarat, and Sandhurst is the head mining centre. They are both distant about one hundred miles from Melbourne, and connected with it by rail. But the whole colony is full of both alluvial and reefing districts, and while the old fields continue to develop, fresh ones are still being discovered. The total yield of gold in 1883 was 808,521 oz. valued at £3,234,124, showing an increase of £133,036 over the yield of 1878; but there is little doubt that if a healthier tone of speculation pervaded the mining market of Victoria, her gold-fields would be developed very much more quickly. The gold-mines of Victoria, however, are an important factor in the money market of the world; and since the discovery of gold in 1851, to the end of the year 1882, the quantity of gold raised amounted to £205,600,216.

The population of Victoria in the last five years has increased over 100,000. The following are the figures:—

POPULATION.

| December 1878 . | 827,439 |
| ,, 1883 . | 931,800 |
| Increase . . | 104,361 |

The revenue has increased even faster than the population, for whereas the increase of the latter was only $12\frac{1}{2}$ per cent. in five years, that of the former was as much as $24\frac{1}{2}$ per cent., in a similar period. This is readily accounted for by two causes, the high protection tariff of the colony, and the extortionate taxation of land recently introduced by the Government, which, of course, for a time increases the revenue, but cannot fail in the end to injure the prosperity of the colony, by deterring immigration, and bringing the transfer of land to a dead-lock.

### REVENUE.

| | |
|---|---|
| 1877–8 . . . . | £4,504,413 |
| 1882–3 . . . . | 5,611,253 |
| Increase . | £1,106,840 |

The imports in 1883 exceeded those in 1878 by over one and a half millions sterling, and the exports in 1883 exceeded those in 1878 by nearly that amount.

### IMPORTS and EXPORTS.

| | Imports. | Exports. |
|---|---|---|
| 1878 | £16,161,880 | £14,925,707 |
| 1883 | 17,713,484 | 16,394,936 |
| Increase | £1,551,604 | £1,469,229 |

### RAILWAYS.

| Year. | Miles open. | Receipts. |
|---|---|---|
| 1878 . . . | 1,052 . . . | £1,391,701 |
| 1883 | . 1,562 . . . | 1,898,311 |
| Increase | 510 . . . | £506,610 |

### AGRICULTURE.

| Year. | Acres under cultivation. | Acres under crop. | Wheat Bushels raised. |
|---|---|---|---|
| 1879 | 1,688,275 | 707,188 . | 9,898,858 |
| 1883 | 2,208,652 | 1,099,944 | 15,499,143 |
| Increase . | 520,877 . . | 392,756 . | 6,100,285 |

It will be seen that the average yield of wheat per cent. is very low, being under $2\frac{1}{2}$ quarters to the acre.

In 1880 3,580,000 bushels of wheat were exported, and in 1884 it is calculated that the amount will rise to 9,000,000 bushels.

WOOL PRODUCED (excess of exports over imports).

| Year. | Quantity. lbs. | Value. £ |
|---|---|---|
| 1878 | 52,639,293 | 3,447,451 |
| 1883 | 64,095,489 . | 5,178,081 |
| Increase | 11,456,196 | 1,730,630 |

LIVE STOCK.

| Year. | Horses. | Cattle. | Sheep. |
|---|---|---|---|
| 1878 | 203,150 | 1,169,576 | 10,117,867 |
| 1883 | 280,874 . | . 1 287,088 . | . 10,174,246 |
| Increase | 77,724 | 117,512 | 56,379 |

The fact that whereas the number of sheep in five years has only increased 56,379, the amount of wool produced during the same period has increased 11,456,196 lbs. at first sight seems rather curious. It is accounted for by three causes. In the first place in the last few years a great many people have given up washing their wool. In the second place, whereas at the end of 1878 the sheep in Victoria were almost entirely merinos, there are now a great number of cross-breds, which, of course, carry greater weight of wool per sheep. In the third place, and this is the most important cause of all three, the wool-growers of Victoria, by improving the breed of their sheep, have during the last few years, in many instances, increased the wool produced by their flocks considerably over one pound per head.

The increase indicated above in cattle and sheep in the colony is ridiculously small. But during the next few years it is pretty certain that the returns will show a considerable decrease. A stock tax was passed a year or two ago, of 5s. per head on all cattle, and 1s. per head on all sheep in Victoria. The public revenue derives little benefit from it, for it costs as much to collect as it is worth, but it is a ruinous imposition on the growers of stock, and is driving sheep and cattle out of the colony in great numbers. Quite recently over two hundred thousand fat sheep have passed from Victoria into New South Wales, where, of course, they will be slaughtered, and their fleeces go to swell the returns of that colony.

The existence of immense freeholds in Victoria has aroused the fiercest class-hatreds in that democratic community, and has provoked legislation which can only be described as free plunder. It is not long since *The Times* drew the attention of England to the astonishing fact that one tenth of the revenue from taxation is paid by a few individuals.

Now, as the population of a country increases, the continued existence of large tracts of land, whether freehold or leasehold, held for pastoral purposes, is to a certain extent a barrier to the advance of civilisation. But we must remember that, had these lands never been taken up and improved by their owners and holders, civilisation could never have advanced at all.

Throughout the whole of Australia rages an interne-
cine war between the two great rival classes competing
for the possession of the land, the squatters and the
selectors. The squatter is the pioneer of civilisation.
His profits are often great, but they are no greater than
his risks deserve, and it is his capital and enterprise
alone that open up the country. At his heels follow the
selectors, an impecunious tribe of jackals armed with
manhood suffrage, who rob him of his hard-earned
gains.

Now it would be utterly unreasonable that the squatter
should expect to remain unmolested in possession of
vast tracts of country, requiring a very few hands to
work. When the proper time comes, he must give way
to the advancing tide of population, and move on
further away from civilisation. But when we consider
that at great risk to himself he has made life
possible in a country where it was impossible before,
it is evident that every consideration is due to the
squatter, and, at any rate, that he is entitled to some
compensation for being forcibly ejected. Had it not
been for the squatter's water-tanks some of the railways in Victoria and new South Wales could never
have been made, and, as has been already said, it is
his capital and enterprise alone that have developed the
country.

But in Victoria the possession of a large estate is
considered as a crime, and the holder a fair mark for
reprisals. The recent land legislation in the colony is
perfectly indefensible.

A few years ago a land-tax was passed, which, until it
was surpassed by a still worse measure, stood alone for

a piece of villainous legislation. It was directed entirely against one class, the holders of large freeholds, for all town-lands and anything under the value of £2,500 was exempt. The value of the whole tax is about £200,000, and it is paid by a little over 800 individuals.

If anything could be worse than the Land Bill itself, it is the way in which the provisions of it are carried out. The assessment of the land was entrusted to the hands of publicans, newspaper editors, and school-masters; and the way in which it has been carried out is a perfect scandal. I have seen a large open plain, divided merely by a wire fence, the land on one side of which was taxed at threepence per acre, and on the other side at a shilling. Extensive bribery prevails, of course, the assessors being generally amenable to the influence of a ten-pound note; but where this induce-ment is not forthcoming, the assessment is regulated by purely political considerations.

A friend of mine, a Conservative, pays the same rent for 7,000 acres of land as his next neighbour, a Radical, pays for 17,000 acres of exactly the same class of country. The classification of the land is itself a most phenomenal piece of absurdity, involving not only rotten legislation but false arithmetic. The land is assessed as follows :—

| | | | | |
|---|---|---|---|---|
| 1st class | . | . | . | 1s. per acre. |
| 2nd ,. | . | . | . | 9d. ,. |
| 3rd . | . | . | . | 6d. |
| 4th ,, | . | . | . | 3d. ,, |

Thus the rise in the tax from the fourth to the third class is 50 per cent., from the third to the second class is 33⅓ per cent, and from the second to the first is only 25 per cent.

As a matter of course the value of land all over the colony went down 30 per cent. ; but the land tax has been entirely eclipsed by the infamous Bill that has just now been passed. The original leases of the squatters having all of them expired some years ago, they have been holding their runs under yearly lease from the Crown. The Government have now resumed all lands so held, without option of purchase, and without any compensation for improvements of any kind, and are going to put them up to auction with all improvements standing on them. It is impossible to imagine more wholesale and unjustifiable robbery, and the effect to many of the squatters will be disastrous.

There is no doubt that the high protection tariff of Victoria and recent land-legislation are doing a great deal to retard the progress of the colony, and to darken her future prospects. Though the tables of statistics above show fairly satisfactory progress, we must remember that they were taken just after a run of five remarkably good seasons, and before the evil effects of the Land Acts were beginning to be severely felt.

In the next decade the progress of Victoria will not be anything like so rapid, and, as it is, she has chiefly her enormous yield of gold to thank for the position she holds. That position she is doing her best to forfeit, and she will very soon be eclipsed by the sister colonies of Queensland and New South Wales. It has been calculated that over fifteen millions of capital have been driven from Victoria into Queensland and New South Wales during the last three years.

In Victoria there is manhood suffrage, and the members of the Lower House of Parliament receive a salary of £300. The Upper House has recently been Liberalised to a very considerable extent, by reducing the qualifications both of its members and of those by whom they are elected. While this has had the effect, if indeed that were possible, of lowering the tone of the Upper House, it has materially strengthened its position. To any attempt to raise an outcry against the Upper House as being representatives of merely a class, the answer is obvious, that the Upper House now represents the people, and is elected by them just as much as the Lower House. The language used in the latter assembly is disgraceful; some of its members are not unfrequently intoxicated, and occasionally there is a fight on the floor.

In Victoria, as in new South Wales and in Queensland, Members of Parliament are principally collected from the scum of the community, and politics are looked down on as being unfit either for the occupation of a gentleman or the profession of an honest man.

It is pleasant to turn from the spectacle of a mob of selfish ruffians struggling to fill their own pockets by ruining a colony, to the society of Melbourne, which is one of the cheeriest and pleasantest in the world.

# CHAPTER XXI.

## MELBOURNE.

To know what real hospitality means, a man must needs go to Australia. Let him journey through the length of the land, in the solitude of the back country or in the busiest of the towns, he has nothing to do but to say he is a stranger to ensure him a welcome. Whether he brings letters of introduction or not, as long as he behaves like a gentleman he will find no door in the country closed against him; and if he stays any length of time he will ever after attach a meaning to the word hospitality, such as he never realised in any other country in the world.

In England hospitality is a lukewarm and cheerless commodity, occasionally doled out in the form of patronage to those from whom no return can be expected, but generally only extended in carefully measured quantities to those from whom an equivalent in kind is anticipated at no distant date. In Australia the word has a very different significance. Hospitality

23

there is no respector of persons, but is extended alike
to rich and to poor, to those who have come from
ten miles off, or to people from the other side of the
world, who are extremely unlikely ever to be able to
return it.

Prompted neither by a recollection of past benefits,
nor by expectation of favours to come, it originates
in a real honest care for the comfort of others, and
looks for no other reward than that of giving happi-
ness, and for no other thanks than a kindly recollection on the part of those to whom it is offered.

It is deeply to be regretted that even this small
return is so frequently not forthcoming.  Too many of
our own countrymen are, I fear, open to a charge of the
basest ingratitude in this respect.  They go out to visit
Australia with a sort of notion that they are conferring
a favour on the inhabitants by doing so.  While they
are there they avail themselves to the utmost of the
kindness that is everywhere shown them, and on their
return to England they abuse the country that they have
just left, and run down its institutions and inhabitants
in every possible way.

It is difficult to imagine a more disgusting picture of
humanity than a young man, educated as a gentleman,
who does not scruple to extract all the pleasure and
profit he can from people upon whom he has not the
slightest claim, and who, as soon as his back is turned,
has not the generosity to acknowledge the kindness with
which he has been treated, or to refrain from laughing
at some solecism which the extreme delicacy of his
insular breeding imagines it has been able to detect in
his entertainers.

And yet it is a picture that I have seen only too
often. Many of my own countrymen only think it
necessary to behave like gentlemen so long as they are
in England, and when they get to Australia offer but
a sorry sample of the manners and customs of the
country that raised them. They seem to consider that
because they are in a new country they can behave just
as they please, and often do not wait till their return
to requite with rudeness the hospitality they seem to
expect as a right.

The rampart of pseudo-refinement and class prejudice
behind which that portion of English society known as
the " Upper Ten " is accustomed to shelter itself is
usually supposed to be the result of birth, breeding, and
education. Since I have had an opportunity of observing the altered behaviour of the members of that
mystic guild who find their way to Australia, I have
come to the conclusion that their " insular reserve,"
is not so much a question of class as of climate.

Probably there is something in the genial atmosphere
of Australia that so quickly thaws the reserve of
Englishmen, and causes them to enter heart and soul
into all the amusement that is to be found there, and
to accept without hesitation the hospitality that is
offered them by perfect strangers.

It must be the warmth of the climate that does this,
for I have noticed that the reverse process takes place
when they return to the lower temperature of their
mother country. There, if chance throws them, as it
often does, into the society of those with whom they
have made merry in Australia, they find it convenient
once more to esconce themselves behind the barrier of

their own society's law, which holds that except in a foreign land a man cannot associate with anyone out of his own set without losing caste, and at home must not introduce any outsider into its enchanted circle unless he be the possessor of fabulous wealth.

Armed with this, the Australian in London may hope for a certain per-centage of return hospitality from those whom he may have entertained in his own country. If he takes a house in a fashionable situation, he may even hope to find a few people so inquisitive as to wish to make his acquaintance. But, wherever he goes, he must always expect to be reminded that he is only there on sufferance ; and, if he has a wife, he must not mind her being stared at as if she were a wild beast, by members of a society that prides itself on being the most refined in the world. If people who consider themselves in the best society in London were simply to declare that anyone who was born south of the equator is unfit to associate with them, and refuse to recognise Australians at all, such conduct, though open to a charge of prejudice, would at least have the merit of consistency.

What is difficult to understand, is how people who pride themselves on the perfection of their breeding can ask Australians to their houses and then be gratuitously rude to them. The prejudice that exists in England against Australians is a perfect discredit to an age so enlightened as the present, and is calculated to do serious injury to the prospect of maintaining the permanent union of the two countries, which is of such vital importance to both. There is no doubt that this prejudice is partly owing to the bad impression created by some few Australians, who have brought their money to England to make such fools of themselves with it, that many people are only too ready to tar all their compatriots with the same brush.

But this is not the real origin of the feeling. The real indictment brought against the Australians is that they come from a land where there was once a penal settlement, and consequently are open to the suspicion of being descended from those who have worked for the good of their country. This may have been all very well in the infancy of the colonies, but we must remember that Australia is no longer a very young country, and it is fully time that her early social history were relegated to the annals of the past. It is inconceivable how any class of people can be found so bigoted as to keep such a prejudice up.

Any Englishman who is so fortunate as to be able to trace his family history back a couple of centuries, will certainly come across several relations who were executed for treason, if for nothing worse; and if he pursues his inquiries any further he must inevitably run his ancestors to ground in a rabbit-warren of immorality, from which no College of Heraldry can ever really extricate them. It is difficult to follow the subtle reasoning of a pride that looks up to an ancestor whose head was certainly chopped off for conspiracy, and looks down on an acquaintance whose grandfather was possibly transported for fraud.

Many Englishmen who visit Australia form an erroneous opinion of its society because they persist in applying to it the standard of the one that they have just left. They stay sufficiently long to discover that in some points it differs from what they have been accustomed to, and not long enough to discover that difference does not necessarily imply inferiority. Having in too many cases brought with them the prejudice, and left behind them the polish of England's society, their views are occasionally still further warped by the discovery that, even in Australia, a man cannot behave otherwise than like a gentleman without an occasional rebuff.

It is from the views of such critics as these that English notions of Australian society are chiefly derived, and upon no point are they more unjustly censorious than upon what they are pleased to call the fastness of the women of Australia. If the canons of English society of the nineteenth century were a fixed standard for determining the propriety of woman's behaviour, there might be some show of justice in condemning anything that falls short of it. But we all know that nothing of the kind is the case. Society's laws are constructed on a sliding scale that varies from one generation to another. In the words of Macaulay, " we change the fashion of our morals with our coats and our hats, and wonder at the depravity of our ancestors."

We have only to look at the relative measure of justice that the same society deals to a man and to a woman for the same offence, to see that it is regulated by arbitrary laws, which have little reference to abstract principles of right and wrong.

Nothing can be more unjust than to try one community by the social laws which govern another ; for although there are certain broad rules which cannot with impunity be transgressed in any society at present, still, in minor matters, what constitutes a breach of propriety in one society does not necessarily do so in another.

The frank demeanour and the entire absence of affectation that make an Australian girl such a pleasant companion after ten minutes' acquaintance, would in England, of course, be set down to fastness, if to nothing worse. Society in England holds affectation in an unmarried woman to be an integral part of modesty, and in order, therefore, to guard against the imputation of forwardness, reserve with a recent acquaintance must be pushed to the verge of stupidity.

Now, as long as critics upon this point recognise that it is simply the veneering of outward demeanour that they are discussing, no harm is done. But any inference as to the morality that may lie beneath it, is most reprehensible. Whether it be a more excellent thing in woman to try and entertain a man to whom she is introduced, or to make it next to impossible for him to entertain her, is a question which should be decided entirely upon its own merits. But it is infamous to say that the absence of reserve, which in some women is the natural outcome of good spirits and a desire to please, argues the slightest inferiority of moral principles to those who have been brought up to consider that purity can only be preserved in ice.

In point of actual immorality, it is doubtful whether fashionable society has varied very much in any country since the age that evoked the satires of Horace and Juvenal. There are periods during which open immorality is fashionable, just as there are some summers

hotter than others, but in the end the mean temperature is maintained. Certainly just now there seems
to be a fall in the moral thermometer all over the
world.

A poet not long dead has declared that London is
no better than the cities for whom " God heard Abra-
ham pray in vain." And assuredly we do not seem far
off the time when the words, *quæ jussa coram non sine
conscio surgit màrito*, will cease to convey any great
reproach to those to whom they may apply. At present,
however, even in London a departure from the path of
virtue derives an additional piquancy from the danger
of social ostracism to which detection exposes the
offender.

As long as Australia is not more lax than London
in upholding the Eleventh Commandment, no one has
the slightest right to disparage the tone of her society.
But it must be indeed a captious and cynical disposition
that would prevent a man, at least during his stay in
Australia, from flinging all such considerations as these
to the winds, and abandoning himself to the charm of
his surroundings.

In Melbourne, especially, it is impossible for a man
to stay long without feeling that he is in an atmosphere
of cheerfulness, and amongst people who are determined
to enjoy life thoroughly. A single introduction makes
him free of the guild, and before he has been there a
week he will know everyone in the place. In this
respect Melbourne has a great advantage over Sydney,
where society is split up into several sets, each of which,
for some unaccountable reason, refuses to mix with the
others.

Whatever a man's tastes may be, it must be his own fault if they are not gratified in Melbourne. If he is inclined for sport, from October to March he will see as good racing as he ever saw in his life, and during the remainder of the year he will have an excellent opportunity of breaking his neck with the Melbourne hounds. If he is fond of good living, he will find that it is with good reason that the "viveurs" of Melbourne pride themselves on the excellence of their wines, and the proficiency of their "chefs." After dinner, if he wishes to gamble, at either of the clubs he will find a certain number of congenial spirits, and, whether he win or lose, it is extremely unlikely next morning that he will complain of the smallness of the stakes.

There are two exceedingly comfortable clubs, the "Australian" and the "Melbourne," both of which admit honorary members for a period of not more than six months in two years; a very liberal allowance, which adds considerably to the pleasure of a visitor's stay in the place, without putting him to any expense. Occasionally rather heavy play goes on at both the clubs. I have known a single player to drop over ten thousand pounds at a sitting.

For several miles to the south-east the suburbs consist of nothing but detached houses, each surrounded by more or less extensive gardens and grounds. Many of these houses have been constructed at an enormous expense, and fitted up by their owners with every comfort and luxury that can be imagined. The grounds of some of them are really beautifully laid out, and there is invariably a well-kept, prosperous kind of look about the whole concern, from the gate-post to the weather-cock.

A glorious ball-room is a very common appendage to one of these Melbourne houses. Dancing, with the people of Melbourne, is a passion; and, like everything else that they go in for, they do it well. The ball-room is strictly sacred to its legitimate use, and no profane feet are allowed to invade its precincts between whiles. All the anxious care of a mother for a delicate child is lavished by the hostess on her ball-room floor, when she is about to give a dance. The music is generally excellent, and they have a happy knack in Melbourne of filling their rooms without crowding them.

Most of the women dance divinely. All through Australia dancing seems to come as naturally to girls as walking; and in Melbourne it is as rare to find a woman between fifteen and fifty who dances badly, as it is in England to find one who dances well. Altogether, if a man goes to a ball to dance and not to lean against a door-post, it is odd if he does not look back to some of these small dances in Melbourne, where everyone knows each other, as amongst the pleasantest he ever was at in his life.

Lawn-tennis is everywhere immensely popular. Young men and maidens, old women and children, at it they go, with the enthusiasm which, whether in the pursuit of business or of pleasure, is a distinctive feature of the inhabitants of Melbourne. Really the energy with which some of the fair sex devote themselves to the game savours rather of work than of play. Those who do play, play for four hours every day of their lives,

and those who do not, come to look on. A round of
afternoon calls means visiting the various lawn-tennis
courts in succession. Here, between the hours of three
and seven, the youth, beauty, and fashion of the place
are every day to be found, comfortably located in a
summer-house overlooking the court, drinking tea and
talking scandal, and watching the enthusiasts below,
who are playing as if their lives depended upon every
stroke of the game.

Hotbeds of scandal are these lawn-tennis parties, but
here the people of Melbourne show their wisdom by
declining to spoil two good things by mixing them.
No one who plays is expected to talk scandal on ·the
same afternoon. The players may sit down to rest
their aching limbs, and if there is time they may have
some tea; but they must be prepared to put down
their cups untasted, and start up again at a moment's
notice to make up another set, lest a minute's interval
in the play should take place. To display the slightest
inclination to sit still, is to risk offending an otherwise
most indulgent hostess, who is certain to be an inde-
fatigable player herself.

Many a time have I watched a recent arrival in the
colony, whose ignorance of its customs leads him to
suppose that an hour's hard play under a broiling sun
entitles him to a few minutes' repose. Having secured
a cup of tea, and asked permission to smoke, he lights
a cigar, and, establishing himself comfortably in an
arm-chair, prepares to enjoy the society of one of his
fair neighbours who does not play. Just then the set
is finished. The relentless eye of his hostess marks
him out for another, and he is forthwith invited to play

again. It is no use refusing. He will have to give in. His hostess is going to play again herself, and for very shame he cannot say he is too tired. There is something sublime in the vitality of a woman who can handle a lawn-tennis racquet for three hours at a stretch, under the afternoon fire of an Australian sun. Gradually he will find himself infected by such heroism, and by the time that he has been a week in the town he will never dream of refusing to play when he is asked.

The climate of the town itself is rather enervating at times, especially in summer, when hot winds blow occasionally for one or two days at a time ; and before a stranger has been long in Melbourne society, especially if he goes much into the bachelor portion of it, he will find that he needs a good constitution and a hard head to drink fair with some of his entertainers. The excellent quality of the wine he is drinking is apt to make him rather careless about the quantity. One of these hot winds, therefore, coming on the top of a " Burgundy night " at the Melbourne Club, will probably recall to a visitor's mind the numerous invitations that he is certain to have received to go and spend a few days in the country.

Away to the north of Melbourne the plain country rises gradually for about forty miles to an elevation of about fifteen hundred feet. Beyond this are heavily-timbered mountain-ranges, on the southern slopes of which are some of the most exquisitely situated country houses in the world. The owners of many of them seem to keep open house the whole year round, and are never happy unless they have a succession of visitors from Melbourne to keep their houses full. When Melbourne is suffocated with dust and heat, the climate up here is delightfully cool and pleasant. Anything more beautiful than some of these places cannot be imagined. Of course the grounds around them are artificially made, being clearances in the endless forest of huge gum-trees, but they have been turned by the genius of their owners into perfect paradises of beauty. Ornamental trees, flowering shrubs, and creepers of every description, grow as if they were determined to make up for lost time in never having been planted before. Wild flowers flourish as if nature had upset her basket here and never stopped to pick it up, and exotics are scattered around with a profusion that quite takes a stranger's breath away, and makes him rub his eyes to be sure that good living in Melbourne has not had the effect of making him see double.

Here the exhausted lawn-tennis player from Melbourne can stretch his weary limbs in perfect peace, idly drinking in the pure mountain air, and feasting on the beauty of the scene around him, without risk of any less pleasant interruption than a stroll round the garden and through the fern-tree gullies. With a pipe to keep away musquitoes, and the conversation of one of Australia's daughters to keep away care, a man must be indeed hard to please who cannot enjoy himself thoroughly. He need not exert himself. He has nothing to do but to allow his fair companion to entertain him. She will do it with an ease that no other woman in the world is so thoroughly mistress of as an Australian.

The scene is one which is not readily forgotten. Around on three sides rise wild mountain ranges, covered to the very summit with dense masses of dark-green forest. Behind them the sun sinks to rest—

> Not, as in northern climes, obscurely bright,
> But one unclouded blaze of living light.

In front a garden bright with every conceivable shade of colouring slopes gently down to a miniature lake, whose glassy surface, unmarred by a single ripple, reflects with startling distinctness the trees that fringe its edges. Beyond this the plains go rolling down to Melbourne, forty miles away, dimly visible, except on a very clear day ; but its whereabouts is distinctly marked by a murky cloud of smoke, which rises up and drifts away to seaward over the shining expanse of Port Philip harbour. It is pleasant to watch the storm-clouds gathering in the south, and to see the steamers creeping out to sea, to fight their way along the most pitiless coast in the world. " Suave mari magno " rises to the spectator's lips, and as he turns to the home-like comfort and fairy beauty of the scene around him, the conviction comes across him that by no race in the world is the philosophy of life better understood than by the inhabitants of Australia.

Small wonder if the lawn-tennis player who comes up here to recruit, occasionally imbibes something else besides mountain air. The perfect repose of his surroundings, the sensation of " masterly inactivity " in himself, which is never felt to perfection out of a hot climate, will make him feel that the world is very pleasant to live in ; an impression that will deepen as he listens to his entertainer's refreshing views of life, and notes her unaffected interest in everything, which proclaims her a stranger to the meaning of the word *ennui*.

The stillness of the evening air is heavy with the scent of orange-flowers, gardenias, and stephanotis; and as the charm of his companion's manner grows upon him, he will own to himself that some of the daughters of the South are wondrous fair.

# CHAPTER XXII.

## IMPERIAL FEDERATION.

IT is impossible for anyone to visit Australia without speculating upon the future that awaits a country possessing such enormous natural wealth and resources. The rapid development that has taken place in every part of this continent during the past thirty years, a development for which there is no parallel in history, makes it certain that before long Australia will form a very considerable item in making up the balance of political power throughout the world. Already she has become a financial power of the first magnitude, and the annual yield of gold in Victoria alone has no small share in determining the value of money in every market from Hong-Kong to London.

It is obvious that a country with the natural advantages of Australia, inhabited, as she is, by the only race who have ever proved themselves able to rise from a colony into a nation, has before her, if she choose to claim it, an existence as one of the independent powers of the world. The question, therefore, naturally arises as to whether she will elect to remain a portion of the British Empire, or whether she will prefer to sever the connection that binds her to the mother country.

In the whole history of the world there has probably never been a question raised of such stupendous importance. The remarks which apply to Australia apply with equal force to Canada, and the subject involves a consideration of the British Empire as a whole, its possible development, its possible disintegration, and the relation of both these contingencies to the future of England herself, of her colonies, and of the whole world.

The Imperial Federation of the British Empire is too vast a subject to be considered at any length in a work of this kind, but it is one with which the future of Australia is so intimately connected that it is impossible to pass over it in silence. Imperial Federation has long been regarded as a mere vision of theorists, sufficiently alluring as a sentimental idea, but wholly incapable of being worked out as a practical problem.

Because no definite scheme has as yet been propounded, the unthinking majority, a class ever the foremost to criticise, have sneered at the notion as utterly unpractical, and relegated it in their own minds to the Millennium.

Opinion on the subject may be divided into three classes.

Firstly, there is the opinion of those who believe that the existing relations between England and her colonies are sufficiently close to secure the permanent unity of the Empire, in spite of the causes which at present threaten to break it up. This opinion may fairly be taken as an epitome of the ignorance of those who know nothing whatever about the subject.

Secondly, there is the opinion of those who recognise the likelihood of disintegration, but who face it with perfect equanimity, and entirely deny the possibility of framing any scheme of Federation that will avert it. This is a much more comprehensive class of ignorance than the first, a species of perverted knowledge which has been crystallized into drivelling similes. Colonies are compared to children who leave their parents as soon as they are grown up, or to fruit dropping off a tree when it is ripe. It is impossible to condemn too harshly such mischievous fallacies as these. Our Colonies are not the fruit, they are the branches of the tree itself, stalwart limbs of a mighty empire, and they drop off, not when they are ripe, but when the connection between them and the mother country is rotten.

Thirdly, there is the opinion of those who share neither the false security of the optimists, nor the apathy of the pessimists, and who, while they see clearly the disintegrating causes that are undermining the fabric of the Empire, have set themselves resolutely to work to elaborate a practical scheme for reconstructing its political organization upon a permanent basis. These are the men who, with a full recognition of the danger of doing nothing, and of the difficulty of doing anything, have rescued Imperial Federation from the misty regions of dream-land, and brought it within the scope of practical politics.

The standard of Imperial Federation has been set up, and the alacrity with which men of all political parties, in every part of the Empire, have hastened to enlist in the ranks of its supporters, proves conclusively how powerful a hold the idea has over all the leading spirits of the age. The extraordinary support which it has received at the outset, has almost entirely silenced the enemies of the League which has now been formed. Here and there some editor of a newspaper, determined to prove that his ignorance does not arise from want of information, but from inability to digest it, exposes the petrifaction of his intellect in the shape of an article sneering at the promoters of Imperial Federation, because they have as yet laid down no definite scheme.

Fortunately it is not by babbling critics such as these that the matter will be decided.

Imperial Federation is a question that will be tried entirely upon its own merits, and if ever any practical form of it be carried out, it will be due to the " masterly inactivity " of those who forebore to hamper its development at the outset by any premature discussion of details. The time is rapidly approaching when some well-defined and precise scheme for the Federation of the Empire must be laid down.

But in the meantime it is the wise policy of the League to arouse popular enthusiasm in every British community, to point out the dangers that threaten, and the necessity for immediate action; so that when the time comes for the details of any scheme to be considered, the various portions of the Empire may be prepared to make mutual concessions to avert a common evil, and to secure a common good.

The ever-increasing majority in whose hands the power of deciding the destiny of their country has been placed, are men who, in the struggle for existence, have little leisure to devote to the consideration of politics. When a fair statement is laid before them, the working

classes are marvellously shrewd in discerning in which
direction their best interests lie ; but it is too much to
expect them to evolve, out of their inner consciousness,
a knowledge of what may be termed the unwritten
current history of the world.

It is the solemn duty of every statesman worthy of
the name, to enlighten the minds of the working-classes
upon those momentous questions which have now, by
an extended suffrage, been surrendered into their
hands for decision. The masses of the people have
not the means for forming an independent judgment
upon foreign affairs, and are only too ready to take
their opinions at second hand from those who, from
their position, are supposed to be qualified to direct
them.

A change so momentous as the dismemberment of
the Empire of Greater Britain is not accomplished in
a day. It is a process so gradual that, unless we look
carefully both at the past and at the present, we do
not recognise that it is taking place. He alone reads
history aright who, observing the events which conduce
to the rise and fall of nations, traces those events back
to their true cause, and applies the experience so gained
to the solution of the problems of the present. Unfortunately the people of England at the present time
are likely to gain but a scant insight into Imperial policy,
from observing the flounderings of a Ministry whose
actions have alienated every single European Power,
and who have carried War with dishonour into almost
every portion of their own Empire.

Whatever questions of colonial policy have been
brought before them have been treated by the present

Ministry with a mixture of stupidity and indifference which clearly proves them to be unworthy of the name of statesmen. It is evident that in the hearts of more than one of them the cry of " Perish India " finds only too ready an echo. The importance of retaining India is a question which cannot be discussed here, for its abandonment is bound up with the Disintegration of the Empire, and with the ruin of millions of the working classes in Great Britain. It is sufficient that " Perish India " is identified with the name of a veteran agitator, a retrospect of whose long and still unfinished career shows that, under the mask of hypocritical friendship, he has never neglected an opportunity of injuring the working classes.

We should be sorry to believe that the present Ministry in any way represents the feeling of England toward the Colonies. Most of its members neither know nor care anything whatever about foreign affairs, and the few whose political and geographical knowledge is not entirely bounded by the ". silver streak " are consistent in nothing but a fixed determination to alienate the Colonies.

Mr. Gladstone repudiates the idea of Imperial Federation as " wholly visionary," and declares that the most he hopes for as a statesman is to effect a separation from the Colonies without bloodshed.

If Lord Derby and Lord Granville are allowed to pursue their present treatment of Colonial interests much longer, it is probable that even the modest hope of Mr. Gladstone will not be realised.

The Colonial correspondence during the last twenty years shows that neither Lord Granville nor Lord Derby have ever lost an opportunity of insulting Colonial susceptibilities, and injuring Colonial interests.

In 1870 it was openly stated in the Dominion Parliament of Canada by Sir Alexander Galt and Mr. Huntington that it was with unfeigned regret that they were obliged to conclude that it was the deliberate intention of Her Majesty's Ministers to effect a separation between the two countries. Even stronger was the feeling which was aroused in New Zealand at the same time.

But all previous blunders of Colonial policy fade into insignificance when compared with the New Guinea question, and we can conceive nothing better calculated to produce a revolution in Australia than the conduct of the English Government in the matter. That it has not done so is entirely due to the fact that the Australians are able to discriminate between the English Government and the English people.

But no one can pretend that distinctions of this kind are a basis upon which the unity of the Empire can be long maintained.

Those who imagine that the existing relations between England and her Colonies are satisfactory will do well to study the New Guinea question, for it is one which conclusively proves that the Empire cannot remain united upon its present political basis.

The main facts connected with the case are well known to all. New Guinea is an island off the northeast coast of Queensland. Its southern shores form one side of Torres Straits, which is one of the main approaches to Australia, and altogether the island bears about the same geographical relation to Queensland that Ireland does to England.

For many years New Guinea has always been looked upon as belonging by natural right to the continent of Australia; but it was not until the danger of foreign annexation was felt, that Australian statesmen realised the importance of at once securing the island for their country.

So great was the scare lest France should secure a foothold in the island, that even the delay of applying to the English Government was felt to be dangerous, and Queensland annexed the whole unoccupied portion of the island, with the full consent of Australia, and then invited the English Government to sanction the annexation.

The contemptuous incivility with which the Australian proposals were met proves, not only that Lord Derby had no sense of the delicate relations between a mother country and her colonies, but also that he entirely failed to realise the intrinsic importance of the question.

Setting aside any question of good feeling or decent behaviour, so as to bring the matter as far as possible within the scope of the present Foreign Office, it was surely most impolitic to irritate Australia by an uncivil demurrer to her just claims, when there was nothing whatever to be gained by opposing them.

Finding that open opposition was arousing a feeling in Australia which it would be difficult to deal with, Lord Derby then had recourse to treachery to accomplish his object of thwarting the wishes of the Australians. Yielding so far to the pressure which was brought to bear upon him, he annexed a portion of the island, and allayed the fears of Australia on the score of foreign intervention, by giving the most unqualified assurances that no other Power should be allowed to touch New Guinea.

While these very assurances were on their way out to the Colonies, it now transpires that Lord Derby and Lord Granville were engaged in handing over a portion of New Guinea to Germany, for no other conceivable purpose than at once to insult and to injure the most loyal of communities.

We look in vain for the motive which prompted this betrayal of Australian interests, but the result is, unfortunately, only too apparent. The question is not one of sentiment, but of real and tangible interest.

In annexing New Guinea, Australia was simply making a wise and politic effort to avail herself of geographical advantages, to secure a peaceful future. But the presence of the most powerful military nation in Europe, in an island adjacent to her shores, has entirely altered the prospects of Australia, and has inflicted a lasting injury upon her future.

It is not by the geographical advantages of an isolated position, but by an enormous addition to her naval and military force, that Australia must in future be prepared to secure herself from foreign aggression; and for this she has only the English Government to thank.

The surrender of Australian interests to Germany by English statesmen has aroused a feeling of bitter resentment and humiliation throughout the Colonies, and the feeling is not likely to be weakened by the discovery that while the action itself was discreditable to statesmen, the manner in which it was done was unworthy of gentlemen.

The recent offer of military assistance from the Colonies must awake enthusiastic admiration in the heart of every true Englishmen for the patriotism and loyalty of our kin beyond the sea. But the joy with which we in England hail the offer must be considerably lessened by the reflection that while the troops are embarking in Sydney for Suakim, the Colonial Secretary is being burnt in effigy in various parts of Australia.

Too many of us will be only too ready to jump to the conclusion that because the Colonies have shown themselves willing to take an active part in fighting our battles, therefore Imperial Federation is a *fait accompli*, and that nothing more remains to be done. A more mischievous delusion can hardly be imagined, and it is of the utmost importance that the present attitude of the Colonies should not be misunder· stood.

The present offer of military assistance proves, indeed, that the Colonies are able and willing to bear their share of Imperial Defence. But we must remember that the offer is coupled with a protest against the recent action of the English Government, which no statesman will be wise to neglect.

The tone of the Australian Press with regard to the New Guinea question is a solemn warning that the present relations between the mother country and the Colonies cannot exist much longer.

The enthusiasm which prompted Australia to send her money and her men to help England in the Soudan, while still smarting under her betrayal to Germany by the English Government, is indeed the triumph of loyalty over exasperation. It is, in fact, a direct overture for Imperial Federation, and we shall do well to accept it as such, and as nothing more.

The sixteen Cabinet Ministers who have brought dishonour and disaster upon their country in every quarter of the globe, and who still cling desperately to office like barnacles to the bottom of a wreck, undoubtedly do not represent either the intelligence or the feeling of the country which they still pretend to govern. This the Australians recognise; but while their loyalty at present remains unshaken, they see clearly that where such a state of things exists their own interests cannot fail to be compromised, of which fact they have lately had a most disastrous example.

Let all those who believe that Imperial Federation now exists ask themselves if it is likely that the Colonies will continue to supply men and money for wars in the conduct of which they have no voice, and which are carried on upon purely party principles by a Government in whose imbecility they originated.

Is it likely that, after the warning of New Guinea, the Colonies will continue to surrender their interests to the arbitrary control of statesmen who betray every determination to repeat the blunders which caused the American Revolution?

It is possible that in years to come England may alienate Australia in the same way that she alienated America. Undoubtedly a prolonged succession of such statesmen as at present guide her foreign policy would have the effect of forcing every one of England's Colonies, who were strong enough to do so, to declare their independence.

Fortunately, however, Imperial Federation is not a

matter that will be left to be manipulated into a party question by politicians whose blunders have made all Europe merry for four years. It will be decided by the working men of Great Britain and her Colonies, whose interests are most deeply affected by the question ; and it is probable that when the time comes, as it shortly will, that the matter must be settled one way or the other, they will decide in favour of retaining their respective positions as portions of one Empire.

There exists in Australia, among all classes, a feeling of loyalty and affection for the old country that has been well described as a passion. To those who look below the surface, there is something very instructive in the sentiment that prompts all Australians, born and bred in the colony, invariably to speak of England as "home," though very possibly they may never have been there, and never intend to go. But although sentiment is undoubtedly an important element, there are other and far more weighty considerations which nearly affect the future of England and her Colonies.

The cardinal point upon which Imperial Federation turns is Imperial Defence ; and the more closely we investigate both questions, the more impossible we shall find it is to separate them. The growing population of England, combined with her fiscal policy during the last thirty years, have made her dependent upon foreign supply for the necessaries of life, to an extent that it is impossible to contemplate without the gravest misgivings.

The only precaution that could neutralize the danger would be an enormous addition to the strength of her navy, and this has been neglected. At the same time the increase in the navies of other Powers has been so great, that it is now doubtful whether, in the event of war, England could defend her own shores and at the same time afford sufficient protection to her commerce to avert the horrors of starvation.

It is evident, then, that if the Empire is to hold together, the Colonies must be prepared to contribute their due share towards its defence. That they are perfectly willing to do so, there is little doubt, provided that their true position as integral portions of the Empire be recognised. England lost America because in the days of her weakness she never made it worth her while to continue as part of the Empire. She made the fatal mistake of treating her as an outlying estate, from which as much as possible was to be squeezed for her own benefit; and the consequence was, as soon as America was strong enough she severed the connection.

The slightest attempt on the part of England to repeat the same tactics with regard to Australia at the present time, or to treat with her otherwise than as an equal in the matter of Federation, would inevitably be followed by separation. And very justly so ; for the question of Imperial Federation, though it is undoubtedly for the advantage both of England and of Australia, is of infinitely greater importance to the future of the mother country than to that of the colony. Both Australia and Canada have before them a glorious future, whether they remain portions of the Empire or become independent. But the future of England herself, deprived of her Colonies, is too gloomy a picture to dwell upon for a moment.

Indeed, the Disintegration of the Empire would be a sufficiently deplorable catastrophe, supposing that it were inevitable. It is rendered doubly so by the brilliant prospect that is opened up by the possibility of Federation.

There is now, outside of England herself, a population of ten millions of Englishmen, inhabiting a territory of almost boundless extent, and with unlimited capabilities for development. In about fifty years these ten millions will have increased to fifty, which, with the population of the mother country, will make a total of at least one hundred millions.

The question, therefore, for Englishmen in every quarter of the globe to ask themselves is this: Are we, by a wise and far-seeing policy, going to unite this enormous nationality in the close relations of an Imperial Federation; or are we, by neglecting the lessons of the past, and by ignoring the warnings of the present, going to allow the vast mass to resolve itself into hostile and helpless fragments, most of which will fall into obscurity among the increasing Powers of the world?

Shall our children and our grand-children see the sublime spectacle of one hundred millions of the most highly-civilised race in the world, inhabiting an Empire upon which the sun never sets, united by the bonds of race and religion, and still more closely united by the interests of an inter-dependent trade, secure from the attack of any foe from without, and developing an ever-increasing prosperity within; or shall they be forced to mourn over the ruins of the finest Empire that the world has ever seen, to watch one after another of its provinces detached from their centre, whether alienated

by England's own folly, or torn from her by a Power
which she can no longer resist; and, finally, to watch
England herself, shorn of the strength which her
remote Dependencies alone can give her, sinking beneath
the burden of a paralysed trade and an enormous population, into an obscurity among the nations from which
she will never rise again ?

A Federation of all parts of the British Empire
would form by far the most mighty Power that has
ever existed in the world, and could laugh at any possible combination of hostile nations.   England's future
as one of the leading Powers depends upon the success
of the movement that has now started ; and we believe
that although an independent existence is open to more
than one of her Colonies, they will one and all prefer
the still more glorious future that awaits them as portions of the Empire of Greater Britain.

# INDEX

# J.

# K.

# L.

# M.

London: Printed by W. H. Allen & Co., 13 Waterloo Place. S.W

Moresby I.

LOUISIADE ARCH

NEW
CALEDONIA

TIMOR

Reef of Coral

Pioneer R.
Mackay
C. Palmerston

Rockhampton
Keppel Bay
C. Capricorn

Burnett R.
Bundaberg
Maryborough
Breaksea Spit

Gt Sandy I.
Wide B.

Gympie

Brisbane R.
Jamine R.
BRISBANE

Moreton I
Moreton B
Stradbroke I.
Pt Danger & Tweed R.

Shark
ay

Murchison R.

PACIFI

Richmond R.
Clarence R.

Port Macquarie

T H
Liverpool
Plains

Port Stephens
Newcastle
Broken B. & Hawkesbury R.
Port Jackson
Botany B.

OCEAN

EY

Freemantle

R. Pe

Jervis B.

Twofold B.
C. Leeuwin
C. Howe

Pt d' Entre

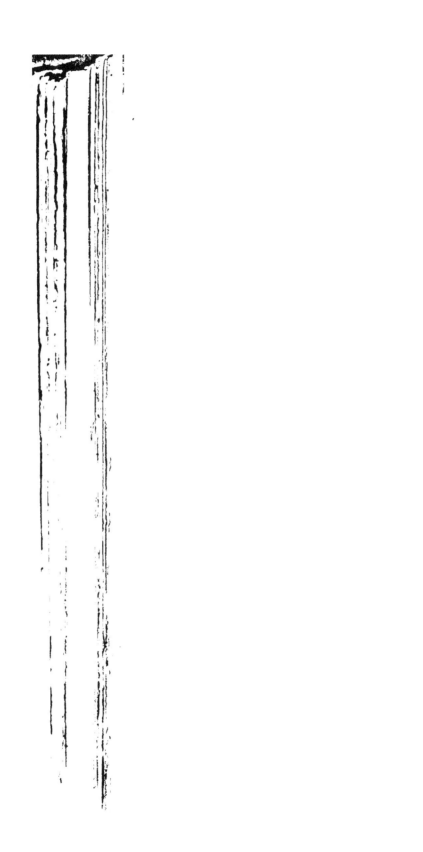

JULY 1885.

# BOOKS, &c.,

ISSUED BY

# MESSRS. W. H. ALLEN & Co.,

Publishers & Literary Agents to the India Office

COMPRISING

MISCELLANEOUS PUBLICATIONS IN GENERAL
LITERATURE.

MILITARY WORKS, INCLUDING THOSE ISSUED
BY THE GOVERNMENT.

INDIAN AND MILITARY LAW.

MAPS OF INDIA, &c.

LONDON:

W. H. ALLEN & CO., 13 WATERLOO PLACE,
PALL MALL, S.W.

# Works issued from the India Office, and sold by
# W. H. ALLEN & Co.

**Illustrations of Ancient Buildings in Kashmir.**
Prepared at the Indian Museum under the authority of the Secretary of
State for India in Council   From Photographs, Plans, and Drawings
taken by Order of the Government of India. By Henry Hardy Cole, Lieut.
R E , Superintendent Archæological Survey of India, North-West Provinces. In 1 vol. ; half-bound, Quarto.   58 Plates.   £3 10s
      The Illustrations in this work have been produced in Carbon from the
original negatives, and are therefore permanent.

**Pharmacopœia of India.**
Prepared under the Authority of the Secretary of State for India.   By
Edward John Waring. M D.  Assisted by a Committee appointed for the
Purpose  8vo   6s.

**The Stupa of Bharhut.  A Buddhist Monument.**
Ornamented with numerous Sculptures illustrative of Buddhist Legend
and History in the Third Century B C.  By Alexander Cunningham, C.S L,
C.I E , Major-General, Royal Engineers (Bengal Retired) ; Director-
General Archæological Survey of India  4to.  57 Plates.  Cloth gilt.
£3 3s.

**Archæological Survey of Western India.**
Report of the First Season's Operations in the Belgâm and Kaladgi
Districts   January to May 1874   Prepared at the India Museum and
Published under the Authority of the Secretary of State for India in
Council  By James Burgess, Author of the "Rock Temples of Elephanta,"
&c &c , and Editor of "The Indian Antiquary."  Half-bound   Quarto
58 Plates and Woodcuts   £2 2s.

**Archæological Survey of Western India.  Vol. II.**
Report on the Antiquities of Kâthiâwâd and Kachh, being the resul of
the Second Season's Operations of the Archæological Survey of West$^e$rn
India   1874-1875   By James Burgess, F.R G S , M R A.S, &c , Archæo
logical Surveyor and Reporter to Government, Western India.   1876.
Half-bound   Quarto.  74 Plates and Woodcuts.  £3 3s.

**Archæological Survey of Western India.  Vol. III.**
Report on the Antiquities in the Bidar and Aurungabad Districts in the
Territory of H H. the Nizam of Haidarabad, being the result of the Third
Season's Operations of the Archæological Survey of Western India.
1875-1876   By James Burgess, F R G S , M R A S., Membre de la Societé
Asiatique, &c , Archæological Surveyor and Reporter to Government,
Western India.  Half-bound   Quarto   66 Plates and Woodcuts.  £2 2s.

**Illustrations of Buildings near Muttra and Agra.**

Showing the Mixed Hindu-Mahomedan Style of Upper India. Prepared at the India Museum under the Authority of the Secretary of State for India in Council, from Photographs, Plans, and Drawings taken by Order of the Government of India By Henry Hardy Cole, Lieut R.E, late Superintendent Archæological Survey of India, North-West Provinces. 4to With Photographs and Plates £3 10s.

**The Cave Temples of India.**

By James Ferguson, D C L , F R A S., V.P R.A S , and James Burgess, F.R G S , M.R A S , &c. Printed and Published by Order of Her Majesty's Secretary of State, &c Roy. 8vo. With Photographs and Woodcuts. £2 2s

# MESSRS. W. H. ALLEN & CO.'S CATALOGUE
# OF BOOKS, &c.

[*All bound in cloth unless otherwise stated.*]

*ABERIGH-MACKAY, GEORGE*
**Twenty-one Days in India.** Being the Tour of Sir Ali Baba,
K.C.B  Post 8vo. 4s. An Illustrated Edition. Demy 8vo. 10s 6d.

*ABBOTT, Capt. JAMES.*
**Narrative of a Journey from Herat to Khiva, Moscow, and
St. Petersburg, during the late Russian Invasion of Khiva.**
With some Account of the Court of Khiva and the Kingdom of Khaurism.
With Map and Portrait. 2 vols  Demy 8vo.  24s.

**Academy Sketches,** including Various Exhibitions  Edited by Henry
Blackburn, Editor of "Academy" and "Grosvenor" Notes  Third
year, 1885, 200 Illustrations  Demy 8vo.  2s

**Æsop, the Fables of, and other Eminent Mythologists.** With
Morals and Reflections  By Sir Roger L'Estrange, kt.  A facsimile
reprint of the Edition of 1669. Fcap. Folio, antique, sheep. 21s.

**Aids to Prayer.** Thirteenth Thousand. 24mo , cloth antique. 1s. 6d.

**Akbar: An Eastern Romance.** By Dr. P A. S. Van Limburg-
Brouwer. Translated from the Dutch by M. M.  With Notes and
Introductory Life of the Emperor Akbar, by Clements R. Markham,
C B , F.R S  Cr. 8vo. 10s. 6d

*ALBERG, ALBERT.*
**Snowdrops: Idylls for Children.** From the Swedish of Zach
Topelius. Cr. 8vo. 3s. 6d.
**Whisperings in the Wood:** Finland Idylls for Children. From the
Swedish of Zach Topelius. Cr. 8vo. 3s. 6d
**Queer People.** A Selection of Short Stories from the Swedish of
"Leah" 2 vols  Illus.  Cr 8vo 12s.

**Alexander II., Emperor of all the Russias, Life of.** By the Author
of "Science, Art, and Literature in Russia," "Life and Times of Alexander I ," &c. Cr. 8vo. 10s 6d.

*ALFORD, HENRY, D D., the late Dean of Canterbury.*
**The New Testament.** After the Authorised Version. Newly com-
pared with the original Greek, and Revised. Long Primer, Cr. 8vo.,
cloth, red edges, 6s ; Brevier, Fcap. 8vo., cloth, 3s. 6d.; Nonpareil,
small 8vo , 1s. 6d , or in calf extra, red edges, 4s 6d.
**How to Study the New Testament.** Vol. I. The Gospels and the
Acts  Vol II. The Epistles, Part 1  Vol. III. The Epistles, Part 2, and
The Revelation  Three vols  Small 8vo  3s. 6d each.

*AMEER ALI, SYED, MOULVI, M.A., LL.B , Barrister-at-Law*
**The Personal Law of the Mahommedans (according to all the Schools).** Together with a Comparative Sketch of the Law of Inheritance among the Sunnis and Shiahs Demy 8vo. 15s

*ANDERSON, EDWARD L.*
**How to Ride and School a Horse.** With a System of Horse Gymnastics. Cr 8vo 2s 6d.
**A System of School Training for Horses.** Cr. 8vo. 2s. 6d.

*ANDERSON, P.*
**The English in Western India.** Demy 8vo. 14s.

*ANDERSON, THOMAS, Parliamentary Reporter, &c.*
**History of Shorthand.** With an analysis and review of its present condition and prospects in Europe and America. With Portraits Cr. 8vo 12s 6d
**Catechism of Shorthand;** being a Critical Examination of the various Styles, with special reference to the question, Which is the best English System of Shorthand ? Fcap 8vo 1s

*ANDREW, Sir WILLIAM PATRICK, C I E , M.R A S , F R G.S , F S.A*
**India and Her Neighbours.** With Two Maps. Demy 8vo. 15s
**Our Scientific Frontier.** With Sketch-Map and Appendix Demy 8vo. 6s.
**Euphrates Valley Route,** in connection with the Central Asian and Egyptian Questions. Lecture delivered at the National Club, 16th June 1882 Roy. 8vo., with 2 Maps. 5s
**Through Booking of Goods between the Interior of India and the United Kingdom.** Demy 8vo. 2s.
**Indian Railways as Connected with the British Empire in the East.** Fourth Edition. With Map and Appendix. Demy 8vo. 10s. 6d

*ANGELL, H C., M D*
**The Sight, and How to Preserve it.** With Numerous Illustrations Fifth Thousand. Fcap 8vo. 1s 6d.

*ANSTED, Professor DAVID THOMAS, M A , F.R.S , &c*
**Physical Geography.** Fifth Edition. With Illustrative Maps. Post 8vo 7s
**Elements of Physiography.** For the Use of Science Schools. Fcap. 8vo. 1s. 4d.
**The World We Live In.** Or, First Lessons in Physical Geography. For the use of Schools and Students. Twenty-fifth Thousand, with Illustrations. Fcap. 8vo 2s.
**The Earth's History.** Or, First Lessons in Geology. For the use of Schools and Students Third Thousand. Fcap. 8vo. 2s.
**Two Thousand Examination Questions** in Physical Geography. pp 180. Fcap 8vo. 2s
**Water, and Water Supply.** Chiefly with reference to the British Islands Part I.—Surface Waters With Maps. Demy 8vo 18s.
**The Applications of Geology to the Arts and Manufactures.** Illustrated. Fcap. 8vo , cloth. 4s.

**Antiquity and Genuineness of the Gospels.** With some Prefatory Remarks on the Remoter Sources of Unbelief Cr. 8vo. 2s.

*AQUARIUS.*
> **Books on Games at Cards.** Piquet and Cribbage—Games at Cards for Three Players—Tarocco—Familiar Round Games at Cards—Norseman—New Games with Cards and Dice—Écarté  Cr 16mo.  1s. each.

*ARCHER, Capt. J. H LAWRENCE, Bengal H P*
> **Commentaries on the Punjaub Campaign—1848-49,** including some additions to the History of the Second Sikh War, from original sources. Cr 8vo. 8s

*ARMSTRONG, ANNIE E.*
> **Ethel's Journey to Strange Lands in Search of Her Doll.** With Illustrations by Chas Whymper. Cr 8vo. 2s. 6d.

**Army and Navy Calendar for the Financial Year 1884-85.** Being a Compendium of General Information relating to the Army, Navy, Militia, and Volunteers, and containing Maps, Plans, Tabulated Statements, Abstracts, &c  Compiled from authentic sources  Published Annually. Demy 8vo  2s. 6d.

**Army and Navy Magazine.** Vols I to VIII are issued  Demy 8vo. 7s. 6d each  Monthly, 1s.

*AYNSLEY, Mrs. J. C MURRAY.*
> **Our Visit to Hindustan, Kashmir, and Ladakh.** 8vo. 14s.

*BAILDON, SAMUEL, Author of "Tea in Assam."*
> **The Tea Industry in India.** A Review of Finance and Labour, and a Guide for Capitalists and Assistants  Demy 8vo  10s 6d.

*BARNARD, H*
> **Oral Training Lessons in Natural Science and General Knowledge :** Embracing the subjects of Astronomy, Anatomy, Physiology, Chemistry, Mathematics and Geography. Cr. 8vo.  2s. 6d

*BATE, J. D , M.R A S.*
> **An Examination of the Claims of Ishmael as viewed by Muhammadans** (being the first chapter of Section I. of " Studies in Islam "  Demy 8vo.  12s

*BAYLISS, WYKE.*
> **The Higher Life in Art :** with a Chapter on Hobgoblins, by the Great Masters. Illustrated. Cr. 8vo  6s.

**Belgium of the East, The.** By the Author of "Egypt under Ismail Pasha," "Egypt for the Egyptians," &c.  Cr 8vo  6s

*BELLEW, Captain.*
> **Memoirs of a Griffin;** or, A Cadet's First Year in India  Illustrated from Designs by the Author. A New Edition  Cr 8vo  10s 6d

*BENTON, SAMUEL, L R C P., &c.*
> **Home Nursing, and How to Help in Cases of Accident.** Illustrated with 19 Woodcuts  Cr. 8vo.  2s. 6d.

*BEERDMORE, SEPTIMUS (NIMSHIVICH).*
> **A Scratch Team of Essays never before put together.** Reprinted from the "Quarterly" and "Westminster" Reviews. The Kitchen and the Cellar — Thackeray — Russia — Carriages, Roads, and Coaches  Cr. 8vo.  7s. 6d

*BLACK, Rev. CHARLES INGRAM, M A , Vicar of Burley in Wharfedale, near Leeds.*
> **The Proselytes of Ishmael.** Being a short Historical Survey of the Turanian Tribes in their Western Migrations  With Notes and Appendices. Second Edition. Cr. 8vo.  6s.

BLANCHARD, SIDNEY LAMAN.
**Yesterday and To-day in India.** Post 8vo. 6s.

BLENKINSOPP, Rev. E L , M A , Rector of Springthorpe.
**Doctrine of Development in the Bible and in the Church.**
Second Edition. Cr 8o. 6s.

BOILEAU, Major-General J. T.
A New and Complete Set of Traverse Tables, showing the Differences of
Latitude and the Departures to every Minute of the Quadrant and to
Five Places of Decimals Together with a Table of the Lengths of
each Degree of Latitude and corresponding Degree of Longitude from
the Equator to the Poles , with other Tables useful to the Surveyor and
Engineer Fourth Edition, thoroughly revised and corrected by the
Author. 1876. Roy 8vo 12s.

BOULGER, DEMETRIUS CHARLES, M R A S.
**History of China.** Demy 8vo. Vol I , with Portrait, 18s. Vol. II , 18s.
Vol. III , with Portraits and Map, 28s

**England and Russia in Central Asia.** With Appendices and Two
Maps, one being the latest Russian Official Map of Central Asia. 2 vols.
Demy 8vo. 36s.

**Central Asian Portraits;** or, The Celebrities of the Khanates and
the Neighbouring States. Cr. 8vo 7s. 6d.

**The Life of Yakoob Beg,** Athalik Ghazi and Badaulet, Ameer of
Kashgar. With Map and Appendix. Demy 8vo 16s

BOWLES, THOMAS GIBSON, Master Mariner
**Flotsam and Jetsam.** A Yachtsman's Experiences at Sea and Ashore.
Cr. 8vo 7s 6d.

BOYD, R. NELSON, F.R.G S , F.G S , &c
**Chili and the Chilians,** during the War 1879–80 Cloth, Illustrated.
Cr. 8vo 10s 6d.
**Coal Mines Inspection:** Its History and Results Demy 8vo. 14s.

BRADSHAW, JOHN, LL D., Inspector of Schools, Madras
**The Poetical Works of John Milton,** with Notes, explanatory and
philological 2 vols., Post 8vo. 12s. 6d.

BRAITHWAITE, R , M.D , F.L.S , &c
**The Sphagnaceæ,** or Peat Mosses of Europe and North America.
Illustrated with 29 Plates, coloured by hand. Imp. 8vo 25s

BRANDE, Professor, D C.L., F R S , &c , and Professor, A S TAYLOR, M.D ,
F.R.S , &c
**Chemistry, a Manual of.** Fcap 8vo. 900 pages. 12s. 6d.

BRANDIS, Dr , Inspector-General of Forests to the Government of India.
**The Forest Flora of North-Western and Central India.** Text
Demy 8vo. and Plates Roy. 4to £2 18s.

BRERETON, WILLIAM H., late of Hong Kong, Solicitor.
**The Truth about Opium.** Being the Substance of Three Lectures
delivered at St. James's Hall. Demy 8vo. 7s. 6d Cheap edition, sewed,
Cr. 8vo , 1s

BRIGHT, W., late Colour-Sergeant 19th Middlesex R.V.
**Red Book for Sergeants.** Fifth and Revised Edition, 1880. Inter-
caved. Fcap. 8vo., 1s.

BRISTOWE, J S , M.D., F R.C.P., Senior Physician and Joint Lecturer on Medicine, St Thomas's Hospital.
  **The Physiological and Pathological Relations of the Voice and Speech.** Illustrated. Demy 8vo. 7s. 6d.

**British Painters of the 18th and 19th Centuries.** With 80 Examples of their Work, engraved on Wood. Handsomely bound in cloth, gilt. Demy 4to  21s.

BUCKLAND, C.T , F.Z S.
  **Whist for Beginners.** Second Edition  Cr. 16mo.  1s
  **Sketches of Social Life in India.** Cr. 8vo  5s.

BUCKLE, the late Captain E , Assistant Adjutant-General, Bengal Artillery.
  **Bengal Artillery.** A Memoir of the Services of the Bengal Artillery from the formation of the Corps. Edited by Sir J. W. Kaye. Demy 8vo  10s.

BUCKLEY, ROBERT B., A.M I.C.E , Executive Engineer to the Public Works Department of India.
  **The Irrigation Works of India,** and their Financial Results. Being a brief History and Description of the Irrigation Works of India, and of the Profits and Losses they have caused to the State. With Map and Appendix  Demy 8vo. 9s.

BURBIDGE, F. W.
  **Cool Orchids, and How to Grow Them.** With Descriptive List of all the best Species in Cultivation  Illustrated with numerous Woodcuts and Coloured Figures of 13 varieties  Cr 8vo.  6s.

BURGESS, Captain F , Bengal Staff Corps.
  **Sporting Fire-arms for Bush and Jungle;** or, Hints to Intending Griffs and Colonists on the Purchase, Care, and Use of Fire-arms, with Useful Notes on Sporting Rifles, &c. Illustrated by the Author  Cr. 8vo. 5s.

BURGOYNE, Lieutenant-Colonel Sir JOHN M , Bart.
  **Regimental Records of the Bedfordshire Militia.** Cr 8vo.  5s

BURKE, PETER, Serjeant-at-Law.
  **Celebrated Naval and Military Trials.** Post 8vo.  10s 6d

BURROWS, MONTAGU, Captain R.N , Retired List, Chichele Professor of Modern History in the University of Oxford.
  **Life of Edward Lord Hawke,** Admiral of the Fleet, Vice-Admiral of Great Britain, and First Lord of the Admiralty from 1766 to 1771. Demy 8vo  21s.

**Byron Birthday Book, The.** Compiled and edited by James Burrows. New Edition  16mo. 2s 6d.

**By the Tiber.** By the Author of "Signor Monaldini's Niece "  2 vols. Cr. 8vo. 21s

CANNING, The Hon. ALBERT S G.
  **Thoughts on Shakespeare's Historical Plays.** Demy 8vo. 12s.

CARLYLE, THOMAS.
  **Memoirs of the Life and Writings of,** With Personal Reminiscences and Selections from his Private Letters to numerous Correspondents. Edited by Richard Herne Shepherd, Assisted by Charles N. Williamson  vols. With Portrait and Illustrations. Cr. 8vo.  s.

*CARRINGTON, B , M D., F.R S.*

**British Hepaticæ.** Containing Descriptions and Figures of the Native Species of Jungermannia, Marchantia, and Anthoceros. Imp. 8vo , sewed, Parts 1 to 4, each 2s 6d plain ; 3s 6d coloured. To be completed in about 12 Parts

*CAVENAGH, Gen  Sir ORFEUR, K C S.I.*

**Reminiscences of an Indian Official.** Cr 8vo. 10s. 6d

*CHAFFERS, WILLIAM, Author of " Hall Marks on Plate."*

**Gilda Aurifabrorum :** A History of London Goldsmiths and Plate-workers, with their Marks stamped on Plate, copied in fac-simile from celebrated Examples and the Earliest Records preserved at Goldsmiths' Hall, London, with their Names, Addresses, and Dates of Entry. 2,500 Illustrations  Roy. 8vo   18s

**Challenge of Barletta, The.**   By Massimo D'Azeglio.   Rendered into English by Lady Louisa Magenis   2 vols., Cr. 8vo   21s.

*CHAMISSO, ADALBERT VON.*

**Peter Schlemihl.**  Translated by Sir John Bowring, LL D , &c trations on India paper by George Cruikshank   Large paper, Cr 4to., half-Roxburghe, 10s. 6d

*CLARKE, Mrs. CHARLES, Lady Superintendent of the National Training School for Cookery, S Kensington, S.W. ●*

**Plain Cookery Recipes as Taught in the School.** Paper cover. Cr 8vo. 1s

**High-Class Cookery Recipes.** Cloth  Cr 8vo. 2s 6d.

**Clever Things said by Children.**   Edited by Howard Paul   Roy. 16mo. 2s 6d

**Collection Catalogue for Naturalists.** A Ruled Book for keeping a Permanent Record of Objects in any branch of Natural History, with Appendix for recording interesting particulars, and lettered pages for general Index  Strongly bound, 200 pages, 7s 6d , 300 pages, 10s , and 2s 6d. extra for every additional 100 pages  Working Catalogues, 1s. 6d. each

*COLLETTE, CHARLES HASTINGS*

**The Roman Breviary.** A Critical and Historical Review, with Copious Classified Extracts  Second Edition. Revised and enlarged. Demy 8vo 5s

**Henry VIII.** An Historical Sketch as affecting the Reformation in England  Post 8vo  6s

**St. Augustine (Aurelius Augustinus Episcopus Hipponiensis),** a Sketch of his Life and Writings as affecting the Controversy with Rome  Cr 8vo   5s

*COLLINS, MABEL*

**The S       of Helena Modjeska** (Madame Chlapowska). Cr. 8vo. 7s 6d.**tory**

*COLOMB, Colonel.*

**Bluestockings.** A Comedy in Five Acts  Adapted from the French of Moliere. Cr 8vo. 3s. 6d.

*COLQUHOUN, Major J. A S , R A*

**With the Kurrum Force in the Caubul Campaign of 1878-79.** With Illustrations from the Author's Drawings, and two Maps  Demy 8vo. 16s.

**Companion to the Writing-Desk.** How to Address Titled People, &c. Roy 32mo. 1s

COOKE, M C , M A., LL.D
   **The British Fungi:** A Plain and Easy Account of. With Coloured Plates of 40 Species  Fifth Edition, Revised. Cr 8vo. 6s.
   **British Hepaticæ.** Sewed 8d
   **Rust, Smut, Mildew, and Mould.** An Introduction to the Study of Microscopic Fungi  Illustrated with 269 Coloured Figures by J. E. Sowerby. Fourth Edition, with Appendix of New Species  Cr 8vo. 6s.
   **A Manual of Structural Botany.** Revised Edition, with New Chemical Notation  Illustrated with 200 Woodcuts  Twenty-fifth Thousand. 32mo 1s.
   **A Manual of Botanic Terms.** New Edition, greatly Enlarged  Illustrated with over 300 Woodcuts  Fcap. 8vo. 2s 6d

COOKE, M C., M A , A.L.S , et L  QUELET, M D , O.A , Inst et Sorb laur.
   **Clavis Synoptica Hymenomycetum Europæorum.** Fcap. 8vo. 7s. 6d

COOLIDGE, SUSAN.
   **Crosspatch,** and other Stories  New Edition. Illustrated. Cr. 8vo. 3s 6d.

**Cooper's Hill Royal Indian Engineering College, Calendar of.** Published (by Authority) in January each year  Demy 8vo. 5s

CORBET, Mrs. M. E
   **A Pleasure Trip to India,** during the Visit of H R H  the Prince of Wales, and afterwards to Ceylon  Illustrated with Photos. Cr. 8vo. 7s 6d.

CRESSWELL, C N , of the Inner Temple.
   **Woman, and her Work in the World.** Cr. 8vo  3s. 6d

CROLL, JAMES, LL.D , F R S.
   **Climate and Time in their Geological Relations.** Illustrated with 8 Coloured Plates and 11 Woodcuts  577 pp  Demy 8vo  24s.

CROSLAND, Mrs. NEWTON
   **Stories of the City of London:** Retold for Youthful Readers. With 10 Illustrations  Cr 8vo  6s

**Crown of Life, The.** By M. Y. W.  With elegantly illuminated borders from designs by Arthur Robertson, Fcap 4to  6s.

**Cruise of H.M.S. "Galatea,"** Captain H R.H the Duke of Edinburgh, K G , in 1867-1868.  By the Rev  John Milner, B A , Chaplain , and Oswald W Brierly.  Illustrated by a Photograph of H R H. the Duke of Edinburgh ; and by Chromo-lithographs and Graphotypes from Sketches taken on the spot by O. W Brierly  Demy 8vo  16s.

CUNNINGHAM, H. S , M A., one of the Judges of the High Court of Calcutta, and late Member of the Famine Commission.
   **British India, and its Rulers.** Demy 8vo. 10s 6d.

CUVIER, BARON.
   **The Animal Kingdom.** With considerable Additions by W B. Carpenter, M D., F.R S., and J O. Westwood, F L S.  New Edition, Illustrated with 500 Engravings on Wood and 36 Coloured Plates.  Imp. 8vo  21s.

DAUMAS, E., General of the Division Commanding at Bordeaux, Senator, &c &c.
**Horses of the Sahara, and the Manners of the Desert.** With
Commentaries by the Emir Abd-el-Kadir (Authorized Edition). Demy
8vo. 6s

DAVIES, THOMAS.
**The Preparation and Mounting of Microscopic Objects.** New
Edition, greatly Enlarged and brought up to the Present Time by John
Matthews, M D., F R M S , Vice-President of the Quekett Microscopical
Club Fcap 8vo. 2s. 6d

DAVIS, GEORGE E , F R M.S , F.C S., F I.C , &c.
**Practical Microscopy.** Illustrated with 257 Woodcuts and a Coloured
Frontispiece Demy 8vo. 7s 6d

DEIGHTON, K., Principal of Agra College
**Shakespeare's King Henry the Fifth.** With Notes and an Introduction Cr 8vo. 5s

DE LISLE, EDWIN
**Centenary Studies: Wyclif and Luther.** Cr 8vo. 3s. 6d
**Destruction of Life by Snakes, Hydrophobia, &c.,** in Western
India By an Ex-Commissioner. Fcap 2s 6d.

DICKENS, CHARLES
**Plays and Poems, with a few Miscellanies in Prose.** Now
first collected Edited, Prefaced, and Annotated by Richard Herne
Shepherd 2 vols. Demy 8vo. 21s.
Edition de Luxe 2 vols Imp. 8vo (Only 150 copies printed )

DICKINS, FREDERICK V , Sc B of the Middle Temple, Barrister-at-law
(translator)
**Chiushingura: or the Loyal League.** A Japanese Romance With
Notes and an Appendix containing a Metrical Version of the Ballad of
Takasako, and a specimen of the Original Text in Japanese character.
Illustrated by numerous Engravings on Wood, drawn and executed by
Japanese artists and printed on Japanese paper Roy 8vo. 10s 6d
**Diplomatic Study on the Crimean War, 1852 to 1856.** (Russian
Official Publication ) 2 vols. Demy 8vo. 28s.

DORAN, Dr J., F S.A
**"Their Majesties' Servants":** Annals of the English Stage Actors
Authors, and Audiences, from Thomas Betterton to Edmund Kean.
Post 8vo 6s

DOUGLAS, Mrs MINNIE
**Countess Violet ; or,** What Grandmamma saw in the Fire A Book for
Girls Illustrated. Cr 8vo 3s. 6d
**Grandmother's Diamond Ring.** A Tale for Girls Cr 8vo , 2s 6d.

DRURY, Col HEBER
**The Useful Plants of India,** with Notices of their chief value in
Commerce, Medicine, and the Arts Second Edition, with Additions
and Corrections Roy. 8vo. 16s.

DUKE, JOSHUA, F R A S , Bengal Medical Service.
**Recollections of the Kabul Campaign 1879-1880.** Illustrations
and Map. Demy 8vo 15s

DUMERGUE, EDWARD, M R.A S , Member of the Leyden Society of Orientalists.
**The Chotts of Tunis; or,** the Great Inland Sea of North Africa in
Ancient Times With Map Cr 8vo., 2s. 6d

DURAND, HENRY MARION, C S I., Bengal Civil Service, Barrister-at-law
**The Life of Major-General Sir Henry Marion Durand,**
**K.C.S.I., C.B.,** of the Royal Engineers With Portrait 2 vols.
Demy 8vo 42s

*DUTTON, Major the Hon. CHARLES.*
**Life in India.** Cr. 8vo. 2s. 6d

*DWIGHT, HENRY O.*
**Turkish Life in War Time.** Cr. 8vo. 12s.

*DYER, The Rev T. F. THISTLETON, M.A*
**English Folk-lore.** Second Edition. Cr 8vo. 5s.

*EDWARDS, G. SUTHERLAND.*
**A Female Nihilist.** By Ernest Lavigne. Translated from the French by G Sutherland Edwards  Cr 8vo. 9s

*EDWARDS, H. SUTHERLAND.*
**The Lyrical Drama :** Essays on Subjects, Composers, and Executants of Modern Opera. 2 vols. **Cr. 8vo  21s.**
**The Russians at Home and the Russians Abroad.** Sketches, Unpolitical and Political, of Russian Life under Alexander II  2 vols. Cr. 8vo.  21s.

**EMINENT WOMEN SERIES.** Edited by *JOHN H. INGRAM.* Cr 8vo. 3s. 6d.

> *BLIND, MATHILDE.*
> **George Eliot.**
> *ROBINSON, A. MARY F.*
> **Emily Bronte.**
> *THOMAS, BERTHA.*
> **George Sand.**
> *GILCHRIST, ANNE*
> **Mary Lamb.**
> *HOWE, JULIA WARD.*
> **Margaret Fuller.**
> *ZIMMERN, HELEN.*
> **Maria Edgeworth.**
> *PITMAN, Mrs E R*
> **Elizabeth Fry.**
> *LEE, VERNON.*
> **Countess of Albany.**
> *MILLER, Mis FENWICK*
> **Harriet Martineau.**
> *PENNELL, ELIZABETH ROBINS*
> **Mary Wollstonecraft Godwin.**

*ENSOR, F. SYDNEY, C E*
**Incidents of a Journey through Nubia to Darfoor.** 10s 6d.
**The Queen's Speeches in Parliament,** from Her Accession to the present time  A Compendium of the History of Her Majesty's Reign told from the Throne. Cr. 8vo  7s 6d

*EYRE, Major-General Sir V , K C.S I , C B.*
**The Kabul Insurrection of 1841-42.** Revised and corrected from Lieut. Eyre's Original Manuscript  Edited by Colonel G B Malleson, C S.I  With Map and Illustrations. Cr. 8vo. 9s.

*FARRAR, The Rev FREDERIC W., D D , F R S., Canon of Westminster, &c.*
**Words of Truth and Wisdom.** Cr 8vo. 5s

*FEARON, ALEC.*
**Kenneth Trelawny.** 2 vols. Cr 8vo  21s.

**FINCH-HATTON, HON. HAROLD.**

**Advance Australia!** An Account of Eight Years Work, Wandering, and Amusement in Queensland, New South Wales, and Victoria. Map and Plates. Demy 8vo 18s.

*FORBES, Capt. C. J. F S., of the British Burma Commission.*|

**Comparative Grammar of the Languages of Further India.** A Fragment; and other Essays, being the Literary Remains of the Author. Demy 8vo. 6s.

**Foreign Office, Diplomatic and Consular Sketches.** Reprinted from "Vanity Fair." Cr 8vo 6s.

*FOURNIER, ALFRED, Professeur à la Faculté de Médecine de Paris, Médecin de l'Hôpital Saint Louis, Membre de l'Académie de Médecine*

**Syphilis and Marriage:** Lectures delivered at the Hospital of St. Louis. Translated by Alfred Lingard Cr. 8vo. 10s. 6d

*FRASER, Lieut.-Col. G. T., formerly of 1st Bombay Fusiliers, and recently attached to the Staff of H.M. Indian Army.*

**Records of Sport and Military Life in Western India.** With an Introduction by Colonel G. B. Malleson, C S I. Cr. 8vo 7s. 6d.

*FRY, HERBERT.*

**London in 1885.** Its Suburbs and Environs Illustrated with 18 Bird's-eye Views of the Principal Streets, and a Map Fifth year of publication. Revised and Enlarged Cr. 8vo. 2s.

**Gazetteer of Southern India.** With the Tenasserim Provinces and Singapore. Compiled from original and authentic sources. Accompanied by an Atlas, including plans of all the principal towns and cantonments. With 4to. Atlas. Roy. 8vo £3 3s.

**Gazetteers of India.**

*THORNTON*, 4 vols. Demy 8vo. £2 16s.
Demy 8vo. 21s
„ (N.W.P , &c ) 2 vols. Demy 8vo. 25s

**Geography of India.** Comprising an account of British India, and the various states enclosed and adjoining pp. 250 Fcap. 8vo. 2s.

**Geological Papers on Western India.** Including Cutch, Scinde, and the south-east coast of Arabia To which is added a Summary of the Geology of India generally. Edited for the Government by Henry J. Carter, Assistant Surgeon, Bombay Army. With folio Atlas of Maps and Plates; half-bound. Roy 8vo £2 2s.

*GIBNEY, Major R. D., late Adj 1st Wilts R.V.*

**Earnest Madement;** a Tale of Wiltshire Dedicated by permission to Lieut.-Gen Sir Garnet Wolseley, G C B. Cr 8vo 6s.

*GILLMORE, PARKER (UBIQUE)*

**Encounters with Wild Beasts.** With 10 full-page Illustrations. Cr. 8vo. 7s. 6d

**Prairie and Forest.** A description of the Game of North America, with Personal Adventures in its Pursuit With 37 Illustrations. Cr. 8vo. 7s. 6d

· **The Amphibion's Voyage.** Illustrated. Cr. 8vo 7s. 6d.

*GOLDSTÜCKER, Prof THEODORE, The late*
   **The Literary Remains of.** With a Memoir   2 vols. Demy 8vo.   21s.

*GRAHAM, ALEXANDER*
   **Genealogical and Chronological Tables,** illustrative of Indian History. Demy 4to.   5s

*GRANT, JAMES.*
   **Derval Hampton ;** A Story of the Sea.   2 vols   Cr 8vo.   21s

*GRANVILLE, J. MORTIMER, M D.*
   **The Care and Cure of the Insane.**   2 vols   Demy 8vo.   36s
   **Change as a Mental Restorative.**   Demy 8vo   1s
   **Nerves and Nerve Troubles**   Fcap. 8vo   1s.
   **Common Mind Troubles.**   Fcap. 8vo.   1s.
   **How to make the Best of Life.**   Fcap 8vo.   1s
   **Youth :** Its Care and Culture   Post 8vo   2s. 6d
   **The Secret of a Clear Head.**   Fcap 8vo.   1s.
   **The Secret of a Good Memory.**   Fcap 8vo   1s
   **Sleep and Sleeplessness.**   Fcap 8vo.   1s.

*GREENE, F. V., Lieut. U.S. Army, and lately Military Attaché to the U. S Legation at St Petersburg*
   **The Russian Army and its Campaigns in Turkey in 1877-1878.**   Second Edition.   Roy 8vo   32s
   **Sketches of Army Life in Russia.**   Cr 8vo   9s.

*GRIESINGER, THEODOR*
   **The Jesuits ;** a Complete History of their Open and Secret Proceedings from the Foundation of the Order to the Present Time   Translated by A. J. Scott, M.D. Illustrated.   Second Edition.   One Volume.   Demy 8vo.   10s. 6d

   **Mysteries of the Vatican, or Crimes of the Papacy.**   2 vols., post 8vo   21s.

*GRIFFIS, WILLIAM ELLIOT, late of the Imperial University of Tokio, Japan.*
   **Corea, the Hermit Nation.**   Roy 8vo.   18s

*GRIFFITH, RALPH T H*
   **Birth of the War God.**   A Poem   By Kalidasa   Translated from the Sanskrit into English Verse.   Cr. 8vo   5s.

**Grove's System of Medical Book-keeping.**   The Complete Set, 4to., £4 14s. 6d

*HAINES, C. B.*
   **A Vindication of England's Policy with regard to the Opium Trade.**   Cr 8vo   2s 6d.

*HALL, E. HEPPLE, F.S.S.*
   **Lands of Plenty for Health, Sport, and Profit.**   British North America   A Book for all Travellers and Settlers   With Maps. Cr. 8vo.   6s.

*HALL, The Rev. T. G., M.A , Prof. of Mathematics in King's College, London.*
   **The Elements of Plane and Spherical Trigonometry.**   With an Appendix, containing the solution of the Problems in Nautical Astronomy.   For the use of Schools.   12mo.   2s.

*HAMILTON, LEONIDAS LE CENCI, M A.*
   **Ishtar and Izdubar.**   The Epic of Babylon, or the Babylonian goddess of love, and the hero and warrior king.   Illustrated.   Demy 8vo.   8s. 6d.

HANCOCK, E. CAMPBELL.
**Copies for China Painters.** With Fourteen Chromo-Lithographs and other Illustrations. Demy 8vo. 10s.

**Handbook of Reference to the Maps of India.** Giving the Lat and Long of places of note Demy 18mo. 3s 6d.
*₊* This will be found a valuable Companion to Messrs. Allen & Co.'s Maps of India

HARCOURT, Maj. A. F. P , Bengal Staff Corps.
**Down by the Drawle.** 2 vols in one, Cr 8vo 6s.

**Hardwicke's Elementary Books,** paper covers Chemistry, 6d.; Mechanics, 2 parts, 4d., Hydrostatics, 2d , Hydraulics, 2d,; Pneumatics, 2d

HARDWICKE, HERBERT JUNIUS, M.D , &c.
**Health Resorts and Spas;** or, Climatic and Hygienic Treatment of Disease. Fcap 8vo. 2s 6d

HARTING, JAMES EDMUND.
**Sketches of Bird Life.** With numerous Illustrations. Demy 8vo 10s. 6d.

HAWEIS, Rev H R.
**Music and Morals.** Thirteenth Edition. Cr 8vo 7s 6d
**My Musical Life.** With Portraits. Cr. 8vo. 15s.

HAWEIS, Mrs.
**Chaucer's Beads:** A Birthday Book, Diary, and Concordance of Chaucer's Proverbs or Sooth-saws. Cr 8vo , vellum. 5s , paper boards, 4s. 6d

**Health Primers.** 1. Premature Death. 2. Alcohol. 3. Exercise and Training. 4 The House 5. Personal Appearances. 6 Baths and Bathing. 7. The Skin 8. The Heart 9 The Nervous System. 10. Health in Schools Demy 16mo 1s. each

HEAPHY, THOMAS
**The Likeness of Christ.** Being an Enquiry into the verisimilitude of the received Likeness of our Blessed Lord. Edited by Wyke Bayliss, F S A. Illustrated with Twelve Portraits Coloured as Facsimiles, and Fifty Engravings on Wood. Handsomely bound in cloth gilt, atlas 4to., price £5 5s.

HEATLEY, GEORGE S , M R C.V S.
**Sheep Farming.** With Illustrations. Cr. 8vo 7s. 6d

HEINE, HEINRICH.
**The Book of Songs.** Translated from the German by Stratheir. Cr. 8vo. 7s 6d.

HELMS, LUDWIG VERNER.
**Pioneering in the Far East,** and Journeys to California in 1849, and to the White Sea in 1878 With Illustrations from original Sketches and Photographs, and Maps. Demy 8vo. 18s.

HENNEBERT, Lieutenant-Colonel.
**The English in Egypt;** England and the Mahdi—Arabi and the Suez Canal Translated from the French (by permission) by Bernard Paunce-tote. 3 Maps. Cr. 8vo 2s 6d.

*HENSMAN, HOWARD, Special Correspondent of the "Pioneer" (Allahabad), and the "Daily News" (London)*

**The Afghan War, 1879-80.** Being a complete Narrative of the Capture of Cabul, the Siege of Sherpur, the Battle of Ahmed Khel, the brilliant March to Candahar, and the Defeat of Ayub Khan, with the Operations on the Helmund, and the Settlement with Abdur Rahman Khan. With Maps. Demy 8vo. 21s.

*HERRICK, SOPHIE BLEDSOE.*

**The Wonders of Plant Life under the Microscope.** With numerous Illustrations   Small 4to.   6s.

*HERSCHEL, Sir JOHN F W , Bt , K.H., &c , Member of the Institute of France, &c.*

**Popular Lectures on Scientific Subjects.** Cr. 8vo.   6s.

*HOLDEN, EDWARD S., United States Naval Observatory.*

**Sir William Herschel:** His Life and Works   Cr. 8vo.   6s

**Holland.** Translated from the Italian of Edmondo Amicis, by Caroline Tilton.   Cr 8vo.   10s 6d.

*HOLMES, T R. E.*

**A History of the Indian Mutiny,** and of the Disturbances which accompanied it among the Civil Population. With Maps and Plans Demy 8vo.   21s

*HOOKER, Sir W J , F.R S , and J G. BAKER, F L S.*

**Synopsis Filicum;** or, a Synopsis of all Known Ferns, including the Osmundaceæ, Schizæaceæ, Marratiaceæ, and Ophioglossaceæ (chiefly derived from the Kew Herbarium), accompanied by Figures representing the essential Characters of each Genus   Second Edition, brought up to the present time.   Coloured Plates   Demy 8vo   £1 8s

*HOSSAIN, SYED M.*

**Our Difficulties and Wants in the Path of the Progress of India.** Cr. 8vo.   3s. 6d.

*HOWDEN, PETER, V S*

**Horse Warranty:** a Plain and Comprehensive Guide to the various Points to be noted, showing which are essential and which are unimportant. With Forms of Warranty. Fcap. 8vo   3s. 6d.

*HOUGH, Lieutenant-Colonel W*

**Precedents in Military Law.** Demy 8vo.   25s.

*HUGHES, Rev. T P.*

**Notes on Muhammadanism.** Second Edition, revised and enlarged. Fcap 8vo.   6s.

*HUNT, Major S LEIGH, Madras Army, and ALEX. S. KENNY, M R C.S E , A K C , Senior Demonstrator of Anatomy at King's College, London.*

**On Duty under a Tropical Sun.** Being some Practical Suggestions for the Maintenance of Health and Bodily Comfort, and the Treatment of Simple Diseases, with Remarks on Clothing and Equipment for the Guidance of Travellers in Tropical Countries   Second Edition.   Cr. 8vo   4s

**Tropical Trials.** A Handbook for Women in the Tropics. Cr. 8vo. 7s. 6d.

*HUNTER, J , late Hon Sec of the British Bee-Keepers' Association*

**A Manual of Bee-Keeping.** Containing Practical Information for Rational and Profitable Methods of Bee Management   Full Instructions on Stimulative Feeding, Ligurianizing and Queen-raising, with descriptions of the American Comb Foundation, Sectional Supers, and the best Hives and Apiarian Appliances on all systems.   With Illustrations Fourth Edition.   Cr. 8vo.   3s. 6d.

HUTTON, JAMES.
    **The Thugs and Dacoits of India.** A Popular Account of the Thugs and Dacoits, the Hereditary Garotters and Gang Robbers of India. Post vo 5s.

**India Directory, The.** For the Guidance of Commanders of Steamers and Sailing Vessels Founded upon the Work of the late Captain James Horsburgh, F.R S.
    Part I.—The East Indies, and Interjacent Ports of Africa and South America. Revised, Extended, and Illustrated with Charts of Winds, Currents, Passages, Variation, and Tides. By Commander Alfred Dundas Taylor, F R G S., Superintendent of Marine Surveys to the Government of India Sup. roy 8vo £1 18s
    Part II —The China Sea, with the Ports of Java, Australia, and Japan, and the Indian Archipelago Harbours, as well as those of New Zealand Illustrated with Charts of the Winds, Currents, Passages, &c. By the same (*In preparation* )

INGRAM, JOHN H
    **The Haunted Homes and Family Traditions of Great Britain.** First Series Cr 8vo , 7s 6d
    Second Series Cr. 8vo , 7s 6d

**In the Company's Service.** A Reminiscence. Demy 8vo. 10s. 6d

IRWIN, H C , B A , Oxon, Bengal Civil Service.
    **The Garden of India;** or, Chapters on Oudh History and Affairs. Demy 8vo 12s.

JACKSON, LOWIS D'A , A M I C.E , Author of "Hydraulic Manual and Statistics," &c.
    **Canal and Culvert Tables.** With Explanatory Text and Examples New and corrected edition, with 40 pp of additional Tables. Roy 8vo. 28s
    **Pocket Logarithms** and Other Tables for Ordinary Calculations of Quantity, Cost, Interest, Annuities, Assurance, and Angular Functions, obtaining Results correct in the Fourth Figure 16mo. Cloth, 2s 6d leather, 3s 6d
    **Accented Four-Figure Logarithms,** and other Tables For purposes both of Ordinary and of Trigonometrical Calculation, and for the Correction of Altitudes and Lunar Distances. Cr 8vo 9s
    **Accented Five-Figure Logarithms** of Numbers from 1 to 99999, without Differences Roy 8vo. 16s
    **Units of Measurement** for Scientific and Professional Men. Cr 4 to 2s

JAMES, Mrs A. G F. ELIOT
    **Indian Industries.** Cr. 8vo. 9s

JENKINSON, Rev THOMAS B , B A,, Canon of Maritzburg.
    **Amazulu.** The Zulu People their Manners, Customs, and History, with Letters from Zululand descriptive of the Present Crisis Cr 8vo. 6s

JERROLD, BLANCHARD
    **At Home in Paris.** Series I., 2 vols., Cr. 8vo , 16s. Series II , 2 vols , Cr. 8vo , 21s

JEVONS, SHIRLEY B
    **Private Lawrie and his Love.** A Tale of Military Life Cr. 8vo 10s 6d

JEWITT, LLEWELLYN, F S A.
    **Half - Hours among English Antiquities.** Contents . Arms, Armour, Pottery, Brasses, Coins, Church Bells, Glass. Tapestry, Ornaments, Flint Implements, &c With 304 Illustrations. Second Edition Cr 8vo. 5s

*JOHNSON, R. LOCKE, L R C.P., L.R C I , L S A , &c.*
**Food Chart.** Giving the Names, Classification, Composition, Elementary Value, Rates of Digestibility, Adulterations, Tests, &c , of the Alimentary Substances in General Use  In wrapper, 4to , 2s 6d ; or on roller, varnished, 6s.

*JOYNER, Mrs A BATSON*
**Cyprus: Historical and Descriptive.** Adapted from the German of Herr Franz von Löher. With much additional matter. With 2 Maps. Cr. 8vo.  10s. 6d

*KAYE, Sir J. W.*
**History of the War in Afghanistan.** New Edition. 3 vols. Cr. 8vo.  £1 6s
**Lives of Indian Officers.** 3 vols  Cr 8vo  6s each.
**The Sepoy War in India.** A History of the Sepoy War in India, 1857-1858. By Sir John William Kaye. Demy 8vo  Vol. I., 18s. Vol II , £1.  Vol III., £1.
> (For continuation, *see* **History of the Indian Mutiny,** by Colonel G. B. Malleson, Vol I of which is contemporary with Vol III of Kaye's work )

*KEATINGE, Mrs.*
**English Homes in India.** 2 vols  Post 8vo.  16s

*KEENE, HENRY GEORGE, C I.E., B.C S , M R A.S., &c.*
**A Sketch of the History of Hindustan.** From the First Muslim Conquest to the Fall of the Mughol Empire  By H G. Keene, C I.E., M R A S , Author of "The Turks in India," &c  8vo.  18s
**The Fall of the Moghul Empire.** From the Death of Aurungzeb to the overthrow of the Mahratta Power. Second Edition. With Map. Demy 8vo.  10s. 6d.
> *This Work fills up a blank between the ending of Elphinstone's and the commencement of Thornton's Histories.*

**Administration in India.** Post 8vo.  5s.
**Peepul Leaves.** Poems written in India  Post 8vo  5s.
**Fifty-Seven.** Some account of the Administration of Indian Districts during the Revolt of the Bengal Army  Demy 8vo.  6s.
**The Turks in India.** Historical Chapters on the Administration of Hindostan by the Chugtai Tartar, Babar, and his Descendants. Demy 8vo.  12s 6d

*KEMPSON, M , M.A.*
**The Repentance of Nussooh.** Translated from the original Hindustani tale, with an introduction by Sir Wm. Muir, K C.S.I. Cr. 8vo  3s. 6d.

*KENNY, ALEXANDER S , M R.C.S. Edin , &c.*
**The Tissues, and their Structure.** Fcap. 8vo.  6s

*KENT, W SAVILLE, F.L.S., F.Z S , F.R.M.S., formerly Assistant in the Nat. Hist Department of the British Museum.*
**A Manual of the Infusoria.** Including a Description of the Flagellate, Ciliate, and Tentaculiferous Protozoa, British and Foreign, and an account of the Organization and Affinities of the Sponges  With numerous Illustrations.  Super-roy. 8vo  £4 4s.

*KINAHAN, G. H.*
**A Handy Book of Rock Names.** Fcap 8vo , cloth  4s
**Knots, the Book of.** Illustrated by 172 Examples, showing the manner of making every Knot, Tie, and Splice  By "Tom Bowling." Third Edition  Cr. 8vo , 2s 6d.

*KING, DAVID BENNETT, Professor in Lafayette College, U.S A.*
**The Irish Question.** Cr. 8vo. 9s

*LAERNE, C F VAN DELDEN.*
**Brazils and Java.** Report on Coffee Culture in America, Asia, and Africa, to H E the Minister of the Colonies. Demy 8vo   Map, Plates, and Diagrams   21s

*LANE-POOLE, STANLEY, Laureat de l'Institut de France*
**Studies in a Mosque.** Demy 8vo   12s.

*LANKESTER, Mrs.*
**Talks about Health :** A Book for Boys and Girls   Being an Explanation of all the Processes by which Life is sustained. Illustrated. Small 8vo.   1s

**British Ferns :** Their Classification, Arrangement of Genera, Structures, and Functions, Directions for Out-door and Indoor Cultivation, &c   Illustrated with Coloured Figures of all the Species   New and Enlarged Edition   Cr 8vo   3s 6d

**Wild Flowers Worth Notice :** A Selection of some of our Native Plants which are most attractive for their Beauty, Uses, or Associations With 108 Coloured Figures by J. E Sowerby. New Edition   Cr 8vo   5s.

*LANKESTER, E , M D , F R S , F L.S*
**Our Food.** Illustrated   New Edition. Cr. 8vo   4s

**Half-hours with the Microscope.** With 250 Illustrations   Seventeenth Thousand, enlarged   Fcap 8vo , plain, 2s 6d , coloured, 4s.

**Practical Physiology :** A School Manual of Health   Numerous, Woodcuts   Sixth Edition   Fcap 8vo   2s 6d

**The Uses of Animals** in Relation to the Industry of Man   Illustrated. New Edition   Cr 8vo.   4s

**Sanitary Instructions :** A Series of Handbills for General Distribution —1. Management of Infants , 2 Scarlet Fever and the best Means of Preventing it ; 3 Typhoid or Drain Fever, and its Prevention ; 4. Small Pox, and its Prevention , 5 Cholera and Diarrhœa, and its Prevention , 6. Measles, and their Prevention. Each, 1d , per dozen, 6d ; per 100, 4s ; per 1,000, 30s.

*LATHAM, Dr R G*
**Russian and Turk,** from a Geographical, Ethnological, and Historical Point of View   Demy 8vo   18s.

*LAURIE, Col W. F B*
**Burma, the Foremost Country : A Timely Discourse.** To which is added, How the Frenchman sought to win an Empire in the East. With Notes on the probable effects of French success in Tonquin on British interests in Burma. Cr. 8vo   2s

**Our Burmese Wars and Relations with Burma.** With a Summary of Events from 1826 to 1879, including a Sketch of King Theebau's Progress   With Local, Statistical, and Commercial Information. With Plans and Map. Demy 8vo   16s.

**Ashe Pyee, the Superior Country ;** or the great attractions of Burma to British Enterprise and Commerce   Cr. 8vo.   5s

**LAW AND PROCEDURE, INDIAN CIVIL.**
**Mahommedan Law of Inheritance, &c.** A Manual of the Mahommedan Law of Inheritance and Contract , comprising the Doctrine of Soonee and Sheea Schools, and based upon the text of Sir H. W. Macnaghten's Principles and Precedents, together with the Decisions of the Privy Council and High Courts of the Presidencies in India   For the use of Schools and Students   By Standish Grove Grady, Barrister-at-Law, Reader of Hindoo, Mahommedan, and Indian Law to the Inns of Court. Demy 8vo   14s

**Hedaya, or Guide, a Commentary on the Mussulman Laws,** translated by order of the Governor-General and Council of Bengal   By Charles Hamilton. Second Edition, with Preface and Index by Standish Grove Grady. Demy 8vo.   £1 15s.

Law and Procedure, Indian Civil—*cont.*

**Institutes of Menu in English.** The Institutes of Hindu Law or the *Ordinances* of Menu, according to Gloss of Collucca. Comprising the Indian System of Duties, Religious and Civil, verbally translated from the *Original*, with a Preface by Sir William Jones, and collated with the Sanscrit Text by Graves Chamney Haughton, M A , F R.S , Professor of Hindu Literature in the East India College. New Edition, with Preface and Index by Standish G. Grady, Barrister-at-Law, and Reader of Hindu, Mahommedan, and Indian Law to the Inns of Court. Demy 8vo.  12s

**Indian Code of Civil Procedure.** Being Act X of 1877. Demy 8vo. 6s.

**Indian Code of Civil Procedure.** In the form of Questions and Answers, with Explanatory and Illustrative Notes. By Angelo J Lewis. Barrister-at-Law  Imp. 12mo.  12s. 6d.

**Hindu Law.** Defence of the Daya Bhaga  Notice of the Case on Prosoono Coomar Tajore's Will.  Judgment of the Judicial Committee of the Privy Council.  Examination of such Judgment.  By John Cochrane, Barrister-at-Law  Roy 8vo.  20s

**Law and Customs of Hindu Castes,** within the Dekhan Provinces subject to the Presidency of Bombay, chiefly affecting Civil Suits.  By Arthur Steele  Roy. 8vo.  £1 1s.

**Moohummudan Law of Inheritance,** and Rights and Relations affecting it (Sunni Doctrine). By Almario Rumsey  Demy 8vo.  12s.

**A Chart of Hindu Family Inheritance.**  By Almario Rumsey  Second Edition, much enlarged.  Demy 8vo.  6s 6d.

**INDIAN CRIMINAL.**

Including the Procedure in the High Courts, as well as that not in the Courts not established by Royal Charter; with Forms of Charges and Notes on Evidence, illustrated by a large number of English Cases, and Cases decided in the High Courts of India : and an Appendix of selected Acts passed by the Legislative Council relating to Criminal matters. By M H. Starling, Esq , LL B , and F. B Constable, M A  Third Edition  Medium 8vo  £2 2s

**Indian Code of Criminal Procedure.** Being Act X of 1872, Passed by the Governor-General of India in Council on the 25th of April 1872. Demy 8vo  12s.

**Indian Penal Code.** In the form of Questions and Answers  With Explanatory and Illustrative Notes  By Angelo J Lewis, Barrister-at-Law  Imp 12mo  7s 6d

**Indian Code of Criminal Procedure, Act of 1882.**  Roy. 8vo. cloth  6s

**MILITARY.**

**Manual of Military Law.** For all ranks of the Army, Militia, and Volunteer Services  By Colonel J  K. Pipon, Assistant Adjutant-General at Head-quarters, and J. F Collier, Esq., of the Inner Temple, Barrister-at-Law.  Third and Revised Edition  Pocket size.  5s.

**Precedents in Military Law;** including the Practice of Courts-Martial ; the Mode of Conducting Trials ; the Duties of Officers at Military Courts of Inquests, Courts of Inquiry, Courts of Requests, &c. &c  By Lieut -Col W. Hough, late Deputy Judge-Advocate-General, Bengal Army, and Author of several Works on Courts-Martial.  One thick Demy 8vo. vol.  25s.

**The Practice of Courts-Martial.**  By Hough and Long  Thick Demy 8vo  London, 1825.  26s.

*LEE, The Rev. F. G , D.D.*
  **The Church under Queen Elizabeth.** An Historical Sketch.
  2 vols. Cr. 8vo 21s
  **Reginald Barentyne;** or, Liberty without Limit. A Tale of the
  Times. With Portrait of the Author. Second Edition. Cr 8vo. 5s.
  **The Words from the Cross:** Seven Sermons for Lent, Passion-Tide,
  and Holy Week Third Edition revised Fcap. 8vo. 3s 6d.
  **Order Out of Chaos.** Two Sermons Fcap 8vo 2s. 6d

*LEES, Col WILLIAM NASSAU, LLD.*
  **The Drain of Silver to the East.** Post 8vo 8s

*LE MESSURIER, Maj. A., R E , Brigad. Major with the Quetta Column*
  **Kandahar in 1879.** Cr 8vo 8s.

*LETHBRIDGE, ROPER, C I E., M.A.*
  **High Education in India.** A Plea for the State Colleges. Cr 8vo. 5s.

*LEWIN, Capt. T. H., Dep Comm. of Hill Tracts.*
  **Wild Races of the South-Eastern Frontier of India.** Including
  an Account of the Loshai Country. Post 8vo. 10s 6d.
  **Indian Frontier Life. A Fly on the Wheel, or How I helped to**
27 **govern India.** Map and Illustrations. Demy 8vo. 18s.

*LIANCOURT, COUNT C. A. DE GODDES, and FREDERIC PINCOTT, M R A S.,*
  *&c.*
  **The Primitive and Universal Laws of the Formation and**
  **Development of Language;** a Rational and Inductive System
  founded on the Natural Basis of Onomatops. Demy 8vo. 12s. 6d.

*LLOYD, Mrs JESSIE SALE*
  **Shadows of the Past.** Second Edition Cr 8vo. 6s.
  **Honesty Seeds and How they Grew;** or, Tony Wigston's Firm Bank.
  Illustrated Cr. 8vo. 2s 6d

*LOCKWOOD, EDWARD, B S.C.*
  **Natural History, Sport and Travel.** With numerous Illustrations.
  Cr 8vo 9s

*LOVELL, The late Vice-Adm WM STANHOPE, R N , K.H*
  **Personal Narrative of Events from 1799 to 1815.** With Anecdotes Second Edition Fcap. 8vo. 4s.

*LOW, CHARLES RATHBONE.*
  **Major-General Sir Frederick S. Roberts, Bart., V.C., G.C.B.,**
  **C.I.E., R.A.:** a Memoir With Portrait Demy 8vo. 18s
  **Pollock, Field-Marshal Sir George, The Life and Correspon-**
  **dence of.** With Portrait. Demy 8vo 18s.

*LUPTON, JAMES IRVINE, F.R.O.V S*
  **The Horse, as he Was, as he Is, and as he Ought to Be.** Illustrated. Cr 8vo. 3s. 6d.

*MACDONALD, The late DUNCAN GEO. FORBES, LL D., C E., J P , F.R G S.*
  **Grouse Disease; its Causes and Remedies.** Illustrated. Third
  Edition Demy 8vo. 10s 6d

*MACGREGOR, Col C.M , C S.I., C I E., Beng. Staff Corps*
  **Narrative of a Journey through the Province of Khorassan**
  **and on the N.W. Frontier of Afghanistan in 1875.** With
  Map and Numerous illustrations. 2 vols. 8vo. 30s.
  **Wanderings in Balochistan.** With Illustrations and Map. Demy
  8vo 18s.

*MACKAY, CHARLES, LL.D.*
  **Luck; and what came of it.** A Tale of our Times. 3 vols Cr. 8vo.
  31s. 6d.

*MACKENZIE, Capt. C. F (El Musannif).*
**The Romantic Land of Hind.** Cr. 8vo 6s.

*MACKENZIE, —.*
**Educational Series ;** Commercial, Arithmetical and Miscellaneous
TABLES, paper covers, 2d ; Arithmetic, 6d., Murray's Grammar, 4d.,
paper covers, 2d.; Phrenology, paper covers, 2d ; Shorthand, 4d ;
Spelling, 2 parts, paper covers, 4d.

*MALABARI, BEHRAMJI, M.*
**Gujerat and the Gujeratis.** Pictures of Men and Manners taken from
Life Cr 8vo 6s

*MALLESON, Col G B , C S I*
**Final French Struggles in India and on the Indian Seas.** Including an Account of the Capture of the Isles of France and Bourbon,
and Sketches of the most eminent Foreign Adventurers in India up to
the Period of that Capture With an Appendix containing an Account
of the Expedition from India to Egypt in 1801 New Edition Cr.
8vo 6s.

**History of the Indian Mutiny, 1857-1858,** commencing from the
close of the Second Volume of Sir John Kaye's History of the Sepoy
War Vol I. With Map. Demy 8vo 20s —Vol II With 4 plans
Demy 8vo 20s.—Vol III With plans Demy 8vo. 20s

**History of Afghanistan,** from the Earliest Period to the Outbreak of
the War of 1878. Second Edition. With Map Demy 8vo 18s

**The Decisive Battles of India,** from 1746-1819. Second Edition.
With a Portrait of the Author, a Map, and Four Plans Demy 8vo.
18s.

**Herat: The Garden and Granary of Central Asia.** With Map
and Index Demy 8vo. 8s.

**Founders of the Indian Empire.** Clive, Warren Hastings, and Wellesley Vol. I —LORD CLIVE With Portraits and 4 Plans. Demy
8vo 20s

**Captain Musafir's Rambles in Alpine Lands.** Illustrated by G
Strangman Handcock Cr 4to 10s 6d.

**Battle-fields of Germany.** With Maps and Plan Demy 8vo. 16s.

*MALLOCK, W H.*
**A Chart** showing the Proportion borne by the Rental of the Landlords
to the Gross Income of the People. Cr. 1s.

*MANGNALL, Mrs.*
**Historical and Miscellaneous Questions** (generally known as
"Mangnall's Questions") New and Improved Edition 18mo. 1s.

*MANNING, Mrs*
**Ancient and Mediæval India.** Being the History, Religion, Laws,
Caste, Manners and Customs, Language, Literature, Poetry, Philosophy, Astronomy, Algebra, Medicine, Architecture, Manufactures, Commerce, &c. of the Hindus, taken from their Writings With Illustrations. 2 vols Demy 8vo 30s.

*MARVIN, CHARLES.*
**The Eye-Witnesses' Account of the Disastrous Russian Cam-
paign against the Akhal Tekke Turcomans:** Describing the
March across the Burning Desert, the Storming of Dengeel Tepe, and
the Disastrous Retreat to the Caspian. With numerous Maps and Plans
Demy 8vo. 18s.

Marvin, Charles—*cont.*

**The Russians at Merv and Herat**, and their Power of invading India. With 24 Illustrations and 3 Maps. Demy 8vo. 24s

**Merv, the Queen of the World; and the Scourge of the Man-stealing Turcomans.** With Portraits and Maps. Demy 8vo 18s.

**Colonel Grodekoff's Ride from Samarcand to Herat,** through Balkh and the Uzbek States of Afghan Turkestan. With his own March-route from the Oxus to Herat With Portrait Cr. 8vo. 8s.

**The Region of the Eternal Fire.** An Account of a Journey to the Caspian Region in 1883. 21 Maps and Illustrations. Demy 8vo. 21s.

*MATEER, The Rev SAMUEL, of the London Miss. Soc*

**Native Life in Travancore.** With Numerous Illustrations and Map. Demy 8vo 18s.

*MATSON, NELLIE.*

**Hilda Desmond, or Riches and Poverty.** Cr 8vo 10s 6d.

*MAYHEW, EDWARD, M R C.V.S.*

**Illustrated Horse Doctor.** Being an Accurate and Detailed Account, accompanied by more than 400 Pictorial Representations, characteristic of the various Diseases to which the Equine Race are subjected; together with the latest Mode of Treatment, and all the requisite Prescriptions written in Plain English. New and Cheaper Edition. Half-bound Demy 8vo. 10s 6d.

**Illustrated Horse Management.** Containing descriptive remarks upon Anatomy, Medicine, Shoeing, Teeth, Food, Vices, Stables; likewise a plain account of the situation, nature, and value of the various points, together with comments on grooms, dealers, breeders, breakers, and trainers, Embellished with more than 400 engravings from Original designs made expressly for this work A new Edition, revised and improved by J. I Lupton, M R.C V S. New and Cheaper Edition. Half-bound Demy 8vo 7s. 6d.

*MAYHEW, HENRY.*

**German Life and Manners.** As seen in Saxony. With an account of Town Life—Village Life—Fashionable Life—Married Life—School and University Life, &c. Illustrated with Songs and Pictures of the Student Customs at the University of Jena With numerous Illustrations 2 vols. Demy 8vo 18s. A Popular Edition of the above. With Illustrations. Cr. 8vo. 7s.

*MAYO, Earl of.*

**De Rebus Africanis.** The Claims of Portugal to the Congo and Adjacent Littoral With Remarks on the French Annexation. With Map. Demy 8vo 3s. 6d

*McCARTHY, T. A.*

**An Easy System of Calisthenics and Drilling,** including Light Dumb-Bell and Indian Club Exercises Fcap. 8vo 1s. 6d.

*McCOSH, JOHN, M D.*

**Advice to Officers in India.** Post 8vo. 8s.

*MENZIES, SUTHERLAND.*

**Turkey Old and New:** Historical, Geographical, and Statistical. With Map and numerous Illustrations Third Edition. Demy 8vo. 21s.

*MICHOD, C. J.*

**Good Condition:** A Guide to Athletic Training for Amateurs and Professionals Small 8vo. 1s

**Microscope, How to Choose a.** By a Demonstrator. With 80 Illustrations. Demy 8vo. 1s.

## MILITARY WORKS.

**A Treatise on Scales.** By Major F. Hart-Dyke. 2s.

**Red Book for Sergeants.** By William Bright, Colour-Sergeant, 19th Middlesex R.V Fcap. 8vo. 1s.

**Volunteer Artillery Drill-Book.** By Captain W Brooke Hoggan R A , Adjutant 1st Shropshire and Staffordshire V A. Square 16mo. 2s

**Principles of Gunnery.** By John T. Hyde, M.A., late Professor of Fortification and Artillery, Royal Indian Military College, Addiscombe. Second Edition, revised and enlarged. With many Plates and Cuts, and Photograph of Armstrong Gun. Roy 8vo. 14s.

**Treatise on Fortification and Artillery.** By Major Hector Straith Revised and re-arranged by Thomas Cook, R N., by John T. Hyde, M.A. Seventh Edition. Illustrated and 400 Plans, Cuts, &c. Roy. 8vo. £2 2s.

**Elementary Principles of Fortification.** A Text-Book for Military Examinations By J. T. Hyde, M A. With numerous Plans and Illustrations. Roy. 8vo. 10s. 6d.

**Military Surveying and Field Sketching.** The Various Methods of Contouring, Levelling, Sketching without Instruments, Scale of Shade, Examples in Military Drawing, &c. &c. &c As at present taught in the Military Colleges. By Major W. H. Richards, 55th Regiment, Chief Garrison Instructor in India, Late Instructor in Military Surveying, Royal Military College, Sandhurst. Second Edition, Revised and Corrected. Roy. 12s.

**Celebrated Naval and Military Trials.** By Peter Burke. Post 8vo. 10s. 6d.

**Military Sketches.** By Sir Lascelles Wraxall Post 8vo. 6s.

**Military Life of the Duke of Wellington.** By Jackson and Scott 2 vols Maps, Plans, &c Demy 8vo. 12s.

**Single Stick Exercise of the Aldershot Gymnasium.** Paper cover. Fcap 8vo. 6d.

**An Essay on the Principles and Construction of Military Bridges.** By Sir Howard Douglas. Demy 8vo. 15s.

**Hand-book Dictionary for the Militia and Volunteer Services,** containing a variety of useful information, Alphabetically arranged. Pocket size, 3s 6d.; by post, 3s. 8d.

**Lectures on Tactics for Officers of the Army, Militia, and Volunteers.** By Major F. H Dyke, Garrison Instructor, E.D. Fcap. 4to. 3s. 6d

**Precedents in Military Law.** By Lieut.-Col. W. Hough. Demy 8vo. 25s.

**The Practice of Courts-Martial.** By Hough and Long Demy 8vo. 26s.

**Reserve Force;** Guide to Examinations, for the use of Captains and Subalterns of Infantry, Militia, and Rifle Volunteers, and for Sergeants of Volunteers. By Capt. G. H. Greaves. Second Edition. Demy 8vo. 2s.

Military Works—*cont.*

**The Military Encyclopædia;** referring exclusively to the Military Sciences, Memoirs of distinguished Soldiers, and the Narratives of Remarkable Battles  By J. H. Stocqueler.  Demy 8vo   12s.

**Cavalry Remounts.** By Capt Nolan.  With Illustrations  Demy 8vo. 10s 6d.

> *Messrs W. H ALLEN and CO. are Agents for the Sale of Government Naval and Military Publications.*

*MILL, JAMES.*

**History of British India,** With Notes and Continuation by H. H. Wilson  9 vols  Cr 8vo.  £2 10s.

**Misterton,** or, Through Shadow to Sunlight  By Unus.  Cr. 8vo  5s.

*MITCHINSON, ALEXANDER WILLIAM.*

**The Expiring Continent;** A Narrative of Travel in Senegambia, with Observations 'on Native Character; Present Condition and Future Prospects of Africa and Colonisation.  With 16 full-page Illustrations and Map.  8vo.  18s

*MITFORD, EDWARD L.*

**A Land March from England to Ceylon Forty Years Ago.** With Map and numerous Illustrations  2 vols.  Demy 8vo   24s.

*MITFORD, Major R C. W , 14th Bengal Lancers.*

**To Caubul with the Cavalry Brigade.** A Narrative of Personal Experiences with the Force under General Sir F. S Roberts, G C B  With Map and Illustrations from Sketches by the Author.  Second Edition. Demy 8vo.  9s.

**Modern Parallels to the Ancient Evidences of Christianity.** Being an attempt to Illustrate the Force of those Evidences by the Light of Parallels supplied by Modern Affairs.  Demy 8vo.  10s 6d.

*MULLER, MAX.*

**Rig-Veda-Sanhita.** The Sacred Hymns of the Brahmins, together with the Commentary of Sayanacharya.  Published under the Patronage of the Right Honourable the Secretary of State for India in Council. Demy 4to.  6 vols.  £2 10s. per volume.

*NAVE, JOHANN.*

**The Collector's Handy-Book of Algæ, Diatoms, Desmids, Fungi, Lichens, Mosses, &c.**  Translated and Edited by the Rev. W. W. Spicer, M.A.  Illustrated with 114 Woodcuts.  Fcap. 8vo.  2s. 6d.

*NEVILLE, RALPH.*

**The Squire's Heir.** 2 vols.  Cr. 8vo.  21s.

*NEWMAN, The Late EDWARD, F.Z.S*

**British Butterflies and Moths.**  With over 800 Illustrations. Super-roy. 8vo , cloth gilt.  25s.

> *The above Work may also be had in Two Volumes, sold separately  Vol. I., Butterflies, 7s. 6d. , Vol II., Moths, 20s*

*NEWMAN, The Rev. JOHN HENRY (now Cardinal).*

**Miscellanies from the Oxford Sermons of John Henry Newman, D.D.**  Cr 8vo.  6s.

*NICHOLSON, Capt. H. WHALLEY*

**From Sword to Share;** or, a Fortune in Five Years at Hawaii  With Map and Photographs.  Cr 8vo.  12s. 6d.

**Nirgis and Bismillah.** NIRGIS, a Tale of the Indian Mutiny, from the Diary of a Slave Girl, and BISMILLAH, or, Happy Days in Cashmere. By Hafiz Allard. Post 8vo 10s. 6d.

*NORRIS-NEWMAN, CHARLES L , Special Correspondent of the London " Standard."*
**In Zululand with the British, throughout the War of 1879.** With Plans and Four Portraits Demy 8vo 16s.
**With the Boers in the Transvaal and Orange Free State in 1880-81.** With Maps. Demy 8vo 14s.

**Notes on Collecting and Preserving Natural History Objects.** Edited by J E Taylor, F L S , F G S., Editor of "Science Gossip." With numerous Illustrations Cr. 8vo. 3s. 6d.

**Notes on the North-Western Provinces of India.** By a District Officer Second Edition. Post 8vo 5s

*O'DONOGHUE, Mrs. POWER.*
**Ladies on Horseback.** Learning, Park Riding, and Hunting. With Notes upon Costume, and numerous Anecdotes With Portrait. Second Edition Cr. 8vo 5s.

*OLDFIELD, The Late HENRY ARMSTRONG, M D , H M. Indian Army*
**Sketches from Nipal,** Historical and Descriptive, with Anecdotes of the Court Life and Wild Sports of the Country in the time of Maharaja Jung Bahadur, G C.B , to which is added an Essay on Nipalese Buddhism, and Illustrations of Religious Monuments, Architecture, and Scenery, from the Author's own Drawings 2 vols Demy 8vo. 36s.

*OLIVER, Capt. S P.*
**On and Off Duty.** Being Leaves from an Officer's Note Book, in Turania, Lemuria, and Columbia. With 38 Illustrations. Cr. 4to. 14s.
**On Board a Union Steamer.** A compilation, to which is added "A Sketch Abroad," by Miss Doveton With Frontispiece. Demy 8vo. 8s.

*OSBORNE, Mrs WILLOUGHBY*
**A Pilgrimage to Mecca.** By the Nawab Sikandar Begum of Bhopal. Translated from the original Urdu by Mrs. Willoughby Osborne. Followed by a Sketch of the History of Bhopal by Colonel Willoughby Osborne, C.B. With Photographs. Dedicated, by permission, to Her Majesty Queen Victoria. Post 8vo. £1 1s.

*OSWALD, FELIX S*
**Zoological Sketches:** a Contribution to the Out-door Study of Natural History. With 36 Illustrations by Hermann Faber. Cr. 8vo. 7s. 6d.

*OWEN, SIDNEY, M A.*
**India on the Eve of the British Conquest.** A Historical Sketch. Post 8vo. 8s.

*OXENHAM, Rev. HENRY NUTCOMBE, M A*
**Catholic Eschatology and Universalism.** An Essay on the Doctrine of Future Retribution. Second Edition, revised and enlarged. Cr. 8vo. 7s. 6d.
**Catholic Doctrine of the Atonement.** An Historical Inquiry into its Development in the Church, with an Introduction on the Principle of Theological Development. Third Edition and enlarged. 8vo 14s.
**The First Age of Christianity and the Church.** By John Ignatius Döllinger, D.D., Professor of Ecclesiastical History in the University of Munich, &c. &c Translated from the German by H. N. Oxenham, M.A. Third Edition 2 vols., Cr. 8vo 18s.

*OZANAM, A. F.*
**History of Civilisation in the Fifth Century.** Translated from the French by the Hon. A C Glyn. 2 vols., Post 8vo. 21s.

*PANTON, J. E.*
**Country Sketches in Black and White.** Cr 8vo. 6s

*PAYNE, JOHN.*
**Lautrec.** A Poem  New Edition  Paper cover  Fcap 8vo  2s. 6d.
**Intaglios.** New Edition. Fcap. 8vo  3s 6d.
**Songs of Life and Death.** New Edition. Cr 8vo. 5s.
**Masque of Shadows.** New Edition. Cr. 8vo  5s
**New Poems.** New Edition  Cr. 8vo. 7s 6d.

*PEBODY, CHARLES.*
**Authors at Work.** Francis Jeffrey—Sir Walter Scott—Robert Burns—Charles Lamb—R. B Sheridan—Sydney Smith—Macaulay—Byron—Wordsworth—Tom Moore—Sir James Mackintosh  Post 8vo  10s. 6d.

*PEILE, Rev. W. O , M.A.*
**Tay.** A Novel. Cr 8vo. 10s 6d

*PELLY Colonel Sir LEWIS, K.C B , K C S I , &c.*
**The Miracle Play of Hasan and Husain.** Collected from Oral Tradition by Colonel Sir Lewis Pelly, K.C B , K.C.S I  Revised, with Explanatory Notes, by Arthur N. Wollaston, H.M. Indian (Home) Service, Translator of Anwar-i-Suhaili, &c. 2 vols , Roy 8vo  32s.

**Pen and Ink Sketches of Military Subjects.** By "Ignotus" Reprinted, by permission, from the "Saturday Review." Cr. 8vo. 5s.

**Personal Piety:** a Help to Christians to walk worthy of their Calling. 24mo. 1s 6d

*PHILLIPS, Mrs. ALFRED.*
**Man Proposes.** A Novel. 3 vols., Cr. 8vo. 31s. 6d.

*PINCOTT, FREDERIC, M R.A.S.*
**Analytical Index** to Sir John Kaye's History of the Sepoy War, and Colonel G B. Malleson's History of the Indian Mutiny. (Combined in one volume.) Demy 8vo. 10s 6d.

*PINKERTON, THOMAS A.*
**Agnes Moran:** A Story of Innocence and Experience  3 vols , Cr. 8vo  31s 6d

*PITTENGER, Rev. W.*
**Capturing a Locomotive.** A History of Secret Service in the late American War  With 13 Illustrations. Cr 8vo. 6s.

**Plutarch, Our Young Folks'.** Edited by Rosalie Kaufmann. With Maps and Illustrations. Small 4to. 10s 6d

*POPE, Rev G. U., D D., Fellow of Madras University.*
**Text-Book of Indian History;** with Geographical Notes, Genealogical Tables, Examination Questions, and Chronological, Biographical, Geographical, and General Indexes. For the use of Schools, Colleges, and Private Students. Third Edition, thoroughly revised  Fcap. 4 to. 12s.

*PRICHARD, I. I.*
**The Chronicles of Budgepore, &c.;** or, Sketches of Life in Upper India  2 vols , Fcap. 8vo. 12s

*PRINSEP, H. T.*
**Historical Results.** Deducible from Recent Discoveries in Afghanistan. Demy 8vo  15s.
**Tibet, Tartary, and Mongolia.** Second Edition. Post 8vo.  5s.
**Political and Military Transactions in India.** 2 vols., Demy 8vo. 18s.
**Private Theatricals.** Being a Practical Guide to the Home Stage, both Before and Behind the Curtain. By an Old Stager. Illustrated with Suggestions for Scenes after designs by Shirley Hodson  Cr. 8vo.  3s. 6d.
*PROCTOR, RICHARD A., B A , F R A.S.*
**Half-Hours with the Stars.** Demy 4to  3s 6d.
**Half-Hours with the Telescope**  Illustrated  Fcap 8vo.  2s. 6d.
*PROCTER, WILLIAM, Stud Groom.*
**The Management and Treatment of the Horse** in the Stable, Field, and on the Road.  New and revised edition.  Cr 8vo  6s
*RALFE, CHARLES H , M A , M D. Cantab., F.R C P. Lond.; late Teacher of Physiological Chemistry, St. George's Hospital, &c.*
**Demonstrations in Physiological and Pathological Chemistry.** Arranged to meet the requirements for the Practical Examination in these subjects at the Royal College of Physicians and College of Surgeons. Fcap 8vo  5s.
*RAMANN, Fraulein L.*
**Franz Liszt, Artist and Man.** Translated from the German by Miss E Cowdery. 2 vols., Cr. 8vo.  21s.
*RANSOME, A. H.*
**Sunday Thoughts for the Little Ones.** 24mo  1s 6d
*RICE, WILLIAM, Major-General (Retired) Indian Army*
**Indian Game: from Quail to Tiger.** With 12 Coloured Plates. Imp. 8vo.  21s.
*RIDLEY, MARIAN S.*
**A Pocket Guide to British Ferns.** Fcap. 8vo.  2s. 6d.
*RIMMER, R., F.L.S.*
**The Land and Fresh Water Shells of the British Isles.** Illustrated with  Photographs and 3 Lithographs, containing figures of all the principal Species. Cr. 8vo  10s. 6d.
*ROWE, RICHARD.*
**Picked up in the Streets :** or, Struggles for Life among the London Poor. Illustrated. Cr 8vo.  6s.
*SACHAU Dr C EDWARD, Professor Royal University of Berlin.*
**The Chronology of Ancient Nations.** An English Version of the Arabic Text of the Athar-ut-Bâkiya of Albirûni, or "Vestiges of the Past "  Collected and reduced to writing by the Author in A H 390–1, A D. 1000  Translated and Edited, with Notes and Index  Roy. 8vo  42s.
*SANDERSON, G P., Officer in Charge of the Government Elephant Keddahs at Mysore*
**Thirteen Years among the Wild Beasts of India ;** their Haunts and Habits, from Personal Observation. With an account of the Modes of Capturing and Taming Wild Elephants. With 21 full-page Illustrations and 3 Maps. Second Edition  Fcap 4to. £1 5s
*SCHAIBLE, CHARLES H., M.D., Ph.D*
**First Help in Accidents :** Being a Surgical Guide in the absence, or before the arrival of medical assistance  Fully Illustrated  32mo. 1s

SCHLEIDEN, J M., M D
  **The Principles of Scientific Botany.** Translated by Dr. Lankester.
  Numerous Woodcuts and Six Steel Plates. Demy 8vo    10s. 6d

SCUDAMORE, FRANK IVES, C.B.
  **France in the East.** A Contribution towards the consideration of the
  Eastern Question. Cr. 8vo. 6s.

SECCOMBE, Lieut.-Col. T. S.
  **Comic Sketches from English History.** For Children of various
  Ages. With Descriptive Rhymes. With 12 full-page Illustrations and
  numerous Woodcuts. Oblong 4to    6s.

SEWELL, ROBERT, Madras Civil Service.
  **Analytical History of India.** From the earliest times to the Aboli-
  tion of the East India Company in 1858. Post 8vo.   8s

**Shadow of a Life (The).** A Girl's Story   By Beryl Hope   3 vols. Cr
  8vo. 31s. 6d.

SHERER, J. W , C S.I.
  **The Conjuror's Daughter.** A Tale   With Illustrations by Alf   T.
  Elwes and J. Jelhcoe   Cr. 8vo.   6s.
  **Who is Mary?** A Cabinet Novel, in one volume.   Cr 8vo    10s 6d.
  **At Home and in India.** A Volume of Miscellanies.   With Frontis-
  piece   Cr 8vo   5s.

SHERIFF, DANIEL.
  **An Improved Principle of Single Entry Book-keeping.** Roy.
  8vo    3s. 6d.
  **The Whole Science of Double Entry Book-keeping.** Third
  Edition 8vo.   4s.

**Signor Monaldini's Niece.** A Novel of Italian Life. By the Author of
  "The Jewel in the Lotus." Cr. 8vo.   6s

SIMPSON, HENRY TRAILL, M.A , late Rector of Adel.
  **Archæologia Adelensis ;** or, a History of the Parish of Adel, in the
  West Riding of Yorkshire   Being an attempt to delineate its Past and
  Present Associations, Archæological, Topographical, and Scriptural
  With numerous etchings by W Lloyd Ferguson   Roy 8vo   21s.

**Skobeleff, Personal Reminiscences of General.** By Nemirovitch.
  Dantchenko. Translated by E. A Brayley Hodgetts. With 3 Portraits
  Demy 8vo.  10s. 6d.

SMALL, Rev. G , Interpreter to the Strangers' Home for Asiatics
  **A Dictionary of Naval Terms, English and Hindustani.** For
  the use of Nautical Men trading to India, &c.  Cr 8vo   2s 6d.

SMITH, J., A L.S.
  **Ferns: British and Foreign.** Fourth Edition, revised and greatly
  enlarged, with New Figures, &c.  Cr 8vo   7s 6d.

SMITH, WORTHINGTON, F.L.S.
  **Mushrooms and Toadstools:** How to Distinguish easily the Difference between Edible and Poisonous Fungi  Two large Sheets, containing
  Figures of 29 Edible and 31 Poisonous Species, drawn the natural size,
  and Coloured from Living Specimens. With descriptive letterpress, 6s ;
  on canvas, in cloth case for pocket, 10s 6d ; on canvas, on rollers and
  varnished, 10s 6d. The letterpress may be had separately, with key.
  plates of figures, 1s.

SOLYMOS, B (B. E. Falkonberg, C E )
   **Desert Life.** Recollections of an Expedition in the Soudan    Demy
   8vo. 15s.

**Soldiers' Stories and Sailors' Yarns:** A Book of Mess-Table Drollery
   and Reminiscence picked up Ashore and Afloat by Officers, Naval, Military, and Medical    Cr 8vo.  9s

**Songs of a Lost World.** By a New Hand.  Cr 8vo   6s

STANLEY, ARTHUR P , D.D , Dean of Westminster.
   **Scripture Portraits,** and other Miscellanies   Cr 8vo   6s

STEINMETZ, A.
   **The Smoker's Guide, Philosopher, and Friend :** What to Smoke
   —What to Smoke with—and the whole " What's What " of Tobacco,
   Historical, Botanical, Manufactural, Anecdotal, Social, Medical, &c.
   Roy 32mo  1s

STENT, GEORGE CARTER, M R A.S , Chinese Imperial Customs Service
   **Entombed Alive,** and other Songs and Ballads   (From the Chinese )
   With 4 Illustrations  Cr 8vo   9s

   **Scraps from my Sabretasche.** Being Personal Adventures while in
   14th (King's Light) Dragoons   Cr 8vo.  6s

   **The Jade Chaplet,** in Twenty-four Beads   A Collection of Songs
   Ballads, &c from the Chinese.  Second Edition   Cr. 8vo   5s

STOTHARD, ROBERT T , F S.A
   **The A B C of Art.** Being a system of delineating forms and objects
   in nature necessary for the attainments of a draughtsman  Fcap 8vo  1s.

**Sunday Evening Book (The):** Short Papers for Family Reading   By
   J. Hamilton, D D , Dean Stanley, J Eadie, D.D , Rev W. M Punshon,
   Rev. T Binney, J R Macduff, D D   Cloth antique   24mo   1s 6d.

SYMONDS, Rev W. S , Rector of Pendock.
   **Old Bones ;** or, Notes for Young Naturalists. With References to the
   Typical Specimens in the British Museum   Second Edition, much im-
   proved and enlarged   Numerous Illustrations.  Fcap 8vo   2s. 6d

SWINNERTON, Rev. C   Chaplain in the Field with the First Division,
   Peshawur Valley Field Force
   **The Afghan War.** Gough's Action at Futtehabad   With Frontis-
   piece and 2 Plans.  Cr 8vo   5s

SWINTON, A. H.
   **An Almanack of the Christian Era,** containing a legitimate pre-
   diction of the Weather, Disasters by Wind and Rain, Shipwrecks and
   River Floods, Prognostics of the Harvest, Havoc by Vermin and Infec-
   tion, Famines and Panics, Electrical Disturbances, Calamities by Earth-
   quakes and Volcanic Eruptions, with much that is Important or Curious.
   A Record of the Past and Glimpse into the Future, based on Solar
   Physics.  4to   6s

TAUNTON, ALFRED GEORGE.
   **The Family Register.** A Key to such Official Entries of Births,
   Marriages, and Deaths at the Registrar-General's Office as may refer to
   any particular family.  Half-bound. Demy folio. 21s.

*TAYLER, WILLIAM, Retired B C S., late Commissioner of Patna*
**Thirty-eight Years in India,** from Juganath to the Himalaya Mountains 200 Illustrations from Original Sketches 2 vols. Demy 8vo 25s. each.
**The Patna Crisis;** or, Three Months at Patna during the Insurrection of 1857. Third Edition. Fcap 8vo. 2s

*TAYLOR, J E , F.L S., F.G S , &c.*
**The Aquarium:** Its Inhabitants, Structure, and Management. With 238 Woodcuts Second Edition. Cr 8vo. 3s. 6d
**Flowers:** Their Origin, Shapes, Perfumes, and Colours Illustrated with 32 Coloured Figures by Sowerby, and 161 Woodcuts. Second Edition Cr 8vo 7s. 6d
**Geological Stories.** Numerous Illustrations Fourth Edition. Cr. 8vo 2s 6d.
**Nature's Bye-paths:** A Series of Recreative Papers in Natural History Cr 8vo. 3s. 6d
**Half-Hours at the Sea-side.** Illustrated with 250 Woodcuts Fourth Edition Cr 8vo 2s 6d
**Half-Hours in the Green Lanes.** Illustrated with 300 Woodcuts Fifth Edition Cr 8vo 2s 6d

*THOMS, JOHN ALEXANDER.*
**A Complete Concordance to the Revised Version of the New Testament,** embracing the Marginal Readings of the English Revisers as well as those of the American Committee Roy. 8vo 6s.

*THOMSON, DAVID*
**Lunar and Horary Tables.** For New and Concise Methods of Performing the Calculations necessary for ascertaining the Longitude by Lunar Observations, or Chronometers; with directions for acquiring a knowledge of the Principal Fixed Stars and finding the Latitude of them. Sixty-fifth Edition Roy 8vo. 10s.

*THORNTON, EDWARD.*
**The History of the British Empire in India.** Containing a Copious Glossary of Indian Terms, and a Complete Chronological Index of Events, to aid the Aspirant for Public Examinations. Third Edition With Map 1 vol Demy 8vo 12s.
*\*\* The Library Edition of the above in 6 volumes, 8vo., may be had, price £2 8s.*

**Gazetteer of India.** Compiled from the records at the India Office. With Map 1 vol. Demy 8vo , pp. 1015 21s
*\*\* The chief objects in view in compiling this Gazetteer are —*
*1st. To fix the relative position of the various cities, towns, and villages with as much precision as possible, and to exhibit with the greatest practicable brevity all that is known respecting them; and*
*2ndly To note the various countries, provinces, or territorial divisions and to describe the physical characteristics of each, together with their statistical, social, and political circumstances.*
*To these are added minute descriptions of the principal rivers and chains of mountains; thus presenting to the reader, within a brief compass, a mass of information which cannot otherwise be obtained, except from a multiplicity of volumes and manuscript records*
*The Library Edition.*
4 vols. Demy 8vo, Notes, Marginal References and Map. £2 16s.

Thornton, Edward—*cont.*

**Gazetteer of the Punjaub, Affghanistan, &c.** Gazeteer of the Countries adjacent to India, on the north-west, including Scinde, Affghanistan, Beloochistan, the Punjaub, and the neighbouring States. 2 vols Demy 8vo. £1 5s.

*THORNTON, PERCY M.*

**Foreign Secretaries of the Nineteenth Century.** Lord Grenville, Lord Hawkesbury, Lord Harrowby, Lord Mulgrave, C J Fox, Lord Howick, George Canning, Lord Bathurst, Lord Wellesley (together with estimate of his Indian Rule by Col G B. Malleson, C S I ), Lord Castlereagh, Lord Dudley, Lord Aberdeen, and Lord Palmerston Also, Extracts from Lord Bexley's Papers, including lithographed letters of Lords Castlereagh and Canning, bearing on important points of public policy, never before published. With Ten Portraits, and a View showing Interior of the old House of Lords. Second Edition 2 vols Demy 8vo 32s. 6d

Vol III Second Edition. With Portraits Demy 8vo. 18s.

**Harrow School and its Surroundings.** Maps and Plates. Demy 8vo. 15s.

*THORNTON, T.*

**East India Calculator.** Demy 8vo. 10s.

**History of the Punjaub,** and Present Condition of the Sikhs. 2 vols. Cr 8vo. 8s.

*TILLEY, HENRY A*

**Japan, the Amoor and the Pacific.** With Notices of other Places, comprised in a Voyage of Circumnavigation in the Imperial Russian Corvette Rynda, in 1858-1860. Eight Illustrations Demy 8vo. 16s

**Time's Footprints:** A Birthday Book of Bitter-Sweet. 16mo. 2s 6d

*TINCKER, MARY AGNES*

**The Jewel in the Lotos.** A Novel. By the Author of "Signor Monaldini's Niece," &c 5 Illustrations Cr 8vo. 7s 6d

*TORRENS, W T. McCULLAGH, M.P.*

**Reform of Procedure in Parliament** to Clear the Block of Public Business Second Edition Cr 8vo. 5s

**Treasury of Choice Quotations:** Selections from more than 300 Eminent Authors. With a complete Index Cr 8vo 3s 6d

*TRIMEN, H., M B (Lond ), F L S , and DYER, W T , B A.*

**The Flora of Middlesex:** A Topographical and Historical Account of the Plants found in the County With Sketches of its Physical Geography and Climate, and of the Progress of Middlesex Botany during the last Three Centuries. With a Map of Botanical Districts Cr. 8vo. 12s 6d.

*TRIMEN, Capt. R , late 35th Regiment.*

**Regiments of the British Army,** Chronologically arranged. Showing their History, Services, Uniform, &c Demy 8vo 10s 6d.

*TROTTER, Capt. LIONEL JAMES, late Beng Fusiliers*

**History of India.** The History of the British Empire in India, from the Appointment of Lord Hardinge to the Death of Lord Canning (1844 to 1862) 2 vols. Demy 8vo. 16s. each

**Lord Lawrence.** A Sketch of his Career Fcap 8vo 1s 6d.

**Warren Hastings, a Biography.** Cr. 8vo. 9s.

*TROTTER, M.E.*

**A Method of Teaching Plain Needlework in Schools.** Illustrated with Diagrams and Samplers New Edition, revised and arranged according to Standards. Demy 8vo. 2s 6d.

*TUPPER, MARTIN F , Author of " Proverbial Philosophy," &c.*
**Three Five-Act Plays and Twelve Dramatic Scenes.** Suitable for Private Theatricals or Drawing-room Recitation. Cr. 8vo. 5s.

*TURGENEV, IVAN, D.C.L.*
**First Love,** and **Punin and Baburin.** Translated from the Russian by permission of the Author, with Biographical Introduction, by Sidney Jerrold. With Portrait. Cr 8vo 6s

**Under Orders.** By the Author of  Invasions of India from Central Asia." Third Edition  3 vols., Cr. 8vo. 31s 6d.

*UNDERWOOD, ARTHUR S , M R C S, L D S E , 'Assistant-Surgeon to the Dental Hospital of London*
**Surgery for Dental Students.** Cr. 8vo. 5s

*VALBEZEN, E. DE, late Consul-General at Calcutta, Minister Plenipotentiary.*
**The English and India.** New Sketches. Translated from the French (with the Author's permission) by a Diplomate. Demy 8vo. 18s

*VAMBERY, ARMENIUS.*
**Sketches of Central Asia.** Additional Chapters on My Travels and Adventures, and of the Ethnology of Central Asia  Demy 8vo  16s.

*VAN GELDER, Mrs JANE.*
**The Storehouses of the King, what they are and who built them.** Gilt. Demy 8vo  21s.

*VIBART, Major H M , Royal (late Madras) Engineers.*
**The Military History of the Madras Engineers and Pioneers.** 2 vols  With numerous Maps and Plans. Demy 8vo. 32s. each.

**Victoria Cross (The), An Official Chronicle of Deeds of Personal Valour** achieved in the presence of the Enemy during the Crimean and Baltic Campaigns, and the Indian, Chinese, New Zealand, and African Wars, from the Institution of the Order in 1856 to 1880  Edited by Robert W. O'Byrne  With Plate  Cr. 8vo.  5s.

*VYSE, GRIFFIN W , late on special duty in Egypt and Afghanistan for H M.'s Government*
**Egypt : Political, Financial, and Strategical.** Together with an Account of its Engineering Capabilities and Agricultural Resources. With Maps  Cr. 8vo.  9s

*WALFORD, M A , &c &c.*
**Holidays in Home Counties.** With numerous Illustrations  Cr. 8vo. 5s.

**Pleasant Days in Pleasant Places.** Illustrated with numerous Woodcuts. Second Edition. Cr. 8vo  5s

*WALL, A J , M.D , F R C S , Med Staff H M 's Indian Army*
**Indian Snake Poisons,** their Nature and Effects  Cr 8vo.  6s.

*WATSON, Dr J FORBES, and JOHN WILLIAM KAYE.*
**Races and Tribes of Hindostan,** A series of Photographic Illustrations of ; prepared under the Authority of the Government of India ; containing about 450 Photographs  on mounts, in Eight Volumes, super royal 4to  £2 5s. per volume

*WATSON MARGARET.*
**Money.** Translated from the French of Jules Tardieu  Cr. 8vo.  7s 6d.

*WEBB, Dr. ALLAN, B M.S.*
**Pathologia Indica.** Based upon Morbid Specimens from all parts of the Indian Empire. Second Edition. Demy 8vo  14s

**"Where Chineses Drive."** English Student-Life at Peking. By a Student Interpreter. With Examples of Chinese Block-printing and other Illustrations Demy 8vo. 12s

**Wellesley's Despatches.** The Despatches, Minutes, and Correspondence of the Marquis Wellesley, K G , during his Administration in India. 5 vols With Portrait, Map, &c Demy 8vo. £6 10s.

**Wellington in India.** Military History of the Duke of Wellington in India. Cr. 8vo. 1s

*WHINYATES, Col F A , late R H A , formerly commanding the Battery*
**From Coruna to Sevastopol.** The History of " C " Battery, " A " Brigade, late " C " Troop, Royal Horse Artillery. With succession of officers from its formation to the present time With 3 maps. Demy 8vo 14s

*WHITE, Col S. DEWÉ, late Beng. Staff Corps.*
**Indian Reminiscences.** With 10 Photographs. Demy 8vo 14s

*WILBERFORCE, SAMUEL, D.D , Bishop of Winchester*
**Heroes of Hebrew History.** New Edition Cr. 8vo 5s.

*WILBERFORCE, E .*
**Franz Schubert.** A Musical Biography Translated from the German of Dr Heinrich Kreisle von Hellborn Cr 8vo 6s.

*WILKIN, Mis (Mârâ).*
**The Shackles of an Old Love.** Cr 8vo 7s 6d.

*WILKINS, WILLIAM NOY.*
**Visual Art;** or Nature through the Healthy Eye. With some remarks on Originality and Free Trade, Artistic Copyright, and Durability. Demy 8vo. 6s.

*WILLIAMS, FOLKESTONE.*
**Lives of the English Cardinals,** from Nicholas Breakspeare (Pope Adrien IV.) to Thomas Wolsey, Cardinal Legate. With Historical Notices of the Papal Court. 2 vols Demy 8vo. 14s.

**Life, &c. of Bishop Atterbury.** The Memoir and Correspondence of Francis Atterbury, Bishop of Rochester, with his distinguished contemporaries Compiled chiefly from the Atterbury and Stuart Papers 2 vols Demy 8vo. 14s.

*WILLIAMS, S. WELLS, LL.D. Professor of the Chinese Language and Literature at Yale College.*
**The Middle Kingdom.** A Survey of the Geography, Government, Literature, Social Life, Arts, and History of the Chinese Empire and Its Inhabitants Revised Edition, with 74 Illustrations and a New Map of the Empire 2 vols. Demy 8vo. 42s

*WILSON, H. H.*
**Glossary of Judicial and Revenue Terms,** and of useful Words occurring in Official Documents relating to the Administration of the Government of British India. From the Arabic, Persian, Hindustani, Sanskrit, Hindi, Bengali, Uriya, Marathi, Guzarathi, Telugu, Karnata, Tamil, Malayalam, and other Languages. Compiled and published under the authority of the Hon the Court of Directors of the E. I. Company Demy 4to £1 10s.

*WOLLASTON, ARTHUR N.*

**Anwari Suhaili,** or Lights of Canopus. Commonly known as Kalilah and Damnah, being an adaptation of the Fables of Bidpai. Translated from the Persian. Royal 8vo., 42s.; also with illuminated borders, designed specially for the work, cloth, extra gilt. Roy 4to £3 13s 6d

*WOOLRYCH, HUMPHREY W., Serjeant-at-Law*

**Lives of Eminent Serjeants-at-Law of the English Bar.** 2 vols Demy 8vo. 30s.

*WORDSWORTH, W.*

**Poems for the Young.** With 50 Illustrations by John Macwhirter and John Pettie, and a Vignette by J. E Millais, R.A. Demy 16mo. 1s. 6d

*WRAXALL, Sir LASCELLES, Bart*

**Caroline Matilda,** Queen of Denmark, Sister of George 3rd, from Family and State Papers. 3 vols Demy 8vo 18s

*WYNTER, ANDREW, M.D , M R.C P*

**Subtle Brains and Lissom Fingers:** Being some of the Chisel Marks of our Industrial and Scientific Progress Third Edition, revised and corrected by Andrew Steinmetz Fcap 8vo. 3s 6d.

**Our Social Bees:** Pictures of Town and Country Life. New Edition. Cr. 8vo 5s.

**Curiosities of Civilization.** Being Essays reprinted from the *Quarterly* and *Edinburgh Reviews.* Cr. 8vo 6s.

*YOUNG, Prof. J. R.*

**Course of Mathematics.** A Course of Elementary Mathematics for the use of candidates for admission into either of the Military Colleges; of applicants for appointments in the Home or Indian Civil Services; and of mathematical students generally. In one closely-printed volume. pp. 648. Demy 8vo. 12s

*YOUNG, MINNIE, and TRENT, RACHEL*

**A Home Ruler.** A Story for Girls. Illustrated by C. P Colnaghi. Cr. 8vo. 3s. 6d.

*ZERFFI, G. G , Ph.D., F.R.S L.*

**Manual of the Historical Development of Art**—Prehistoric, Ancient, Hebrew, Classic, Early Christian With special reference to Architecture, Sculpture, Painting, and Ornamentation Cr. 8vo 6s.

# A Selection from Messrs. ALLEN'S Catalogue of Books in the Eastern Languages, &c.

## HINDUSTANI, HINDI, &c.'

*Dr. Forbes's Works are used as Class Books in the Colleges and Schools in India.*

ABDOOLAH, SYED.
>   **Singhasan Battisi.** Translated into Hindi from the Sanscrit. A New Edition Revised, Corrected, and Accompanied with Copias Notes. Roy 8vo. 12s. 6d.
>   **Akhlaki Hindi,** translated into Urdu, with an Introduction and Notes. Roy 8vo. 12s 6d.

BALLANTYNE, JAMES R.
>   **Hindustani Selections,** with a Vocabulary of the Words    Second Edition  1845   5s
>   **Principles of Persian Caligraphy.** Illustrated by Lithographic Plates of the Ta"lik Character, the one usually employed in writing the Persian and the Hindustani   Prepared for the use of the Scottish Naval and Military Academy.  Second Edition.  4to   3s. 6d

EASTWICK, EDWARD B.
>   **The Bagh-o-Bahar**—literally translated into English, with copious explanatory notes  8vo   10s. 6d.
>   **Hindostani Grammar.** Post 8vo.  5s.
>   **Prem Sagar.** Demy 4to   £2 2s.

FORBES, DUNCAN, LL D
>   **Hindustani-English Dictionary,** in the Persian Character, with the Hindi words in Nagari also, and an English-Hindustani Dictionary in the English Character; both in one volume. Roy. 8vo. 42s.
>   **Hindustani-English and English-Hindustani Dictionary,** in the English Character. Roy. 8vo.  36s.
>   **Smaller Dictionary,** Hindustani and English, in the English Character. 12s.
>   **Hindustani Grammar,** with Specimens of Writing in the Persian and Nagari Characters, Reading Lessons, and Vocabulary  8vo.  10s 6d.
>   **Hindustani Manual,** containing a Compendious Grammar, Exercises for Translation, Dialogues, and Vocabulary, in the Roman Character. New Edition, entirely revised. By J. T. Platts. 18mo  3s. 6d.
>   **Bagh o Bahar,** in the Persian Character, with a complete Vocabulary. Roy. 8vo.  12s 6d.
>   **Bagh o Bahar,** in English, with Explanatory Notes, illustrative of Eastern Character. 8vo.  8s.
>   **Bagh o Bahar,** with Vocabulary. English Character. 5s.
>   **Tota Kahani;** or, "Tales of a Parrot," in the Persian Character, with a complete Vocabulary. Roy. 8vo.  8s.
>   **Baital Pachisi;** or, "Twenty-five Tales of a Demon," in the Nagari Character, with a complete Vocabulary. Roy 8vo. 9s.

Forbes, Duncan, LL D.—*cont.*

**Ikhwanu-s-Safa;** or, "Brothers of Purity," in the Persian Character. Roy 8vo. 12s 6d.

[*For the higher standard for military officers' examinations* ]

**Oriental Penmanship;** a Guide to Writing Hindustani in the Persian Character. 4to. 8s

*MULVIHILL, P.*

**A Vocabulary for the Lower Standard in Hindustani.** Containing the meanings of every word and idiomatic expression in "Jarrett's Hindu Period," and in "Selections from the Bagh o Bahar." Fcap. 3s. 6d.

*PINCOTT, FREDERIC, M.E A.S., &c &c.*

**Sakuntala in Hindi.** Translated from the Bengali recension of the Sanskrit Critically edited, with grammatical, idiomatical, and exegetical notes 4to. 12s. 6d.

**Alf Laila, ba-Zuban-i-Urdu** (The Arabian Nights in Hindustani) Roman Character. Cr 8vo 10s 6d.

**Hindi Manual.** Comprising a Grammar of the Hindi Language both Literary and Provincial, a complete Syntax , Exercises in various styles of Hindi composition; Dialogues on several subjects, and a complete Vocabulary Fcap 6s

*PLATTS, J T*

**Hindustani Dictionary.** Dictionary of Urdū and Classical Hindī. Super Roy. 8vo £3 3s

**Grammar of the Urdu or Hindustani Language.** 8vo 12s.

**Baital Pachisi;** translated into English 8vo 8s

**Ikhwanu-s-Safa;** translated into English. 8vo 10s 6d

*ROGERS, E. H.*

**How to Speak Hindustani.** Roy 12mo 1s

*SMALL, Rev. G.*

**Tota Kahani;** or, "Tales of a Parrot." Translated into English. 8vo 8s

**Dictionary of Naval Terms,** English and Hindustani For the use of Nautical Men Trading to India, &c. Fcap 2s 6d

## SANSCRIT.

*COWELL, E. B*

**Translation of the Vikramorvasi.** 8vo. 3s 6d

*GOUGH, A. E.*

**Key to the Exercises in Williams's Sanscrit Manual.** 18mo. 4s.

*HAUGHTON, —*

**Sanscrit and Bengali Dictionary,** in the Bengali Character, with Index, serving as a reversed dictionary. 4to. 30s

**Menu,** with English Translation 2 vols. 4to -24s.

**Hitopadesa,** with Bengali and English Translations 10s. 6d.

*JOHNSON, Prof. F.*

**Hitopadesa,** with Vocabulary 15s

*PINCOTT, FREDERIC, M.R A S, Corresponding Member of the Anjuman-i-Panjab.*

**Hitopadesa.** A new literal Translation from the Sanskrit Text of Prof. F. Johnson For the use of Students. 6s

*THOMPSON, J. C.*

**Bhagavat Gita.** Sanscrit Text 5s

*WILLIAMS, —.*
**English-Sanscrit Dictionary.** 4to , cloth. £3 3s.
**Sanscrit-English Dictionary.** 4to. £4 14s 6d.

*WILLIAMS, MONIER.*
**Sanscrit Grammar.** 8vo 15s
**Sanscrit Manual;** to which is added, a Vocabulary, by A. E. Gough. 18mo. 7s 6d.
**Sakuntala,** with Literal English Translation of all the Metrical Passages, Schemes of the Metres, and copious Critical and Explanatory Notes Roy. 8vo. 21s
**Sakuntala.** Translated into English Prose and Verse. Fourth Edition. 8s.
**Vikramorvasi.** The Text 8vo 5s.

*WILKIN, Sir CHARLES.*
**Sanscrit Grammar.** 4to. 15s.

*WILSON —.*
**Megha Duta,** with Translation into English Verse, Notes, Illustrations, and a Vocabulary. Roy. 8vo. 6s.

## PERSIAN.

*BARETTO, —*
**Persian Dictionary.** 2 vols. 8vo 12s.

*CLARKE, Captain H WILBERFORCE, R E.*
**The Persian Manual.** A Pocket Companion.
    Part I —A Concise Grammar of the Language, with Exercises on its more Prominent Peculiarities, together with a Selection of Useful Phrases, Dialogues, and Subjects for Translation into Persian.
    Part II.—A Vocabulary of Useful Words, English, and Persian, showing at the same time the Difference of idiom between the two Languages. 18mo 7s 6d
**The Bustan.** By Shaikh Muslihu-d-Dín Sa'di Shírází. Translated for the first time into Prose, with Explanatory Notes and Index. With Portrait 8vo 30s.
**The Sikandar Nama,e Bara,** or, Book of Alexander the Great. Written, A D 1200, by Abu Muhammad Bin Yusof Bin. Mu'ayyid-i-Nizámu-d-Dín Translated for the first time out of the Persian into Prose, with Critical and Explanatory Remarks, and an Introductory Preface, and a Life of the Author, collected from various Persian sources Roy 8vo 42s.

*FORBES, DUNCAN, LL D*
**Persian Grammar, Reading Lessons, and Vocabulary.** Roy. 8vo. 12s. 6d

*IBRAHEEM, —*
**Persian Grammar, Dialogues, &c.** Roy. 8vo. 12s 6d.

*KEENE, Rev H G.*
**First Book of The Anwari Soheili.** Persian Text. 8vo. 5s.
**Akhlaki Mushini.** Translated into English 8vo. 3s. 6d.

*OUSELEY, Col.*
**Anwari Soheili.** 4to 42s.
**Akhlaki Mushini.** Persian Text. 8vo 5s.

*PLATTS, J. T.*
**Gulistan.** Carefully collated with the original MS., with a full Vocabulary. Roy. 8vo. 12s 6d
**Gulistan.** Translated from a revised Text, with copious Notes. 8vo. 12s 6d

*RICHARDSON —.*
**Persian, Arabic, and English Dictionary.** Edition of 1852 By F. Johnson 4to £4

*TOLBORT, T W. H , Bengal Civil Service.*
**A Translation of Robinson Crusoe into the Persian Language.** Roman Character Cr 8vo 7s.

*WOLLASTON, ARTHUR N.*
**Translation of the Anvari Soheili.** Roy. 8vo. £2 2s
**English-Persian Dictionary.** Compiled from Original Sources 8vo. 25s.

## BENGALI.

*BATRI, —.*
**Singhasan.** Demy 8vo. 5s.

*FORBES, DUNCAN, LL.D.*
**Bengali Grammar,** with Phrases and Dialogues. Roy 8vo. 12s. 6d.
**Bengali Reader,** with a Translation and Vocabulary. Roy. 8vo. 12s. 6d.

*HAUGHTON, —.*
**Bengali, Sanscrit, and English Dictionary,** adapted for Students in either language, to which is added an Index, serving as a reversed dictionary. 4to. 30s.

**Nabo Nari.** Anecdotes of the Nine Famous Women of India. [Text-book for examinations in Bengali ] 12mo. 7s.

**Tota Itihas.** The Tales of a Parrot Demy 8vo. 5s

## ARABIC.

*FORBES, DUNCAN, LL D.*
**Arabic Grammar,** intended more especially for the use of young men preparing for the East India Civil Service, and also for the use of self-instructing students in general Royal 8vo , cloth. 18s.
**Arabic Reading Lessons,** consisting of Easy Extracts from the best Authors, with Vocabulary. Roy 8vo , cloth 15s.

*KAYAT, ASSAAD YAKOOB*
**The Eastern Traveller's Interpreter;** or, Arabic Without a Teacher. Oblong 5s.

*PALMER, Prof E. H , M.A., &c.*
**Arabic Grammar.** On the principles of the best Native Grammarians 8vo. 18s
**The Arabic Manual.** Comprising a condensed Grammar of both Classical and Modern Arabic; Reading Lessons and Exercises, with Analyses and a Vocabulary of useful Words. Fcap. 7s 6d.

*RICHARDSON, —.*
**Arabic, Persian, and English Dictionary.** Edition of 1852 By F. Johnson 4to , cloth. £4

*STEINGASS, Dr F.*
**Students' Arabic-English Dictionary.** Demy 8vo 50s.
**English-Arabic Dictionary.** Demy 8vo 28s.

## TELOOGOO.

BROWN, —.
   **Dictionary,** reversed; with a Dictionary of the Mixed Dialects used in
   Teloogoo 3 vols. in 2. Roy. 8vo £5.
   **Reader.** 8vo. 2 vols. 14s
   **Dialogues,** Teloogoo and English. 8vo. 5s 6d

CAMPBELL, —.
   **Dictionary.** Roy. 8vo 30s

**Pancha Tantra.** 8s

PERCIVAL, —.
   **English-Teloogoo Dictionary.** 10s 6d.

## TAMIL.

BABINGTON, —.
   **Grammar** (High Dialect). 4to 12s.
   **Gooroo Paramatan.** Demy 4to. 8s

PERCIVAL, —.
   **Tamil Dictionary.** 2 vols 10s. 6d

POPE, Rev G. U.
   **Tamil Handbook.** In Three Parts. 12s. 6d. each. Part I. Introduc-
   tion—Grammatical Lessons—General Index Part II Appendices—
   Notes on the Study of the "Kurral"—Key to the Exercises Part III.
   Dictionaries I Tamil-English—II English-Tamil

ROTTLER, —.
   **Dictionary,** Tamil and English. 4to. 42s.

## GUZRATTEE.

MAVOR, —.
   **Spelling,** Guzrattee and English. 7s. 6d.

SHAPUAJI EDALJI.
   **Dictionary,** Guzrattee and English. 21s.

## MAHRATTA.

BALLANTYNE, JAMES R , of the Scottish Naval and Military Academy.
   **A Grammar of the Mahratta Language.** For the use of the East
   India College at Hayleybury 4to 5s.

**Æsop's Fables.** 12mo. 2s 6d

MOLESWORTH, .
   **Dictionary,** Mahratta and English. 4to. 42s
   **Dictionary,** English and Mahratta 4to 42s

## MALAY.

BIKKERS, Dr. A J. W
   **Malay, Achinese, French, and English Vocabulary.** Alphabeti-
   cally arranged under each of the four languages With a concise Malay
   Grammar. Post 8vo. 7s 6d

MARSDEN, —.
   **Grammar.** 4to £1 1s

## CHINESE.

MARSHMAN, —.
**Clavis Sinica.** A Chinese Grammar. 4to. £2 2s.

MORRISON, —.
**Dictionary.** 6 vols , 4to.

**View of China,** for Philological Purposes. Containing a Sketch of Chinese Chronology, Geography, Government, Religion, and Customs, designed for those who study the Chinese language 4to. 6s

## PUSHTO.

RAVERTY, Major H G , Bombay Infantry (Retired), Author of the Pus'hto Grammar, Dictionary, Selections Prose and Poetical, Selections from the Poetry of the Afgháns (English Translation), Æsop's Fables, &c. &c.
**The Pus'hto Manual.** Comprising a Concise Grammar; Exercises and Dialogues, Familiar Phrases, Proverbs, and Vocabulary Fcap. 5s.

HUGHES, Rev. T. P
**Ganj-i-Pukto, or Pukto Treasury.** Being the Government Text-Book for the Lower Standard of Examination in Pukto, the Language of the Afghans With Glossary of Words Post 8vo. 10s. 6d.

## MISCELLANEOUS.

COLLETT, —.
**Malayalam Reader.** 8vo. 12s, 6d.

**Æsop's Fables in Carnatica.** 8vo , bound 12s 6d.

MACKENZIE, Captain C. F , late of H.M 's Consular Service.
**A Turkish Manual.** Comprising a Condensed Grammar with Idiomatic Phrases, Exercises and Dialogues, and Vocabulary 6s.

REEVE, —.
**English-Carnatica and Carnatica-English Dictionary.** (Very slightly damaged.) £8

SCHNURMANN, J. NESTOR
**Russian Manual.** 6s (For details see next page )

TIEN, REV. ANTON, M R A S
**Egyptian, Syrian, and North African Handbook.**

**REEDS** for Oriental Writing may be obtained from Messrs. **W. H. Allen & Co. Price 6d.**

# W. H. ALLEN & Co.'s Oriental Manuals.

CLARKE, Captain H. W, R E

**The Persian Manual.** Containing a Concise Grammar, with Exercises, Useful Phrases, Dialogues, and Subjects for Translation into Persian, also a Vocabulary of Useful Words, English and Persian. 18mo    7s 6d.

GOUGH, A E.

**Key to the Exercises in Williams's Sanscrit Manual.** 18mo    4s

MACKENZIE, Captain C F.

**A Turkish Manual.** Comprising a Condensed Grammar with Idiomatic Phrases, Exercises and Dialogues, and Vocabulary. Fcap. 6s

PALMER, Professor E H., M A

**The Arabic Manual.** Comprising a Condensed Grammar of both Classical and Modern Arabic, Reading Lessons and Exercises, with Analyses and a Vocabulary of Useful Words    Fcap. 7s 6d

PINCOTT, FREDERIC, M.R.A S , Corresponding Member of the Anjuman-i-Panjab, Editor and Annotator of the " S'akuntalá in Hindí," Editor of the Urdú " Alf Lailá," and Translator of the Sanskrit " Hitopadés'a."

**The Hindi Manual.** Comprising a Grammar of the Hindi Language both Literary and Provincial, a Complete Syntax; Exercises in various styles of Hindi Composition, Dialogues on several subjects; and a Complete Vocabulary    Fcap. 6s.

PLATTS, J. T.

**Forbes's Hindustani Manual,** Containing a Compendious Grammar, Exercises for Translation, Dialogues, and Vocabulary, in the Roman Character    New Edition, entirely revised. 18mo    3s 6d.

RAVERTY, Major H. G.

**The Pus'hto Manual.** Comprising a Concise Grammar    Exercises and Dialogues, Familiar Phrases, Proverbs, and Vocabulary. Fcap. 5s.

SCHNURMANN, J. NESTOR.

**The Russian Manual.** Comprising a Condensed Grammar, Exercises with Analyses, Useful Dialogues, Reading Lessons, Tables of Coins, Weights and Measures, and a Collection of Idioms and Proverbs, alphabetically arranged    Fcap. 6s.

TIEN, Rev. ANTON, Ph.D , M.R A S.

**Egyptian, Syrian, and North-African Handbook.** A Simple Phrase-Book in English and Arabic for the use of the British Forces, Civilians, and Residents in Egypt    Fcap 4s

**Manual of Colloquial Arabic.** Comprising Practical Rules for learning the Language, Vocabulary, Dialogues, Letters and Idioms, &c in English and Arabic    Fcap    7s. 6d

WILLIAMS, MONIER.

**Sanscrit Manual.** To which is added a Vocabulary, by A. E Gough. 18mo. 7s. 6d.

## Oriental Works in the Press.

NICHOLL, Prof G. F., Lord Almoner's Professor of Arabic, Oxford
**Bengali Manual.**

PALMER, the late Prof E. H., M.A
**Oriental Penmanship.** (See p 44 )

# Maps of India, &c.

*Messrs Allen & Co's Maps of India were revised and much improved during 1876, with especial reference to the existing Administrative Divisions, Railways, &c.*

**A General Map of India.** Corrected to 1884. Compiled chiefly from Surveys executed by order of the Government of India. On six sheets —size, 5ft. 3in. wide, 5ft. 4in. high, £2, or on cloth, in case, £2 12s. 6d ; or rollers, varnished, £3 3s.

**A Relievo Map of India.** By Henry F. Brion. In frame. 21s.

**District Map of India.** Corrected to 1884 Divided into Collectorates with the Telegraphs and Railways from Government Surveys On six sheets—size, 5ft. 6in. high, 5ft 8in. wide, £2; in a case, £2 12s 6d., or rollers, varnished, £3 3s.

**Handbook of Reference to the Maps of India.** Giving the Latitude and Longitude of places of note. 18mo   3s. 6d.

**Map of India.** Corrected to 1876 From the most recent authorities. On two sheets—size, 2ft. 10in wide, 3ft 3in high, 16s , or on cloth, in a case, £1 1s.

**Map of the Routes in India.** Corrected to 1874. With Tables of Distances between the principal Towns and Military Stations. On one sheet—size, 2ft. 3in. wide, 2ft. 9in. high, 9s , or on cloth, in a case, 12s.

**Map of the Western Provinces of Hindoostan**—the Punjab, Cabool, Scinde, Bhawulpore, &c.—including all the States between Candahar and Allahabad On four sheets—size, 4ft 4in wide, 4ft 2in. high, 30s ; or in case, £2; rollers, varnished, £2 10s.

**Map of India and China, Burmah, Siam, the Malay Peninsula, and the Empire of Anam.** On two sheets—size, 4ft 3in. wide, 3ft. 4in. high, 16s ; or on cloth, in a case, £1 5s

**Map of the Steam Communication and Overland Routes** between England, India, China, and Australia In a case, 14s· on rollers and varnished, 18s.

**Map of China.** From the most authentic sources of information. One large sheet—size, 2ft. 7in wide, 2ft 2in high, 6s ; or on cloth, in case, 8s.

**Map of the World.** On Mercator's Projection, showing the Tracts of th Early Navigators, the Currents of the Ocean, the Principal Lines of great Circle Sailing, and the most recent discoveries. On four sheets— size, 6ft 2in. wide, 4ft. 3in high, £2, on cloth, in a case, £2 10s., or with rollers, and varnished, £3

**Russian Official Map of Central Asia.** Compiled in Accordance with the Discoveries and Surveys of Russian Staff Officers up to the close of the year 1877. In two sheets.   10s. 6d ; or in cloth case, 14s.

# Works in the Press.

**Men of Character.**
By the late Douglas Jerrold. With 12 Original Illustrations by W. M. Thackeray    Edited by the late Blanchard Jerrold

**The Orders of Chivalry.**
By Major Lawrence Archer. With an Illustration of Every Order    4to.

**A History of the Press.**
By the late Blanchard Jerrold.

**Soldiers' Tales.**
By J. Menzies.

**Linnæus, the Floral King.**

**Street Idylls.**

**Anomalous Tales.**
By Albert Alberg.

**Essays.**
By W. Stigand.

**A History of Gujarat.**
By the late Professor Dowson.

**Poems.**
By H. G. Keene.

**Oriental Penmanship:** comprising Specimens of Persian Handwriting. Illustrated with Facsimiles from Originals in the South Kensington Museum, to which are added Illustrations of the Nagari Character. By the late Professor Palmer.

**A Dictionary of Islam.** Being a Cyclopædia of the Doctrines, Rites, Ceremonies, and Customs, together with the Technical and Theological Terms, of the Muhammadan Religion. By Thomas Patrick Hughes, B.D., M R A S , Fellow of the Punjab University, Missionary of the Church Missionary Society, Peshawur, Afghanistan. 8vo. With numerous Illustrations.

**Mythical Monsters.**
By Charles Gould    Profusely illustrated.

**Ambushes and Surprises.** By Colonel G. B. Malleson, C S.I.

**Reminiscences of Sport in India.** By General E F. Burton

**Life of General Francis Rawdon Chesney.** Edited by Stanley Lane Poole